CAPITAL SPACES

Critiques of contemporary public space argue that free rein has too often been given to the market to shape urban public space in its own interests whilst the public sector has been relegated to the edges of the space-making process. The result, it is argued, is public space that, whilst meeting a certain set of private objectives (profitable, safe, unchallenging, etc.), fails to meet the needs of a wider public interest and of the diversity of users that make up society.

Is it really that bad? Crudely, that is the question that this book attempts to address through a detailed investigation of the complex and evolving public spaces that have been designed and developed, used and managed in London since 1980. Through the crucible of this pre-eminent global city with all its attendant economic, social and political complexities, the book navigates the contemporary debates on public space, and reveals important conclusions of relevance to both the local practice and international theory of public space creation and recreation in the twenty-first century.

Matthew Carmona is Professor of Planning and Urban Design at UCL's Bartlett School of Planning. His research has focused on processes of design governance and on the design and management of public space. Matthew was educated at the University of Nottingham, from which he holds a PhD. He is an architect planner. His recent books include *Public Places Urban Spaces: The Dimensions of Urban Design* and *Urban Design Reader* (both for Architectural Press). Also, *Public Space: The Management Dimension* and *Measuring Quality in Planning: Managing the Performance Process* (both for Routledge).

Filipa Matos Wunderlich is Lecturer in Urban Design at UCL's Bartlett School of Planning. Her research has focused on place temporality and the rhythmicity of everyday urban places, and also on walking and the urban design process. Filipa was educated at the University of Porto, the Technical University of Delft and latterly at UCL, from which she holds a PhD. After completing her PhD she worked as a Research Fellow with Professor Carmona. She is an architect urban designer.

CAPITAL SPACES

THE MULTIPLE COMPLEX PUBLIC SPACES OF A GLOBAL CITY

Matthew Carmona and Filipa Matos Wunderlich

Routledge
Taylor & Francis Group

LONDON AND NEW YORK

First published 2012 by Routledge
2 Park Square, Milton Park, Abingdon, Oxon OX14 4RN

Simultaneously published in the USA and Canada by Routledge
711 Third Avenue, New York, NY 10017

Routledge is an imprint of the Taylor & Francis Group, an informa business

British Library Cataloguing in Publication Data
A catalogue record for this book is available from the British Library

Library of Congress Cataloging in Publication Data
Carmona, Matthew.
Capital spaces : the public spaces of a global city / Matthew Carmona and Filipa Matos Wunderlich.
p. cm.
1. City planning--England--London. 2. Public spaces--England--London. I. Wunderlich, Filipa. II. Title.
HT169.E52L63 2012
307.7609421--dc23
2011046104

ISBN: 9780415527088 (hbk)
ISBN: 9780415527095 (pbk)
ISBN: 9780203118856 (ebk)

Designed and typeset in ITC Officina Sans and Avenir
by Sutchinda Rangsi Thompson/Crown4to

Printed and bound in India by Replika Press Pvt. Ltd.

CONTENTS

CONTENTS

LIST OF FIGURES

ACKNOWLEDGEMENTS

The research on which this book is based has been long and complex and we are indebted to all those who have freely given up their time to discuss the projects with which they have been involved or simply the spaces they happened to be using as we passed by.

We are particularly indebted to the following collaborators who at various times and in various ways have significantly contributed to the research:

- Adriana Portella
- Ruth Blum
- Reetuparna Sarkar
- Chadkiran Nath
- Matthias Wunderlich

Thank you!

The empirical phase of this project was funded by the Economic and Social Research Council, for which we are profoundly grateful.

1   PUBLIC SPACE: IS IT REALLY THAT BAD?

INTRODUCTION

Go to any academic conference with a focus on public space (of which there are many) and one can never fail to be struck by the pessimistic, almost despairing, view that many researchers purvey about the state of contemporary public space in Western (and increasingly Eastern) cities. The critiques of public space that result are situated within and emerge from a wider critique of the neo-liberal orthodoxy that pervaded political and policy agendas in the latter years of the twentieth and early years of the twenty-first centuries. This orthodoxy, the argument goes, gave free rein to the market to shape urban space in its own interests – the shopping mall, corporate business park, gated residential enclave, etc. – whilst the public sector was relegated to the margins; providing the infrastructure for the necessary car-borne movement between the fragmented episodes of development, or dealing with the fall-out from a market that ignores that to which it has no relationship: the poor and the dispossessed and the places in-between. The result, it is argued, is public space that whilst meeting a certain set of private objectives for those who are lucky enough to own it (profitable, value adding, cost-effective), or the needs of those who are fortunate enough to be able to use it (clean, safe, convenient), may fail to meet the requirements of a wider public interest (open, equitable, sustainable) and of the full diversity of users that make up society.

Is it really that bad? Crudely, that is the question that this book seeks to address through a detailed investigation of the multiple, complex and evolving public spaces that have been designed, developed, used and managed in one global city – London – since 1980 (a date after which postmodern and neo-liberal thinking came firmly to the fore). The research that underpins this book is both global and local in its relevance: global in its focus on public space trends that much of the literature views as universal (or at least pervasive); local in its focus on one city chosen as an exemplar of the sort of neo-liberal trends that have been so derided in terms of their impact on public space.

This chapter, first, briefly introduces some of the key theoretical arguments that have been informing the discussions of public space referred to above. It does this through classifying the discussions into 'critiques' and 'counter-arguments' and through identifying four 'conundrums' that these categories reveal. The chapter also introduces the research project on which this book is based.

CRITIQUES, COUNTER-ARGUMENTS AND CONUNDRUMS

The critiques

An earlier book *Public Space: The Management Dimension* (Carmona *et al.* 2008) suggested that within the international academic literature, a range of reoccurring critiques characterise discussions about public space. These critiques are diverse, highly nuanced and range from the prosaic to the abstract. Most are based on a view about what public space should offer, often predicated on an idealised notion of public space as an open and inclusive stage for social interaction, political action and cultural exchange. Although there are distinct historical antecedents for such qualities, it is also probably true to say that public space has rarely, if ever, achieved such a utopian state, not least because the 'public' in 'public space is not a coherent unified group, but instead a fragmented society of different socio-economic (and often cultural) groups, further divided by age and gender. Each part of this diverse society will relate to public space in different and complex ways, pursuing separate and sometimes incompatible goals.

The literature itself and the critiques will be explored throughout this book (see in particular Chapters 5–10), but, in summary, those public and private actors with responsibility for the design, development and management of contemporary public space have been criticised for failing to prioritise an open and inclusive view of public space, leading to:

- **Neglected space:** Neglecting public space, both physically and in the face of market forces (**1.1a**).

- **Invaded space:** Sacrificing public space to the needs of the car, effectively allowing movement needs to usurp social ones (**1.1b**).

- **Exclusionary space:** Excluding the least mobile and most vulnerable in society through physical and psychological barriers to their participation (**1.1c**).

- **Segregated space:** Following the desire of affluent groups in many societies to separate from the rest of society reflecting a fear of crime and simply the desire to be exclusive (**1.1d**).

- **Insular space:** Failing to halt a more general retreat from public space into the technology-enhanced domestic realm or into virtual worlds.

1.1a-d London – (a) neglected, (b) invaded, (c) exclusionary and (d) segregated public space

a

b

c

d

1.2a-d London – (a) privatised, (b) consumption, (c) invented, and (d) scary space

a

b

c

d

Perversely, they have also been widely criticised for accepting or promoting schemes and strategies that in some localities are actively denying opportunities to some sections of society, or that are sterilising public space and homogenising the urban experience:

- **Privatised space:** Allowing public space to be privatised, with knock-on impacts on political debate and social exclusion (**1.2a**).

- **Consumption space:** Failing to address the relentless commodification of public space and the dangers of the financial exclusion of less prosperous segments of society (**1.2b**).

- **Invented space:** Condoning the spread of placeless formulae-driven space formats (**1.2c**).

- **Scary space:** Where crime and – more often – fear of crime have been allowed to dominate perceptions of place, and where crime prevention strategies – public and private – impact on the freedom with which space is used and enjoyed (**1.2d**).

- **Homogenised space:** Resulting from standard approaches to design and management, derived from a detached view of the urban realm as functional space instead of characteristic place.

As Carmona (2010a) argues, these sets of critiques may simply represent two sides of the same coin, with each directly and indirectly contributing to the other. Thus a poorly designed and inadequately managed public realm (the first set of concerns) leads directly to the desire of key commercial and community interests to desert publicly managed space in favour of their own more highly managed and exclusionary space (the second set). Indirectly this perpetuates itself by withdrawing investment from traditional public space, to which perceived antisocial elements are now relegated. Removing key civil groups from the public space ambit also perpetuates public space trends and ultimately the criticised management practices.

As such, many of the second set of critiques can be seen as a consequence of the first set, causing in turn a flight from truly public space into private and semi-private domains. Equally, more recent critiques around the over-design and over-management of publicly owned and managed space may be viewed as a response to the need of these spaces to compete with their pseudo-public counterparts as a means to redress the situation. The discussion shows a complex relationship between the two groups of criticisms and the types of space to which they relate. They are potentially both the cause and consequence of each other.

Some counter-arguments

On the face of it, the critiques are damming of contemporary public space, but, returning to the question posed at the start of this chapter – Is the situation really as bleak as much academic discussion would have us believe? – a range of arguments can be marshalled against the critiques. These arguments were summarised by Carmona (2010b: 160–4) as follows:

- **It is not as bad as you think:** There is a tendency amongst commentators to exaggerate what they see as 'negative' trends in public space design and management and underplay positive ones, extrapolating issues identified in the most extreme cases of segregation and securitisation as if they were universal and ubiquitous. Moreover, there can be two sides to every critique, thus invaded and consumption characteristics, for example, in many contexts, may be simply signs of the health and vitality of public space (**1.3**).

- **It is nothing new:** There is also a tendency to romanticise the

1.3 London – vital consumption space

1.4 London – private space as public realm

history of public space – be it the agora of ancient Greece, the village green or streets of terraces filled with the sound of children at play. In fact, public space was rarely as inclusive, democratic and valued as many commentators would have us believe. Much (if not most) public space has always been neglected and scary, much of it privatised, and often, to varying degrees, exclusionary.

- **It is not necessarily inferior:** Some have argued that the fact

1.5   London – dedicated youth space

1.6:   London – revitalised traditional public space

that something is private rather than public, suburban rather than urban, or commercial rather than civic does not determine either its quality as a place or its potential role as part of the public realm. In these arguments, the quintessential quality of public space is determined by those who occupy it and how comfortable they feel there, not by who owns and/or manages it, or where it is (**1.4**).

- **Society (and space) is changing:** Reflecting the notion that as society changes, we need to expand our concepts of public space beyond the traditional spaces of the neighbourhood or civic city to a wide range of new spaces where the public gather, and which have expanded opportunities for association and exchange – for example activities in community facilities, shopping malls, cafes, car boot sales, etc. This argument can easily be extended to the new forms of domestic and virtual spaces that are so heavily criticised in the literature.

- **Different groups seek different spaces:** The idea that we live in a homogenised society where all citizens should aspire to the same types of public space is also open to challenge. Thus today, most societies are divided along lines of wealth, education, opportunity, and increasingly ethnicity and culture, and it is almost inevitable that different segments of society will seek out different types of space. As such, we should not criticise space if it fails in being fully welcoming and accessible to all (**1.5**).

- **Different spaces have different purposes:** A consequence of varying needs of different groups, and of the varying functional needs imposed on space, is that different spaces will be designed and managed with different purposes in mind. It would seem churlish to criticise a space provided for quiet contemplation for failing as an entertainment space, or a space primarily meant for civic ceremony for failing to cater for rough sleepers.

- **Things are on the up:** Finally, some have noted an improvement and re-investment in traditional public space, with a con-sequential improvement in the quality of public space and resurgence in public life. This may be a consequence of cities competing for investment through enhancing their public realm, of private corporations recognising the value of better public space, or simply of a more active and (perhaps) enlightened state seeking to improve the quality of life for its citizens (**1.6**).

The conundrums

Clearly many of the critiques and counter-arguments seem to conflict. Over the last 20 years, as the literature on public space has burgeoned, contributions have come to reflect a wide range of perspectives, from the philosophical and theoretical to the practical and technical, and everything in-between. A number of conundrums are raised by this literature, and together these inspired the research project on which this book is based. The first addresses the key conflict that has already been identified.

The critiques and counter-arguments conflict

A first obvious conundrum, and the original inspiration for the research, is that the critiques and counter-arguments outlined above seem to conflict with each other. Indeed, a reading of the literature on public space demonstrates how partisan and polemical much of it is, but also that particular views about public space – either negative or positive – are espoused on the basis of remarkably little evidence, with the evidence that does exist sometimes distorted to fit a particular thesis, for example the discussion of London's much hyped surveillance culture (see Chapter 4). In this regard, the literature commonly generalises from individual cases, from unsubstantiated theories, or from particular types of space and contexts to make universal and sweeping arguments about the nature of contemporary public space. Although intellectually stimulating, if accepted in an unquestioning manner (as it often is), such literature can be misleading, offering a false impression of public space that can then be applied inappropriately to very different contexts.

Design and social sciences views conflict

Sometimes – it seems – there is simply a gulf in understanding between those approaching the subject from a social sciences perspective and those hailing from a design background. Thus the literature is replete with critiques of design-led approaches to development, dismissing such perspectives as physically deterministic or simply irrelevant when placed alongside socio-economic considerations. On the other side, large numbers of well-documented grand projects (both buildings and spaces) have been incorrectly promoted on the basis of their social benefit, when such benefits have turned out to be marginal. Others are described as 'iconic' as if such a label – whether deserved or not – makes them unquestionably desirable (Punter 2010b: 345–6).

Both perspectives are equally troubling: the first advancing a space-less (political economy) perspective and the second a place-less (aesthetic) vision for a phenomena that will always be rooted in both place and space. In reality, physical form will impact decisively on the socio-economic potential of space, just as the socio-economic context should always inform the design solution adopted. Equally, neither will determine absolutely the outcomes. The conundrum therefore concerns how to reconcile these perspectives, bringing a social science and design understanding to bear on the analysis of public space in order to move beyond partial views of the territory. Ultimately, the story of public space in London (as anywhere) cannot be grasped without understanding the range of design, development and political economy influences that act together to shape the outcomes of public space development projects. The research (and this book) was rooted in such an understanding of public space, and in the need to evaluate public space both as a physical entity and as a place for people, set within a particular political economy.

Disciplinary views conflict

If academic discourse is divided by traditions of thought, so to are professional perspectives that remain notoriously siloed, with designers, developers, regulators and managers each bringing their own preoccupations to bear, be these aesthetic, market, technical, legal, etc. The professional press in particular remains starkly divided, with few public space schemes subjected to analysis that compares outcomes with processes of delivery. Thus the architectural press typically reviews schemes just before completion, omitting discussion of use or serious debate about development process, and focusing instead on image. Real estate professionals, by contrast, focus on marketing and procurement processes.

Rarely is a view taken across the entire development process, and almost never are public spaces subjected to post-occupancy review in the way that buildings are. The result, when combined with the somewhat partial academic discourses, are a series of crude judgements about the quality or otherwise of public spaces based on limited evidence and an almost entirely product or process-based view of projects, for example that they are iconic, corporate, securitised, pastiche, etc. without a full understanding of the design and development processes that gave rise to them, how they are used and by whom, the manner in which they are managed and why, etc. To overcome this conundrum, the research deliberately explored public space creation and performance across four interrelated processes:

- **Design** – the key aspirations and vision, and contextual and stakeholder influences

- **Development** – the power relationships, and processes of negotiation, regulation and delivery

- **Use** – who uses the space, how, why, when and with what conflicts, and how the space performs

- **Management** – the responsibilities for stewardship, security, maintenance and ongoing funding

Theoretical and experiential views conflict

A final further conundrum reflects the observed tendency that public views (across social classes) relating to public space often focus on the most prosaic dimensions of use and management and miss altogether the sorts of issues that the academic literature (and critiques) reveal. Thus some qualities are consistently regarded as significant in helping to improve or undermine the quality of people's lives: that spaces should be 'clean and tidy', 'safe and secure' and should help to support a sense of 'community and belonging'. At the other end of the scale, qualities such as 'attractive', distinctive' and 'functional' are considered less important, in part reflecting a belief that such qualities relate more to the initial design of an environment than to its subsequent management, and are therefore fixed and not open to influence by the users of public space (Carmona & de Magalhaes 2009).

Many of the concerns summarised in the critiques above are nowhere to be seen when everyday users of space are freely asked about their experience of space quality. This may reflect a lack of awareness of the potential dangers of such trends (if they are trends) or an absence of everyday language through which to engage with these concerns. Alternatively, it may demonstrate a disconnect between public space theory and the real experience of users, with critics raising spectres that simply aren't there, at least not in the experience of the proverbial man on the Clapham omnibus. The result is that policy-makers reflect the everyday concerns of the public in their prescriptions for public space, but may be missing gradual creeping trends such as

privatisation, with the potential for long-term harm unless checked. The research attempted to capture both perspectives in order to better understand the public space stories discussed in Chapters 5–10.

GLOBAL PLACE, CONTESTED SPACE – THE RESEARCH

The conundrums described above emerged through a series of earlier research projects. They provided the inspiration for the work underpinning this book – in particular a determination to cut through some of the conflicting theory and rhetoric on public space and to explore through detailed empirical study the issues behind the critiques and counter-arguments.

Unfortunately, public space defies simplistic understanding: a space that is problematic in one respect may be highly successful in another. Leicester Square in London's West End, for example, represents a hopeless space if one is seeking peace, seclusion and gentle relaxation, but if one is seeking stimulation, human contact and vitality, it is the place to be (**1.7a**). For some, the space will be alienating, for others, highly stimulating. Similarly, London's parks typically offer few commercial opportunities, but as places to relax in the sun and watch the world go by, their value is undeniable (**1.7b**). Successful spaces may not be all things to all people, but arguably, cities should offer something for everyone if they are to avoid being alienating and exclusionary for some.

In order to overcome the complexity wrapped up in any single space, the project aimed to take a single (albeit hugely diverse) city – London – and understand, as far as possible, debates around public space through examination of a particular type of space – the urban square – across the city at large.

London and the urban square

London represents an ideal context in which to study the critiques of contemporary public space, not least because of the very obvious and pervasive pressures that the global property market brings to bear on this 'global' city and its local spaces. In this respect it provides a microcosm for the property-led development processes that are now impacting on urban design outcomes around the globe. At the same

1.7a-b Leicester Square and the Diana Fountain, Kensington Gardens – spaces of fun and relaxation

a

b

time, the resurgence of the urban square in London as a morphological type, encouraged by the 100 Spaces initiative of the first London-wide Mayor – Ken Livingstone – (see Chapter 3), offered a valuable focus for such a study.

The urban square was chosen as the focus for the work because of the perceived importance (rightly or wrongly) of such spaces in

the design of large-scale development and regeneration projects (Corbett 2004). This is combined with their historic role as the venue for public discourse, protest, encounter, collective experience and communication (Merrifield 1996). In this respect, Goheen (1998) has identified the unique status of public squares in marking the changes and continuities in civic confidence and the public life of cities, whilst Zukin (1995) identifies their role as an important interface between public, private, and community interests. Richard Rogers (1992: xv) neatly sums this up: 'The paradigm of public space is the city square or piazza: without it the city scarcely exists. City squares are special because their public function almost eclipses any other use they might have – people come to them principally to talk, demonstrate, celebrate; all essentially public activities.'

In the case of London, he cautioned, in doubling up as traffic intersections, some of its great squares do not act as squares at all. Certainly it is within the city square that the public realm is (or should be) at its most public. It follows that it is also within this space that the balance between these public functions and other essentially private ones can most easily be corrupted.

The 'new' London squares

The research was situated in a belief that to fully understand the success or failure of public space creation, an in-depth understanding of the stakeholder, development and institutional context in which it was created is first required; in this case, the infinitely complex and dynamic context of London. Writing in the 1930s, the Danish architect Steen Eiler Rasmussen described London as 'the unique city': 'On a summer day when the sun is shining you can walk for hours from one square to another under fresh green trees and see thousands of little circular spots cast by the sun on the green leaves. But in the dark season, the old squares are no less attractive' (Rasmussen 1948: 200–1). London's historic garden squares, most dating from the Georgian expansions of the eighteenth century, are now rightly famous throughout the world. Since their creation, this network of spaces have continued to deliver 'value' to their owners, residents, and (more recently) to wider London society (English Heritage 2000).

These arguments that public space adds value – economic, social and environmental (Woolley et al. 2004) – are increasingly used in urban competitiveness strategies of cities around the globe. For London, this renewed interest in public space globally has ignited a resurgence

1.8   Duke of York Square, Chelsea – a 2003 retail, residential and commercial development by one of the original aristocratic landed estates, the Cadogan Estate owned by the Earl Cadogan. With privately owned and managed public spaces at its heart, the scheme has opened up a site that, for military purposes, had been closed to the public for 200 years

of interest in London's urban space. Rasmussen (1948: 166) commented about the Georgian squares that 'The great landlord and the speculative builder found each other and together they created the London square with its character of unity surrounded as it is by dignified houses'. In today's London, many new urban spaces continue to be driven by private interests, a movement sparked in the late 1980s and 1990s by the arrival on the scene of two influential devel-opments at Broadgate in the City and Canary Wharf in the Docklands (Chapter 2). Each used space as a means to differentiate their 'products' in the market, in so doing creating a strong sense of place and eliciting premium rental returns. Since then, the formula has been repeated time and time again, at More London, Paddington Basin, Spitalfields, Paternoster Square, Duke of York Square (**1.8**), and now in King's Cross (see Chapter 3). It represents London's dominant commercial development model, creating in the process a new privatised public realm much as the Georgian expansions did in the eighteenth century; although this time largely corporate rather than residential in nature.

1.9 Tower Hill – historic site of public executions next to the Tower of London. In 2004 Historic Royal Palaces led the redesign of this space to create a proper setting for the Tower, and a space for visitors to London

Following the private sector lead, the public sector increasingly accepted arguments about the value of public space. For example, Ken Livingstone's 100 Public Spaces programme attempted to deliver a network of new and improved public spaces across London (Chapter 3). Thus in the 2000s, a series of new and regenerated urban squares have been delivered, including Monument Yard, Acton Town Square, Horse Guards Parade, Gillett Square, Wembley Stadium Station Square, and a rejuvenated Trafalgar Square, Peckham Square, Somerset House Courtyard, Stratford Station Square, Barking Town Square and Tower

1.10 Potters Fields – adjacent to City Hall, this space was refurbished in 2006-07, and although privately owned as part of the More London estate is managed by a not-for-profit trust with representatives from the GLA, Southwark Council, community groups and More London on its board

Hill (**1.9**), to name but a few. These, unlike the private spaces are primarily in public or pseudo-public ownership.

Yet, whilst the Georgian squares continue to receive universal praise for their restrained functionality and beauty (Lawrence 1993), the initial reaction of architectural critics to London's 'new' spaces often seemed to support many of the critiques discussed above, that London's new public squares are privatised, exclusionary, architecturally deterministic, over-designed, and sometimes, simply cheap. Heathcote (2007a), for example, writing in the *Financial Times*, argued that London's new public spaces are characterised by chain coffee and sandwich stores, fountains filled with chlorine, security guards, sculptural light fittings spiked with CCTV cameras, and signs forbidding skateboarding. For him, singling out for particular criticism a new green space – Potters Fields (**1.10**) – and a major new corporate space – Paternoster Square (see Chapter 5) – these spaces are often public in appearance only.

The truth of such statements can only be determined through empirical study. The quantity and variety of 'new' public squares in London, their diverse socio-economic and cultural settings, and their relative geographical proximity, make the city an ideal context for such evaluation.

Conducting the research

Funded by the UK's Economic and Social Research Council (ESRC), the empirical phase of research lasted two and a half years from late 2007 to early 2011. It encompassed:

- A London-wide survey enlisting the help of London's local authorities to map new and substantially regenerated squares across London, built or refurbished since 1980.

- An impressionistic on-site visual survey of 130 squares in ten London boroughs across central, inner and outer London locations. Observations focused on three main areas: physical form (shape, clarity of form, access and linkages, image, sense of place, and authenticity); function (variety of activities, degree of sociability, diversity, adaptability, and comfort); and rights and responsibilities (ownership, degree of maintenance and control, signage and lightning, and degree of exclusion).

- Fourteen detailed multi-dimensional case studies of London

squares focusing on the 'context for', 'process of', and 'outcomes from', each project. This stage involved analysis of the policy context; stakeholder interviews with key individuals involved in the design, planning, development and ongoing management of each space (70 detailed interviews in total); time-lapse observation of each space to capture use across the day; and interviews with actual users of each space (650 across the 13 realised projects).

Methodologically, the diversity of approaches helped to overcome known potential weaknesses with each in order that a more rounded and robust view of the subject could be obtained.

CAPITAL SPACES

The book

Capital Spaces can be broadly divided into three groups of chapters. The first four chapters set the scene by exploring a range of contexts for public space generation and regeneration in London. In this chapter, a series of public space critiques, counter-arguments and conundrums have been briefly rehearsed; these discussions are returned to in Chapters 5–10 as the core basis against which London's squares are interrogated. Chapter 2 sets the historical context and Chapter 3 the more recent political and policy context for exploring new and regenerated squares in London. Chapter 4 begins the empirical phase of the work, first discussing evidence of an urban renaissance, and then presenting a tangible outcome of 'renaissance thinking', the spread of new and refurbished squares across London.

In a second group of chapters (5–10), the results of the 14 detailed case studies of new, regenerated and proposed spaces in London are presented. Each chapter presents two or three spaces that illustrate observed trends across the 'types' of square revealed by the surveys. The case studies are situated where they best fit against the critiques, but many are relevant to a range of discussions and could have been located in a number of these chapters.

Two final chapters draw out conclusions from the work. First, Chapter 11 focuses on practical findings about the evolving nature of space in London, and about the design, development, use and management processes that shape and reshape that space. Second, Chapter 12 examines, in the light of the empirical evidence, the more theoretical issues encompassed in the critiques and counter-argument introduced above, concluding with what the research reveals about the future of public space in London and what this implies for public space in cities today.

A word of warning

Collectively, the research deals with big themes of global significance, and reveals conclusions, both process and outcome-oriented, that are of relevance to processes of public space generation and stewardship internationally. However, because the book draws its evidence from one city, in one region, of one country (and a 'world city' at that) no claim is made that the findings can be applied universally without question or due consideration to local context. To do so would be to fall into the same trap as much of the existing public space literature that is riven with wild and unsubstantiated extrapolations from the particular to the general, and from the theoretical to unquestioned received wisdom, without serious grounding in evidence.

So whilst the big themes from this research will surely be relevant elsewhere, the specific findings should only be extrapolated from London with care. By contrast, the continually questioning approach that the research espouses to the diversity of issues impacting on the even greater diversity of public space types in cities around the world, should be accepted universally. Public space researchers should reject the needlessly political, polemical and partisan – except as a valuable stimulus to thinking – and embrace instead the evidence of what works and what does not: how to make good cities from good public spaces, whatever their type. On this, the book attempts to throw a little light.

2 A CITY OF SQUARES, OPPORTUNITY AND NEGLECT

2.1   London 1832 – London's Roman roads can be seen leaving the city in all directions, whilst the city is growing to encompass outlying settlements, although some, such as Greenwich to the southeast, still remain distinct. To the west, the Georgian expansions are growing fast, whilst much of the rest of the city has expanded in an incremental unplanned manner

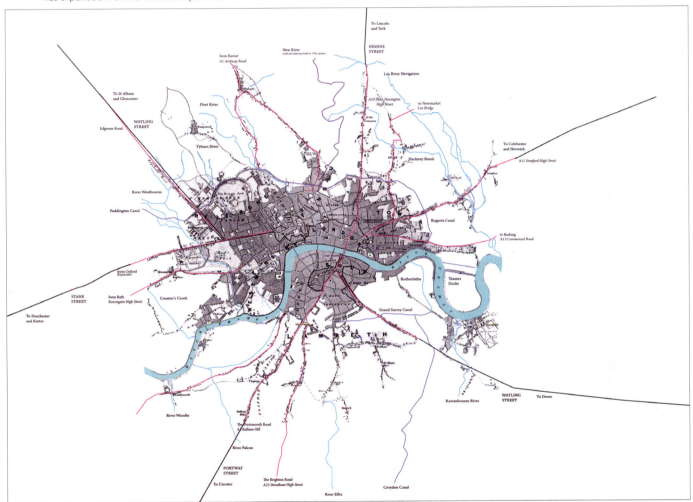

THE FACES OF LONDON THROUGH TIME

London is a metropolis with almost 2,000 years of history, but for three-quarters of its history it occupied little more than the square mile of what is today the City of London, and later a smaller area to the west, part of today's City of Westminster (Trent 1965). It was not until the seventeenth century and, more significantly, the eighteenth century that London really began to expand. It is not the intention of this book to offer a history of London's urban form and expansion, that is well covered elsewhere, but it would be remiss in a book on contemporary London public space not to discuss the city's great gift to international urbanism, the garden square, or to establish a historical lens through which to view public space in London today.

This chapter first examines the history of formal public spaces in London with an emphasis on the types of squares that have been dominant in London through its history. It goes on to reveal some of the essential characteristics of London's development and governance through time, and draws this together with a discussion of the period from 1979 to 1997 when the neo-liberal ideology of the Conservative governments of the time exemplified the laissez-faire approaches that have characterised much of London's history. The chapter covers the first 1,950 years of the city's history, bringing the story up to the election of New Labour in 1997. It leaves the next 15 years to Chapter 3.

A CITY OF SQUARES

The growth of London

Historic maps of London reveal three primary explanations for the structure of London today. First, a story rooted in the early development of London as a Roman settlement from the invasion of AD 43 to the end of occupation approximately 350 years later. During this period, the construction of Roman roads from the city to other Roman settlements – Bath, Lincoln, Canterbury, etc. – provided a network of links – Watling Street, Portway Street, Ermine Street, etc. – the routes of which have largely survived through to today (**2.1**). As London began to grow beyond its walls from the sixteenth century onwards, these created a structuring device for the growing city. Along them development of all types naturally spread, taking advantage of the increased opportunities for trade that was to be had beside these busy roads and the advantages of direct links back into the City of London. From this period onward, London was an open city, no longer hemmed in by defensive walls, and taking advantage of the relative lack of threats from outside to grow.

A second type of development has grown up independently of these major radial routes, growing instead as a consequence of pre-existing settlements. The Danish architect and town planner Steen Eiler Rasmussen (1948: 3) famously applauded the scattered, seemingly unplanned and open fabric that had derived from the agglomeration of London's numerous historic towns and villages. The origins of many of these is uncertain, but it is likely that some grew up around the convergence of particular local routes, whilst others may have derived initially from particular locational advantages – a river, a well, a protected position, etc. – only later becoming part of the wider

movement network. Today these previously outlying settlements such as Hampstead, Greenwich and Dulwich are buried deep within the Greater London metropolis, but are still recognisable as towns or villages in their own right.

These first two types of development can in large part be characterised as incremental and unplanned, with development happening along key routes and around pre-existing settlements in a manner unguided by a consciously conceived masterplan or other coordinating vision. By contrast, a third type of development has been 'designed' in the sense that it is characterised by a highly ordered and consciously conceived physical structure at the local scale, although often unplanned at the larger scale, with development occurring as a result of market opportunity as landowners, in a largely uncoordinated manner, realised the potential of their land holdings. Such development includes the major Georgian expansions of the eighteenth century and the Victorian and Edwardian suburbs, followed by the inter-war expansions (along new infrastructure lines out of the city) and by much speculative housebuilding ever since.

Today, the city is still largely dependent on the historic routes through its fabric that connect and pass through its towns and villages. In this regard it is distinct from cities such as Paris or Barcelona in that, whilst it has its 'designed' neighbourhoods (Bloomsbury, Hampstead Garden Suburb, etc.), it is not a city of grand boulevards and civic set pieces. Instead, it is characterised by its continuous network of everyday streets, and by a classic concentric pattern, with high densities in the centre (and at a few other strategic points), quickly reducing to a medium- and low-density expansive city form until halted by its green belt.

London squares: four historic models

Within this structure, English Heritage (2000) claim there are 600 squares across London, whilst Wikipedia lists over 500 of these, although it is not entirely clear on what basis they were selected and how comprehensive the list is (Wikipedia, Squares [n.d.]). Whatever the final number, it is probably true to say that the linear mixed-use street remains London's primary structuring device, whilst squares (as a type) reflect a continental European tradition that remained relatively unimportant until Renaissance influences began to be felt from the late sixteenth century onwards. From then on, squares became increasingly more popular as an urban element, and today many parts of central and inner London are sprinkled heavily with such spaces.

Continental European models of urbanism had visited London before – Roman Londinium had its amphitheatre and forum, but no traces of these survive above ground today. Setting these aside therefore, prior to 1980 London featured four types of public square:

1 medieval marketplaces

2 garden squares

3 civic set-pieces

4 modernist plazas.

London's medieval marketplaces

Although structured primarily through its street network, London has always featured spaces of greater consequence as the foci of public life; spaces left over for certain purposes, be they social (e.g. Tower Hill, the site of punishment and public executions), economic (e.g. Smithfield, a livestock market) or spiritual (e.g. St Paul's Churchyard). The medieval marketplace was the precursor to the formally designed squares of today and literally provided the 'place' for the market in which agricultural and other goods could be traded. Although the reasons for both the origins and the physical form that such markets took are often lost in time, most are organic in form, often more 'street-like' than 'square-like', and unlikely to be the result of conscious design processes. In other words, they emerged as the result of numerous uncoordinated decisions made over time.

For Postles (2004: 41), such markets became sites of negotiation and conflict, both commercial and social, but also of civic pride. Since they possessed this attribute of civic dignity, they also quite naturally became the sites of resistance and subversion, whether collective or individual. Conversely, this very pride meant that any abuse in this space was an abuse against the dignity of the town. This ranged from a host of what were seen as deviant behaviours to loitering. The marketplace was also, typically, the place of punishment, where ritual humiliation of 'offenders' was commonplace. Thus, although the crowded nature of public space allowed a measure of private subversion by users (Postles 2004: 42), marketplaces were by no means tolerant, equitable or associated with 'higher-order' pastimes.

2.2   Traditional marketplace, Kingston upon Thames

Instead, they were commercial, usually highly regulated and often physically uncomfortable spaces.

In the City of London, most markets occupied commercial streets rather than squares, for example the market held in what came to be known as Cheapside, which sold all kinds of goods and which remained for many years the City's principal marketplace (Calabi 2004: 40, 86–7). Over time, the form and function of the medieval market system in London was spatially reorganised, with a greater degree of product specialisation between markets, and the formalisation of pitches outside the City boundaries; for example Ingsrock in Westmouthfield took the clear form of a square (Calabi 2004: 87–91). Despite this, the purpose of these markets was almost entirely commercial, while other functions of the space, including civic ones, were negligible (Clout 1991: 148–9). The exception was Cheapside, which was often the site of royal and civic pageantry and popular celebration.

Significantly, public space in the City of London tended to be more differentiated than in the rest of the country, something explained by the size and relative organisation of the City through the auspices of the City of London Corporation, whose roots date back at least 1,000 years (City of London, History [n.d.]). The result was greater choice offered to users, although this was not a choice born of true democracy but rather of the particular governance of the Corporation, dominated (as it still is today) by business interests, with most decisions made for sound commercial reasons, including, when commercial dictates suggested otherwise, the disbanding of particular markets. As such, marketplaces outside the City are most representative of this type today. Examples include those of Kingston upon Thames (**2.2**), Enfield, Woolwich, Barnet and Romford, each featuring markets with ancient roots that once served the scattered villages surrounding London, but which today still function as marketplaces within Greater London.

Garden squares

A number of ancient village greens, originally with the status of common land, have also been incorporated into London as its boundaries have expanded. Like the marketplaces, today these spaces are surrounded by buildings and provide an important focus for a range of social (including sporting) functions in some of London's outlying centres, for example Islington Green, Turnham Green and Twickenham Green. Unlike the marketplaces, these are green spaces, but, like them, they were never consciously designed, and remain organic spaces today. Their size, however, usually prohibits them from being perceived as squares.

The majority of London's 'green' squares (which also form the majority of squares in London) fall under a separate category for which London is rightly famed, its garden squares, most originating from the seventeenth and eighteenth centuries. These 'London Squares', as they are sometimes termed, represented one of the first effective ways of integrating elements of the natural landscape into the urban fabric. In the main, they have survived the wars, post-war rebuilding and (in many cases) the wholesale conversion of their surrounding building stock into offices. Today, they are recognised as one of the most precious features of London's heritage, as well as desirable places to live and work (Barry 2003a: 8; Goodman 2003: 8–9). They offered a social model for the first modern public parks, and represented an early expression of the desires for social segregation and privatised domesticated open space that, arguably, later inspired the landscapes of suburbia. As such, the garden square offered a model of urban planning adopted and adapted the world over, which also informed much of the urban landscape constructed during the twentieth century (Lawrence 1993: 115).

In the beginning, the garden squares were not designed to be places for strolling or relaxing in the open, to be green spaces, or to be 'English' in design at all. They were instead formal hard piazzas in the

continental European mode, places for parking carriages, for resting, watering and feeding horses, and places to offset the elegant facades that surrounded them. Covent Garden, for example, the first of these new residential squares, was created by Inigo Jones in 1630 in the Italianate style. But with insufficient space provided for back gardens in the houses that surrounded them, pressure subsequently came to bear to transform these blank open spaces into a common garden or park. In London, this was the beginning of the garden square as a place for social purposes (Goodman 2003: 4–5; Catt 1995: 18).

After the Great Fire of London in 1666, as the urban area of London spread slowly to the east and more rapidly to the west and north of the city, the residential square became one of the major forms used to establish new districts for the wealthier classes. A few of the garden squares have their origin in former burial grounds or open grazing, such as Coram's Fields and Lincoln's Inn Fields, but most were the creation of the aristocratic landlords who laid out much of residential London from 1660 onwards (Binney 2001: 3). From the beginning, they were intended to be amenities that increased the value of the property surrounding them (Goodman 2003: 1–5; Lawrence 1993: 95). Collectively, however, they were quite unplanned and there was no coherent plan at any time until the nineteenth century to provide open spaces for the enjoyment of common people (Trent 1965: 233–45).

In most cases, the land remained in the ownership of the original landowner, who leased it to speculators or directly to the tenants, usually on long leases (up to 99 years) rather than selling it outright. Often, the landowners, or more rarely the developers, had control over the design of the buildings surrounding the square and most strove to achieve unified facades, though many fell short of this goal owing to vagaries in the pace of construction and the will of contractors and leaseholders. Most of the landowners also had restrictive covenants that limited the ability of leaseholders to modify their premises and in their use of open space. These prohibited such activities as the dumping of refuse, building of sheds or planting private gardens (Lawrence 1993: 91–100).

The history of London's garden squares demonstrates how these places were not designed as gardens for the general populace but instead as exclusive enclaves of attached houses fronting onto private spaces where the aristocracy could live alongside their peers. In essence,

2.3   Bedford Square, Bloomsbury – dating from 1783, built for the Dukes of Bedford (now the Bedford Estates), the central garden is open to key holders only

they were exclusionary and exclusive spaces, often situated within larger development schemes that were themselves gated (e.g. large parts of Bloomsbury), whilst increasingly the squares themselves were fenced-in as they transmuted from hard open spaces into green garden squares.

Through this process, the residential squares played a pivotal role in introducing trees and gardens into the urban layout and in shaping subsequent environmental ideals of urban life. Indeed, the transformations of the residential squares of London during the eighteenth and nineteenth centuries can be seen as an important chapter in the development of the city in its own right, transforming

not only the appearance of these places but also their functions (Goodman 2003: 1; Lawrence 1993: 90), although their exclusive and exclusionary nature became more pronounced in the process. What is clear is that London gained these green spaces (and its parks) by establishing a customary right or privilege for aristocrats, not for Londoners at large.

The process of actually enclosing the squares was often initiated by the residents of the squares, not by the landed freeholder. Petitions to Parliament were put forward by groups of leaseholders to protect the space in front of their houses, their personal amenity, and by landlords attempting to maintain the value of their properties. According to

Lawrence (1993: 99), the process represented a major step away from the feudal forms of property relations and towards capitalist forms. The first parliamentary enclosure act was passed in 1726 to enable the residents of St James's Square to restrict public access to the square and to levy a rate on themselves for its improvement and maintenance. Others in a similar vein followed rapidly, and still today the centres of many squares are accessible only to residents of the surrounding buildings (**2.3**).

However, by the 1880s, serious efforts were under way to open many of the garden squares to public use (Royal Commission on London Squares, 1928) and at the end of the nineteenth century the private street barriers were removed. According to Leendertz (2006: 72) 'London squares have been called the city's lungs because of the pollution-filtering and oxygen-pumping action of all that foliage'. But whilst 'the trees may provide fresh air for all ... the squares themselves are not for the likes of most of us to actually walk in and enjoy; they are private and we are destined to peer, urchin-like, through the railings'. For others, reflecting on the poor state that some of these spaces had been allowed to degenerate to by the turn of the twenty-first century, the first step to their restoration was the return of their railings (removed for the war effort) in order to keep people out at night and users safe by day (Barry, 2003b: 9). Whether public or private, they are undeniably enriching to the London streetscene.

Civic set-pieces

If London's medieval market spaces grew incrementally over time and not through a conscious design process, and its garden squares were designed as private spaces to be enjoyed by the privileged few; then before the twentieth century only a tiny number of London's squares were consciously designed for the mass of Londoners, as truly public spaces. In large part these were designed as civic set-pieces, variously as places to off-set important buildings, mark important junctions, to reflect the grandeur of a growing empire, places for statues and monuments, and as sites for public gathering, celebration and, even, protest. Spaces of this type include Piccadilly Circus, Sloane Square, and. most notably, Parliament and Trafalgar Squares. Guildhall Yard in the City (or parts thereof) has been through many incarnations in its long history, from the site of the original Roman amphitheatre, to churchyard, to the dumping ground for the carcasses of skinned cats (Colson 2009), but the space has also been subject to a series of formal design processes, resulting in today's ceremonial set-piece.

Trafalgar and Parliament Squares are visited by people from around the world, include more than 30 Grade I listed buildings, and represent key civic set-pieces. Both these squares also have specific political purposes as sites of public protest and demonstration in which citizens press public claims (Parkinson, 2006: 5). Farrell (2010: 262) identifies them as two corners of a triumvirate that reflect a hidden order at the heart of the capital. The triumvirate encompasses the key power relationships in the city, namely government and church (Parliament Square), the people (Trafalgar Square), and the monarch as represented by the site of the Queen Victoria Memorial outside of Buckingham Palace, being the third point on the triumvirate and the space of national celebration and mourning.

Since its foundation in the mid nineteenth century, Trafalgar Square has been the site of public gatherings and demonstrations, from the Chartists who assembled there in 1848 to the thousands of anti-Iraq-war protesters who passed through the square on the way to a mass rally in Hyde Park in 2003. Thus Keller (2007: 9) comments that in the nineteenth century, places such as Hyde Park and Trafalgar Square became test-beds for how public spaces would or would not be used for civic purposes. 'Such defined areas had not existed since ancient times. For the first time in the modern era, citizenry and government tested legal boundaries regarding personal liberties and public space.'

Today, Trafalgar Square has a further important function as a venue for large-scale external events and a key social and activities space for London (see Chapter 6), yet the very 'civic' and 'monumental' intentions of the Square remain obvious in its original 1812 design by John Nash, who spearheaded an early and uncharacteristic flowering of formal civic design in Regency London. Named in honour of a great naval victory and dominated by its statue of Nelson and the presence of the National Gallery on its north side, the space celebrates power and oozes the national self-confidence of its era. However, this imposed grandeur and civic pretention brought with it concerns that the private garden squares avoided, namely that because it was open, it also needed adequate lighting to prevent those with bad intentions from lurking in the shadows whilst making it more difficult for the homeless to rest there unseen (Mace 2005: 12–17, 88).

Mace (2005) recounts the history of protests in Trafalgar Square, and that throughout its history the attitude of the state to such protests has swung from tolerance to opposition and back again. These swings

2.4   Parliament Square, site of the 2010 Peace Camp

included the adoption of specific regulations promulgated at the end of the nineteenth century to severely curtail such activities, and the construction of a tiny police station in 1927 in the southeast corner of the Square as a lookout post for a policeman in order to monitor protests and other activities. In recent times, however, the regulations have been greatly relaxed and throughout the 1980s a continuous anti-apartheid protest was held outside South Africa House on the Square. The Square was also scene to a large vigil held shortly after the terrorist bombings in London on 7 July 2005, bombings that followed the day after the Square had been the focus for scenes of

jubilation as London won the right to host the 2012 Olympic Games. Such activities have ensured that Trafalgar Square has become an enormously important symbolic political and social location, whilst its near neighbour, Parliament Square, had increasingly become the site of conflict between activists and the state over the right to protest.

Parliament Square, another civic set-piece, was part of Sir Charles Barry's designs for the rebuilding of the Houses of Parliament following the fire of 1834. The Square was laid out in 1868 in order to open up the space around the Palace of Westminster, improve traffic

2.5   Lakeside Terrace, the Barbican, City of London

flow and form a key part of the ceremonial route between Westminster Abbey (on the south side of the Square) and Westminster Hall (used for state funerals and other civic occasions) (Heath 1998: 16). Along with Trafalgar Square, the central garden area was transferred from government control to the Greater London Authority (the Mayor) in 1999. The GLA now has responsibility to light, cleanse, water, pave, and repair the garden, and has power to make by-laws for the Square.

The east side of Parliament Square, lying opposite one of the key entrances to the Houses of Parliament, has historically been a common site of protest against government action, with notorious confrontations recorded on the site involving the Tolpuddle Martyrs, Chartists and Suffragettes, all pressing for civil liberties, and more recently between the police and supporters of the pro-hunting Countryside Alliance (Tames 2005: 80–1). Between 2001 and 2011, the Square was also home to veteran peace campaigner Brian Haw and in 2010 hosted a 'Peace Camp' occupied by protesters against the war in Afghanistan (**2.4**), eventually removed by bailiffs at the behest of Mayor Boris Johnson, who argued at the Court of Appeal that the self-styled Democracy Village was unsightly, damaged the historic fabric of the site, and undermined the right of other Londoners and 'responsible protestors' to use the site (Bingham 2010). For others, this is 'not a mere public space, but a location of huge democratic significance' that the peace camp encapsulated (Tony Benn, quoted in Bindmans 2010).

Parliament Square has also been the setting for more mainstream political display, as a site of monuments to celebrate the lives of important political figures – contrasting with the military figures displayed in Trafalgar Square. In 1926, the Square became the first official roundabout (or gyratory) in Britain (Nairn 1988: 28), and, unlike Trafalgar Square, remains one today – in 2008 Mayor Boris Johnson pulled funding for a large-scale redevelopment scheme that had been planned by his predecessor, Ken Livingstone. With debates raging in the press in 2010 about the right to peaceful protest versus the rights of other users in public space (e.g. tourists), or indeed the rights of one group of protesters over another, the case of Parliament Square demonstrated how these civic spaces of high public use and high public and political emotion can also become the most controversial sites for regeneration, leading, in the case of Parliament Square, to stagnation (see Chapter 3). In general, however, the small numbers of these spaces in London ensures they will remain the exception rather than the rule, albeit exceptions with a unique and vital role.

Modernist plazas

From the mid nineteenth century onwards, the garden square increasingly fell out of fashion as owners of residential properties increasingly preferred their own gardens. Thus most new housing after 1850 took the form of suburban villas or semi-detached houses, each with its own private garden front and back (Catt 1995: 20). From that point on, new squares in London became a rarity, at least until the plazas of the modernist housing estates began to appear.

The modernist project was not known for its construction of urban squares, which, as urban elements, might instead be viewed as part of the traditional urban canon. Instead, modernism favoured buildings as sculptural objects seen within space (e.g. a landscape setting), rather than buildings defining space (streets, squares, courtyards, etc.) as cities up to that point had been. However, when modernism came up against traditional urban settings such as a war-damaged London, some modification of the modernist precepts were often made in order to respond to the setting and obtain the necessary support from still-conservative regulatory authorities and funders. In this way a sort of intermediate (modernist/traditional) urban form emerged.

Whilst outer London sometimes exhibited purer forms of the modernist genre in its many post-war housing estates, central London became dotted with examples of the intermediate forms, many following the post-war rebuilding of London. Examples included cultural spaces such as those around the Southbank Centre and the Royal Festival Hall (now remodelled, see Chapter 7); residential squares such as those of the Barbican (**2.5**) in the City, or the green spaces at Robin Hood Gardens in the East End or on the Aylesbury Estate in Southeast London (both being redeveloped); corporate plazas, such as that below Centrepoint on Charing Cross Road in the West End (being remodelled), or the original post-war Paternoster Square (now redeveloped, see Chapter 5); and those associated with infrastructure, such as the somewhat later Euston Station Plaza (now substantially modified, see Chapter 7).

As the examples suggest, the history of modernist piazzas has often been short, with spaces being substantially remodelled or included within large-scale redevelopment schemes from the 1980s onwards. The last hurrah for modernist piazzas came in 1984 when a scheme by Mies van der Rohe for Mansion House Square (the site of No.1 Poultry in the City) was rejected at a high-profile public inquiry following the savaging of the tower block component of the development by the Prince of Wales, who described it as a 'glass stump'. The project had included a grand modernist piazza at the base of the tower – Seagram style – but the failure of this project to get off the ground concluded a short-lived and largely unsuccessful genre, at least in London, where few of this type now remain.

The legacy of London squares

Despite the rather ad hoc and informal manner in which London has grown, it is a city with a rich heritage of squares, from the iconic to the unknown, from great architectural set-pieces to architectural disasters, and everything in between. According to English Heritage, squares in London help to combine high-density urban development with a quality urban environment, creating in the process more sustainable neighbourhoods. But, whether public or private, not all of London's historic squares are well maintained, and some suffer from a lack of funds and a downward spiral of degradation and vandalism. In some historic spaces, later insensitive design interventions such as the insertion of underground car parks with vehicle ramps, air vents and inappropriate signs, poor-quality surfacing and planting, and the random introduction of unwanted facilities have spoilt their character (Catt 1995: 33–4; Hillman 1988: 67–74; Clout & Wood 1986: 142–3).

2.6   Type of gardens, squares and enclosures in London according to the Report of the Royal Commission in 1927 (adapted from Catt 1995: 5)

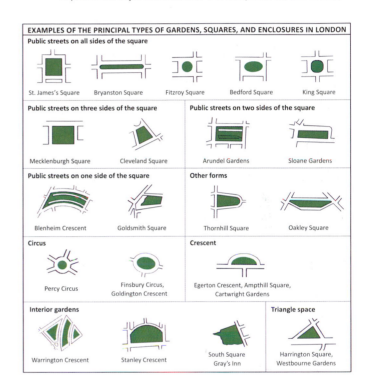

In fact repeated attempts have been made since 1855 to deal with the management problems associated with London's squares. In 1927, for example, the London County Council (LCC) asked the then government to institute an inquiry to look at squares and enclosures in London. In September 1928, the resulting Royal Commission produced a report, the focus of which was limited to the garden squares, of which it identified 461. This included general recommendations, such as visually opening them up in order to increase their amenity value 'to the inhabitants of the houses facing the enclosure as well as the public' (cited in Catt 1995: 34–7). The report also typologically classified London's garden squares, revealing in the process the sheer variety and potential complexity of these spaces (**2.6**). It led to the London Squares Preservation Act 1931 and to statutory protection for all the squares identified in the report. The act states that 'a protected square may not be used for any purpose other than an ornamental garden, pleasure ground or ground for play, rest or recreation, and that no

2.7 St James's Square, laid out in the 1670s

building, structure or erection shall be created or placed on or over any protected square except such as may be necessary or convenient for the use or maintenance of the square for an authorised purpose'.

Today, these spaces remain a top conservation priority across the capital, although actual practice varies locally. For English Heritage (2000: 3–9) they offer a traditional device to 'link communities through a network of socially interactive focal points'. They identify four types of benefit that the historic squares continue to deliver:

- **social and cultural** – an oasis for workers to relax and talk, promoting community spirit amongst residents, and space for play and active recreation;

- **aesthetic** – effecting a seamless unification of architecture, street and open space, breaking up the dense grain of the city and making it more legible;

- **environmental** – offering a home to trees, plants and animals that link city dwellers to the natural world and to the changing rhythm of the seasons;

- **economic** – one of the main reasons visitors and businesses come to London is the quality of its historic buildings, parks and open spaces.

Some of these are collective benefits to society and others accrue just to the users of the space. In many of London's garden squares, these are still the resident or corporate keyholders immediately surrounding the space.

A CITY OF OPPORTUNITY

A lesson from history

For Steen Eiler Rasmussen (1948: 23), from its evolution as a Roman city to modern times, the importance of London was primarily due to its position as the great centre of commerce. For him, the free spirit and determination to resist absolutism that accompanies such an open and unfettered view of the world can be traced in the built form of the city, characteristics best reflected in the almost immediate rejection of Sir Christopher Wren's grand plans for the rebuilding of the City of London in the monumental continental style following the 1666 Great Fire of London. Thus Rasmussen (1948: 110–21) recounts how the King (Charles II), who had lived for many years in the French Court, was quickly seduced by Wren's plans and proclaimed that any rebuilding should await his full consideration of the proposals. Yet, just three days later, the plans had been soundly rejected in favour of speedy rebuilding upon existing plots and foundations when pressure had been brought to bear on the King by representatives of the City shocked by the seeming impracticality of an idealised plan, not least in what it meant for existing property rights. The result was a further proclamation setting down, instead of a grand plan, plans for a series of regulations (the minimum deemed 'absolutely necessary') to ensure the safe rebuilding of the City in a manner that reduces the risk of fire spread. These included that buildings should be of brick and stone, and controls on the width of streets (to widen them), and on building heights.

The episode, although 350 years ago, demonstrates three continuing characteristics of the development of London:

1   the reluctance of the state to commit large-scale investment to undertake works of deemed public benefits when a functioning market will do the job instead, albeit in its own image and based on market opportunity and preferences rather than social good;

2   that power is fragmented and uncoordinated, leading to ad hoc and uncertain decision-making, to complicated lines of responsibility for urban space, and to the privileging of landowners who exploit the lack of clear public policy;

3   a preference for 'light touch' public regulation over 'heavy handed' public vision, with the market providing the direction for the state to follow and the state thereafter influencing at the edges to ensure that the worst excesses of unfettered capitalism are avoided.

For Farrell (2010: 12), London is a natural city, collectively planned over time, built by many hands, with no superimposed order. He quotes Peter Ackroyd, who remarks that London has 'never followed a theory or an idea. It had never been driven by a coherent philosophy. It has simply grown in an organic fashion, opportunistic, haphazard, market-led. Yet [despite this] every building seems part of a general pattern, of a general will to exist in this shape and in no other' (Farrell 2010: 170).

Emergence of a speculative development model

The age of the garden square demonstrated exactly these same characteristics. Thus, between 1650 and 1800, the population of London jumped from just 375,000 inhabitants to almost one million, with huge pressure to provide new housing development – and not just for the gentry. This marked the beginning of a fully-fledged property market in London as speculators rose to the challenge.

The speculators ranged from members of the nobility such as the Earl of Bedford, to architects and tradesmen, to entrepreneurs with no background in land ownership or construction. For example, St James's Square was developed by Henry Jermyn, the Lord of St Albans, close to St James's Palace, where Charles II wanted to encourage 'respectable' neighbours (**2.7**). The Lord of St Albans had not inherited the land, but was granted a 60-year lease as a favour from the Crown on the basis that he would build large mansions around the new square to be occupied by only the best families, including his own. Such families, however, were not prepared to lay out for large houses on the basis of a 60-year lease, and following further negotiations Jermyn was granted the freehold, allowing him to increase the number of plots and begin building (Catt 1995: 17). In these circumstances, the building lease represented a convenient device by which the land could be rendered profitable over and over again, with the family retaining their long-term interest in the land and its ongoing profitability. Provision of high quality amenities, including the residential squares, but also often a church and market (nearby), were part of the package.

The most celebrated non-aristocratic speculative builder of the seventeenth century was Dr Nicholas Barbon, who was active all over London, perfecting the method of dividing large land parcels into smaller lots and selling each segment to workmen for as much as possible whilst putting his own buildings on plots that he could not sell. Barbon, for example, demolished two riverside palaces, Essex House and York House in the Strand, and covered their sites with streets; he also built Red Lion Square (Catt 1995: 17–18). Barbon and others of his ilk in large part invented the Georgian terrace, a model that, along with its handsome streets and squares, spread throughout the world, and was able to cover large areas in a unified and coherent manner on the basis of very little, if any, pre-planning. Hebbert (1998: 30) quotes Rasmussen's original interpretation of this process in three elements that also echo point for point the three characteristics of the London development process described above:

1   consumer preference, expressed in the evolution of architectural taste through the classicism that unified the London terraces;

2   private landlordism in the freedom of landowners around London to develop their holdings;

3   public regulation under the London Building Acts.

Even the major public investments that did happen in London, such as the northerly bypass of the mid eighteenth century (now the Marylebone, Euston, Pentonville and City Roads) and the Embankment projects over a century later, were driven by absolute necessity (e.g. to solve the 'Great Stink' created by the then putrid Thames) rather than through any sense that a particular type of London should be created. Until the twentieth century, most other major investments (e.g. the rail and underground lines, dock systems, the housing stock, local roads, etc.) were provided by private enterprise and on the basis of opportunity and what the market would provide; an attitude to infrastructure that persists today, with upgrades to the Docklands Light Railway (from the 1980s), Jubilee line extension (1990s), Channel Tunnel Rail Link (2000s) and the new east/west train line, Crossrail (from 2018), each made possible only following direct private sector investment or negotiated contributions.

Hebbert (1998: 33) recounts how efforts to hold back the tide of free enterprise in London have historically been doomed to failure. These included an early attempt to constrain the outward growth of London by preventing, via the Parliamentary Bill that enabled its construction, residential development within 50 feet either side of the new northern bypass. This soon came to naught, however, as continuous frontages developed along its full length. Later, in the nineteenth and twentieth centuries, unbridled development continued on two fronts:

● first, as a continuation of the terraced forms westward out of London, following the unwritten urban code of the Georgians with well-mannered streets and garden squares adorned, by this time, with more expressive Victorian facades;

● second, around this expanded inner London core, where a much larger expansion into the new suburbs was underway, led by an army of small-scale speculative developers who, at a tremendous rate, built out along and between the new rail lines from London wherever the availability of land, capital and demand took them.

In these cases, the urban code of the Georgians was increasingly dispensed with, and replaced from 1874 onwards with by-laws and then planning and highways standards that guaranteed minimum standards for light, air and traffic flow but, despite pretence to the contrary, often failed to deliver the other amenities that the earlier developments had (Carmona 2001: 19–23). Today, the speculative development model still predominates in the residential sector, although the developers today are no longer aristocrats, but instead national housebuilding companies (and their subsidiaries) with interests that are short term and market-driven, rather than long term and embedded in the places they create.

A fragmented governance

If the expanding London exhibited a laissez-faire approach to its own destiny and a contentment to let private interests pursue those interests largely uninhibited, then at least part of this must be put down to the fragmented governance that characterised London from the moment it spread outside the historic boundaries of the square mile. Thus the City through its Corporation had a very clear and unified organisation for its governance, and retains many of its ancient rights through to today. Outside those boundaries, however, a competing patchwork of monarchy, national government, local

administration (liberties, district boards, parishes and hundreds), the church (e.g. the civil vestries), landed estates and, from 1855, the Metropolitan Board of Works, provided a patchwork of authority and little coordinated vision for how London might grow. So, for example, whilst Paris was rebuilding itself under Baron Haussmann as the grand imperial capital, private business ran London, with London's burgeoning business community using (and effectively running) the array of local administrative authorities to redevelop the city in their own image. In the process, during the mid Victorian era, public space took a back seat.

However, from the late Victorian period onwards, greater attention started to be paid to London governance. The fragmented local structures that surrounded the City transmuted first, in 1900, into metropolitan boroughs alongside unitary authorities for Croydon, East Ham and West Ham, and then, in 1965, into London boroughs. This was matched at the London-wide scale by the journey from the Metropolitan Board of Works to the London Country Council in 1888, to the Greater London Council in 1965, to no strategic authority from 1986, and finally, in 2000, to today's Greater London Authority headed by the Mayor of London. Throughout, a patchwork of responsibilities has remained, as have frequent tensions between the layers of government (including with central government) (**2.8**). This contributes to a sense of drift.

Decisions on the types of major development in the capital that are likely to generate new public spaces will almost certainly cut across the interests and remits of local, London-wide and national government, as well as a host of government agencies and commissions. In some parts of London, the landed estates remain as powerful as ever, as does, within its boundaries, the City Corporation, although now subject to the strategic precepts of the Mayor's London Plan. The result, arguably, has been a rather ad hoc decision-making framework that survives in its essentials through to today, and around which adept private interests weave their way.

In the era of New Labour (post-1997 – see Chapter 3), this fragment-ation of responsibility multiplied, with the multiple bodies of local government also followed by a host of Local Strategic Partnerships (LSPs) with responsibility for coordinating the voice of local business, local community and local government through the production of Community Strategies. At various scales and in various ways with

2.8   London's 32 Boroughs and the City of London

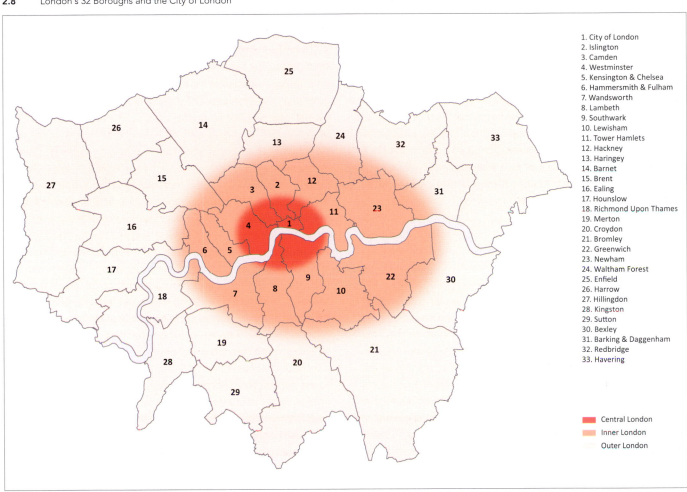

1. City of London
2. Islington
3. Camden
4. Westminster
5. Kensington & Chelsea
6. Hammersmith & Fulham
7. Wandsworth
8. Lambeth
9. Southwark
10. Lewisham
11. Tower Hamlets
12. Hackney
13. Haringey
14. Barnet
15. Brent
16. Ealing
17. Hounslow
18. Richmond Upon Thames
19. Merton
20. Croydon
21. Bromley
22. Greenwich
23. Newham
24. Waltham Forest
25. Enfield
26. Harrow
27. Hillingdon
28. Kingston
29. Sutton
30. Bexley
31. Barking & Daggenham
32. Redbridge
33. Havering

Central London
Inner London
Outer London

various influence, these sprung up all over London, although the strategies they spawned were often little more than motherhood and apple pie aspirations, requiring the development plan to give them a sense of spatial meaning. In the Thames Gateway (the 80,000 hectare great eastern development opportunity for London), this process of governance overload came to its nadir under New Labour, with government quangos, local strategic partnerships, regeneration agencies, traditional local government, the GLA family, national government departments, offices and committees, community organisations, and a slew of major landowners wallowing in a largely

directionless and uncoordinated space of governance and little else. There 'it took the private ruminations of one individual architect, Sir Terry Farrell, to mobilise a single big idea capable of sustaining momentum' (Nicolaou & Chaplin 2010: 228, 232).

A departure from normal business

Faced with a fragmented governance and a powerful private sector, even the 'heroic' – Hebbert says 'lethal' – Abercrombie plans for the post-war reconstruction that aimed to 'eliminate the life and variety of the streets and parcel London into a series of self-contained new-built enclaves' were continually frustrated in favour of retaining the 'curious street network' (Hebbert 1998: 75). For Hebbert, drawing a direct parallel with the frustrated grand plans of 1666, the structure of London survived after the Second World War more by fortune than design, a combination of austerity (initially), opposition from vested interests and local opinion formers, and intra- and inter-governmental discordance (between government departments and between governance tiers). The result was that although ad hoc 'improvement' schemes dotted London (and dominated the East End), including a range of comprehensive redevelopment and roads schemes, criticism of large-scale redevelopment had become rife by the 1960s and so wholesale restructuring of London never came.

Despite this, the period from 1945 to 1979 represented a short-lived departure from normal business in London. It was a period when development became primarily a state-led activity though the offices of the LCC/GLC, and at the local level via the London boroughs. The priority was housing, and this was seen as a public good to be provided by a benevolent state. Although private housebuilders continued to build in the suburbs, their projects were in the main small scale (by comparison), without civic pretention, and shaped by the types of planning and highways standards referred to above, wielded by the boroughs to control what was seen as the rump of housing provision (the main event being housing produced by the state itself). For Jenkins (1975), this was a reversal in fortunes that saw the decline of the private landlord and a rise in public ownership – a state of being that extended to the ownership of the types of new residential public spaces that were being produced.

The results are well documented, that although these places were technically in public ownership, in reality they often seemed to belong to no one in particular, and so, at best, were ignored, poorly managed and gradually decayed. At worst, they were appropriated by anti-social groups with exclusionary consequences for almost all other potential users, including their tenants. Public in name only, when the physical and social problems surrounding these newcomers to the London squares scene began to be addressed in the 1990s and 2000s, the answer was usually a clean sweep.

By contrast, in the commercial sphere during this period, private capital still dominated, although with an increasingly strong guiding hand from the public authorities and public funding for the more ambitious infrastructure elements. Thus armed with their grand plans for megastructures, grade-separated roads and towers, London's transport and land-use planners attempted to free themselves from what they saw as the shackles of their traditional city. Parts of these schemes were built across the capital, usually part of some grand plan of which only relatively small fragments were built, including, for example, the Euston underpass.

Significantly, it was the attempt to obliterate key London spaces such as Piccadilly Circus (**2.9**) and Covent Garden (see below) with such megastructure schemes (projects finally killed off by government in 1972 and 1973 respectively) that really galvanised opinion against these alien insertions and awoke an appreciation of the city as it was, rather than as it could be. Moreover, as the criticisms steadily grew, the public sector finances steadily shrank, portending both a removal of the redevelopment threat to London's historic neighbourhoods, but also a general and growing new appreciation of the city's Georgian and Victorian heritage and a determination to preserve it. Instead, from the late 1960s onwards, large parts of London were progressively covered by conservation designations, including all the now highly valued eighteenth-century neighbourhoods.

By the 1980s, the state had effectively withdrawn as a developer in London, in favour of a new role, as conserver. In this endeavour, and hand in hand with English Heritage (who have had an enhanced role in London), London government has been highly successful – at least if measured by the extent of conservation designations that cover the city rather than by the extent of activity to systematically enhance this heritage. The City of Westminster, for example, has 11,000 listed buildings and 55 conservation areas covering 75% of its territory. Less historic parts of London have far less, including the London Borough of Barking and Dagenham, which has just four conservation areas.

Post 1980, the identification and pursuit of opportunity lay once more in the hands of the private sector, although now restricted in many parts of London (particularly in the centre) by historic constraints that, until recently, were not part of the development landscape. As such, the departure during the 1950s to 1970s from the normal business of London as city of private opportunity was replaced with a further departure that ramped up from the late 1960s onwards in the form of conservation restrictions imposed by the state on the

2.9   Piccadilly Circus – site of the 1962 plans for a double-decker megastructure proposed by William Holford

free market, including on the provision and re-provision of public space.

A CITY OF NEGLECT

Conflict and change

The period from 1980 to the early 1990s is well covered in the literature on British politics, planning, governance and development. It was a period of hugely divisive 'conviction' politics, laissez-faire planning, increasingly centralised governance, weakened local government and (outside historic areas) of largely unfettered free-market development. For London, normal business seemed to have resumed as the city once again saw a flourishing of market opportunity, reversing ground lost to its international competitors during the 1970s (Simmie 1994: 157). Arguably, however, this was at the expense of many public interests as the state's involvement in London reverted to a regulatory role and as a stimulator of market opportunity.

The political story as it relates to London's development is well told elsewhere (Pimlott & Rao 2002; Newman & Thornley 1997), but, in essence, London initially stood out against the right-wing doctrines of the Thatcher governments of the period, in 1981 electing the

(then) left-wing Labour politician Ken Livingstone to lead the GLC, leading to inevitable conflict and to the eventual abolition of the GLC at the behest of Margaret Thatcher. This was a period in which the politics of London was at its most divergent, with grassroots activists opposing many key development projects, and with hugely varied visions about London's future and the future of its communities apparent at national, London-wide and borough scales. If the period saw a rapid return of the market to dominate the development scene, it also witnessed a departure from the relative stability in London's political scene that had existed at least up to the mid 1960s, and that increasingly diverged thereafter (Gyford 1994: 84–6).

The result was that planning, already marginalised by the government, was further marginalised in London, where the regional tier was stripped away, leaving only the 32 boroughs and City Corporation to represent London, or 'vie with each other like so many Italian principalities' (Hillman 1988: 101). This situation quickly worsened when even the boroughs refused to talk to each other, with the Labour-controlled boroughs leaving the London Boroughs Association (the forum for exchanging information and coordinating interests) to establish their own rival group, the Association of London Authorities. In its absence at a London scale, London-wide governance (including planning and transport) reverted to the national level, which waited until 1989 to issue RPG3, strategic planning guidance for London (Regional Planning Guidance 3: London), a permissive set of policies containing little strategic vision for the capital and virtually no policy on London's environmental quality beyond policies protecting strategic views of St Paul's and the Palace of Westminster, and some very generic aspirations to maintain the vitality and character of town centres and sustain 'residential amenity'. The policy in London, as elsewhere, was one of a presumption in favour of development, with early development in Docklands demonstrating what such an entirely permissive environment would spawn (**2.10**).

Unlike Scotland and Wales, and despite its larger population and multiple endemic problems, London had no dedicated Minister, and was simply one of the many conflicting responsibilities of the Secretary of State for the Environment (alongside all other English towns and cities). It was not until 1994 that the government of John Major finally established the Government Office for London (GOL) and instigated a Cabinet Sub-Committee for the capital in an attempt to fill an increasingly obvious gap.

2.10   The market given a free hand in London's Docklands

position of planning and the politicisation of the decision-making processes that this gave rise to – in particular the battle between local and national government – but also to the impact of a number of underlying trends that London was gripped by. These included, first, an increasingly strong emphasis on efficiency in the delivery of public services, for example the spread of Compulsory Competitive tendering for many public space management functions, with whole swathes of previously public sector activities being tendered out to the private sector. Planning was certainly not immune from this trend, and London's planning authorities were often cut to the bone, with forward planning activities in particular being marginalised and often split from development management functions.

Second, there was a new emphasis on urban regeneration, although initially (as in Docklands) with a strong emphasis on private investment and very little concern for development quality. Third, there was an increasing obsession with international competitiveness, with London's position as a 'World City' seen to be under threat from the ambitious plans of international competitors, whilst its lack of a strong strategic planning framework left the city weak both in terms of making the case for new transport investment and in terms of promoting the quality-of-life factors that were required to compete at the top table. Fourth, the Thatcherite policies of the 1980s, although delivering the required structural change to the economy, were also resulting in a polarisation of London's population, with the wealthy and middle-class homeowners doing well out of the new opportunities that the city presented, whilst low earners were finding it difficult to survive in an increasingly expensive city where a growing underclass was being largely ignored and was choosing to opt out from society altogether, with knock-on impacts on crime, drug use, vagrancy, social breakdown and long-term unemployment. It was in such a context that the outputs from a final trend identified by Hall (1994: 179) – the growth of the mega-project – seemed often to be particularly divisive.

Return of the square

With the deregulation of financial services in the City of London, a huge demand for floor space was unleashed: deep-plan, highly serviced spaces that could not easily be shoehorned into the historic buildings and tight urban grain of the City. Instead, developers looked for opportunities where large sites had become available because of the presence of large areas of obsolete buildings and infrastructure or where the air rights above infrastructure could be

In reality, from the demise of the GLC in 1986 to the creation of the GLA in 2000, London saw a period of weak governance, weak planning and a resurgent market, and in the 1980s and 1990s the direction was firmly away from London as a place where things were made to London as a place where things (mostly shares, commodities and money) were traded. Thus, in the early 1990s, Coupland (1992: 25) queried whether every job needed to be an office job, and raised the spatial implications of a trend such that London might become less a city of villages and much more focused on its centre. In fact, when London-wide governance returned to the capital once again, this market-driven trend was anyway endorsed as official policy (see Chapter 3).

For Peter Hall (1994), the changing circumstances in which London found itself during the period were down not just to the weakened

utilised. The larger scale of individual buildings was matched by a larger scale of project overall, frequently exceeding 100,000 square metres in size, and often incorporating retail uses and a new public realm (Punter 1992: 70–1).

The best known and most divisive was undoubtedly London's Docklands which encompasses each of the five trends discussed above:

1   a planning process designed to by-pass local accountability and local aspirations in favour of administrative efficiency and national need;

2   a new emphasis on urban regeneration, although initially in an anything-goes guise;

3   a stress on expanding London's truly global industry as a financial centre;

4   a complete disregard (at least initially) for the impact of new Docklands developments on surrounding local communities;

5   a truly mega-scale of aspiration.

Within the wider Docklands, the case of Canary Wharf and the Isle of Dogs is brought up to date by Carmona (2009a), in which a critical impact of this scheme on other mega developments in London is discussed. The project spearheaded a move back to design-led development, with the developer spurning the absence of a public plan by imposing their own detailed urban design framework in an attempt to create a new 'place' and thereby safeguard a long-term investment in a marginal location. Circumstances and over-ambition initially conspired against this approach resulting in the well-publicised liquidation of developer Olympia and York. Later it came good, however, through the careful stewardship of successor Canary Wharf Group and, elsewhere on the Isle of Dogs, the auspices of a (once more) engaged local planning authority (Carmona 2009a: 138).

A critical place-making feature of Canary Wharf has been its high-quality (if completely privately owned and managed) public realm with its network of well-used public spaces (**2.11**). It is a model adopted at roughly the same time in the City of London for the Broadgate development by Rosehaugh Stanhope Developments, and later in Paddington Basin (Westminster), for Paternoster Square, also in the City (see Chapter 5), for More London (Southwark), and latterly

2.11   Canary Wharf Phase Three – high-quality animated (if corporate and private) public space

at King's Cross Railway Lands (Camden), where various abortive schemes throughout the 1980s and 1990s adopted this strategy, as did the scheme that finally received outline consent in 2006. From the 1980s, therefore, as power returned to the private sector, their critical innovation in a highly competitive climate was a new emphasis on urban design and public realm, with a revival of the urban square at its heart.

Reflecting the times, sometimes this was a simple unadorned space in the Modernist piazza ilk, as had been proposed at Mansion House Square (see above); increasingly it was a postmodern landscape (as at Canary Wharf), the most audacious of which was John Simpson's design for the final phase of what later became More London. This took the form of a replica of St Mark's Square in Venice (but on the Thames), which the inspector at public inquiry endorsed precisely because of its urban grain, streets and spaces (Punter 1992: 76–7), but which (perhaps fortunately) was a victim of the property crash of the early 1990s alongside many of London's planned and actual mega-projects of the period.

Most successful, commercially, and perhaps also in urban design terms, was the Broadgate development that utilised the air rights over Liverpool Street Station on the edge of the City. 'A sea-change project, transforming developers' understanding of the commercial

2.12 Broadgate Arena – demonstrating the potential of the square, and of private sector innovation

2.13 Covent Garden – a rescued and resurgent place

advantages that might ensue from investment in architecture' (Woodman 2010: 11), Broadgate 'stands as a testament to those who argue that the key to improved design in Britain is a recognition by developers that quality will ensure both higher rents and greater longevity for development' (Punter 1992: 77). Here, architecturally, the buildings were modern but well articulated and the three key new public spaces each had their own character, from animated and heavily programmed, to quiet and reposed (**2.12**). For Punter (1992: 79), however, this was a development that also showed the impact of local planning policy – in this case how the relaxation of permissible plot ratios in the City in the mid 1980s (see below) was quickly reflected in the form of the development, where the later phases were compromised and overdeveloped as a result.

Despite these shortcomings, once again development around a square or sequence of spaces was firmly established as a viable commercial model in London, and once again this was to be a private 'public' space, generated for clear commercial reasons and market advantage. Some argued that the trend readily demonstrated the impact of Thatcherism, that the sorts of culturally driven spaces that were commonplace on the continent, particularly in Paris (the focus of endless envious comparisons in the 1980s and 1990s) were off the agenda in London, and instead commercially driven schemes were creating the new 'public' realm of the city. Yet, bar a few

exceptions such as the much derided (and by a minority much loved) Barbican in the City or the Southbank Centre on the South Bank, in modern times (from the eighteenth century onwards) this was almost always the way.

An alternative narrative

Despite their dominance in the commercial world, in contemporary critiques, and in the political discourse of the time, commercial mega-projects were not the only show in town. A significant group of exceptions are worth noting whose narrative began with the conservation movement of the 1960s and 1970s and which flourished during this period on the back of small-scale entrepreneurial activity, often helped by targeted public sector intervention (particularly by the GLC before its demise) and the low rents available in London's obsolete (but centrally located) industrial and wholesale spaces. Covent Garden, the first of the London squares, is, today, the most high profile of these spaces.

Privately developed, Covent Garden had been privately owned until 1974 when the famous fruit, vegetable and flower market was moved out and the space was purchased for demolition and redevelopment by the GLC. Huge local protest in 1974 followed by the spot listing of over 250 buildings in the area by the then Secretary of State for the Environment presaged a dramatic rethink based on the restoration of the market buildings as set down in the GLC Covent Garden Area Action Plan. In 1980 the market buildings re-opened and in 1988 the estate was sold to Guardian Royal Exchange, with the market itself and some other key buildings leased on a long-term peppercorn rent to the community group, Covent Garden Area Trust (Covent Garden Area Trust [n.d.]). With its mix of small independent shops, a craft market, street entertainments, the opera house, and fine-grained mix of commercial and residential accommodation, the area is now one of London's

primary attractions for tourists and Londoners alike, with its vital and highly managed public spaces providing a key draw for visitors (**2.13**). Yet it is a success story that could so easily have never happened if the first inclination of the public sector, to redevelop, had carried sway.

Elsewhere, the pattern has been repeated on a number of occasions, often with the involvement of Urban Space Management, who since the 1970s has been spearheading the regeneration of historic

2.14 Bishops Square, Spitalfields – after the closure of the wholesale fruit and vegetable market by its owners, the Corporation of London, in 1991, Spitalfields reinvented itself as a space for alternative food, clothes and culture. In 2005, after a long battle by the community group SMUT (Spitalfield Market Under Threat) to prevent it, the Norman Foster-designed corporate public space and office building was opened, demolishing a large part of the historic market buildings and irreversibly changing the character of the market that remained

buildings and spaces for imaginative retail, workshop and community uses. Schemes of this type include Camden Lock, Gabriel's Wharf (Chapter 7), Spitalfields Market, Greenwich Market, Bishopsgate Goodsyard and Merton Abbey Mills. Typically the spaces are derelict or underperforming (and therefore cheap), the refurbishment is basic (and also cheap), the uses often temporary (at least initially), the tenants small-scale artisans, artists, specialist importers, or producers of high-quality farm or other produce, and the role of the public sector minimal. This is a model often ignored in the literature, but widely emulated by larger corporate owners and managers of space across London and elsewhere, for example at Hays Galleria near London Bridge or in numerous shopping centres around London. In such locations, however, the requirement to make a high return to cover a much higher initial investment ensures that the model rarely translates.

Although these exceptions were few in number, their impact was significant, and widely seen as part of 'the capital's unique buzz', which, from the mid 1990s onwards contributed towards reversing the population decline by building a new and more positive image for London (London Pride Partnership 1994: 18). Eventually, however, success breeds market interest, and the phenomenal success of many of these ventures led to commercial opportunities that have been increasingly exploited. Covent Garden, Camden Lock, Spitalfields Market (**2.14**) and Bishopsgate Goodsyard all fall into this camp, and in the 2000s started to attract criticisms that they were becoming over-commercialised and homogenised as a result.

Stewardship gone to pot

For Thornley (1999: 1) and many academic commentators, London in the 1980s and early 1990s was 'in a mess': a mess that started with the poor quality of life experienced by many of its citizens, many of whom were unemployed, homeless or simply struggling to get by in an increasingly expensive and hostile (high-crime) environment. This extended to the lack of housing, particularly affordable housing and was compounded by problems in getting around the city as a consequence of the poor state of London's public transport and its gridlocked traffic network. All this manifested itself in the everyday physical experience of the city, its streets and public spaces. In this regard Punter (1992: 82) argued that London failed (or perhaps, in the absence of a strategic authority, had no mechanism) to learn from the experiences of its competitor cities (Paris, Copenhagen, Munich, Vienna, New York, Barcelona, etc.) many of which were making signifi-

cant investments in public space and environmental quality, largely in remodelling existing spaces, but also selectively in creating new public spaces.

A survey conducted in the early 1990s for the London Planning Advisory Committee (LPAC), who, following the demise of the GLC had been set up as an advisory body to the Secretary of State for the Environment on strategic planning matters, compared London with its (then) world city and premier European city competitors – New York, Tokyo, Paris, Frankfurt and Berlin. It revealed in the process that although access to open green space was extremely good (by quantum), London's public spaces had become neglected and degraded in quality over the previous decades (Kennedy 1991: 98). The emphasis of the report reflected the preoccupation of London policy before and since with World City status, and with what was required to maintain its position in the top rankings of this select group. The survey of businesses undertaken as part of the study suggested that quality of life issues were critical to maintaining this status, and the availability of clean, safe and pleasant public space was an important dimension of this. In this regard London's position was inferior to that of all its comparator cities, with the exception of New York (Kennedy 1991: 200).

In the late 1980s and early to mid 1990s, a series of reports focused on the quality of London's urban environment, and on its perceived deterioration, often blamed on the lack of civic leadership. The first, commissioned by the Royal Fine Art Commission (the forerunner to CABE) from Judy Hillman, cut to the heart of the problem: 'Too much of London has become dirty, degraded and depressing. ... there is absolutely no reason why the city should tolerate this decline in the quality of the environment. Improvements will however require popular pressure and involvement, political will and imagination.' For her, much of the problem was with how the existing spaces of the city were managed and maintained, rather than with the quality of new developments. The problems were aesthetic, but also profoundly social, with London's population being alienated from the streets and spaces they inhabited. It was time both for a general clean-up, but also to return a greater proportion of the space in the capital to pedestrians, and generally to restrain London's drivers in order to civilise space. Although not couched in such terms, the arguments reflected a belief that the quality of London's built environment had a direct impact on its citizens' quality of life and deserved greater attention from public and private sectors alike.

Despite Hillman (1988: 101–4) placing the lack of a London-wide voice and governance at the heart of her critique, the report was endorsed by the Prime Minister, Margaret Thatcher, who wrote the foreword. It was followed in 1992 by a more ambitious and broader call for 'A New London' from architect Richard Rogers and Mark Fisher (then the Official Opposition Spokesman on Media and the Arts). The book began with 'A Call for Action' from Rogers. For him, the deterioration of London's urban environment was forcing people out of the city – deterioration matched by a decline in the city's social fabric (less social housing, more ghettoisation, more physical segregation and disruption) and in its infrastructure. In turn this was leading, he argued, to a range of market solutions to city space: the shopping centre, residential cul-de-sac, business park, etc. as single-minded private spaces that may be sanitary, safe and prosperous, but were no longer forums for public life with certain groups (e.g. groups of youths) increasingly treated with suspicion. By these means, Rogers argued, the public life of London was being sucked out of the city, the most galling aspect of which was the decline in the 'people places – streets, squares and parks – that ... make up the greater part of the public domain' (Rogers & Fisher 1992: xl).

Mark Fisher argued that few spaces in London were actively welcoming to pedestrians – for example, few pubs, restaurants or cafes had external seating (particularly in the winter) and few public spaces were designed for lingering. Thus although 'central public spaces are invariably full, even crowded, ... in the main people are moving, going somewhere, walking with a purpose. Strolling is not a common London activity' (Rogers & Fisher 1992: 104). The observation revealed the distance London had come by this time from the ambitions of the landed Georgians to create places in which to see and be seen, and the late Victorians who under the newly formed and ambitious LCC set out to create and regenerate London's parks to encourage healthy activity (as an alternative to the debauchery of the industrial city). For Fisher, this represented a missed opportunity for a city otherwise blessed with open space. In a series of devastating criticisms, Rogers and Fisher suggested that London was becoming a 'traffic dominated, segregated, non-place, unjust city' (Rogers 1992: xxxi).

Portending the agenda of New Labour to come and the influential role Richard Rogers was yet to play in that wider project (see Chapter 3), the book echoed Hillman's call for a return of London-wide governance.

This was envisaged to be a slimline strategic body to coordinate the macro planning landscape and provide a framework within which more proactive local planning could occur at the borough level. At the same time a re-investment in the city needed to occur in order to make urban life more attractive whilst restricting further suburbanisation (Rogers & Fisher 1992: 33–5). The pursuit of environmental quality and good urban design, it was argued, should be at the heart of this drive for a more liveable city, with the public sector learning from the private sector's lead in developments such as Broadgate and Canary Wharf and investing itself in a high-quality public realm and in spaces that prioritise pedestrians over vehicles.

A new sensitivity (and procrastination)

In 1990, John Major took over from Margaret Thatcher as Prime Minister, and in 1993, appointed John Gummer to the position of Secretary of State for the Environment. Gummer brought with him a new sensitivity to design and a profound interest in environmental issues that had not been a feature in many of his predecessors. He set about launching a spate of initiatives both nationally and in London (for which, in the absence of a strategic authority, he was responsible) in order to move design up the policy agenda. At the national level, the Quality in Town and Country Initiative was launched which led eventually to a new national planning framework for design in 1997 (see Carmona 2001: 69–78). In London, a range of more systematic analyses began with the London Planning Advisory Committee (LPAC) commissioning Tibbalds Colbourne Karski Williams Monro (1993) to investigate 'London's Urban Environmental Quality' with a focus on whether such concerns should be reflected in revised regional planning guidance for the capital.

The resulting report was extremely comprehensive (**2.15**). On the positive side, it identified a growing concern for design quality and for preserving the existing physical and environmental qualities of the city, for example through the spread of a stronger conservation credo, pedestrianisation schemes (e.g. Union Square in Kingston upon Thames) and more sensitive infill developments (e.g. Richmond Riverside – **2.16**). On the negative side, they confirmed many of the concerns of Hillman, Rogers and Fisher, adding that extreme development pressures in the capital were continuing to erode the scale, character, grain and intricate mix of uses in parts of London through the internationalisation and standardisation of development forms. The study concluded that a consistent and coordinated focus

2.15   London's Urban Environmental Quality – eight critical factors in
        London's urban environmental quality

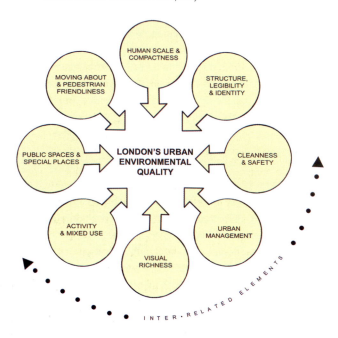

2.16   Richmond Riverside – 1987 mixed-use development and public
        spaces by Quinlan Terry Architects, reflecting the strong historical
        conservation credo that emerged in the 1980s

on urban quality and urban design was absent in London, and that support for these issues should feature strongly in any London-wide strategic policies for the city.

The analysis led to the inclusion of a chapter on the built environment in the 1994 'Advice on Strategic Planning Guidance for London' from LPAC, with the government's advisor on planning for London arguing that the pursuit of a good quality of life should be a critical objective for London, alongside a strong economy (LPAC 1994: 4–5); that urban quality represented an appropriate matter for revised regional planning guidance (RPG3) to address; and should be a stronger focus of local policy as and when the boroughs reviewed their development plans (LPAC 1994: 108–9). In this document, the conflation between urban quality and London's position as a competitive World City was clear, and reflected an increasing concern at the time that the relative neglect of the capital was leading to its decline on the world stage.

In the absence of a strategic authority for London, these concerns rested with government, who, following their political instincts, subcontracted the problem to the private sector to address (Thornley 1999: 5). Thus, in 1993, John Gummer launched the City Pride initiative in London (as well as in the Birmingham and Manchester metropolitan regions, where strategic-level government had also been abandoned). City Pride represented an attempt to bring together the key civic and business leaders to prepare a prospectus setting out a vision for their city's strategic development over the next ten years. In London, the job of coordinating the prospectus was given to London First, a business membership organisation set up to promote London as a location for business.

The initiative was short term in its duration and impact, but in London it was successful in bringing together many of the key players, including the rival Association of London Authorities and London Boroughs Association (who re-merged in 1995), The London Chamber of Commerce, LPAC, The Confederation of British Industry (London Region), the London Training and Enterprise Councils, the London Voluntary Service Council, and, separately, the Cities of London and Westminster. The prospectus itself, published in 1994, was long on warm words and generic aspirations, including the need for consensus on tackling the city's physical decay and promoting environmental quality. It was short on specifics or the means to effect a coordinated

2.17   Core Contributions to the Quality of London's Urban Environment

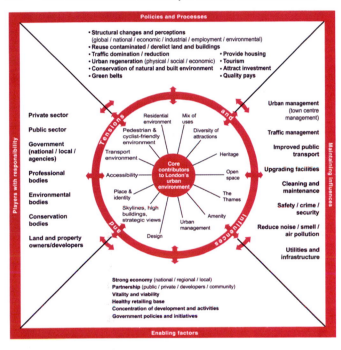

response from the organisations involved in its production (London Pride Partnership 1994).

It looked, for example, to the Government Office for London (GOL) to benchmark London's progress towards its aspirations. Instead, GOL commissioned BDP to undertake another research project to evaluate London's urban environment as a feed into the still to be revised regional planning guidance for London. The resulting report (BDP Planning 1996a, b), unsurprisingly, looked remarkably similar to that commissioned by LPAC three years earlier, covering broadly the same set of issues in the same admirable detail (**2.17**), and with similar recommendations, including that major projects in the capital should be accompanied by significant public realm benefits based on strategies produced by London's local authorities.

In 1997, by the end of their 18 years in office, the Conservative government had completed a U-turn in their attitude to design and planning, if not yet on London governance. In London, the BDP report for GOL went as far as to admit 'The time now seems to be right for a

move towards more serious, relevant and positive planning. This should learn from a period of high development activity and a more laissez faire approach to planning' (BDP Planning 1996a: 10). In 1996, new Strategic Guidance for London Planning Authorities (revised RPG3) was issued, replacing the earlier slimline and permissive version of the guidance (see above), in which questions of quality had been barely addressed. By contrast, the new strategic framework began with a statement by John Gummer in which he argued that critical to London's success is that it should be an attractive place to live, work and do business, offering a good quality of life and range of opportunities to its inhabitants (Government Office for London 1996: 1).

The new guidance extended to 129 pages and (unlike its predecessor) was centrally based on the detailed analysis of LPAC and featured a clear spatial strategy. This alone signalled a much greater commitment to actively planning London, as did its new requirement for the boroughs to set out policies that incorporated goals for urban quality. It represented a major shift in focus for London, and a move towards a far more holistic vision of urban quality than had ever been the case before, including in the halcyon days of post-war planning when the ambition of planners was only matched by the conviction, and therefore narrowness, of their vision. Delivery, as previously, however, remained largely out of government hands, and London's local planning authorities after years of retrenchment and disinvestment were in no position to step up to the plate (LAPSDC 2004: 14–15). Effectively, the private sector remained in the driving seat, although now just a little more directed by a stronger vision of what the capital should aspire to be.

A non-plan city (or perhaps too many plans)

Since the reforms of 1965, the London boroughs had been local planning authorities and up to the abolition of the GLC in 1986 had the power to produce local plans for either all or just parts of their areas. The result was inconsistent practice, with some boroughs opting for borough-wide plans, others adopting numerous plans to cover their borough, and yet others opting for very partial or even no coverage by formally adopted plans (Collins 1994: 116–22). These boroughs used a combination of draft plans and informal 'bottom drawer' strategies to maintain their flexibility in decision-making. A minority adopted, from the 1970s onwards, very detailed sets of design standards as part of their plans, and over time these became some of the most comprehensive and sophisticated compilations of design policies found in the UK (Punter & Carmona 1997: 2, 329). In the main, however, design received scant treatment in the local plans beyond broad aspirations and basic control policies to deal with some of the most common problems.

With the demise of the GLC, the boroughs became the sole planning tier in London and were required under the Local Government Act of 1985 to prepare borough-wide Unitary Development Plans (UDPs). Following national guidance about their content and structure, the new plans were more systemised, but despite this, those boroughs that already had a significant concern for design (e.g. Westminster or Camden) continued to develop and refine their policies under the new label (Punter & Carmona 1997: 347), whilst others continued to produce policy that remained 'somewhat descriptive, repetitive, vague and not particularly user friendly' (Collins 1994: 131). Detailed design concerns – local views, control of advertisements, design of shop fronts, etc. were well covered (Collins 1994: 136) – but not, in the main, a concern for more fundamental issues around the design and provision of public space. The London Borough of Wandsworth offered the exception with a more sophisticated set of public realm policies (Punter & Carmona 1997: 171), although there was little obvious implementation of these principles on the ground by the borough in how it managed its public space. These were development control manuals to control the development of private developers, rather than statements of public sector aspiration and intent.

For Farrell (2007: 58), the structure of planning in London presented a fundamental obstacle to a more proactive stance on such issues, namely that the post-1965 boroughs (in contrast to those before) followed a logic of political and administrative expediency, rather than any connection to coherent communities of interest relating to logical geographies. The result was a disconnection of 'place' from management responsibilities, the severance of key London development opportunities by borough boundaries, and an undermining of a place-based urban design approach to addressing local development opportunities.

Approaches to planning in the (by then) three London business poles – the West end, Canary Wharf and the City – demonstrated the divergence in approaches across London. The departure point for the City of Westminster was a profound concern for conservation (Punter & Carmona 1997: 188), reflecting the fact that the vast majority of

the borough was designated as conservation area whilst its highly vocal resident population was keen to see its character preserved. The London Borough of Tower Hamlets, by contrast, had given up any attempt to plan the area around Canary Wharf, and the London Docklands Development Corporation (in existence as development control authority until 1998) were happy to let the market run its course with little or no significant intervention (Carmona 2009a: 119–20). The City, however, was caught between these two stools.

As Punter (1992: 71) recounts, the pressure generated by the 1980s property boom, the competition from abroad, and, more specifically, the competition from Canary Wharf, was clearly expressed in the redrafting of the City of London Local Plan between 1984 and 1986. Initially, the lack of development interest during the 1970s and the realisation of the destruction wrought by some of the post-war reconstruction projects in the City gave rise to a conservation-led draft of the plan. However, the realisation from the mid 1980s onwards that this would greatly disadvantage the City if it could not accommodate the types of developments required by the market panicked members into a pro-office development stance, removing lesser conservation designations, encouraging the use of air rights over major infrastructure and raising plot ratios across much of the territory. 'It was an invitation to large-scale redevelopment and the response was immediate and dramatic' (Punter 1992: 74).

The diversity in approaches to planning and design was also reflected in London's suburban boroughs. Richmond upon Thames, for example, echoed the strict conservation-based stance of Westminster, Greenwich showed little interest in design (or planning), whilst Harrow instigated a worthy but ultimately largely ineffective character-based strategy in their territory. Housebuilders continued to weave their merry way around the absence of any clear policy (**2.18**) (Carmona 2001: 200–4).

Reflecting on the London planning scene at the end of the 1980s, Richard MacCormac concluded that London's local planning authorities were failing to generate any real vision for key sites across the capital beyond crude density, height and land-use designations: 'Planning tries to mediate, but fails to do so because the visual implications of density and built form are insufficiently understood' (MacCormac 1990: 70). For him, the sorts of generic standards and policies that were being used by local authorities at the time were not

2.18   The poor quality of suburban housing in London

Hebbert (1998: 200) concludes his history of London's planning and development by returning to Steer Eiler Rasmussen's classic text *The Unique City*, arguing that Rasmussen was able to see through the inferiority complex of Londoners that led them to do their city down when compared against what were seen as truly urban cities such as Paris. Instead, Rasmussen was able to see the positives in a city that reflected a culture of 'private ownership and management and the historical dispersal of power within the unwritten British constitution', that had planned itself not through heavy-handed imposition of the grand vision, but instead through a light-touch unifying framework of public interest and urbanistic essentials. Yet for Hebbert (1998: 208) there was a second major message of Rasmussen's book, that 'London was the case study for a larger argument about domesticity, public spaces and the conventional street', and that these qualities of the city represented universal qualities that have since informed urban design agendas worldwide, and that are enduring.

For most of London's history, the city has exhibited a remarkable fortitude based on resisting the imposed visions of the state (in whichever fragmented and frequently chaotic guise), of embracing the market (wherever that has led) and in building on what has gone before, on the layers and layers of accumulated history, eschewing a clean sweep mentality. Arguably, therefore, it was not the neo-liberal ideology of Margaret Thatcher and the neglect of the 1980s and 1990s that was the aberration in its long history, but instead the short post-war period up to the 1970s when the state took on a far more active role as instigator and provider of development, as opposed to laissez-faire enabler. This is not to make the case for such an opportunistic approach to city design and planning, merely to point out that it has been the London way. It is an approach that has, historically, been able to deliver rich diversity and innovative urbanism, not least in its embrace of the square as an urban typology in all its many guises.

sufficient to make their 'civic values explicit'. This stemmed from a failure to feature urban design as part of the planning framework in London from the outset of the development process. Consequently, the private sector took the lead by commissioning their own commercially inspired master plans, particularly where land was under a single ownership.

THE LONDON WAY

In tracing the history of London's development, Hebbert (1998: 203) notes that the tendency of London to eschew grand planning in favour of going its own merry incremental way (largely through indecision and inaction rather than intention), has, in the main, been a positive thing. By these means, it avoided the monumental restructuring plans of the post-war planners, just as it did those of Sir Christopher Wren three centuries before. In so doing, it largely avoided the planned arterial network and rebuilding of its neighbourhoods in the modernist mould that the post-war plans advocated, and this has exerted its own limits on car growth, necessitating instead a model of walking, flexible working, and public transport. 'London's high pedestrian densities are channelled into a street net that survives substantially intact from Victorian times' (Hebbert 1998: 205), whilst its key public spaces have a heightened significance and value as a result.

3   A CITY OF GROWTH, RETRENCHMENT AND DISJOINTED LOCAL ACTION

THE LAST FIFTEEN YEARS

If the pre-1945 history of London, and then again from 1980 to 1997 demonstrated the typical processes of development in the city – namely, let the market (or those with land and money) decide – then this equates directly to the capitalist 'first way' in political parlance. Similarly, the post-war period saw an attempt at an alternative, 'second way', just as it did in the national politics of the era, with the state taking on a much stronger leadership role, although often constrained in what could be achieved by available resources and already well-established patterns of interests and ownership. This chapter will explore how an intermediate 'third way' characterised the development of London in the period from 1997, again, reflecting wider trends in the national political scene (Giddens 2000). In this period, the state tried to direct, once again, a stronger vision for the capital, although implementation would largely be through market mechanisms with all the challenges and compromises, but also resources and innovation, which that implied. Although moving beyond the strict neo-liberal approaches of Thatcherism (see Chapter 2), in essence, the period took the neo-liberal experiment to the next stage.

This chapter brings the story of London's development up to date through an exploration of the period 1997–2012. This is the period of a return to London-wide governance and with it a drive for urban renaissance (at least until 2008). Through examining the approaches of London's first two mayors and the boroughs, the chapter will explore the processes, policies and politics of this episode, a period in which the state and the market acting in closer accord have delivered greater change than ever the state or market could have achieved acting alone.

A CITY OF GROWTH

An early priority of New Labour, elected in 1997, was to deal with the 'London problem': a city verdant with opportunity, but directionless and suffering the multiple endemic problems of long-term neglect. The Greater London Authority Act followed in 1999 and the period from the election of a new London-wide government in May 2000 marked a decisive shift in how London was governed. More than that, it reflected a new recognition of London as a unified entity and not simply a collection of disparate boroughs able to go their own merry way without recourse to the whole. Thus if the period following the demise of the GLC in 1986 reflected a return to the mid-nineteenth-century model of local governance, with no overall strategic authority or legitimate voice for the capital, then the period after the election of the Mayor of London and London Assembly (together the GLA) in 2000 has seen a reinvigorated London-wide governance as an increasingly strong counterbalance to the boroughs at the local level, although the boroughs retained most of the powers to actually deliver local services (including local planning). The first two mayors have shown that the position also encompasses a role as the capital's voice, providing a stage from which to speak out and be heard on all issues affecting London, whether or not actually covered by direct mayoral powers. One such issue is public space.

In terms of planning and development, the instigation of the GLA marked a significant shift in power, with greater powers residing in the hands of the Mayor than had resided with the GLC (Bowie 2010: 29). Under the act, not only did the Mayor gain powers as the strategic planning authority for London, in connection with which he was required to prepare a Spatial Development Strategy (first published in 2004 as the London Plan), he also obtained new strategic development control powers. Thus planning applications of more than 500 homes (amended down to 150 in 2007), major commercial or infrastructure projects, and development over 30 metres tall (75 metres in the City or 25 metres next to the Thames) should be referred to the Mayor, who has the power to veto any approvals not in conformity with the plan. Seen from different perspectives, these far-reaching powers either further fragmented responsibilities in London, for example for the sort of large new developments that would give rise to significant new public space, or better coordinated them by establishing in the London Plan and subsequently in supplementary planning guidance a set of design/development policies to which all London's local authorities (including the City Corporation) needed to have regard (see below).

Ken Livingstone – the first Mayor

Coming hard on the heals of the Thatcher years, only partially tempered by John Major and his ministers, the national election of Labour in 1997 followed by Ken Livingstone, with his reputation for radical left-wing politics, as the first Mayor of London in 2000, might on the face of it have portended a return to a less favourable market environment. However, those who looked forward to the state once again expanding its role to become leader of development were to be quickly disappointed.

Although the role of the state did grow, for example with the instigation of a new 'spatial planning' system from 2004 of which the London Plan was the precursor, arguably, New Labour was a little too fond of the bureaucracy of governance, and many of its projects, including spatial planning, all too quickly became mired in the processes of delivery at the expense of the ends they were attempting to deliver (Allmendinger & Haughton 2009). This was certainly the case for borough-level planning in London (see below). Alongside this predisposition, the New Labour government of Tony Blair adopted (or more correctly continued) the neo-liberal approaches of their predecessors, emphasising the vital importance of the market in economic and social policy, and of the state in enabling rather than directing development.

To the surprise of many, Ken Livingstone (who had fallen out with Labour and who in 2000 stood and won the mayoralty as an independent candidate), fully adopted the precepts of neo-liberalism, although with a clear social justice tinge. Thus, from the start, he clearly signalled his intention to work closely with the business sector and the City Corporation, and to pursue an agenda for London based on growth (Bowie 2010: 62). For Bowie (2010: 228), this

was simply a pragmatic recognition that to achieve anything the Mayor needed to work within the prevailing orthodoxy, instead of opposing it as the GLC had done prior to, and in effect inviting, its demise. But it was perhaps also a tacit acceptance that in the absence of direct public sector investment, it was only through growth that many 'public goods' could be provided, including better quality public space.

In many respects it represented a return to the political accommodation and resulting stability that London had enjoyed pre-1970s (Gyford 1994: 86), with Boris Johnson, the Conservative Mayor who succeeded Ken Livingstone in 2008 singing noticeably from many of the same hymn sheets, and largely adopting Livingstone's London Plan without fundamental change (see below). Imrie et al. (2009: 5–6) coin Cochrane's (2007) notion of a 'growth first' logic to describe the situation in London post-2000, with regeneration being 'put to work by politicians as part of a strategy to remove obstacles to economic growth and to create the social and physical infrastructure required to compete for inward investment'. In the absence of any other game in town, Livingstone counted on the social and economic benefits that would trickle down from the city's continued growth. It was the third way in action, although Livingstone himself (never inside the 'big tent' of New Labour and sometimes actively excluded) would never have described it in such terms.

The London Plan that followed in 2004 addressed both this growth agenda and, to some commentators (Rydin et al. 2004), a seemingly contrasting environmental agenda. For Bowie (2010: 61), however, it was not these wider environmental debates that tempered the drive for growth, but instead the design-led urban renaissance ideas of the Mayor's Advisor on Architecture and Urbanism, Richard Rogers. Rogers had chaired the Government's Urban Task Force that reported the year before Ken Livingstone was elected, and which promoted a reinvestment in cities as a means to meet the country's long-term housing needs (Urban Task Force 1999). Significantly, Rogers signed the foreword to the London Plan alongside Nicky Gavron, the Deputy Mayor who actually drove the plan forward and who took a more explicitly environmentalist perspective.

For Rogers (2005), the situation in London post-2000 was of considerable concern: 'London's future quality of life and cultural meaning is in danger because its whole environment is deteriorating

3.1   The renaissance aspiration – to be like Barcelona

and becoming notably worse than those of other major European cities'. For him, the sin was one of omission in failing to invest in the planning and architectural talent that would grapple with what he saw as the fragmentation wrought by ad hoc redevelopment projects. He argued that this 'sin of omission has had an often devastating effect in both public and private sector architecture and infrastructure, especially the architecture of smaller urban spaces, parks and squares, where people watch people' (Rogers 2005: 24). This he contrasted with the situation in cities such as Barcelona, Paris and Copenhagen (**3.1**), arguing that the impact undermined the collective sense of identity and culture.

These arguments had been long pursued by Rogers and were reflective of the prescriptions of the Urban Task Force (1999), which clearly took as its model the higher-density, highly planned cities of continental Europe, and for exactly the opposite of the sorts of reasons for which Rasmussen 65 years earlier had favoured London (see Chapter 2). Thus the focus of the first London Plan was clearly on Central London, and on the provision of higher-density mixed-use development, bringing people back into the city, and emphasising the importance of high-quality design. As such, although the GLA was a strategic authority, in policy and through his strategic development control function, the Mayor quickly found himself getting involved in local urban design matters. This role was bolstered by the establishment of the small but

influential Architecture + Urbanism Unit (A+UU), chaired by Richard Rogers, which, as part of the GLA, helped to fill the very obvious gap in skills that the period since 1980 had bequeathed.

Two early external reports vied to influence the direction of the new Mayor. In 2000, English Heritage launched their Campaign for London Squares. Endorsed by the government, it argued that 'For London to maintain its pre-eminence, there must be greater investment in its public spaces' and that, for them, this investment should begin with the restoration of its heritage of garden squares (English Heritage 2000: 2–3). They argued that although the condition of London's garden squares varied widely, with some well kept and faithful to their origins, many had lost their railings, and suffered from changes to surfaces and layout, underground disturbance, traffic intrusion, clutter and inadequate maintenance, and generally from a downward spiral of decline. For them, even some of London's set-piece spaces were in a poor state, including such historic examples as Gordon Square, Bedford Square and Fitzroy Square. But, although English Heritage recorded considerable success with this agenda, working through the boroughs and Heritage Lottery Fund, heritage never became a major concern for Ken Livingstone, who time and time again overruled the arguments of English Heritage in connection with major development proposals.

In 2001, a similar campaign, but with a focus on design rather than heritage, was coordinated by the Royal Institute of British Architects (RIBA). This focus was to prove more seductive to the Mayor, not least through the auspices of his design advisor, Richard Rogers, who wrote the foreword to the document and who was able to place the importance of design centrally on the GLA's agenda, almost from day one. The document itself amounted to an unashamed attempt to lobby the Mayor through making a statement about the perceived importance of design in a context where 'World class heritage and contemporary architecture jostles with run down and derelict streetscapes' (RIBA London Region 2001: 4). Most usefully, it included a wide range of ideas about how the Mayor could take a role in leading better practice in this previously neglected area, including how he might integrate design within the various strategies that he was obliged by legislation to prepare for spatial development, culture and economic development. Amongst the ideas was that the boroughs should be asked to identify a potential civic square or pedestrianised zone for mayoral backing, one per borough per year. This idea quickly

3.2   An early, but lonely, success, Gillett Square, Dalston

3.3   Parliament Square Gardens – surrounded and isolated by traffic

got backing from Ken Livingstone in perhaps his most high-profile design-related initiative – the 100 Public Spaces programme.

100 Public Spaces

The Mayor launched his 100 Public Spaces programme with a fanfare in 2002, arguing: 'I have always enjoyed walking through London's streets, squares and parks, but am frequently appalled by the shabby and neglected state of some of our public spaces' (Mayor of London 2002a: 1). For him, the quality of public space was seen as having a direct impact on the city's beauty, sustainability, prosperity, connectivity and safety; although the intention of the scheme to create or upgrade 100 public spaces over just five years proved to be over-ambitious, and to some extent undermined the credibility of the initiative as a whole.

Ten projects were announced as a first phase in 2002, with second and third phases following in subsequent years, each announcing a further 14 projects. But, beyond political pressure and cajoling, the Mayor had very little direct power to actually deliver. In reality, huge land ownership, development, funding and planning complexities quickly came to bedevil many of the schemes, with funding proving particularly problematic unless schemes could be cross-funded by large-scale development that included an accompanying 'planning gain' package (Willis 2008).

All that was on offer from the Mayor was some limited technical help

from the A+UU and the oxygen of publicity that came with inclusion in the scheme. Given a general lack of dedicated resources, absence of any statutory role in this area, and lack of responsibility for the vast majority of public space in London beyond the trunk road network controlled by Transport for London (TfL), which, as an agency of the GLA, the Mayor has direct control over, the early ambition thus proved to be rash, leading to a sense of failure when only five schemes had been realised five years later – Acton Town Square, Potters' Fields, Gillett Square (**3.2**), Wembley Station Square and Barking Town Square Phase 1 (Dean 2007) – although more were completed subsequently.

World squares for all

Despite the slow progress on his 100 Spaces programme, the Mayor scored an early success through his involvement in the regeneration of Trafalgar Square. Trafalgar and Parliament Squares at either ends of Whitehall had long been the subject of concern arising from the increasing isolation of the centres of both these great spaces from their peripheries as over time the spaces had been gradually transformed into little more than grand traffic gyratory systems (**3.3**).

In fact attempts to transform these spaces had begun at the instigation of John Gummer, who in 1996 set in train the 'World Squares for All' study involving a number of governmental organisations

3.4   Trafalgar Square – site of regular demonstrations and rallies, large and small

as much as the physical changes. Thus Livingstone announced, 'My vision is to make Trafalgar Square a vibrant and accessible place whilst maintaining its traditional role as a forum for free speech. I have therefore introduced an innovative events programme that celebrates London's cultural and social diversity' (quoted in Mayor of London 2002b: i). Today, traditional Christmas and New Year celebrations are supplemented by a programme of summer events and by other ad hoc activities throughout the year, including the 25,000 that annually fill the space to celebrate Chinese New Year (Mayor of London 2005: 10). In addition, the fourth plinth in the northwest corner of the square hosts a highly successful rotating programme of modern art, the plinth having previously been empty for 160 years. All this operates side by side with public rallies and demonstrations that operate through-out the year (93 between October 2000 and September 2002), coordinated by a dedicated support service in the GLA (Mayor of London 2002b: 11) (**3.4**).

including the Government Office for London, English Heritage and the City of Westminster, that subsequently became the World Squares for All Steering Group (see Chapter 6). This led to the appointment of consultants to undertake the development of a masterplan whose objective was to redefine the heart of London; specifically Trafalgar Square, Parliament Square and the Whitehall conservation area.

The World Squares for All masterplan was published in 1998, just in time for the election in 2000 of Ken Livingstone who saw the project as a ready-made early and highly visible win for his administration and who, starting with Trafalgar Square, pursued the project with gusto. This first phase of the wider masterplan was completed in July 2003 following an 18-month construction project to transform Trafalgar Square, involving the removal of traffic from the north side of the space and improvements to the wider area. The pedestrianised north terrace now links the square to the National Gallery through a new central staircase, and the square houses a café, public toilets and lifts for disabled access (GLA, Trafalgar Square [n.d.]).

The redevelopment had been spurred on by the transfer to the GLA of management responsibilities for Trafalgar Square in 2000. Indeed, following the works, it was the programme of events and more active management of the space, for example actively discouraging the pigeons that had previously flocked to the square (memorably described by Livingstone as 'rats with wings'), that transformed it

Despite the success at Trafalgar Square, Livingstone's plans for the other major space for which he held direct responsibility – Parliament Square – was to prove more frustrating, notwithstanding the GLA also assuming management responsibility for Parliament Square Gardens, in the centre of the space, from 2002. Again, the ambition of 'World Squares for All' was inherited by Livingstone (2002b: i) who announced, 'My vision is that Parliament Square should provide a symbolic and dignified setting for Parliament and the surrounding historic buildings in keeping with its role as a world heritage site.'

The scheme proposed removing the green garden area at the centre of the space that had become isolated by multi-lane roads on all four sides and that cut off the centre of the square to 99 per cent of potential users (Building Design 2008a). Instead, it was to be replaced with a paved piazza extending over to Westminster Abbey on the south side of the square, and closing that side of the space to traffic. Progress remained slow and sensitive to external pressures, not least because of the complex array of stakeholders involved: the GLA, Westminster Abbey, the Parliamentary Estate, the Royal Parks, English Heritage, the Metropolitan Police, and the Cabinet Office representing the government. Despite this, by 2008 and the end of Ken Livingstone's second term in office, the project had reached the detailed design phase, with Hawkins Brown leading a team of urban designers, and Colin Buchanan conducting traffic modelling in order to mitigate the traffic effects (GLA, Parliament Square [n.d.]). The project had support from the complex array of key players but would now be in the hands of Livingstone's successor (see below).

Design policy and control

The relative failure of the 100 Spaces programme (if judged by completions) showed the limitations of mayoral power in the local delivery of public realm projects, whilst the slow progress on Parliament Square revealed the complications and difficulties of public space schemes even where the Mayor had direct responsibility. By contrast, the Mayor's strategic development control function had the potential to be more far-reaching in its significance.

These powers were awarded on the basis that their focus and limits would be articulated in the Mayor's Spatial Development Strategy. The London Plan sought to accommodate the city's growth within its boundaries without encroaching on open spaces, whilst also making London a more attractive, well-designed and green city. The plan aimed to protect and enhance the quality of the townscape through conserving and enhancing the public realm, open spaces and waterways. It also emphasised the creation of new public space resources, recognising their increased importance in a compact city.

On the national scale the New Labour administration continued the work instigated by John Gummer (see Chapter 2), but with a new vigour. In 1999, they launched the Commission for Architecture and the Built Environment (CABE) to drive forward the design agenda; in 2000, they published a long-awaited guide to design and the planning system (DETR/CABE 2000), effectively establishing urban design as a central tenet of planning in England; in 2004, they launched the new 'spatial planning' system with (amongst its key aims) a greater focus on the preparation of proactive local planning documents as part of the new Local Development Frameworks (see below) that all local planning authorities were required to prepare; and in 2007, launching the 'Manual for Streets' which finally extended the urban design agenda to the realm of highways design and planning (DfT 2007).

Following this national lead, the London Plan set out clear principles of good design in seven key policies (Mayor of London 2004a: Chapter 4) as an agenda for the Mayor and for the boroughs in their policy-making and local development control functions. The resulting strategic development control powers and the right to veto were used effectively, but also selectively, by the first Mayor, and his impact

was tangible in sanctioning the renaissance-inspired drive towards an intensified central city, often in the face of opposition from local authorities. It was also tangible in supporting the delivery of higher urban design standards in relation to many major developments such as those planned for the Isle of Dogs. There, the Mayor's strategic development control powers were wielded to great effect in order to encourage a stronger focus on the delivery of a high-quality better-connected public realm in parts of Docklands that had suffered from the incremental sprawl initially sanctioned by the London Docklands Development Corporation before Canary Wharf changed the game (Carmona 2009a: 105). Elsewhere, the Mayor's presence was hardly felt, for example in relation to the massive King's Cross Railway Lands development. This reflected both a lack of resources to intervene everywhere, but also a willingness to leave things well alone if they seemed to be going well (Carmona 2009b: 11).

The Mayor's design infrastructure

The experience of strategic development control revealed an important demand on the Mayor's planning team, namely the need to prioritise, and only to intervene where impact could be maximised and the results reflected in practice elsewhere. This the Mayor did successfully to spread his urban renaissance agenda beyond the GLA to the boroughs and to development interests in London. The A+UU faced the same challenge of how to spread its message despite its isolated position and diminutive size: it was neither part of the London Planning Team of the GLA, with its remit for spatial planning, nor situated within the London Development Agency (LDA), with its extensive resources and responsibility for regeneration projects. Moreover, as a non-statutory responsibility, the A+UU had just seven staff in 2003, rising to ten in 2005 (including Rogers and other part-time staff).

The solution was to work in partnership with other organisations within the GLA family (particularly the LDA and TfL), and with the boroughs and other governmental and local interests. Thus, between its founding in 2001 and 2007, the A+UU was most effective in working with others to produce a range of design strategies across London (mainly in the Thames Gateway), and in well-publicised campaigning fronted by Richard Rogers, including publishing a series of guides to further disseminate key messages. These included advice on 'Housing for a Compact City' (A+UU 2003) and on 'Commissioning a Sustainable Well-designed City' (A+UU 2005). However, in January 2007 the A+UU was wound up, or more correctly morphed into a new unit, Design for

London. The move reflected the frustration of the Mayor with the slow progress made by the A+UU in delivering his 100 Spaces programme, but also a new seriousness about the design agenda.

Initially, Design for London retained its independence as a standalone unit within the GLA, but absorbed urban design staff from the LDA and TfL. The intention was to give the unit a greater weight in its dealings with the boroughs and to deliver a more integrated emphasis on design across the separate parts of the GLA family. Whilst Richard Rogers remained the Chair of Design for London, Peter Bishop, the man who steered through the huge King's Cross Railway Lands development at the London Borough of Camden, was appointed as its first Director. Early on, he defined its agenda: 'If we consider the scale of the billions of pounds of annual investment by the LDA and TfL, if we can influence their quality we can make a significant impact on the quality of development across London. We will write the design briefs, we are party to the appointment of design teams, and we sign off the design at a critical stage before planning permission is granted' (Bishop quoted in Neale 2007). Critical early concerns also included a desire to deliver more and better public space in London, and, as far as possible, to ensure that all new or regenerated spaces in receipt of GLA assistance are controlled and managed by the public sector: 'Keeping public spaces truly public and democratic' (Bishop quoted in Ross 2007).

However, a much trumpeted Design Manifesto to lay out strict use and management strictures was never forthcoming under Ken Livingstone, and despite its ambition and involvement in a wide range of projects – London-wide – at the defeat of Livingstone in May 2008, Design for London still had no real powers or resources beyond those required to run its own operations.

The public realm challenge

Four years earlier, as Livingstone began his second term, three reports reconfirmed the significant public space challenges that London faced. The Association of London Government (2004: 2) focused on the everyday streets and spaces of the city and on the need to address how they are managed: 'Graffiti, litter, abandoned cars and fly-tipping are all too frequent facts of everyday life in parts of the capital' (**3.5**). They argued 'Our councils have a key role to play when it comes to protecting and caring for our environment – in making sure our streets and spaces are more attractive and enjoyable places.'

3.5   The poor state of everyday streets, London early 2000s

A second report from the London Assembly Planning and Spatial Development Committee (LAPSDC 2004: 4) offered a wider critique following its inquiry into the Mayor's ambitions for higher design quality. After taking evidence, the London Assembly (the body charged with holding the Mayor to account) concluded that although progress was being made on raising awareness of the importance of improving the quality of the built environment, results on the ground were largely limited to one-off exemplar projects such as Trafalgar Square or the simplified streetscape at Kensington High Street (see **3.10**). Of most serious concern was the shortage of urban design skills in the public sector, the lack of leadership (both at political and officer level), the absence of the local planning process as a serious player in delivering better design, and the failure to approach London's built environment in an integrated manner instead of as a series of siloed responsibilities. For the Committee, this represented a significant problem when the new London Plan was demanding more compact, intensive, mixed-use development – something, they believed, that was only deliverable if buildings and spaces are carefully designed.

A final report in the same year saw the return of Danish analytical wisdom to the understanding of London exactly seventy years after the publication of Rasmussen's *The Unique City* (see Chapter 2), although this time in the guise of architect and urban consultant Jan Gehl. Gehl had been commissioned by TfL and the Central London Partnership (a partnership of eight Central London boroughs and business interests) to focus on the experience of public space in London. In common with earlier reports (see Chapter 2), Gehl found London full of world-class spaces, but dominated by the needs of vehicular traffic to such an extent that pedestrians and cyclists had become a low priority (despite walking and public transport being the primary means of travelling around the city). Walking had become an essentially functional activity, rather than a pastime undertaken for leisure (**3.6**) and the report argued that the balance needed to shift with more space given over to, and better conditions provided for, pedestrians and cyclists. It suggested, for example, that spaces needed to be found and nurtured within the city where people could rest and interact (Gehl Architects 2004: 12).

Despite its negative findings, the commissioning of Gehl's report by TfL was significant as a visible indication of a direction of travel, namely that a shift in culture was taking place in the constituent parts of the GLA (beyond the A+UU), with the pursuit of better design at its heart. The Mayor, for example, established an ambitious vision for London in his 2004 Walking Plan for the city to become one of the world's most walkable cities by 2015 (Mayor of London 2004b). This, in turn was to benefit from the introduction from 2003 of the Congestion Charge

3.7   Legible London way-finding signage

in central London, and the better cross-river connectivity that had become obvious following the opening of a number of new Thames pedestrian bridges around the millennium.

Gehl's report represented a sign of this new ambition, but also a statement of the very significant barriers that the Mayor faced to deliver such a strategy. By the end of Livingstone's second term it had led to the Legible London Initiative (TfL [n.d.]) aimed at developing an integrated signage system for London in order to improve way-finding across the city (an initiative developed and trialled under Ken Livingstone, but rolled out under Boris Johnson – **3.7**). It also led to the commissioning of a public realm strategy from Alan Baxter & Associates, and to the production of radical new Streetscape Guidance from TfL (first launched in 2005 and regularly updated ever since). This had a strong emphasis on streetscape character and promoted

3.6   Euston Road – despite acting as the front door to world-class organisations – from a university (UCL), hospital (UCH), research funder (The Welcome Trust), library (the British Library); to vital local facilities, including the Town Hall of the London Borough of Camden, three major stations (Euston, St Pancras and King's Cross), five tube stations; and to the headquarters of key companies and unions such as Santander and UNISON – in common with many of London's streets, it offers little more than functional (not pleasure) space

3.8   Walworth Road, southeast London – simplified streetscape scheme, 750 metres of guard railings replaced by 40 street trees and wider pavements

3.9   Café culture spreads across London

a simplified pallet of materials, signage and public realm elements in order to strike a better balance between vehicles and pedestrians (Mayor of London 2009a). Very gradually, a more pedestrian-focused approach to streetscape design has been spreading across the city (**3.8**).

Yet, despite the 100 Spaces programme, the work on Trafalgar Square, and the wide-ranging discussions in policy, professional and academic circles during the period, the subject of London's public space did not seem to capture the popular imagination, at least if measured by column inches, as a review (using the ProQuest-CSA search engine) of articles in the popular national and London press revealed. If, however, the numbers of users of public space in London were to be measured, the story would likely be very different. Although data is not available on such matters, for Londoners this was undeniably a period when a noticeable new embrace of public space was apparent (for the first time since the Victorian parks movement) as café culture came to the capital, with new cafes and bars springing up across the city replete with external seating to meet the growing demand to eat and drink outdoors, and generally to see and be seen in the city's public spaces (**3.9**).

A CITY OF RETRENCHMENT

In May 2008, the charismatic, high-profile, but somewhat unpredictable figure of Boris Johnson replaced Ken Livingstone as Mayor of London. His election coincided with the credit-crunch-driven recession that, with its origins in the failure of financial services, impacted centrally on London (and in 2012, is still doing so). Johnson's period in office was thereby defined by an immediate and increasingly tight squeeze on public sector expenditure in the capital (as elsewhere), with a rise in unemployment, and a dramatic decline in development activity across all sectors, in particular in housing. This was a context that his predecessor had never had to face, having presided over a period of sustained and robust growth for almost all of the eight years he was in power. In 2010, parts of London recorded some of the highest unemployment rates in the country, with Tower Hamlets (in London's East End) recording 14 per cent, a rate, in its severity, comparable to the worst performing post-industrial towns and cities in England (ONS 2010: 10).

Boris Johnson's socially liberal brand of Conservatism appealed to London's suburban middle classes, whilst his 2008 campaign consistently made the case that Outer London had suffered at the hands of Ken Livingstone's centre-focused view of the city. His election was followed two years later by the election to national government of a Conservative-led coalition with an agenda of cutting the national budget and radically reducing the size of the public sector, including the range of Central Government functions based in London. By December 2010, therefore, following the savage cuts of the national Comprehensive Spending Review of that year that preserved Crossrail, the 2012 Olympics and some other large-scale infrastructure projects in London, but delivered the planned closure of the LDA and cut 30 per cent from the capital expenditure budgets of the boroughs, the context for London had dramatically changed. In particular, the future of any strategic engagement with design was in the balance once again, whilst the boroughs looked set to pare their services back to the statutory legal minimum, outside of which design services, public realm investment and enhanced public space management would fall.

Boris Johnson – the second Mayor

From the start, Boris Johnson's interest in planning, design and regeneration seemed limited. He was elected to the mayoralty after a campaign that revealed little focus on the design of public space, but strongly emphasised the constituent elements of the 'Cleaner, Safer, Greener' agenda being pursued by national government at the time (ODPM 2002), despite an absence of power or responsibility in at least the first of these areas. The over-riding emphasis was on leafy outer London, with Johnson strongly criticising Livingston's London Plan as 'a Zone 1 plan' (Johnson 2008a: 34). Thus, instead of 100 new public spaces, Johnson promised 10,000 new residential street trees and the protection of large back gardens from the types of development that had been increasing densities across London (Johnson 2008b: 3). In doing so, he made it very clear that to him much planning was a local matter and that as Mayor he would institute a more flexible approach to the planning decisions of the boroughs, criticising Ken Livingstone for using the London Plan 'as a means to consistently undermine councils' in order to impose his will upon them (Johnson 2008c: 9).

On coming to power, Johnson immediately set about his new agenda, launching, for example, the Outer London Commission and issuing guidance within months of coming to office on how his approach to planning would change. In this, the Mayor set out a stronger emphasis

on the needs of all London (not just the centre), including his goal of protecting London's distinctive character and heritage (Mayor of London 2008: 29). True to his word, Johnson also adopted more of a partnership approach with the boroughs, and although there was a stronger emphasis on the suburban boroughs than had previously been the case, he was also willing to collaborate with Labour administrations, such as the joint vision for the Royal Docks prepared for the Mayor of London and Mayor of the London Borough of Newham (Labour) (Design for London 2010).

The Draft Replacement London Plan, when it came in 2009, whilst retaining a strong emphasis on maintaining London as a globally competitive city, also emphasised the need to spread the benefits of development beyond the Central Activities Zone. Less detailed and more strategic in nature, the plan (adopted in July 2011) was also more traditional in its structure, with topic-focused sections, including one on 'London's living places and spaces', containing detailed policies on neighbourhood design, inclusive design, designing out crime, local character, public realm design, architectural design and a range of local and strategic conservation themes.

In his foreword to the draft plan, Boris Johnson strongly emphasised the importance of public space, arguing that more than half of the London landscape – by area – is shared space, 'This shared space is a vast and complex environment in which millions of perfect strangers must move, meet and negotiate. ... The genius of a big city lies in the way it organises that shared space, for the benefit of visitors and inhabitants alike. ... To make that shared space safer, we need to make it more beautiful. That is why we are seeking a world reputation for new and improved public spaces that Londoners will cherish for decades to come' (Mayor of London 2009b: 5–6). Yet despite this seeming commitment to the public space of the city, Johnson quickly set about dismantling some of the public space programmes of his predecessor, attracting accusations of hypocrisy from Ken Livingstone, who complained that Johnson 'went on about beautiful London ... [but] he's just another bottom-line merchant' (quoted in Henley 2008a).

An early cut was the flagship Parliament Square Improvement Project. A spokesperson announced 'The Mayor was concerned about the cost of the proposed scheme and the traffic implications. He was also extremely anxious about aesthetics, particularly the proposal to pave over a precious square of green space in central London'

3.10   Kensington High Street – public realm improvements by the Royal Borough of Kensington and Chelsea

(Building Design 2008b). Characteristically, the Mayor put it in more poetic language: 'This scheme would have turned a green glade of heroes into a vast, blasted, chewing-gummed piazza. ... There is absolutely no sense in Londoners paying £18m from their already stretched transport budget in order to reduce capacity on London's roads' (Boris Johnson quoted in BBC News 2008a). In making the cut, the Mayor rejected advice from his Design for London team that the scheme was a modest cost for potentially highly visible and significant gains (Building Design 2008c), whilst the decision was subsequently

condemned in Parliament itself by his own architectural advisor Richard Rogers (a life peer) who proclaimed himself 'stunned by the decision'.

The decision was revealing, illustrating two key tensions in debates about London's public space. First, the tension between space for traffic versus pedestrians. Reports discussed above and in Chapter 2 had, since the 1980s, consistently criticised the dominance of London's public space by traffic, and the poor deal suffered by pedestrians. The late 1990s and early 2000s had seen some progress in this direction through schemes such as Trafalgar Square, the Millennium and Golden Jubilee Bridges over the Thames and the Streetscape scheme at Kensington High Street (**3.10**) (CABE, Kensington High Street [n.d.]) reclaiming and civilising space for pedestrians. Most significantly, the Congestion Charge introduced in 2003 had led by 2006 to a 21 per cent reduction in traffic, with congestion down 26 per cent. It also resulted in a reduction of 13 per cent in nitrogen oxide and 15 per cent in particulates. By contrast, Mayor Boris Johnson campaigned on abandoning the Western Extension of the Congestion Charge Zone (introduced in 2007 and removed in January 2011). Unnamed sources within the GLA commented: 'We've got a Tory [Conservative] Mayor and Parliament Square is in a Tory borough. Neither wants to lose votes because of stopping people driving across London' (Building Design 2008c).

A second tension concerned that between the continental European paved piazza view of public space and the British garden square view. American landscape designer Martha Schwartz (2009), for example, has argued that the British 'view the landscape much as the Victorians viewed women; as either saints or whores. If an open space is green, it is considered a saint. If it is built, concreted or asphalted, it is a whore.' But whilst the continental view of the design and use of public space had been a critical influence on the urban renaissance project of New Labour, with the notable exception of Trafalgar Square almost all new public spaces in London from the eighteenth century to the immediate post-war period had been of the green type. Boris Johnson therefore supported what he saw as the London tradition, and was not alone in his view. Some argued that it was the traffic, and not the garden, that was the issue (Ball 2008), whilst even the designer of the proposed scheme, Roger Hawkins (Birch 2008: 15), recognised the dangers of an emerging corporate and ubiquitous style, where 'cheap granite from China is used and all the street furniture is stainless steel with a bit of glass in the signage'. For him, however, the opportunity to attract many more of the 33 million visitors who use the space every year into its centre meant that grass was impractical. Therefore, in common with all the other designers who had prepared schemes for the space over the years (Norman Foster in the 1990s, Richard Rogers in the 1980s, Halcrow Fox in the 1970s and Gordon Cullen in the 1940s), he concluded that hard surfaces were a necessity. The abandoning of the project, however, ensures that the debate will go on.

The announcement on Parliament Square was quickly followed by winding up the 100 Public Spaces programme, abandoning work on the London Public Realm Strategy and subsuming Design for London into the LDA. At the time, the new Mayor justified the decisions as a desire to focus much more on delivery. A spokesperson argued, 'the Mayor is committed to delivering important public realm improvements, but the feeling is that the [100 spaces] scheme was too aspirational and we will now be looking at a programme that focuses far more on delivering schemes on the ground' (Regeneration & Renewal 2008).

Predictably, the news of the 100 Spaces demise was widely condemned by practitioners as diverse as avant-garde architect Will Alsop and 'traditional urbanist' John Thompson (Henley 2008b; Willis 2008), although the absorption of Design for London into the much larger Land and Infrastructure Directorate of the LDA under the continued leadership of Peter Bishop did (at least in theory) offer the potential for public realm issues to be better integrated into the wider regeneration programmes, and to take advantage of at least some of the (then) £80 million annual budget of the new directorate. In effect, it was a return by the back door to design-led regeneration, at least insofar as the potential was there for the design expertise of Design for London to infuse the regeneration activities of the LDA from the inside. Thus Bishop (quoted in Daubney 2008) argued 'This is a huge endorsement from the LDA and a commitment that it wants to put design and masterplanning at the heart of its remit'. Ken Livingstone (quoted in Henley 2008b), by contrast, argued that the move sidelined design as it no longer had a direct line to the Mayor: 'We specifically created Design for London … so that it wasn't always subordinated to whatever transport, planners or the LDA developers wanted'.

The Great Spaces Initiative

Despite the initial bonfire of the public space initiatives, 18 months into his mayoralty Boris Johnson launched his own 'Great Spaces Initiative', followed by an innovative set of policy documents. The Mayor's Great Spaces was billed as an initiative to revitalise the capital's unique public spaces: 'It will help transform some of London's recognised and lesser known streets, squares, parks and riverside walks into places Londoners and visitors will want to use and enjoy all year round' (Mayor of London 2009c). For Livingstone (2010), the new initiative was simply a cynical attempt to cover the retreat on the whole public space agenda. On the face of it, however, the initiative seemed remarkably similar to the 100 Spaces programme of his

3.11   Great spaces for pocket money (cartoon from Hurst 2009)

predecessor, re-launched in a different guise and with an initial line up of some 36 projects (some from the previous programme) selected by a Great Spaces Panel (including Richard Rogers) after an open call to the boroughs to put schemes forward.

In fact at least a third of the schemes were in outer London (the focus of the new Mayor), in contrast to the 100 Spaces schemes, which were largely concentrated in central and inner London. The initiative was also less ambitious than its predecessor, and largely aimed at celebrating and supporting work already happening across London, rather than advancing proposals that the Mayor would take a key role in driving forward. In this role, it was argued, the initiative embraced projects at any stage of their development, and in so doing it cleverly, or slyly (depending on your perspective), overcame a key problem of the earlier programme that had favoured proposals in their evolutionary phase, namely the difficulty in getting schemes off the ground. Instead, proposals were carefully selected against delivery expectations, as well as for their design intentions, with successful schemes earmarked for a combination of feasibility funding, design and procurement advice, or an exemplar public space award. In this way support was to be more tailored to the needs of projects, with expectations limited in each case, thus ensuring a greater chance of success. For some, however, the lack of ambition was underscored by the initial budget of £200,000 for the first year, resources that were quickly lambasted by opposition groups on the London Assembly, including as 'great spaces on pocket money' by the then former Deputy Mayor, Nicky Gavron, who had worked with Richard Rogers on the 100 Spaces programme (Hurst 2009) (**3.11**).

For Peter Bishop (quoted in Hopkirk 2009: 8), the new programme had learned from the mistakes of its predecessor by putting the boroughs in the delivery hot seat, rather than the GLA. Thus it was a requirement of the competition that each bid had to be signed off by the leader and chief executive of each borough to ensure their political commitment to deliver. In this regard, the programme was more of an umbrella for existing schemes, although together as a programme they could be seen as part of a new commitment from the Mayor to move public space back on to the policy agenda. In doing so, however, the initiative largely moved the Mayor from a delivery role to a coordinating, cajoling and mentoring one.

London's Great Outdoors

Great Spaces sat within the wider context of 'London's Great Outdoors' a strategy for London's street, green and blue spaces (Hopkirk 2009: 9). 'London's Great Outdoors' was launched with a fanfare in November 2009 and was significant as London's first official policy document dealing with public space (Mayor of London 2009d). Penned as if a personal manifesto from Boris Johnson, the focus was on establishing a set of high level principles for the city's public spaces whilst recognising that the boroughs were the critical agencies to translate the ideas into delivery on the ground, assisted by Design for London, TfL and others. Amongst the key themes in the document were:

1   Restoring a sense of civic pride in the streets and spaces of the city – an accompanying document 'Better Streets' (Mayor of London 2009e) set out a range of principles to be applied across the capital.

2   Protecting, enhancing and linking the green and water assets of London – a further document 'Better Green and Water Spaces' (Mayor London 2009f) set out the key principles.

3   Promoting public spaces as venues for a diverse range of activities – in this, the mayoralty was seen to have a key coordinating and promotion role.

4   Avoiding privatisation and corporatisation of publicly accessible spaces – the Mayor argued that through such practices 'Londoners can feel themselves excluded from parts of their own city'.

To make it happen, the initiative included a 'Strategy for Spatial Investment' and an implementation plan, the latter listing a series of public realm schemes categorised as 'secured', 'in development' and 'aspirational' – 105 in total (including the 36 Great Spaces projects). The Mayor argued that the initiative was not meant to be prescriptive, progress would not 'require huge new resources, just determination, enthusiasm and a willingness to spot and seize opportunities' (Mayor of London 2009d: 8). The initiative certainly proved to be opportunistic.

The Mayor, for example, allocated an impressive-sounding £220 million to public space projects up to the 2012 mayoral election, suggesting 'I doubt that there has ever been such a concentrated effort to make a great outdoors for London.' In reality, this included very little new money above and beyond what the LDA and TfL would normally have spent on physical infrastructure and development over a three-year period. It counted the significant resources that had already been allocated to major projects such as the delivery of the Olympics public realm in 2012, as well as many projects with little or no direct involvement by the Mayor and his agencies. The latter included a wide range of proposals from the boroughs that had been approved by the Mayor (through the auspices of TfL) as part of the normal Local Implementation Plan process for funding the transport schemes of the boroughs.

In 2009, Richard Rogers, who had continued under Boris Johnson as Deputy Chair of his Design Advice and Great Spaces Panels, suddenly quit citing his frustration at the lack of action from the Johnson regime on London public realm issues, and in particular on not being given the resources or commitment necessary 'to lead a professional team to design and deliver public spaces in London' (Rogers quoted in Hurst & Barney 2009). In fact, on the face of it, progress seemed rapid. A year after launching London's Great Outdoors, Councillor Daniel Moylan, Deputy Chair of TfL, announced that 20 projects (including 4 Great Spaces schemes) had already been completed; secured funding for public realm projects had risen to £390 million; and, by the mayoral election in May 2012, 86 new public realm improvements (including 15 Great Spaces schemes) and the original 10,000 street trees promised by Johnson prior to his election, would all be delivered (GLA 2010). In reality, Johnson was benefiting to some extent from the momentum that had gradually built up during (although not always as a result of) the previous administration, including schemes that had begun a long time before he was elected such as Windrush Square in Brixton (see **3.16**).

3.12 Homes for hobbits – the high-density apartments blocks that have come to dominate the London development and property markets

Raising standards

If creative accounting was, to some degree, a feature of Johnson's public space initiatives, a further initiative had a much more direct, if somewhat unexpected, impact on proposals for public space. The Mayor's emphasis from the start had been on the suburban boroughs, with the protection of back gardens and the reduction of high-density development solutions both priorities. As part of his 'Building a Better London' election manifesto, Johnson had promised to amend the London Plan to ensure the delivery of more family-sized dwellings. Whilst the urban renaissance policies of Ken Livingstone had driven up densities to a point where towers situated in communal space were once again being proposed in order to deliver the units demanded by developers, and sanctioned in the London Plan, the demise of the buy-to-let market after 2008 opened up other possibilities again.

Comparing the average floor area of a home in London at 77 m² with the 206 m² in Australia, 109 m² in Germany and 88 m² in the Irish Republic, Boris Johnson asked: 'What's that all about? We're not Hobbits. I am not about building homes for Hobbits. ... I don't want to cast aspersions on particular homes but I do think in this country, where if you read the newspapers we are not getting any thinner ... they [houses] need to be human-sized' (quoted in Hamilton 2008) (**3.12**).

Backing the rhetoric, in 2010 the interim London Housing Design Guide was published, with new housing standards for all housing in London supporting the standards already contained in the draft replacement London plan that covered all tenures. A number of projects immediately moved away from the housing blocks that had increasingly become the norm, and looked instead to traditional urbanism solutions, including high-profile schemes such as the legacy masterplan for the 2012 Olympics site and the re-design of the Chelsea Barracks. In the latter, Richard Rogers' slab blocks became mired in controversy following a damning intervention by Prince Charles and were subsequently replaced by Dixon Jones' more traditional terraces and mansion blocks around a series of green spaces. The original Olympics legacy masterplan was also heavily criticised, this time by its client, the Olympic Park Legacy Company, whose Chief Executive argued that it said little about London, instead presenting a series of 'high-rise and fairly bland' blocks that 'could have been anywhere' (Bloomfield 2010). The design U-turn, which was vocally backed by the Mayor, proposed a move towards lower-rise (largely below five stories) buildings, including family houses with gardens, around a series of Nash-inspired crescents and London squares. Post-2010 the combination of policy and circumstance looked set to presage the return of the 'traditional' garden square once again, playing directly into Boris Johnson's clear preference for traditional London vernacular. In this regard the revised housing standards are likely to have a long-term impact.

SHAPING LOCAL LONDON: THE BOROUGHS

Turning from London's Mayors to its boroughs, although the governance context for the city had been decisively changed from 2000 onwards with the arrival of the GLA, for most of London's existing and everyday public spaces this meant business as usual, with the boroughs retaining control of many of the key levers of power for influencing public space quality. Notably, this included control over the day-to-day management of London's streets, and control of new development through local planning powers. This final section of the chapter explores this local practice and the differential policy and project visions for public space it gave rise to during the period.

Terry Farrell has argued that it is only in the new, mainly privately led developments that much urban planning happens in London. London

in the 2000s, he suggests, was unlike the 1960 and 1970s, when the public sector took the lead with the great housing estates and new towns; instead, it is the private estates of Canary Wharf, Paddington Basin, King's Cross, Stratford City and Greenwich Peninsular, amongst others, that involve the energies and skills of those who make new places. In-between, a network of overlapping controls and authorities remain – 'an area where non-plan prevails'. For Farrell, however, London remains a triumph of town planning, albeit of an informal style, based on mid-scale increments of villages and great estates instead of boulevards and grand gestures,

Local design policies

If this is the case then the boroughs had a golden opportunity to put a new more outcome-focused planning agenda into effect from 2004 onwards when, in common with local planning authorities across the country, they were charged to produce Local Development Frameworks (LDFs) to replace their Unitary Development Plans (UDPs). LDFs were intended to move the planning system from a land-use planning to a spatial planning system, with the development plan acting as the spatial coordinating framework for all public sector investment programmes, as well as for private investment. Rather than a single plan, the LDF was envisaged as a package of documents with a Core Strategy establishing strategic policies and aspirations for more detailed Action Area Plans (AAPs) and Supplementary Planning Documents (SPDs). LDFs were to be in place within a three-year period.

Perhaps revealing something of a lack of priority attached to these documents by the boroughs, seven years after the legislation, just 10 of the 33 local planning authorities in London had an adopted core strategy (with a further four submitted for inquiry as of October 2010), and just nine AAPs and three SPDs formally adopted through the process (Planning Inspectorate [n.d.]). Examining the adopted and emerging LDF documents of the ten boroughs covered by the public space survey discussed in Chapter 4, a range of fairly generic policies were apparent. The boroughs, for example, each aimed to promote high-quality, safe and attractive public realm schemes by employing similar sets of design and development principles to improve the public realm and pedestrian experience.

A range of more specific public space proposals were also apparent, ranging from the provision of individual new spaces (e.g. around Crossrail stations) to more significant but still one-off public realm projects such as the removal of gyratory systems in Swiss Cottage, Aldgate, and Earls Court. Proposals were also included for general public realm standards such as a general endorsement of Legible London signage (see above), whilst the City, Kensington & Chelsea, and Westminster included detailed proposals to extend and unify the public realm throughout their respective boroughs, with specifications for pavement widths, type and height of lighting standards, colour of light bulbs, paving materials, types and materials of bollards, boundary treatments, railings, and colour of street furniture. In addition, either alone or through partnerships, each borough identified the need to properly manage their streets and public spaces. Their aspirations included:

- Improving public transport capacity and reducing traffic and congestion.

- Providing cycle parking spaces.

- Delivering efficient street cleaning, refuse collection, and removal of graffiti.

- Promoting and carefully licensing the evening and night-time economy.

- Introducing more public toilets.

- Addressing questions of safety and security, and reducing anti-social behaviour.

- Continuing to promote street-based cultural, artistic and entertainment activities as well as markets and street vendors to enliven the public realm.

LDF policies, it seemed, were more firmly embracing public space and design issues than had been the case in the 1990s (see Chapter 2). Plans (particularly in central London) were also beginning to move beyond a solely regulatory agenda to a more proactive place-shaping one.

Local projects and propositions

In this (place-shaping) task, Raco and Henderson (2009: 114–15) emphasise the vital role of London's boroughs through their development and regeneration activities. First, in a complex fragmented scene, the boroughs offer much-needed continuity to governance, having been in place for almost half a century (since 1965). Second,

3.13   Acton Town Square – a traditional public space providing a new focus for public life at the heart of Acton town centre

they continue to play an important representational role, fixated as many are on their electorate and on the need to reflect their views (sometimes to the detriment of wider London agendas) in local development politics and partnerships. Third, within the increasingly complex governance scene, the boroughs' coordinating role is becoming more, rather than less important, and without it, local community and development interests may find it difficult to reach consensus. Finally, some boroughs have been proactive in shaping partnerships and policy priorities in a manner that decisively impacts on outcomes, both physically and in delivering wider socio-economic benefits from development.

However, not all boroughs have been equally interested in urban design and public space issues, or able to respond to these issues with the same sophistication and ambition. Middleton (2009: 200), for example, recalls how the Mayor's London Walking Plan (see above) was enthusiastically taken up and promoted in some boroughs such as Islington, whilst neighbouring Hackney had no identified responsibility for walking. In this respect, boroughs fall broadly into four groups.

A first group have seen little significant progress on public space issues in recent years. Typically, these are outer London boroughs such as Barnet, Hounslow, Merton, Harrow, Hillingdon and Sutton, but also

3.14 Peninsular Square – privately owned, highly managed and highly programmed entertainment space in front of the 02

3.15 Sheldon Square – amphitheatre space at the heart of the Paddington Central commercial office development on Paddington Basin

a few inner London boroughs, including Haringey and Wandsworth. Others have seen little systematic or widespread intervention, although have benefited from the occasional high-profile projects, for example, Ealing (Acton Town Square – **3.13**), Kingston upon Thames (Kingston Marketplace), Barking & Dagenham (Barking Town Centre), Lewisham (Peckham Square – see Chapter 8), and Waltham Forest (Walthamstow High Street).

A third group, typically ex-industrial inner London boroughs, have witnessed significant new and regenerated public space projects in their territories, although typically these have been led by others, with the boroughs taking a largely regulatory role. These include:

- Southwark, which has benefited from new developments at Potters Fields (led by More London), Coin Street (Coin Street Community Builders – see Chapter 7), Tate Modern (The Tate), and along the Southbank (Southbank Employers Group – see Chapter 7), as well as at Empire Square (Berkeley Group – see Chapter 9);

- Tower Hamlets, with extensive public realm schemes around the Tower of London (Historic Royal Palaces), on the City fringes, and in and around Canary Wharf (Canary Wharf Group – see Chapter 5);

- Greenwich, which has invested directly in refurbishing Cutty Sark Gardens in Maritime Greenwich and in Woolwich town centre, but, more significantly, has benefited from major interventions at Woolwich Arsenal (Berkeley Group, amongst others – see Chapter 8), Millennium Village (GMV Ltd – see Chapter 9) and elsewhere on Greenwich Peninsular (Meridian Delta Ltd – **3.14**);

- Newham, which has seen the most transformative public realm investments as home to the 2012 Olympics and via the Stratford City development.

A final small group dominated by central London boroughs have been more proactive, not only securing huge investment interest by dint of their location, but also actively creating opportunities and driving through projects themselves. The category includes Kensington & Chelsea, responsible for the transformation of Kensington High Street (see **3.10**) and latterly Exhibition Road and for the abortive Sloane Square scheme (see Chapter 6); the City of London, with its far-reaching Street Scene Challenge programme of public space interventions across the Square Mile, including at Monument Yard (see Chapter 10); and Westminster, which has long invested in a high-quality public realm and continues to do so whilst also being actively involved in perhaps the highest concentration of major public space projects led by others, including Horse Guards Parade, Somerset

3.16   Brixton Windrush Square – clarifying and connecting existing public space fragments in Brixton town centre

House (see Chapter 10), Trafalgar Square (see Chapter 6), Hyde Park Corner and Paddington Basin (**3.15**).

Two inner London boroughs and one outer London borough also join the group: Lambeth, who led on the Brixton central public spaces projects (**3.16**) and who have been overseeing the huge Elephant & Castle masterplanning project; Camden, with their Clear Zones Initiative transforming spaces such as Monmouth Street,

taking a direct involvement in the Swiss Cottage Community Square development (see Chapter 8), and proactively shaping the nature of public space at King's Cross; and Brent, who have been involved in driving significant public realm change in the Wembley area spearheaded by their Wembley Masterplan, who have supported the Kilburn Streets for People community-led public realm project, and who in 2011 published their own Brent Placemaking Guide to focus more systematically on public realm quality across the borough.

Of this latter group, Punter (2010b: 341) distinguishes between the City and the others, arguing that whereas boroughs such as Westminster and Camden have invested in strong and consistent control to actively shape development, the City has been more entre-preneurial in its approach, for example in the pursuit of signature designers and projects. The approach has been led by Peter Rees, the Chief Planning Officer for the City since 1985, who during his period in office has run a uniquely personal and hands-on (some might argue arbitrary and subjective) approach to design regulation – an approach only possible because of the equally unique governance of the City, with its strong business rather than party political representation. The results have demonstrated Rees's strong preference for design innovation, discretionary decision-making and flexible policy frame-works over fixed plans, an approach exemplified in his relaxation of plot ratios in the City (see Chapter 2), preferring instead to judge every scheme on its merits and in relation to its (more subjective) townscape fit (Woodman 2010).

The skills deficit

Collectively, developments in and around central London in the early years of the new millennium led the Royal Institute of British Architects and English Heritage (RIBA/English Heritage 2005: 3) to jointly declare that the importance of the urban realm had been rediscovered in London: 'A programme of works is now in place that is greatly improving the quality of the spaces and places in our capital city. ... London now has the opportunity to create a radically better urban realm in the years ahead.' They argued that London was going though a period of major growth and change – culturally, commercially and demographically – and it was in such periods of change that the city was at its best: 'Much of London's finest architecture and town planning was developed in periods of great growth and expansion' (RIBA/English Heritage 2005: 30).

At the end of the twentieth century and in the first decade of the twenty-first, London was certainly going through such a phase, with much of the major development during this period returning to the urban square as a revitalised or new core to many proposals. Across London, local government remained just one (often minor, but sometimes major) player amongst the array of interests that continued to shape change. In part, this simply reflected the way things had always been done in London, but the lack of a proactive engagement in public space projects and proposals across large parts of the city may also, to some degree, be explained by the skills deficit in urban design across London's local authorities.

Design for London (and before them the A+UU) were able to make some impact on the design skills deficit through a policy of deliberately supporting a wide range of young London architectural practices in the projects in which they were involved. In doing so, they sometimes courted controversy with their selection architects – processes called into question over the favouring of some architects over others (Vaughan 2007). Over time, however, the policy was effectively used to induct a wide range of practices into the urban design canon, and addressed a key early concern of Richard Rogers (2005: 24), namely the need to invest in the city's design talent.

To tackle the wider public sector skills gap, the London Authorities Urban Design Forum (LAUDF) was launched in 2003 as a pan-London best-practice sharing network, initially funded at a very low level by the boroughs. From 2005, following the London Assembly inquiry, funding was ratcheted up to a higher level with significant contributions from TfL, the LDA, the boroughs, and the Housing and Communities Agency (London), and with support from CABE in order to develop and launch a dedicated programme of urban design training for built environment professionals in London. At this point, the Forum became Urban Design London (UDL) and was eventually located alongside Design for London in the LDA Headquarters to take advantage of synergies in both directions.

In the year April 2009 to March 2010, for example, UDL offered about 80 training events focused on raising design skills levels in the boroughs and GLA agencies (UDL [n.d.]), receiving a glowing endorsement for the effectiveness of its work in the same year as an external audit confirmed that it had been a significant contributor to raising urban design skills levels since the launch of its training programmes in 2006 (ECOTEC 2009). Counter-intuitively, however, the auditors also identified a growing urban design skills gap, with 90 per cent or practitioners reporting a gap in 2009, compared with just 74 per cent in 2005 when a baseline survey was conducted to monitor UDL's work.

Through their analysis, ECOTEC (2009: 24) had identified a curious anomaly, namely that the more London's built environment organisations receive urban design training, the larger they perceive the urban design skills gap to be. Moreover, in contrast to the 2005 findings, respondents now felt that this skills gap was not primarily the result of an absence of specialist urban designers in London, but instead derived from the absence of design awareness amongst non-specialists. The findings suggested that a certain level of knowledge is required in order to make a sensible assessment about the scale of the problem; in this case, how wide the skills gap actually was, the range of skills and knowledge required, and by whom. With cuts to the work of UDL in 2011, the question of a lack of design skills looks likely to remain a significant problem for most London boroughs for some time to come.

THE END OF AN ERA?

From October 2010, the context for design and public space changed dramatically, with a national Comprehensive Spending Review leading, first, to the decision, at the national scale, to abolish CABE (40 per cent of whose design review work was in London – Taylor 2011: 80) and second, in London, to abolish the LDA and, with it, Design for London. These two organisations epitomised the experiment with a design-led urban renaissance that had been championed by New Labour; albeit on foundations established in the mid 1990s by the then Conservative administration (see Chapter 2). Rather than delivering a core statutory service such as health, transport or education, the remit of these organisations was largely concerned with adding social, economic and environmental value through better design and an enhanced quality and experience of public space. Yet, in an age of austerity, this value-adding activity was, it seems, not tangible enough to guarantee the future of such a discretionary and modestly funded service, perhaps because the case for its existence had still not been convincingly made.

By March 2011, however, both CABE and Design for London had received a stay of execution: the former shrinking to 20 staff (a fifth of its former size) and merging with the Design Council; the latter through a return to its roots, namely back to the GLA and temporarily shrinking from 18 staff to the original size of the A+UU, 7 core staff (a tiny number with which to deliver a design service across the agencies in the GLA and across London). In fact, Design for London quickly bounced back, clawing back its lost staff capacity by the 2012

mayoral election. Dramatic cuts in the already meagre urban design service of most London boroughs, however, look to be longer lasting, including the closure of a number of local design review panels, with, in 2010, just a third of London boroughs retaining such a panel (UDL 2011). Thus a survey of the urban design and conservation capacity of boroughs at the end of 2010 (prior to many of the anticipated cuts taking effect) revealed just 68 dedicated urban design posts across London (and a further 76 conservation posts) to deal with the outputs of a construction industry worth some £8 billion (on top of London's 1,000 conservation areas, 40,000 listed buildings and 150 registered parks and gardens). This equated to £120 million worth of development for each urban designer or an investment by the public sector in securing quality in the public interest of around 0.03 of the output of this industry in London (Carmona 2011).

In such a context, the public space initiatives of both mayors were incremental and more than a little ad hoc, although Livingstone's intervention at Trafalgar Square, the direct provision of new public space by a small minority of boroughs, and of course the Olympic Park, demonstrate that 'second-way' direct provision of space by the state for purely public (social) purposes is not entirely dead. Moreover, despite the column inches devoted to them, and the hyperbole of successive mayors, the 100 Spaces and London's Great Outdoors initiatives both helped to confirm that responsibility for public space in London in the first decade of the twenty-first century remained hopelessly fragmented, and, given the size and prominence of the city, significantly underfunded. Even Boris Johnson's creative accounting of £220 million into public realm projects only amounted to about £10 per head of population, with cuts announced in 2010 resulting in the cancellation or delay of many of the projects featured in 'London's Great Outdoors' (Fulcher 2010).

Despite this, what had been achieved in the first three terms (12 years) of the GLA was a growing culture of concern for urban design in London, in which the GLA, alongside central government, had played a significant role, not least through recasting TfL's Streetscape Guidance, via the GLA's strategic development control function, and through the detailed support Design for London were able to give on some of London's recent public space success stories (3.17). It was equally obvious, as 100 Spaces showed and Great Places recognised, that mayors (of whichever political colour) remain reliant on the boroughs and private actors to deliver much of the design agenda, and, at that level, interest and expertise in such issues remains patchy.

So, as London moves into more uncertain times (economically), it is possible to conclude that, up to a point, the more active role of the state (post-1997) has secured a range of enhanced outcomes that would otherwise not have been delivered. In doing so, it has largely avoided the mistakes of the overbearing state during the post-war period, and the very different but equally tangible mistakes of the 1980s and first half of the 1990s when the government largely withdrew its guiding hand. In this regard, the period has seen a 'third way' in London's urbanism, just as it did in its politics, with the state taking a stronger role, but embracing the market as the essential means to deliver its ends, the public good. Sometimes 'third way', sometimes 'second' but often 'first way', the last 15 years confirms that this remains the 'London way'.

3.17   Barking Town Square and Arboretum – designed by muf architecture/art, the project includes a hard-landscaped, formal civic 'foreground' to Barking Town Hall (see 6.1) and an urban arboretum of carefully selected trees between the new library and commercial development. Design for London acted as design champion; assisted with consultant selection, funding bids and briefing; and conducted regular design reviews. The square received the 2008 European Prize for Urban Public Space

4 THE 'NEW' SQUARES OF THE RENAISSANCE CITY

A CITY OF RENAISSANCE?

The period following the New Labour victory of May 1997 witnessed momentous change in London, not just in the structure of its government, but also in the attempt to find a new, more balanced, accommodation between market and state. In the public space arena it has sometimes seemed that the public sector resources dedicated to this effort have been minimal, particularly when set against the scale of the issue if reports of decline from the late 1980s onwards are to be believed (see Chapters 2 and 3). Latterly, however, as well as greater resources (human and monetary) and proactive initiatives through which to directly engage with the issue, the state has also had at its disposal a new formidable regulatory instrument, The London Plan.

If Chapter 2 examined the history of London's development and the existence of a 'London way' through its reliance on the market to deliver change, and Chapter 3 brought the story up to date through examining the politics, policies and practices of the last 15 years, then this chapter establishes the contemporary context for public space provision that these periods have bequeathed to London. It examines, first, whether, beyond the rhetoric, an urban renaissance has been achieved in London over the past 15 years – concluding that it has – and, second, what the wider socio-economic context is for that change – concluding that renaissance is not the be-all and end-all in a city that is generally more divided between haves and have-nots than many would suppose such a rich city to be. Finally, it reveals a key physical manifestation of urban renaissance through presenting the results of the London-wide survey of new and substantially regenerated public squares across London.

THE RENAISSANCE CITY

From the publication of the Urban Task Force report in 1999 to the demise of New Labour in 2010, urban policy in the UK was dominated by the urban renaissance agenda. In London, the drive was wholeheartedly adopted by Ken Livingstone, and although the rhetoric changed with the election of Boris Johnson in 2008 – density aspirations were lowered and greater attention directed to the suburbs – the essentials of a growth-based renaissance policy remained. 'Renaissance-light' had replaced 'renaissance-max', both built upon a period of sustained development and re-investment (public and private).

If the 1980s and 1990s represented a period in which London as an entity and many of its constituent parts were somewhat neglected, it was also a period of rapid economic growth, particularly in central London. In the early 1990s, Hoggart and Green (1991) even concluded that large parts of London were in danger of becoming locations for almost exclusively middle- and upper-income citizens. This was in contrast to the decades since the war that had seen a steady and sustained decline in London's population, with middle-class couples often abandoning the city (or at least its inner areas) when children arrived. From 1988, this population decline began to be reversed, driven by a more buoyant economic climate and a generally more positive perception of the city, not least those held by the middle classes, who became likely once more to remain within the city's boundaries, pushing into and gentrifying increasingly larger inner city areas (Butler 2003). The population has grown every year since (Mayor of London [n.d.]).

Arguably, therefore, an urban renaissance of the type sought by the Urban Task Force and successive mayors – if measured by the attraction of an urban area to its residents – had begun in London long before the Urban Task Force commenced their work. Edwards (2010: 192) argues that the proposals of the Urban Task Force were actually never fully relevant to London, a city with generally little brownfield land, where high-income groups had never abandoned the city centre, and where public transport already served a dense and mixed city core. Despite this, policies from 1999 onwards gave regeneration processes in London a boost and started, in a more systematic manner, to mix environmental quality into the recipe for guiding urban London's future development.

UCL renaissance seminar, nine years on

In the summer of 2008 (just as Boris Johnson took the helm and as the credit crunch began to bite), a seminar hosted at UCL to evaluate London's urban renaissance drew on the collective wisdom of 100 academics and practitioners to determine the nature and extent of any renaissance. Discussions over two days revealed a significant degree of unanimity and a range of conclusions about London and its urban renaissance (see Carmona 2009b):

- *London is unique in the UK* – London remains the only UK city with a serious international presence, although arguably its national and international role often takes precedence over local concerns. In fact, the city is a massive net exporter of wealth to the rest of the UK, whilst internally huge international speculation drives up asset values. Despite this, it is one of the richest regions in the EU; has been and continues to be the subject of major infrastructure investment (bus and tube upgrades, Thameslink, Crossrail, etc.); and in many areas and in many respects is an exemplar of principles of sustainable urbanism. Yet, side by side with its prosperity live some of the poorest communities in the UK, coping with the highest costs of living.

- *Central London continues to dominate* – There is undoubtedly a need for a better balance in policy and associated design and regeneration efforts between centre and periphery – urban and suburban. Ken Livingstone's London Plan was clearly focused on central London, while developments such as those at King's Cross Railway Lands or in the Docklands continue to be judged by their contribution to the expansion of the central London activity zone. As a result central London expands ever outwards, whilst the potential renaissance contribution of the suburbs has been largely overlooked. Boris Johnson recognised this, but in 2012 the impact of his revised plan is yet to be seen.

- *Quality development in London takes time* – The story of Docklands regeneration, for example, dates back 40 years and a renaissance (as understood by the Urban Task Force) has only been achieved in some parts of that massive territory over the last ten years. In others – namely the Royal Docks – it still seems some way off, with the 2011 budget announcing the designation of a new enterprise zone in the Royals precisely to stimulate investment. Elsewhere, the massive King's Cross development was finally granted planning permission in 2006 after a litany of failure dating back to the 1980s, Greenwich Peninsular is only partially developed, whilst widespread planned redevelopment in the Thames Gateway still has to build up a head of steam. In none of these places has this been wasted time. In Docklands, the period saw a maturing of the design and planning approach, with, for example, much higher-quality public space in the latter phases of the development, whilst the six years that Argent took to negotiate their planning permission at King's Cross was a period of gradual refinement and convergence of opinion between public and private partners over the masterplan.

- *The private sector continues to lead* – The design and planning vision in London is still largely coming from the private sector, or not at all, whilst public sector planning contends with a crisis of skills and confidence to plan positively. Perhaps this is inevitable in a context where, unlike Paris or Barcelona, the city does not have the freedom necessary to make the sort of investment that is required to transform areas. Instead, it continues to seek private sector solutions. Despite this, where no market exists, huge amounts of public money have been required to kick-start one, as was the experience in the Docklands, although this was only made available grudgingly, and when private sector disaster promised to derail the whole project. The situation is being repeated in the Thames Gateway.

- *Local government is often reactionary* – With some notable exceptions, the ability of local authorities to set the agenda in London has been particularly weak. Lots of design policies exist, some (e.g. those of the City of Westminster) highly refined and very robust (see Chapter 3) but there remains a general lack of clear spatial vision. Moreover, where such a vision does exist, typically it is commissioned from, or led by, the private sector, such as the Urban Forest concept to improve public spaces around London's Southbank, commissioned and led by the Better

Bankside Business Improvement District (BID – see Chapter 5) (**4.1**). This leads to an over-concentration on reactionary development control and on ad hoc regeneration initiatives to ensure that the benefits of development are shared and do not pass the community by. It also leads to big contrasts between highly planned private estates – such as Canary Wharf – and surrounding areas with little or no planning and too much faith placed on market opportunism, exemplified in the late 2000s by the overheating of the buy-to-let market.

- *Private development is funding many 'public goods'* – The area where negotiation is often longest and most complex concerns the agreement of the planning gain package (the Section 106 Agreement) that sits alongside the planning permission, and which defines the developer's contribution to a range of associated 'public goods'. In London, increasingly this has been relied upon to deliver commitments as diverse as energy efficiency measures, affordable housing, a wide range of social infrastructure, and public space. Whilst some argue that planning

4.1   Enhanced public space at Bankside on London's Southbank – the refurbishment, revitalisation and active management of many public spaces on London's Southbank have been led by the Better Bankside BID

authorities should be confident enough to ask for larger contributions, others feel that when the pot is limited the system encourages trade-offs between otherwise essential public goods and in so doing tends to overlook the public liability for some goods (e.g. affordable housing), or to recognise that others, such as high-quality public space, actually add value to new development. Such factors should not be seen as a cost to be negotiated and traded-off, but instead, as a necessary outcome of the development process.

- *Urban design is now accepted* – During the 2000s, urban design came of age in London, being widely accepted as a basis for successful development. Schemes were generally much more outward looking and traditionally urban in nature than their counterparts from the 1980s, with the Canary Wharf/Broadgate model where developers also take on the role of long-term estate owners and managers becoming more the norm. In such cases, developers remain interested in the long-term quality and profitability of their developments, relying on outcomes from the third, fourth and fifth rent reviews to deliver enhanced profits, rather than the initial capital values. As argued in Chapter 2, the experiences of these companies have portended the return of a design-led commercial model to London that emulates the successful private management model of London's great estates, many of which are still generating handsome returns from their garden square developments many generations after the original investment.

4.2   Gordon Square – regenerated and now fully open to the public, seven days a week

Privatisation and gentrification are rife – Major developments across London have increasingly been taking significant parts of the city into private ownership with private management and control regimes. Much of this new London passes the much vaunted 'cappuccino test' (that a continental-style renaissance has truly arrived if you can enjoy an al-fresco cappuccino), but the benefits of regeneration have not been shared equally; communities remain starkly divided, both socially and physically; the second-home and investment markets have grossly inflated prices in some areas, whilst those on middle incomes find it increasingly hard to secure housing of any sort close to work. The danger is that renaissance may itself lead to greater displacement and gentrification as areas of the city with viable low rent economies that cater for the non-corporate and non-profit sectors are swept away in the name of regeneration. In this process, old is too often associated with decay and failure, and new with vitality and progress (see below), leading to areas that are poorly inoculated against the inevitable pressures of gentrification.

Heritage is easily marginalised – Reflecting a basic conflict between the preservation of built heritage and the increasing scale of many development projects across London, heritage is being insensitively adapted or dwarfed by intensification pressures. In this environment, more sensitive approaches to development, or the 'alternative' approaches that came to the fore from the 1970s onwards (see Chapter 2), are increasingly rare. At the same time, the skyline is being increasingly privatised as strategic policies to protect key London-wide views were relaxed under Ken Livingstone (although tightened again under Boris Johnson) and as building high has come back into fashion. In this, the views of English Heritage have often been ignored, although success in driving forward their Campaign for London Squares (see Chapter 2) has managed to rejuvenate key historic garden squares that were previously on the danger list (**4.2**).

Land value is not being captured – Underpinning many of these points is the critical tension between land ownership and regulation. On this front, three final conclusions could be drawn:

❖ First, when land is unified under a single private ownership, the value of 'public goods' such as public space can be identified and internalised within development schemes. In such circumstances, planners need to ensure that clear public

More London – largely corporate development on London's Southbank designed by Foster & Partners and incorporating City Hall, the new headquarters for the Mayor of London

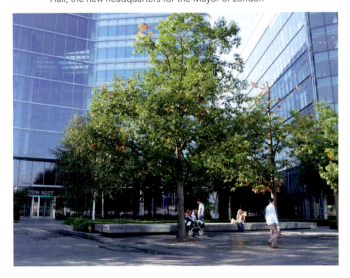

design aspirations are also being met in these large private landscapes.

❖ Second, when land ownership is divided, where major infrastructure is divisive, or where the scale of thinking required is strategic in nature, processes of visioning and the robust control of what the market subsequently brings forward will nearly always be dependent on a strong public sector lead to achieve coherence and quality. In this respect, the UCL renaissance seminar concluded, London has been failed.

❖ In part, this is because, third, despite the huge potential power wielded by the public sector as major landowner and infrastructure provider, this power has not been used as a positive tool in regeneration. As such, land prices and the market dividend from infrastructure upgrades have not been sufficiently captured as a means to fund something better than the standard market products. As elsewhere, but perhaps more so in London given the size of these investments, the public sector operates with one hand tied behind its back.

For Terry Farrell (2010: 276), the last 15 years of London's regeneration has been a success story, but one that derives from the community of London, not its development professionals: 'Like the whole history of London, it has been a pattern of organic change, collective change by many hands, that have brought it about by evolving the form, the shape of London. The metropolis is, in essence, a social creation London is itself, in itself, a great accumulated work.' By contrast, comparing the renaissance in London with that in other UK cities, Punter (2010b: 330) argues that 'even in London it has proved difficult to fund large-scale, high quality investments in public space – as the abandonment of the Mayor's 100 Spaces project illustrates'. Instead, with limited access to national regeneration funds, London shows the benefits of small-scale partnerships and private initiative projects, some funded by BIDs, and others through planning gain.

Roberts & Lloyd-Jones (2010: 176) argue that although many central London developments of the last ten years such as More London (**4.3**), Tower Place in the City, Cardinal Place in Victoria and Exchange Square in Broadgate have many positive features, the spread of a corporate ambience is increasingly a problem: 'Functionally they fulfil their planning requirements to provide public access, public space and mixed uses at ground floor level [but] The anonymity of their styling, the ubiquitous use of glass and granite and the corporate "cloned" replication of chain bars and chain stores at ground level rob these new insertions of any character.' Like Punter, they argue, that a greater success has been the large number of smaller spaces that have been improved, often attached to key historical buildings, often with the input of central London's BIDs, and sometimes tied to the enlightened patronage of London's great estates, including the work of the Crown Estate at Regents Street (and now Oxford Circus). They argue that such examples 'support the urban renaissance ideal of a walkable, human-scaled lively street environment, albeit one that requires an above average salary to participate in' (Roberts & Lloyd-Jones 2010: 177).

THE ECONOMIC, SOCIAL AND CULTURAL CONTEXTS FOR CHANGE

An economically dynamic city

As the discussion suggested, renaissance, if it has arrived, is clearly not without its complications and compromises (although in London urban change was ever that way). Each phase of London's development from the Georgian expansions to the urban renaissance policies of the early twenty-first century has been underpinned by its own political economies, although, throughout, London has remained a permissive city, encouraging of growth and development, and shy of top-down intervention whether from king, government or local authority. The economic fortunes of the city have waxed and waned over its history, but something in its DNA has ensured that it has remained a dynamic centre of commerce and urban life, most recently taking advantage of the long period of growth from the mid 1990s to the 2007 credit crunch to further consolidate the city's position as the UK's economic powerhouse. Even in the period 2008–10 when the rest of the country suffered grievously from the after-effects of the financial crisis in which London-based institutions were heavily implicated, employment in the capital continued to grow, as (after an initial crash) did property prices (Hall 2011).

In this period, arguments raged about whether in recent times the city's economy has become too reliant on financial services. Certainly, the profile of London's economy has shifted over time, most recently seeing a dramatic decline in the city as a centre of manufacturing industry and a huge growth in its service economy. In 2010, just 5 per cent of Londoners worked in manufacturing (a further 5 per cent in construction), but, despite the perceived domination of financial services, only 7 per cent worked in such occupations – a similar number to those working in transport and communications (7 per cent), hospitality (6 per cent) and public administration (5 per cent). Most Londoners worked in a wide range of other business services (27 per cent), in education, health or social work (16 per cent), in retail and distribution (13 per cent), and in a wide range of personal services (9 per cent) (LDA 2010: 11).

In spite of the employment numbers, financial services have undoubtedly been the source of huge wealth generation for the capital, and the provision of space for this industry has been a key driver of many of London's major development opportunities (and new public spaces) since the 1980s. Beyond this, the huge growth in London's service sector has given rise to an equally large expansion in professional, managerial and technical employment, and a sharp decline in non-skilled occupations. The result is that London far outstrips other regions in the UK in terms of its Gross Value Added (GVA) per head as well as in its overall productivity (Swadkin & Virdee 2007). With its ability to suck in bright and dynamic talent from across the UK, Europe and the world, and to continue to attract significant foreign direct investment, it looks likely that London's recent economic success will be self-sustaining, despite some considerable economic bumps in the road, most notably the 2008 credit crunch and subsequent recession. With this comes a potentially more profitable and less risky market for developers who will continue to invest in converting, upgrading and reproducing London's physical building stock and associated public realm (Hamnett 2003: 214).

A socially diverse city

As well as its diverse employment profile, London has long been a socially diverse city, and in the twentieth century became an ethnically diverse one as well. Chapter 2 began by discussing the garden squares of London, the product of an elite homogenous group of wealthy and advantaged families, building for their own kind and to ensure that they could control who their neighbours were. By contrast, the public housing estates built in the mid twentieth century were initially built for an equally homogenous group, albeit at the other end of the wealth spectrum: for the disadvantaged, those without adequate housing, or those surviving in London on a working wage.

In twenty-first-century London, the gap between rich and poor and the Balkanised nature of London's neighbourhoods is just as stark. London is home to the richest and some of the poorest of the UK's inhabitants, and culturally is far from homogenous (if it ever was). Thus Imrie *et al.* (2009: 8) argue that London is characterised by juxtaposed inequalities and processes of social polarisation that are greater than in any comparable city in Europe. Large swathes of the city feature amongst the country's most deprived locations, with 4 of London's 33 local authorities featuring in the top-ten most deprived in England (Hackney (second), Tower Hamlets (third), Newham (sixth) and Islington (eighth) (Imrie *et al.* 2009: 9)).

Culturally, the story has been additive, with new communities 'building like a coral reef on communities with a strong degree of historical continuity and resilience' (Hebbert 1998: 164). Approaching one-third (30.5 per cent) of the city's population is foreign-born, hailing from a far wider range of countries than in the past when the UK primarily attracted immigration from its former colonies (LSE 2007: 13). Peter Hall's book *London Voices, London Lives* vividly traces the great variety of those who today call themselves Londoners (or who at least live and work in the city), concluding that in European terms

London is unique as one of the great global cities of the world. Thus London acts as a magnet for people from across the world, the majority of whom are highly skilled and who come from high-income countries (Hall 2007: 7). This creates tensions, and not always between those from whom you might expect it, but instead between one group of new arrivals and the next. On the whole, however, London has become one of the most multi-ethnic and multi-cultural cities in the world with remarkably few problems (Hall 2007: 469).

More than anywhere, it is on the streets and in the public spaces of the city that these different groups meet and interact, as do London's advantaged and disadvantaged, old and young, women and men. This provides a further important context for discussion of London's public space; London in 2012 is a city whose communities are as ethnically and socially diverse as the spaces they occupy; diversity that can manifest itself in public space aspirations. In 2005/06, for example, a study examining the ethnography of one of London's street markets threatened with redevelopment revealed starkly contrasting narratives of old and new (Dines & Cattell 2006). In this study of Queen's Market in Newham, one of the most deprived and ethnically mixed parts of London, the old was associated with dirty, ugly, old-fashioned, anti-social space by the developer and the new (his proposals) with destruction of diversity, vitality, affordability and social mixing by campaigners against the development. For Dines (2009: 271), the research demonstrated a continuing tension between redevelopment and regeneration agendas in the capital, particularly as they relate to social and economic spaces. It also revealed a considerable constituency in London that recognises and celebrates the ethnic diversity of the capital and the opportunity that some public spaces provide to experience that. However, studies of walking practices in London have suggested that it is through visual rather than verbal interactions that different groups most often experience each other (Middleton 2009: 210), typically passing like strangers, despite occupying and sharing the same public space.

The gentrification issue

For Ruth Glass (1964), who coined the term 'gentrification' through her studies of London's fast-polarising inner city neighbourhoods in the 1960s, London represented a city where the fit (those with money) survived whilst those without were squeezed out, or squeezed into smaller pockets of undesirable or social housing. Forty years later, Hamnett's (2003: 8) analysis of London's social and economic

4.4   Hoxton – London's gentrified public space

transformation in the late twentieth century advances a similar narrative – that the growth in professional and managerial jobs and associated middle classes is being matched by the decline of other, lower-income, groups, particularly in inner London. These trends give rise not only to astronomical growth in property values as demand for owner occupation increases pushing from clearly middle-class areas into hitherto working-class neighbourhoods, but also to increasing inequalities between the larger groups of haves and the (relatively) smaller group of have-nots (Hamnett 2003: 102). The analysis echoes Smith's (2000: 294) broad definition of gentrification: 'the reinvestment of capital in the urban centre, which is designed to produce space for a more affluent class of people than

currently occupies that space'. For Punter (2010b: 343), this has direct resonance with the processes that have been in place in central London, including at King's Cross, calling in to question the aspiration of social mix advanced as part of the drive for urban renaissance.

As a context for the design, delivery and management of public space, such social change has arguably brought with it changing perceptions about places, leading to the re-shaping of whole areas in the image of their gentrifiers – for example Hoxton (**4.4**) and Clerkenwell – processes that are now underway in even the most traditional of East End communities such as Whitechapel and Bow. Crudely, such change also heralded huge development opportunities, both to cater for London's expanding service industries (see above) and taking advantage of sky-rocketing property prices, with average London house prices exceeding £400,000 in 2010, despite the liberalisation of density policy. The nature of London's new and regenerated public spaces may therefore simply reflect the changing nature of the city, change that in recent times has manifested itself socially, economically and culturally, as well as physically.

Crime, security and surveillance

Amongst the renaissance narratives and critiques, particular concerns have been raised about how public space is managed. A concern for cleaner, tidier public space became a particular issue for the Labour government following its re-election in 1991, and whilst some boroughs were able to rise to the challenge, the general concern on these matters persisted into the 1998 mayoral election as an issue on which, Boris Johnson argued, London could do much better. A related key management dimension generating much discussion and dissension has been the issue of crime and security on London's streets.

For much of the twentieth century, London was the preferred target for the IRA, with a particular surge in attacks during the periods 1973–83 and 1990–96, and from the 'Real IRA' during 2000 and 2001. Hard on the heals of the heinous 9/11 attacks in New York (2001), London again came under attack, this time from home-grown Islamist terrorists, with the devastating 7/7 (2005) attacks on London's tube and bus system followed by failed attacks two weeks later and again in 2007. Reflecting the size and ferocity of the attacks in New York and later in London, a legislative reaction was, perhaps, predictable, and this came in the form of the Serious Organised Crime and Police Act

4.5   Rangers patrolling the Heart of London BID

of 2005, threatening, some argued, to limit rights of public assembly and free speech. Thus Keller (2007: 13) refers to the 'chilling effect on civil liberties' of attempts to limit public demonstrations as public spaces in London are declared not suitable for demonstrations. In fact, as regards public space, the provisions of the act were rather tame, namely that demonstrations within one kilometre of Parliament Square (although excluding Trafalgar Square) needed to be notified to the Metropolitan Police at least six days prior to their commencement, and, if this was not reasonably practicable, then within 24 hours.

For Keller (2007: 13), however, the legislative changes go hand in hand with a claim that the UK is the most surveilled nation in the world and that 'London has become the most watched city in the world, with the largest number of closed-circuit cameras in public places anywhere'. Citing extensively quoted evidence that Londoners are caught on security cameras 300 times a day (and that the UK boasts 4.2 million CCTV cameras), she conjures an Orwellian dystopia of a surveillance society on London's streets. In fact, the evidence and the figures are fatally flawed, extrapolating the London-wide totals from a short stretch of Putney High Street; assuming the same coverage across the capital and (without evidence) conjecturing that other cities around the world are less surveilled (Lewis 2009). The example demonstrates the ease with which, in the field of public space, it is possible to get caught up in the assertions of urban theorists, single-issue campaigners or lazy journalists with a dystopian view to spin.

In this case, arguments too often focus on the numbers of cameras per se instead of on their use, or on whether there is any evidence that they undermine the liberties of anyone except those committing offences. One of the few Europe-wide studies on the subject suggested that CCTV is widely supported as a tool against crime, with Londoners (in the survey) reporting the greatest faith in such systems – 90 per cent seeing CCTV as a good thing – and believing that those who have nothing to hide have nothing to fear (78 per cent) (Hempel & Topfer 2004: 42–6).

In reality, in common with many cities around the world, CCTV cameras are indeed ubiquitous in London. The City of Westminster, for example, has a network of 160 cameras from which to monitor public space within the borough (Lewis 2009), whilst the *Evening Standard* has reported that the capital as a whole has 10,000 cameras used to fight crime, but also that a comparison between camera numbers and rates of crime clear-up shows no correlation (Davenport 2007). Similarly, the BBC (2008b) reported that just 3 per cent of London street robberies are solved on the evidence provided by CCTV cameras, whilst the Metropolitan Police argue that, despite the statistics, CCTV cameras remain a valuable weapon in their armoury for tackling crime. Whatever the value or otherwise of CCTV in fighting crime, one thing does seem clear – there is a distinct lack of evidence that CCTV has been used to undermine civil liberties in London. Instead, the widespread acceptance of CCTV in London is part of an unspoken pact: freedom, but freedom tempered by order and, when necessary, by control.

Across Greater London, responsibility for such control falls largely into the hands of the Metropolitan Police, although the City of London has its own police force, which famously threw up a 'ring of steel' around the Square Mile in the early 1990s as a visible security presence to deter IRA terrorist action, the ring consisting of cordons, sentry points and CCTV cameras to record drivers and vehicles entering the City. The Metropolitan Police is funded by the Mayor, who indirectly also controls their strategic direction through his influence on the Board of the Metropolitan Police Authority (MPA), either as its Chair or through appointing the Chair and Vice Chair. On coming to power, Ken Livingstone caused some consternation by arguing that it felt safer to walk the streets of New York (despite that city's much higher murder rate) than the streets of London. For him, levels of street crime were 'unacceptably high, but fear of crime was still higher' and represented the real problem (quoted in Russell 2002).

The solution over the course of his mayoralty was to put more police on the streets (rising from 25,000 officers in 2001 to 36,000 in 2009, with an additional 4,500 Police Community Support Officers). He also supported through London Development Agency (LDA) funding the establishment of BIDs in London, despite critiques in the (mainly American) literature (e.g. Briffault 1999) about their potentially privatising effects on public space. Alongside key promotional and stewardship roles, these have typically provided an additional layer of security through funding teams of rangers or wardens to mount security patrols within their boundaries (**4.5**). This followed the 2003 Local Government Act, which introduced the right to set up BIDs in England and Wales, followed shortly afterwards by the Circle Initiative, which established the first five pilot BIDs in London (see Chapter 10). By March 2006, each of the original BIDs had conducted successful ballots of their local business communities in order to constitute themselves, and by 2012, 25 BIDs were in operation across the capital with a further seven in development. These now mount patrols in some of London's busiest and most high-profile localities.

By 2008, perhaps reflecting this strategy of increasing the uniformed presence on the streets, but more likely reflecting the rising economic fortunes of London, fear of crime as reported in the British Crime Survey had fallen. Fear of violent crime, for example, was down from 29 per cent of respondents reporting a high level of fear in 2001 to around 23 per cent in 2008, although the figures were still well above the national average at 14 per cent or those for any other UK region. In other words, Londoners were more fearful when compared with those living in other parts of the country, although at a lower base level than previously (Defra [n.d.]). In part, the levels of fear may be explained by media coverage of such issues – in particular of crime amongst youth gangs, which, although heavily localised in particular parts of the capital, have typically been reported as if they impact across London and on all Londoners (Travis 2008), and which were heavily implicated in the 2011 London riots, amongst other explanations (Wikipedia, Riots [n.d.]).

In the mayoral race of 2008, the solution advocated was yet more police on the streets, whilst Boris Johnson also made the case for more CCTV, in particular on London's buses. In fact, by 2010, financial

4.6 a, b Mobile CCTV unit – evidence of 'big brother' watching (a), or sensible precaution against nationalist groups (b) during the now annual St George's Day celebration in Trafalgar Square?

a

b

cutbacks were forcing cuts in police numbers, although how this will feed through into rates of crime, and (perhaps more importantly) into perceptions of crime in London's public space is yet to be seen. What is clear is that as these issues play out on the ground (and in the capital's politics), simplistic interpretations of crime figures, and/or methods of preventing crime typically stir up much heat, but rarely shed much light on how people use and experience public space in London.

4.7   The distribution of new and refurbished spaces in London since 1980

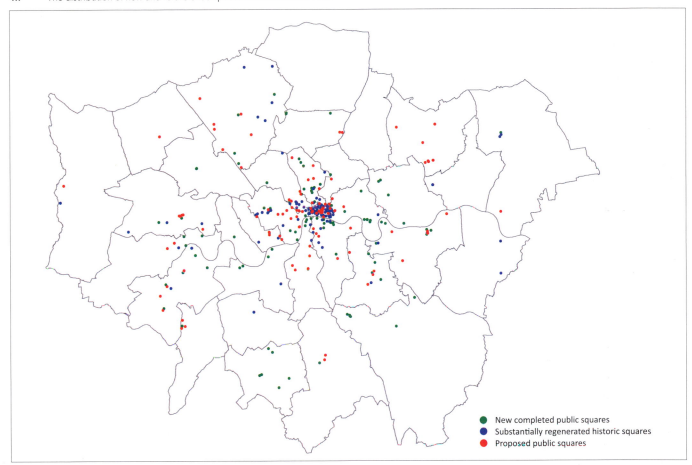

- ● New completed public squares
- ● Substantially regenerated historic squares
- ● Proposed public squares

Worse, as the discussion on CCTV above suggests, they can be grossly distorted in order to support particular polemical views of public space without an evidence base to back them up (**4.6**).

A MANIFESTATION IN SQUARES

The lack of an evidence base with which to back up assertions about public space is, it was hypothesised in Chapter 1, a key reason why so much public space literature is potentially suspect. This in turn explains why it is so important to have a good grasp of the political,

social and economic trends affecting London before their impact on the creation of the physical public realm, including public squares, can be properly understood. In order that subsequent chapters can bring together discussion of all the factors that impact on contemporary public space creation and recreation in London, this final part of the chapter turns to the physical manifestation of these wider trends and presents the results of a survey of new and regenerated squares in London since 1980.

The patterns of public space today

Whilst Mayor Ken Livingstone's 100 Spaces programme may, in hindsight, have seemed hopelessly optimistic in its ambition, and

4.8   Ten boroughs, 130 spaces

NEW LONDON SQUARES PER BOROUGH

CENTRAL LONDON		INNER LONDON						OUTER LONDON		
City of London	Westminster	Tower Hamlets	Southwark	Lambeth	Camden	Kensington & Chelsea	Greenwich	Richmond	Barnet	
Aldermanbury Place	Bessborough Gardens	Bishops Square	Montague Close	Broadwall Square/ Coin Street	Bedford Square	Duke of York Square	Ballast Quay	East Sheen Lane Square	Seaton Square	
Aldermanbury Square	Cardinal Walk	Burrell's Wharf	Borough Market	Festival Riverside	British Library Piazza	Madjeski Garden V&A	Cutty Sark Gardens	Kew Piazza	Tally Ho Corner	
Athene Square	Channel 4 Forecourt	Cabot Square	Empire Square	Gabriel's Wharf	Queen Elizabeth II Great Court	Sloane Square	James Clavell Square	Lower George Street		
Bartlett Passage	Leicester Square	Canada Place	Hays Galleria	Theatre Square	Brunswick Square		Greenwich Station Forecourt	Richmond Riverside		
Basinghall Square	Hyde Park Corner	Reuters Plaza	King's College Square		Community Square		Glaister Street			
Bishopsgate Churchyard	Royal Art Academy Courtyard	Canada Square	More London		Fitzroy Square		Millennium Quay			
Bishopsgate 55 Courtyard	Somerset House Courtyard	Clove Crescent	Oxo Tower Wharf		Euston Station Piazza		GMV Square			
Broadgate Circle	St Andrew's Square	Columbus Square	Peckham Square		Russell Square		Old Pearson Court			
Bury Court	Sheldon Square	Clipper's Quay	Potter Fields		Theatre Square		Peninsular Square			
Carter Lane	Trafalgar Square	Lanark Square	Tate Modern Square		Torrington Square		Royal Arsenal Gardens			
City Point 1 Square	West End Quay	Jubilee Park	Tabard Gardens		Triton Square		Wellington Park Square			
Cross Key Square		Muirfield Crescent	Horselydown Square		UCL Print Room Square					
Devonshire Square		Menton Place								
Dorset Rise 1-2		Maritime Quay								
Exchange Square		Millwall Outer Dock								
Fenchurch Place		New Providence Wharf								
Fetter Lane 86		Selsdon Way								
Finsbury Avenue Square		St David's Square								
Fleet Street 65		Tower Hill Square								
Fleet Place		Watney Market								
Gilbert Bridge Square		Westferry Circus								
Greyfriars Courtyard										
Greyfriars Christ Churchyard										
Guildhall Yard										
Hare Court										
Holborn Circus										
Hope Square										
Johnson's Court										
Little Somerset Street Court										
Minster Court										
Monument Yard										
Moorhouse Square										
Monkwell Square										
New Street Square										
Old Broad Street Courtyard										
Old Change Court										
Paternoster Lane										
Paternoster Square										
Petticoat Square										
Plough Place										
Queen Street Square										
Royal Exchange Courtyard										
St Mary Axe Square										
Salisbury Square										
Tower Place										
West Court Cutlers Gardens										
West Smithfield Place										
Woolgate Exchange Place										

in fact proved impossible to deliver, when compared with the actual extent of public space projects taking place across the capital at the time, it seems less naive. Conducted in 2007 with the help of borough planning departments, a London-wide survey of 'new' public squares across the 32 London boroughs and the City of London mapped over 230 new or substantially regenerated squares (100 new and 130 regenerated), ranging from formal piazzas to incidental spaces, all built or rebuilt since 1980 (the majority since 1990). In addition, another 100 square projects (new or refurbished) were being actively proposed across London at the time of survey. The figure is remarkable in that it follows a period of nearly 150 years during which relatively few new public spaces had been built in London as the focus shifted to suburban and traffic growth, whilst those that were built have since been largely redeveloped (see Chapter 3) as part of the renaissance processes discussed above.

However, although almost all London boroughs can boast new or refurbished schemes, this revival in formal public space building has not been evenly distributed. Instead, it was heavy skewed to inner and central London, with far fewer squares (around 50) in the 20 outer suburban boroughs (**4.7**).

On-site visual analysis of 130 of the spaces across ten London boroughs chosen to represent both the geography of London and the distribution of new and refurbished spaces threw further light on the phenomenon (**4.8**). Positively, the analysis revealed that the majority

of new squares in London are well used, legible, permeable and accessible, distinct and attractive, and comfortable, they have a good microclimate and active frontages, and they are clean, safe and well maintained. They are used most often as 'everyday' sorts of spaces for simply passing through, or for meetings, rest and relaxation, are well respected with few obvious signs of anti-social behaviour, and, in about a third of cases, are vibrant and social in character (**4.9**). Almost inevitably they are covered by CCTV, with around a tenth of spaces exhibiting some form of behavioural signage to limit activities.

Distinguishing London's spaces geographically

When examined in relation to the geographic structure of London, some common characteristics could be distinguished in spaces in outer, inner and central London (the latter including Tower Hamlets, because of the dominance, for this purpose, of the high-density business-oriented Isle of Dogs and City-fringes). Commonalities largely stemmed from the influence of single major land uses (whether corporate in central London or residential in outer London), on the design of spaces, whilst regenerated spaces, particularly in Westminster, were typically dominated by clear single themes or functions, be that entertainment, cultural, memorial, and so forth. Spaces in inner London, by contrast, more often sit within mixed-use developments or multi-functional areas and are therefore more diverse in their character and use, tending to be more obviously inclusive and sociable with a greater degree of adaptability (**4.10**).

Because of these broad differences, new spaces in central London are characterised by contemporary buildings that lack visual interest, human scale and detail when compared with inner and outer London and that often exhibit dead or only partially active frontages (also a feature of some inner London schemes). Moreover, signs of homogenisation were most apparent in central London; in

4.10a–c Spaces of central (a), inner (b) and outer (c) London

a

b

c

4.11   Typical signs of homogenisation

the international architecture, repetitive landscape treatments, and in the types of brands that situated themselves on these high-value spaces (**4.11**). The presence of public art was also ubiquitous in central London, as it was in inner London, but less often seen in outer London, where the range of materials used within public spaces was also more diverse. By contrast, the approach to integrating historical elements divided more along east/south and west/north lines. Thus

boroughs such as Westminster, Kensington & Chelsea, and Camden remained particularly sensitive to historic context, whilst others were more content to see a much greater contrast between new and historic elements, including the City, Tower Hamlets, Lambeth and Greenwich.

A further difference was the presence of clearly privately owned

4.12 Signs of exclusivity and exclusion

and managed public spaces that were most often found in central London (again including Tower Hamlets), whilst clearly public spaces or public spaces with some restrictions were the norm elsewhere in inner and outer London. Because of this (and the presence of high-impact tourist destinations in Westminster) explicit dedicated control was also most obvious in these boroughs and absent or more subtle elsewhere, although it was spaces in the City and in Kensington &

Chelsea that most obviously exuded a sense of exclusivity or exclusion (**4.12**).

Distinguishing by physical form

Focusing on the physical form of the new and regenerated spaces, six different types were identified: piazzas (36 per cent of spaces), courtyards (18 per cent), incidental spaces (16 per cent), garden

4.13 A typology of physical forms

a Piazzas are traditional squares, often distinguished by their hard formal or semi-formal nature

d Garden squares are characterised by their green grassed centre that is itself sometimes enclosed (e.g. by railings) and sometimes not

b Courtyards, are completely surrounded and enclosed by a building or buildings requiring users to pass through or under the building to enter

e Forecourts, act as external pauses and transitions between the public realm of the street and private or semi-private realm of a key building

c Incidental spaces are informal, often low-key small and / or reclaimed spaces

f Other spaces, encompass the amorphous spaces that defy classification, or those that transcend the other physical types

squares (13 per cent), forecourts (9 per cent) and other spaces (7 per cent) (**4.13, 4.14**). Although piazzas, courtyards and incidential spaces typically included green elements (trees and planting), overwhelmingly the sorts of spaces being created in London are harder and more urban than the city's historic garden squares. Here, however, survey results were skewed by the large number of spaces (mainly piazzas, courtyards, forecourts and incedental spaces) being created and recreated in the City of London, which, despite its geographically diminutive size, had well over double the number of spaces of the next nearest borough (Tower Hamlets) (**4.15**).

The six categories of physical form show a range of correlations with aspects of design, although in general there was a great variety in design character across the types. The following correlations were nevertheless apparent:

- Public art is a 'must-have' element of piazzas.

- Incidental and courtyard spaces are generally of a small scale and piazzas and garden squares of a large scale.

- Incidental spaces have a less coherent form than other spaces and are generally more noisy, and less clean and comfortable.

- Courtyards, by their nature, are less connected than other types to the surrounding street network.

- Piazzas tend to be more highly sanitised than other space types.

- Courtyards and piazzas typically feel less inclusive than other types and exhibit higher levels of control.

- Garden squares have a lower level of security patrols and incidental spaces the highest degree of behavioural signage.

- Forecourts are often strongly themed.

4.14 The forms of London's public squares

COURTYARD

Bartlett Passage

Bishopsgate 55 Courtyard

Bishopsgate Churchyard

Hare Court

Cross Key Square

Johnson's Court

Fetter Lane 86

Fleet Street 65

West Court Cutlers Gardens

Greyfriars Courtyard

Old Broad Street Courtyard

Petticoat Square

Royal Exchange Courtyard

Royal Academy of Art

Somerset House Courtyard

St Andrew's Square

Empire Square

King's College Square

Oxo Tower Wharf

Horselydown & Brewery Squares

Muirfield Crescent

Madjeski Garden V&A

Brunswick Square**

UCL Print Room Square

Old Pearson Court

East Sheen Lane square

FORECOURT

Athene Square

Fenchurch Place

Bury Court

Minster Court

Woolgate Exchange Place

Hope Square

Tate Modern**

British Library Piazza

Euston Station Piazza

Queen Elizabeth II Great Court

Greenwich Station Forecourt

Forum Magnum Square

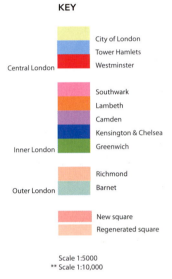

KEY

Central London
- City of London
- Tower Hamlets
- Westminster

Inner London
- Southwark
- Lambeth
- Camden
- Kensington & Chelsea
- Greenwich

Outer London
- Richmond
- Barnet

- New square
- Regenerated square

Scale 1:5000
** Scale 1:10,000

4.14 The forms of London's public squares (cont.)

PIAZZA

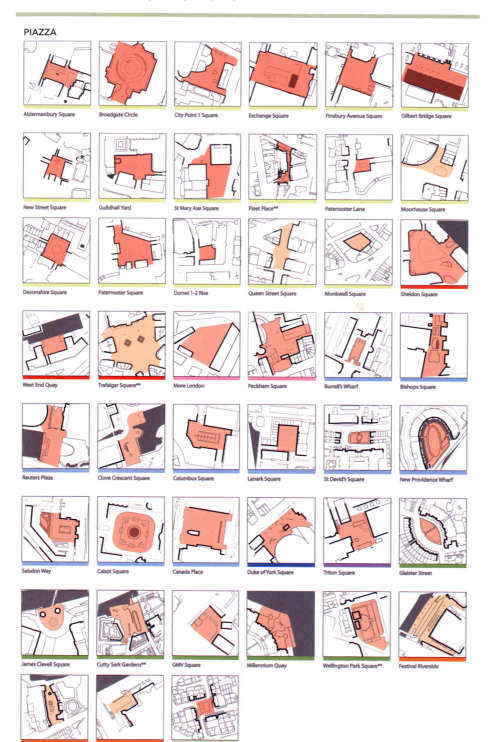

KEY

Central London
- City of London
- Tower Hamlets
- Westminster

Inner London
- Southwark
- Lambeth
- Camden
- Kensington & Chelsea
- Greenwich

Outer London
- Richmond
- Barnet

- New square
- Regenerated square

Scale 1:5000
** Scale 1:10,000

GARDEN

Greyfriars Christ Churchyard · Salisbury Square · Bessborough Gardens · Hyde Park Corner** · Leicester Square** · Potter Fields**

Tabard Gardens** · Maritime Quay · Millwall Outer Dock · Jubilee Park** · Canada Square · Bedford Square

Community Square** · Fitzroy Square** · Russell Square** · Broadwall Square ** · Windrush Square Gardens

KEY

City of London
Tower Hamlets
Westminster

Central London

Southwark
Lambeth
Camden
Kensington & Chelsea
Greenwich

Inner London

Richmond
Barnet

Outer London

New square
Regenerated square

Scale 1:5000
** Scale 1:10,000

INCIDENTAL

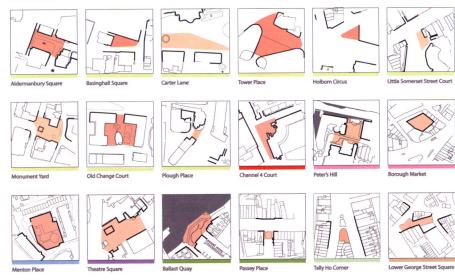

Aldermanbury Square · Basinghall Square · Carter Lane · Tower Place · Holborn Circus · Little Somerset Street Court

Monument Yard · Old Change Court · Plough Place · Channel 4 Court · Peter's Hill · Borough Market

Menton Place · Theatre Square · Ballast Quay · Passey Place · Tally Ho Corner · Lower George Street Square

Kew Piazza

4.14   The forms of London's public squares (cont.)

OTHER

West Smithfield Square**   Cardinal Walk**   Hays Galleria   Clipper's Quay   Watney Market   Westferry Circus**

Torrington Square   Royal Arsenal Gardens**   Peninsular Square   Richmond Riverside

KEY

Central London
- City of London
- Tower Hamlets
- Westminster

Inner London
- Southwark
- Lambeth
- Camden
- Kensington & Chelsea
- Greenwich

Outer London
- Richmond
- Barnet

- New square
- Regenerated square

Scale 1:5000
** Scale 1:10,000

Distinguishing by function

When the dominant function of spaces rather than their physical form was the focus of analysis, eight types could be identified, although some spaces can be categorised in more than one type: community spaces (45 per cent), corporate spaces (23 per cent), undefined spaces (17 per cent), domestic spaces (13 per cent), civic spaces (13 per cent), consumption spaces (8 per cent), service spaces (5 per cent) and transit spaces (4 per cent) (**4.16**). Unsurprisingly, the City and Tower Hamlets had by far the largest number of corporate spaces, and Westminster the largest number of civic spaces. Inner and outer London boroughs, by contrast, featured more community and domestic spaces, whereas consumption spaces are spread across London (**4.17**). Reflecting its Street Scene Challenge programme to reclaim physically 'incidental' street spaces across the City (see Chapter 10), the Corporation of London surprisingly also accounted for the largest number of community and undefined spaces.

Function (rather than physical form or rights and responsibility) has by far the strongest impact on the perceived design of spaces, with strong correlations between functional types and key characteristics of space:

- Consumption, civic and transit spaces exhibit noticeably vibrant characters with active frontages.

- Community and corporate spaces exhibit a background level of activity and domestic and undefined spaces are generally quiet and often deserted.

- Significant greenery is a common feature of all space types, except civic spaces.

- Seating is most prevalent in community squares.

- Corporate, civic and the consumption squares most often feature public art.

- Community spaces tend to be designed with sandstone paving, corporate with granite and sandstone, and consumption and transit space with granite.

4.15   The forms, by borough

FORM

Courtyard	Forecourt	Piazza	Garden	Incidental space	Other
Bartlett Passage	Athene Square	Aldermanbury Square	Greyfriars Christ Churchyard	Aldermanbury Square	West Smithfield Place
Bishopsgate 55 Courtyard	Fenchurch Place	Broadgate Circle	Salisbury Square	Basinghall Square	Cardinal Walk
Bishopsgate Churchyard	Bury Court	City Point 1 Square	Bessborough Gardens	Carter Lane	Hays Galleria
Hare Court	Minster Court	Exchange Square	Hyde Park Corner	Tower Place	Clipper's Quay
Cross Key Square	Woolgate Exchange Place	Finsbury Avenue Square	Leicester Square	Holborn Circus	Watney Market
Johnson's Court	Hope Square	Gilbert Bridge Square	Potter Fields	Little Somerset Street Court	Westferry Circus
Fetter Lane 86	Tate Modern Square	New Street Square	Tabard Gardens	Monument Yard	Torrington Square
Fleet Street 65	British Library Piazza	Guildhall Yard	Maritime Quay	Old Change Court	Royal Arsenal Gardens
West Court Cutlers Gardens	Euston Station Piazza	St Mary Axe Square	Millwall Outer Dock	Plough Place	Peninsular Square
Greyfriars Courtyard	Queen Elizabeth II Great Court	Fleet Place	Jubilee Park	Channel 4 Court	Richmond Riverside
Old Broad Street Courtyard	Greenwich Station Forecourt	Paternoster Lane	Canada Square	Montagues Close	
Petticoat Square	Forum Magnum Square	Moorhouse Square	Bedford Square	Borough Market	
Royal Exchange Courtyard		Devonshire Square	Community Square	Menton Place	
Royal Academy of Art Courtyard		Paternoster Square	Fitzroy Square	Theatre Square	
Somerset House Courtyard		Dorset 1-2 Rise	Russell Square	Ballast Quay	
St Andrew's Square		Queen Street Square	Broadwall Square	Passey Place	
Empire Square		Monkwell Square	Windrush Square Gardens	Tally Ho Corner	
King's College Square		Sheldon Square		Lower George Street	
Oxo Tower Wharf		West End Quay		Kew Piazza	
Horselydown Square		Trafalgar Square			
Muirfield Crescent		More London			
Madjeski Garden V&A		Peckham Square			
Brunswick Square		Burrell's Wharf			
UCL Print Room Square		Bishops Square			
Old Pearson Court		Reuters Plaza			
East Sheen Lane Square		Clove Crescent			
		Columbus Square			
		Lanark Square			
		St David's Square			
		New Providence Wharf			
		Selsdon Way			
		Cabot Square			
		Canada Place			
		Duke of York Square			
		Triton Square			
		Glaister Street			
		James Clavell Square			
		Cutty Sark Gardens			
		GMV Square			
		Millennium Quay			
		Wellington Park Square			
		Festival Riverside			
		Gabriel's Wharf			
		Theatre Square			
		Seaton Square			

4.16 A typology of functions

a Community spaces provide a focus for the local social and community functions of their surrounding neighbourhoods and often have community-type functions located in and on them

b Corporate spaces sit at the heart of large corporate estates or adjacent to major office buildings, and are dominated by the corporate functions that surround them

c Civic spaces have a key representational role and provide a setting for the civic-type activities and functions located on them

d Other spaces, encompass the amorphous spaces that defy classification, or those that transcend the other physical types

e Consumption spaces are dominated by the retail and catering functions both within and around them

f Service spaces are left-over spaces that have been purposefully designed for, or more often appropriated by, service functions such as waste storage, bicycle parking, and so forth

g Transit spaces act as thresholds or external 'waiting rooms' for the transport infrastructure located on them

h Undefined spaces do not have any dominant function, or often any obvious function at all

- Consumption and service spaces are typically less legible than others, with service spaces most often poorly connected to their hinterlands.

- Corporate and service squares are (unsurprisingly) distinguished by their highly corporate appearance.

- Transit spaces typically feature franchised retail outlets, as do many consumption spaces and are often highly adaptable with lower levels of explicit control.

- Civic spaces are often strongly themed reflecting their history and exhibit a strong sense of place.

4.17 The functions, by borough

FUNCTION

Community	Civic	Consumption	Corporate	Transit	Service	Domestic	Undefined
Aldermanbury Place	Gilbert Bridge Square	Royal Exchange Courtyard	Aldermanbury Place	Fenchurch Place	Dorset Rise 1-2	Monkwell Square	Bartlett Passage
Basinghall Square	Greyfriars Christ Churchyard	Cardinal Walk	Aldermanbury Square	Hope Square	Lanark Square	Petticoat Square	Bishopsgate 55 Courtyard
Bishopsgate Churchyard	Guildhall Yard	Leicester Square	Athene Square	Sloane Square Station Forecourt	Selsdon Way	Bessborough Gardens	Carter Lane
Broadgate Circle	Minster Court	Borough Market	Basinghall Square	Euston Station Piazza	Westferry Circus	West End Quay	Cross Key Square
City Point 1 Square	Monument Yard	Bishops Square	Broadgate Circle	Greenwich Station Forecourt	Greenwich Station Forecourt	Empire Square	Devonshire Square
Exchange Square	Channel 4 Forecourt	Reuters Plaza	City Point 1 Square			Horselydown Square	Fetter Lane 86
Finsbury Avenue Square	Hyde Park Corner	Watney Market	Exchange Square			Burrell's Wharf	Fleet Street 65
Fenchurch Place	Royal Academy of Art Courtyard	Brunswick Square	Finsbury Avenue Square			Clipper's Quay	Greyfriars Courtyard
Gilbert Bridge Square	Leicester Square	Euston Station Piazza	Bury Court			Maritime Quay	Holborn Circus
New Street Square	Somerset House Courtyard	Theatre Square	New Street Square			Millwall Outer Dock	Little Somerset Street Court
Greyfriars Christ Churchyard	Trafalgar Square	Peninsular Square	St Mary Axe Square			New Providence Wharf	Old Broad Street Courtyard
Guildhall Yard	More London	Passey Place	Fleet Place			Glaister Street	Old Change Court
Hare Court	Tate Modern Square	Festival Riverside	Paternoster Lane			GMV Square	Plough Place
Johnson's Court	Tower Hill Square	Gabriel's Wharf	Paternoster Square			Old Pearson Court	Montague Close
Moorhouse Square	British Library Piazza	Lower George Street	Tower Place			Wellington Park Square	St Andrew's Square
Queen Street Square	James Clavell Square		Woolgate Exchange Place			Broadwall Square	Menton Place
Salisbury Square	Cutty Sark Gardens		Bishops Square			Seaton Square	Ballast Quay
West Court Cutlers Gardens			Reuters Plaza				Millennium Quay
West Smithfield Place			Clove Crescent				Royal Arsenal Gardens
Leicester Square			Columbus Place				
Sheldon Square			Lanark Square				
More London			Muirfield Crescent				
Tate Modern Square			Selsdon Way				
Hays Galleria			Cabot Square				
King's College Square			Canada Place				
Oxo Tower Wharf			Canada Square				
Peckham Square			Westferry Circus				
Potter Fields			Triton Square				
Tabard Gardens							
Tower Hill Square							
Cabot Square							
Jubilee Park							
Canada Place							
Westferry Circus							
Duke of York Square							
Madjeski Garden V&A							
Bedford Square							
British Library Piazza							
Queen Elizabeth II Great Court							
Brunswick Square							
Community Square							
Fitzroy Square							
Russell Square							
Theatre Square							
Torrington Square							
Triton Square							
UCL Print Room Square							
Cutty Sark Gardens							
Broadwall Square							
Theatre Square							
East Sheen Lane Square							
Kew Piazza							
Richmond Riverside							

- Corporate, service and domestic spaces typically feel less inclusive than other spaces, particularly community and transit spaces, and are less adaptable.

- Service, transit and undefined spaces feel less safe than other spaces and tend also to be the least comfortable spaces.

- Community, corporate, civic and consumption squares exhibit the highest levels of soft and hard controls.

Distinguishing by rights and responsibility

Gauging ownership and management responsibility for spaces from a visual survey was not always easy although often it was easier to infer

4.18   A typology by rights and responsibility

a   Public space denotes publically owned and managed space that is always open and available

b   Public-private space includes space owned the public sector or by a psuedo-public organisation (e.g. a charitable trust, universtity or community organisation) where some restrictions are maintained on use

c   Public-private space reflects space owned and managed by the private sector but where public access is allowed, typically with some restrictions

d   Private space refers to external spaces that are private and not open to the public (spaces in this category were only counted if visible from the public realm)

rights of access. Taken together, four types of space were identified: private–public space (45 per cent), public space (27 per cent), public–private space (26 per cent) and private space (2 per cent) (**4.18**). Of immediate significance is the overwhelming number of privately owned and managed private–public spaces, although it should also be noted that three-quarters of these are situated in either the City of London or Tower Hamlets (**4.19**). The category also includes spaces such as refurbished churchyards and some garden squares whose ownership has long been private but that have also long been open for public use. Many are also spaces within blocks or courtyards within buildings (especially in the City) that were previously private backlands and that have been opened up to public use as part of commercial refurbishment projects. The public–private category includes the wide range of spaces that now exist that are owned and managed by trusts, government agencies, education, health or cultural establishments, and other organisations that might be viewed as pseudo-private (or pseudo-public). Others are owned by boroughs but are closed at night, for example some of Camden's garden squares. Excluding private gardens, the analysis revealed that very few significant new spaces are being built with no public access at all.

Rights and responsibilities vary across the form types, although generally courtyards and piazzas were private–public, and incidental

squares, in the main, public. Functionally, corporate, domestic and consumption spaces were likely to be private–public, whilst transit and undefined were typically public, and community and civic spaces were most often public–private. The four categories of rights and responsibilities show a range of correlations to aspects of design, although there was a great variety in design character across the types:

- Public spaces are the most active, with animated frontages; they are less enclosed and more open and inclusive in character, but often less comfortable than other spaces and less well maintained.

- Private and private–public spaces are usually contemporary in style with a corporate aesthetic and generally show less regard to historical context, whilst public and public–private squares vary more significantly in their architectural treatments.

- Private and private–public spaces also exhibit high levels of sanitation and soft and hard controls and a greater sense of implicit exclusion.

- Public and public–private spaces demonstrate a greater variety of uses and feel more inclusive than their more private counterparts.

- Private–public and public–private spaces both feel very safe places to be.

4.19 Rights and responsibilities, by borough

RIGHTS & RESPONSIBILITIES

Public	Public-Private	Private-Public	Private
Carter Lane	Aldermanbury Place	Athene Square	Minster Court
Fenchurch Place	Aldermanbury Square	Bartlett Passage	Dorset 1-2 Rise
Guildhall Yard	Gilbert Bridge Square	Bishopsgate 55 Courtyard	New Providence Wharf
Moorhouse Square	Johnson's Court	Basinghall Square	
Queen Street Square	Paternoster Square	Bishopsgate Churchyard	
West Smithfield Place	Salisbury Square	Broadgate Circle	
Little Somerset Street Court	Woolgate Exchange Place	City Point 1 Square	
Monument Yard	Holborn Circus	Exchange Square	
Hope Square	Old Change Court	Finsbury Avenue Square	
Plough Place	Petticoat Square	Bury Court	
Hyde Park Corner	Leicester Square	New Street Square	
Trafalgar Square	Somerset House Courtyard	Greyfriars Courtyard	
Montague Close	St Andrew's Square	Hare Court	
Borough Market	Tate Modern Square	St Mary Axe Square	
Peckham Square	King's College Square	Fleet Place	
Tabard Gardens	Potter Fields	Cross Key Square	
Watney Market	Tower Hill Square	Paternoster Lane	
Sloane Square Station Piazza	Madjeski Garden V&A	Devonshire Square	
Community Square	Bedford Square	Fetter Lane 86	
Theatre Square	British Library Piazza	Fleet Street 65	
Greenwich Station Forecourt	Euston Station Piazza	Tower Place	
Cutty Sark Gardens	Queen Elizabeth II Great Court	West Court Cutlers Gardens	
Ballast Quay	Brunswick Square	Greyfriars Courtyard	
Millennium Quay	Fitzroy Square	Old Broad Street Courtyard	
Royal Arsenal Gardens	Russell Square	Monkwell Square	
Passey Place	Torrington Square	Royal Exchange Courtyard	
Gabriel's Wharf	UCL Print Room Square	Bessborough Gardens	
Emma Cos Gardens	James Clavell Square	Channel 4 Court	
Forum Magnum Square	GMV Square	Royal Academy of Art Courtyard	
Windrush Square Gardens	Festival Riverside	Sheldon Square	
Tally Ho Corner	Broadwall Square	West End Quay	
Lower George Street	Theatre Square	More London	
East Sheen Lane Square	Seaton Square	Empire Square	
Kew Piazza		Hays Galleria	
Richmond Riverside		Horselydown Square	
		Oxo Tower Wharf	
		Burrell's Wharf	
		Clipper's Quay	
		Maritime Quay	
		Millwall Outer Dock	
		Bishops Square	
		Reuters Plaza	
		Clove Crescent	
		Columbus Square	
		Lanark Square	
		Muirfield Crescent	
		St David's Square	
		Menton Place	
		Seldson Way	
		Cabot Square	
		Jubilee Park	
		Canada Place	
		Canada Square	
		Westferry Circus	
		Duke of York Square	
		Triton Square	
		Glaister Street	
		Peninsular Square	
		Old Pearson Court	
		Wellington Park Square	

A NEW 'LONDON SQUARE'

Looking back over the period from the election of New Labour (May 1997) to the mayoral election in May 2012, London has certainly seen a positive transformation in large parts of its built environment, although in others (away from the centre) there has been little change. The period has, in a very real sense, witnessed an urban renaissance if measured by the attraction of the city as a place to live. Arguably, however, that was underway from at least the mid 1990s onwards as the economy of the city expanded, and was boosted after 2000 by the changing policy environment in London and beyond.

Yet, if a re-investment in the physical infrastructure of the city and a new relationship between its people and its spaces have been key features of the renaissance then so too has the failure to share in a more equitable manner everything that the rejuvenated city of today has to offer. Thus the resilient nature of London's dynamic economy is certainly matched by the resilient nature of the disadvantage that remains an everyday feature of parts of its increasingly diverse population. Equally, attempts by some to blame renaissance processes for the continuing disparity in opportunities, for the pressures of gentrification or for the responses to the challenges of managing and policing the public realm seem far from the mark. More likely, these are the side effects of a dynamic global city that constantly needs to re-position and reinvent itself in the face of shifting economic pressures, and the changing expectations of its expanding, shifting and generally richer populace. These are the social consequences of the wider political economy. They are not shaped by the built environment, but are both reflected in it and exacerbated or mollified by it.

Thus in launching his 100 Spaces initiative Ken Livingstone announced: 'Creating and managing high quality public spaces is essential to delivering an urban renaissance in London' (Mayor of London 2002a: 1). Later, Boris Johnson argued 'Public spaces are part of what defines a city. ... Well designed and decently maintained public spaces can bring communities and people together ... They can restore a sense of place, identity and pride in an area, and play a big part in attracting businesses and jobs' (Mayor of London 2009d: 1). If the sheer numbers of new and refurbished public spaces in London (particularly in central and inner London) in recent years are anything to go by, then these arguments have been broadly accepted, with the quantity and overall quality of space providing a tangible measure of renaissance.

4.20   Flat Iron Square, Southwark – a new London square

As well as the startling numbers of public spaces that have been created and recreated, it is apparent that a dominant new type of London space has emerged: typically harder and more urban in nature, more clearly an extension of surrounding uses, and frequently well used as a result. In essence, this is a more continental type of space of the type that was promoted through the urban renaissance discourse but that, led by the private sector, emerged in London during the 1980s and before the policy context caught up (**4.20**). Thus, over the period of analysis, over a third of spaces were of the piazza type (albeit often greened with trees and planting), whilst new garden squares seemed rare by comparison.

To some degree, the London-wide analysis tended to confirm some of the stereotypes of public space advanced in the literature: a degree of homogenisation in design and tenant branding; the dominance of spaces by single land uses or by particular themes or functions; signs of control and exclusion (particularly in central London, and not just in private spaces); ubiquitous CCTV and public art; greater sanitation (some spaces excessively so); and large numbers (almost half) of contemporary space being privately owned and managed and revealing, to a greater extent than publicly owned spaces, the characteristics listed above. It demonstrated how a cursory inspection of spaces might confirm a thesis that contemporary public space is loosing its essential qualities of 'publicness'.

Yet despite this, the analysis also recorded a general and surprisingly high quality of space across the wide range of space types – by physical form, function, and rights and responsibility – and a strong resurgence in public and pseudo-public, and privately owned and managed, 'public' space types. Community-type functions, for example, matched piazza-type physical forms in their frequency, with just a fifth of new and refurbished spaces associated with corporate developments that were heavily concentrated in London's business districts. Clearly the London-wide analysis was not telling the whole story, and greater, in-depth, investigation was required.

5 SPACES OF THE CORPORATE CITY

CORPORATE LONDON

If the dominant history of London's development can be encapsulated in the idea of opportunity-driven incremental growth, then the role of business of all types in the city's expansion has been pivotal. Thus Chapter 2 revealed how at key points in London's history, alliances of the city's landowners (often aristocrats) and its entrepreneurial builder/developers (large and small) have driven its growth, sometimes in direct opposition to alternative visions mapped out by the state. London in the neo-liberal era has been subjected to a new development dynamic brought about by a huge and sustained investment of the city as an international financial and service centre.

Edwards (2010: 192) comments that 'A great deal of money-capital was (and is) in the hands of investors and had to be channelled by portfolio managers into assets which they expected to be profitable'. Thus when New Labour came to power, 'London was already subject to a strong version of the hegemonic story which could be paraphrased like this: finance and business services are increasingly the dominant sectors in the UK economy. Because London is overwhelmingly the seat of this sector, London must subordinate all other priorities to serving the needs of finance, business services and the related real estate industry.' Hand in hand with the urban renaissance policies, from 2000 onwards, based on a notion of raising densities in the city, particularly in central and more accessible locations, development in London has increasingly taken three forms:

- First, in the domestic sphere, the provision of a new typology of high-density housing blocks, often bought as buy-to-let or buy-to leave investments (see Chapter 9).

- Second, a wave of corporate developments, often at huge scale to feed the sometimes insatiable demand for central office space. As well as entirely new landscapes such as Canary Wharf, Paddington Basin and now King's Cross, this trend has incrementally transformed London's existing office areas, most notably the City of London, Southbank, the City fringes and, less markedly (reflecting their greater concern for conservation), parts of Westminster. This corporate wave has also extended out to the back-office, governmental and lower-rent markets in places such as Croydon and on key peripheral and radial routes out of London.

- Third, in the late 2000s and early 2010s, the return with a vengeance of the shopping centre to London, initially through smaller schemes such as Cardinal Place in Victoria or the N1 at Angel Islington, but followed by a slew of new mega-malls (e.g. Westfield at Shepherd's Bush, One New Change in the City, Westfield at Stratford, and proposals for major changes to the Brent Cross and Elephant & Castle Shopping Centres).

The third form of development is increasingly significant in its impact on London, but the new spaces associated with the first two forms have become ubiquitous. The second trend, in particular, has produced (since the mid 1980s) a new corporate landscape of towers, mid-rise blocks and lower groundscrapers; the last of these dominating in the City and its surrounds where view corridors of St Paul's and the Palace of Westminster have allowed (5.1). Examining groundscrapers in London, Carmona & Freeman (2005: 327) concluded that even in these largest of commercial developments, it is possible to successfully integrate schemes into their surroundings. Equally, 'compromises nearly always need to be made with such developments, often to meet the real or perceived demands of future occupiers for security, for uninterrupted work spaces, and for retaining ownership rights and management controls over any external spaces that result'. For the market, these are simply rational decisions based on the driving need to satisfy the private requirements of occupiers rather than public urban design objectives. For the public, the consequence

5.1   Triton Square – site of the 18,500m² headquarters for Abbey (now Santander) Bank since 2002, a groundscraper on the Broadgate model

will be 'privatised' and 'invented' spaces about which a wide body of international literature is highly critical, critiques which this chapter explores.

THE CRITIQUES

Privatised public space

Debates about the privatisation of public space are widespread and often polarised, with critics arguing that these trends are creeping, increasingly universal and essentially exclusionary in nature.

Defenders assert the pre-eminence of private property rights and that such practices often enhance rather than undermine public space in the city.

Corporate privatisation

In recent years, a number of trends have arguably stimulated a greater trend towards privatisation practices:

● The gradual acceptance of arguments around the potential of public realm to enhance economic returns on property investment. On the back of this, commercial developers have been looking to include public spaces and other significant public realm elements within their schemes, whilst retaining ownership and management responsibility. At the same time, municipalities, won over by arguments concerning the public interest in better design, have been increasingly supportive of incorporating new public space into development projects whilst remaining unwilling or unable to provide it themselves or to adopt it after completion and take on its long-term management to an acceptable standard.

- Increased security concerns, especially since the 9/11 and 7/7 attacks in New York (2001) and London (2005), although building on trends already inherent in an increasingly fearful urban populace cowered by the sensational reporting of urban crime, and by the commercial decisions of property companies to address this fear through their products, for example with enhanced security measures.

- The widespread decline during the 1980s and 1990s in urban stewardship as hard-pressed municipalities increasingly cut the costs and standards of urban management as a reaction to the withdrawal of the state as a direct provider of key public services and the general squeeze on public funds. These processes have led to a desire amongst private companies to retain control over areas in their ownership and to take greater control over the publicly owned areas within which their interests are located.

- The detachment of some investors and developers from the contexts in which they build, brought about by the involvement of national and multi-national companies in much development. For these companies, their interest in sites may only extend as far as their potential to deliver a return on investment, and not to any wider contribution to the public realm. In such a context, the needs and wishes of the potential occupiers, rather than of the surrounding community, will be of paramount concern, and municipalities (who want the investment) may feel unable or unwilling to demand wider public goods.

For Ellin (1999: 167–8) processes of privatisation are both a consequence of the desire to control private space, growing out of a general decline in public space, and also a cause of it, as facilities move from central locations to less accessible suburban ones where the public space is internalised and external space is dominated by car parking. In such cases, the public realm can be appropriated wholesale by private corporations. In urban locations, Low (2006: 82) has argued that 'privatisation of urban public space has accelerated through the closing, redesign, and policing of public parks and plazas, the development of business improvement districts that monitor and control local streets and parks, and the transfer of public air rights for the building of corporate plazas ostensibly open to the public'.

In the USA today, the argument is widely accepted that urban public spaces are more highly managed and policed owing to the increasing private ownership of public space and the consequent spread of private management strategies. Németh (2008), for example, traces the nature of bonus spaces in central Midtown Manhattan (spaces provided by the private sector in exchange for a floor area ratio bonus), finding that whilst the owners of such spaces actively encourage their use for public purposes, their management practices also actively control who these users are by filtering out some types of (as they see it) less desirable (e.g. less affluent) users (see Chapter 8). He concludes that leaving the provision of public spaces to the market:

- delivers a concentration of new spaces in already advantaged areas (e.g. where the market is willing to invest, and not where they are not)

- places undue power in the hands of private corporations to suppress political and/or religious discourse if they so choose (because of the popularity of some of these spaces)

- undermines accountability and oversight of public space management practices

- situates the profit motive at the forefront of decisions regarding both the provision of spaces and their long-term stewardship .

Likewise, in the UK, Minton has written a persuasive polemic about what she sees as the spread of the Canary Wharf model across British cities, culminating in places which are no longer inspired by the culture of where they are, but instead by their locational advantages and economic potential. Citing Paddington Waterside, Minton (2009: 35) writes that 'this private enclave the size of Soho, is all about office blocks and waterside apartments, with few shops and fewer people to be seen, although there is a very similar feel of sameness and sterility' to other corporate enclaves (**5.2**).

Others argue that it is inappropriate to call something public space when in fact it is not. In central areas, Boyer (1994: 113–14)

5.2   Paddington Waterside – exhibiting a sense of disconnection from the surrounding streets

5.3   Trinity Buoy Wharf, London

suggests, we are witnessing a 'City of illusion' where the emphasis is firmly on the provision of luxury spaces whilst ignoring the everyday places between. Loukaitou-Sideris & Banerjee (1998: 280) agree, suggesting that postmodern design eliminates unwanted and feared political, social and cultural intrusions: 'Space is cut off, separated, enclosed, so that it can be easily controlled and "protected". This treatment succeeds in screening the unpleasant realities of everyday life: the poor, the homeless, the mentally ill, and the landscapes of fear, neglect, and deterioration.' For them, the subjugation of public space to market forces is a recent phenomenon, with the public sector primarily reacting to the initiatives of the private sector for downtown building rather than proactively leading the way. Their analysis of west coast American cities not only revealed a lack of macro-scale strategic direction to steer investment into parts of the city where the public realm was in decline, but also a series of micro-scale design strategies that deliberately foster a sense of the private and exclusive: high blank walls, impenetrable street frontage, sunken plazas, hidden entrances (to new spaces), de-emphasised doorways and openings onto the street, no retail, etc. At the same time the 'privatised' spaces inside can be seen as a series of spectacles or themed environments to be packaged and advertised (Loukaitou-Sideris & Banerjee 1998: 288).

But the notion of public space is itself a slippery concept (Kohn

2004: 12–13), with a continuum from city streets or squares that are government-owned and accessible to all, to the privately owned and restricted home environment. Thus, in identifying at least 20 types of urban space in categories that range across wholly public to wholly private, with a range of ambiguous spaces in between, Carmona (2010b: 276) contends that if a nuanced understanding of public space is to be achieved, it is just as important to understand the day-to-day function and perception of spaces, as well as patterns of ownership and management responsibility. Minton (2009: 199), for example, notes how Trinity Buoy Wharf in London, a Docklands business location for creative enterprises, represents a space that is owned privately (by a trust) whilst being managed 'in ways that benefit the public good' by a private property company, Urban Space Management (USM) (**5.3**).

Reflecting this muddying of the waters, the extent of publicness in fact 'depends on the degree to which the public space, as well as the activities occurring in it and the discussions on, and information about its development and use processes, are open to all, are managed and controlled by public actors, are used by the public and serve the public interest' (Akkar Ercan 2010: 25). In London, this debate came to the fore in 2010, with the Planning and Housing Committee of the London Assembly launching an enquiry into issues surrounding the privatisation of public space following a commitment in the Mayor's

London's Great Outdoors manifesto (see Chapter 3) that public space should remain 'as unrestricted and unambiguous as possible', avoiding in the process the 'corporatisation' of the city's spaces (Mayor of London 2009d: 8). The Mayor's own City Hall, for example, is part of the private More London estate, which has repeatedly denied permission for bike racks to be located on-site and whose permission has to be sought before the Mayor and politicians of the London Assembly can conduct interviews outside their building (Walker 2007). Early briefing papers for the enquiry identified a surfeit of local policies and guidance stressing the importance of high-quality public space, but insufficient knowledge about the level of influence of the commercial sector on public space, with aspirations for an inclusive environment often only vaguely expressed.

The enquiry concluded, 'While private ownership or management of public space is not, in itself, a cause for concern, problems can arise with spaces in which commercial interests prevail over public access'. In such circumstances, 'Through the London Plan policies and other guidance, the Mayor can provide clear and continuous advice to London boroughs and key partners to ensure that the public realm is managed in the most suitable way, to keep it as welcoming and unrestricted as possible' (LAPHC 2011: 11–12). The enquiry called for new Supplementary Planning Guidance on the public realm (including model planning conditions and planning agreement clauses) in order that these issues be fully reflected in directions issued by the Mayor through his strategic development control function and in order that the boroughs be fully cognisant of their responsibilities in this respect and incorporate appropriate policies in their Local Development Frameworks.

State privatisation

But it is not just private corporations that are responsible for the trends towards greater private involvement in public space. Minton (2006) has described the shrinking local government model whereby local councils increasingly act as enablers as opposed to providers of services, with the management of public spaces (and sometimes their security) contracted out to the lowest bidder, or public assets (e.g. housing estates) sold off altogether to the highest bidder. These processes typically happen through public-led urban regeneration initiatives, with the resulting developments being owned and managed by a single private landlord. As Minton notes, this is effectively a transfer of power for the management of public space

from the state to private individuals: 'In terms of public space the key issue is that while local government has previously controlled, managed, and maintained streets and public squares, the creation of these new "private–public" places means that ... they will be owned and managed by individual private landlords who have the power to restrict access and control activities' (Minton 2006: 10).

Minton uses the example of the Liverpool One redevelopment in Liverpool city centre, which has involved Liverpool City Council leasing out streets to a developer to manage for 250 years. Graham (2001) notes an altogether more subtle and pervasive privatisation of the streets, in this case through the move in the UK (and elsewhere) from publicly owned urban infrastructure to privately owned. Although the phenomenon has not yet extended to the roads themselves (new motorways and bridges aside), most of the infrastructure beneath the street has now been privatised, with associated rights transferred to these companies to obstruct, dig up and reinstate public space more or less at will.

A related issue is the rise of Business Improvement Districts (BIDs). BIDs amount to a group of businesses paying an extra financial levy in order to create an attractive external consumer environment. In England, the relevant legislation to allow the creation of BIDs was approved in 2003 and by 2010 there were 120 in England (with 23 rejected following an initial ballot of local businesses – UKBIDs [n.d.]). These, Minton (2006: 17) describes as 'private–public' spaces where private management tightly monitors and controls the public space. For her, BIDs are 'characterised by a uniformed private security presence and the banning of anti-social behaviours, from skateboarding to begging' (although such restrictions are by no means confined to the areas in which BIDs operate). Certainly, in common with many other parts of the world, over the last 30 years the UK has experienced a shrinking local government, a concentration of previously fragmented city centre land ownership in fewer larger estates and private ownership of much new public space, and increasing private control and management in such locations, including an increased focus on cleanliness and security. A key question is, is that a problem?

Citing the impact of the 2001 Patriot Act in the USA as evidence, Low and Smith (2006: 12) conclude that 'the dilemma of public space is surely trivialised by collapsing our contemporary diagnosis into a lament about private versus public'. For them, the cutting edge of efforts to deny public access to places, media and other institutions is occupied by the state, and the contest to render spaces truly public is not always simply a contest against private interests. Critiques of the instigation and spread of BIDs are based on similar concerns; of the state effectively passing aspects of their responsibility for publicly owned space to private interests.

Kohn (2004: 5) identifies a separate dimension of these same trends in what she characterises as a creeping commodification of public space. In this category, she places the renting out of space by local government for commercial events, the sale of advertising space in and around public space, and 'café-creep', or the spread of commercial interests across the pavements of public spaces. Others may argue that these are just the signs of life and vitality that all the very best public spaces exhibit, and that a concern amongst local businesses for the quality of their local public spaces is a healthy sign of local engagement in the future of place, leading to the beneficial extraction of private resources to enhance (rather than supplant) public services. There are often two sides to almost every argument in this contested field, although the preponderance of the literature is certainly critical.

Invented space

Some of the most frequent critiques of the new forms of public space are associated with the perceived loss of authenticity and growth of 'placelessness'. These critiques focus more on over-design than over-management, although the literature suggests they may be coterminous. Various writers have discussed the components of place, typically focusing on the sum of three elements: physical form, human activities, and meaning or image. Others have focused on the qualities of successful places, such as the view of Carr et al. (1992) that space should be 'responsive' to five needs:

- comfort – encompassing safety from harm as well as physical comfort

- relaxation – allowing a sense of psychological ease

- passive engagement with the surroundings and other people (e.g. people-watching)

- active engagement – which some people seek out, but which is often spontaneous if the situation allows

- discovery – reflecting the desire for variety and new experiences.

However, these very qualities help fuel the desire for, and spread of, entertainment spaces where, without effort, participants can indulge in leisure activities. At the same time, the spread of globalisation processes, mass culture and the loss of attachment to place has led to a repetition of certain formulaic responses across the world, a classic example being Baltimore's Inner Harbor, which, since its regeneration in the 1970s and 1980s, has spawned copycat leisure spaces across the globe.

Although many settlements have at some time been 'invented' by their founders, increasingly 'imagineering' techniques are being used to reinvent existing places, with the danger that elements of continuity and character that might have been part of the distinctive qualities of a place are lost. Wilson (1995: 157) takes Paris as an example, arguing that the Parc de la Villette, despite its international reputation, is 'designed for tourists rather than for the hoarse-voiced, red-handed working men and women who in any case no longer work or live there'. Thus, he argues, in cities around the world, 'not only is the tourist becoming perhaps the most important kind of inhabitant, but we all become tourists in our own cities'. In London, the reinvention of the formerly public Millennium Dome to become the private O2 offers a case in point; and, commercially, a very successful one (**5.4**).

Sometimes the process involves the creation of difference as a means to distinguish one place from another, for example the use of place marketing strategies to identify a city, neighbourhood or place. Sometimes the process involves the deliberate creation of sameness, copying a successful formula that has worked elsewhere – for example the emergence of formulaic China Towns in many cities across the world, or the cloning of high streets with the same national and international brands (New Economics Foundation 2004). Criticism of such places is now widespread. Sorkin (1992: xiii), to name but one, reserves particular bile for invented places, arguing, in his case, that America is increasingly devoid of genuine places, which are instead gradually being replaced by caricatures and 'urbane disguises'.

However, although such places can be criticised for being superficial and lacking in authenticity, all such places still necessitate a considered and careful design process. Thus, as Sircus (2001: 30), talking about Disneyland, argues, 'It is successful because it adheres to certain principles of sequential experience and storytelling, creating an appropriate and meaningful sense of place in which both activities and memories are individual and shared.' Zukin (1995: 49–54) agrees that invented places represent one of the most significant new forms of public space from the late twentieth century, although she identifies different factors for their success:

- visual culture – through an aesthetic designed to transcend ethnic, class and regional identities

- spatial control – through a highly choreographed sequence

of spaces, allowing people to watch and be watched, and to participate without embarrassment

- private management – aimed at controlling fear, with no guns, no homeless, no illegal drink or drugs, and promising to 'make social diversity less threatening and public space more secure'.

This manufacturing of place occurs in a wide range of contexts, as do Zukin's factors for success, with the creation of entirely fictitious theme parks at one end of a spectrum, to the reinvention of historic

5.4   Union Square in the O2 arena – the world's busiest concert venue replete with false streets, spaces and stage set facades, all under a continuous glass fibre canopy

5.5   Bankside Gardens – framing the new cultural icon, Tate Modern

urban quarters at the other. In London, for example, former industrial localities have since the 1980s been reinvented as business poles (the Isle of Dogs), sports parks (the lower Lea Valley, site of the 2012 Olympics), cultural quarters (the Southbank – **5.5**), and sites of mass tourism and entertainment (Greenwich). At all scales, there is one over-riding objective, 'to attract attention, visitors and – in the end – money' (Crang 1998: 116–17).

In this sense, such places are undoubtedly popular, and invariably full of human activity. Returning then to the components of place, one might conclude that 'placelessness' is not a product of the lack of activity or carefully considered physical form, but instead an absence of place-derived meaning. For Sircus (2001: 31), even this is not a concern. He argues 'place is not good or bad simply because it is real versus surrogate, authentic versus pastiche. People enjoy both, whether it is a place created over centuries, or created instantly. A successful place, like a novel or a movie, engages us actively in an emotional experience orchestrated and organised to communicate purpose and story'. Ultimately, therefore, the challenge may not be to create authentic or invented places, but simply to create 'good' places, recognising that to do that, many factors over and above the original design will be of concern, not least how such places are subsequently managed, and the restrictions placed on the users of the resulting space. For Merrifield (1996: 67–8) London (and other cities

in the UK) has a distinct advantage in its rich historical antecedence, which ensures that even attempts to bring globalised formulae to the city's public spaces will be subverted by its place-specific quirks. Using Covent Garden, Leicester Square and Russell Square to make his point, he argues that the 'theme park motif has limited explanatory resonance for British cities. Worse, it might even obfuscate and detract from understanding the highly complex economic, political and social dynamics at play'.

CORPORATE SPACES

Reflecting the trends described above, the London-wide survey revealed a surfeit of new corporate squares across London, with a particular concentration in and around London's financial and service hubs – the City, the West End, Canary Wharf, and, increasingly, on the Southbank. Almost a quarter of new and regenerated spaces across London are of this type (see Chapter 4).

As a type, London's corporate spaces come in many shapes and sizes, from the large and imposing spaces of huge corporate campuses, to modest and incidental spaces setting off individual buildings (**5.6**), and everything in between. Typically, these spaces remain in private ownership, are actively managed and often intensively patrolled, and, despite the inclusion of other uses (beyond offices), imbue a corporate ambiance that is derived from the 'polished' design of their architectural and public realm elements, the types of non-office tenants they attract, and predominance of suited and booted individuals who frequent their public spaces. Their vitality is frequently undermined by swathes of dead frontages – a by-product of the large-footprint, single-entrance (for security reasons) buildings that define them – and by the tendency to design fixed elements into the spaces that compromise their adaptability.

Representing the type are two cases that are both reflective of these qualities and also represent London's two most iconic business districts – the City and Canary Wharf: first, the latest reinvention of the historic Paternoster Square, now in the form of a single hard piazza at the centre of a major new commercial development in the heart of the historic Square Mile immediately adjacent to St Paul's Cathedral, and, second, Canada Square, the large formal green space at the

5.6   Channel 4 Headquarters Building and forecourt space, Westminster – featuring here El Anatsui's Big 4 public art project, a commentary on the ubiquitous and ephemeral nature of news

centre of the Canary Wharf estate and one of many newly invented spaces in the locality.

Paternoster Square – corporate compromise

Paternoster Square has a long history (**5.7**). There has been a square on the site since the rebuilding of the City following the Great Fire of 1666, with Newgate Market (a meat market) opening in 1669 in a building within a newly created market square. This was finally named

Paternoster Square in 1872, although only after the meat market had moved to Smithfield and the space vacated was occupied by printers and booksellers (Jackson 2003). The whole area burnt down again in 1940 during the Blitz and was subsequently rebuilt following a design of 1956 by Lord Holford. This scheme moved the square south and for 30 years imposed a Modernist vision of an elevated deck (for pedestrians and retail) set amongst blocks with roads and parking beneath. Comparison of figure ground plans

5.7 Site of Paternoster Square

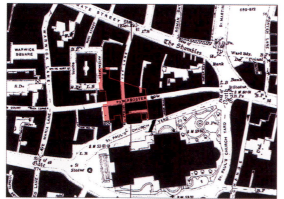

1910s

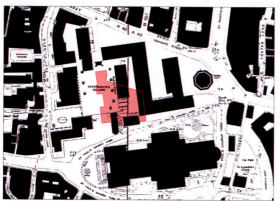

1960s

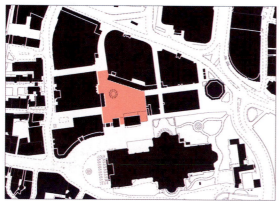

2010

demonstrates how a tightly knit essentially medieval street structure became a more open and geometric arrangement of slab blocks; a clearly Modernist scheme, but one tempered (to some degree) by its context, not least by the inclusion of a Modernist plaza at its heart (see Chapter 2). The scheme wilfully ignored its historic setting (adjacent to St Paul's Cathedral) and street network and quickly failed in functional, aesthetic and economic terms, making way for a further redevelopment in the 2000s, although only after a long, controversial and torturous development process.

In fact, the possibility of redevelopment was being discussed from the early 1980s onwards, although it took 20 years to come to fruition. Following a restructuring of ownerships in 1986 and the appointment of Stanhope as developer, a high-profile design competition was launched, with six of the seven teams proposing one or more new public squares on the site (the exception being proposals by Norman Foster). However, the carefully conceived Arup Associates scheme that won the competition was fatally wounded when Prince Charles intervened, launching a tirade against British planners and architects in his Mansion House Banquet speech of 1987, at which he clearly had the Paternoster proposals in his sights. His support for an alternative classical scheme by John Simpson (championed by the *Evening Standard*) eventually undermined the Arup scheme to such a degree that a new consortium of owners from 1989/90 dropped the proposals and continued instead with the Simpson scheme.

As Simpson's scheme had been produced on-spec without an official client or brief, it quickly proved unviable because of the small floorplates it proposed. At this stage, Terry Farrell was brought in to work with Simpson to re-masterplan the scheme, including large quantities of underground retail. Both Simpson's original scheme and the subsequent Farrell masterplan incorporated central squares, in the latter with a hollowed out central sub-space down to retail below, a feature disliked by Peter Rees, Chief Planner for the City (see Chapter 3), who was also quoted as saying that classical architecture is 'cynical' and 'makes my flesh creep' (quoted in Jackson 2003: 30). In fact, it was the downturn in the property market of the early 1990s that finally killed off the scheme, as well as disagreements within the development consortium and huge complexities associated with site assembly that needed to be overcome in order to construct the mega-structure required by the Farrell proposals. Despite this, by 1993 planning permission had been obtained, and by 1995 all the ownership issues were resolved, with the Mitsubishi Estate Company (MEC) buying out the other partners in the consortium.

In order to better address the new market circumstances, under advice from Stanhope (the original developers), Sir William Whitfield was approached by MEC and appointed as the new masterplanner. Whitfield had been surveyor of the fabric of St Paul's and was deemed acceptable to the Dean and Chapter of the Cathedral, to Prince Charles and to the City of London. Whitfield had been one of the assessors of the original competition in 1987, and was appointed to ensure that a development finally happened. His design concept was also based on a central square with views of the Cathedral and Chapter House, this time surrounded by a loggia (colonnade). In 1999, planning permission was given for the masterplan and demolition began with Stanhope (once again) as developer for MEC as investor.

The scheme was completed in 2003, with buildings designed by six teams of architects. It had taken 13 years to gain consent for a viable scheme, although only three years to build it. As Peter Rees admitted (quoted in Jackson 2003: 66), the result is a compromise between a huge array of complex and competing factors, not least the need to develop a commercial and viable scheme, set against the conservation concerns associated with developing next to St Paul's and the interest this generated from high-profile advocates such as Prince Charles and his ilk.

Canada Square – twenty-first-century garden square

By contrast, obtaining the permissions for Canada Square were plain sailing; although, as part of Canary Wharf, in a very different way, no less controversial. Its actual development, however, was a different matter. The early story of Canary Wharf is well known and is extensively discussed and brought up to date in Carmona (2009a). In a nutshell, the docks on which Canary Wharf stands today were completed in 1802 and run as working docks, initially privately and later by the state-owned Port of London Authority until 1980, when they were shut (**5.8**). As part of the Thatcherite response to the declining inner cities, the walls enclosing the docks were removed and the London Docklands Development Corporation (LDDC) moved in to attempt a market-led regeneration of the area, using the Enterprise Zone that had been established on the Isle of Dogs as a lever to attract private developers.

5.8 Site of Canada Square

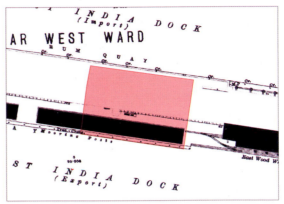

1920s

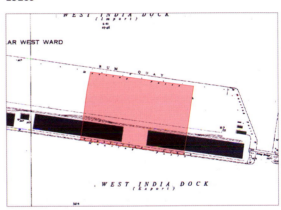

1950s

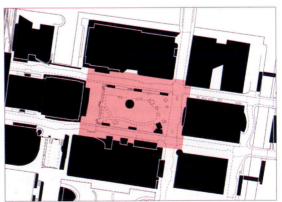

2010

Following some small-scale and largely rudderless regeneration activity from 1980 to 1985, it took the intervention of G. Ware Travelstead (an American developer and entrepreneur) to see the potential of the site. He proposed 10 million square feet of space with three 60-storey office towers and a series of public spaces, all designed in an international office style by Chicago-based architects SOM. However, this quickly morphed into a formal beaux-arts masterplan with a 50-storey tower accompanied by two shorter towers to the east, all designed around a large new space that became Canada Square. In the face of opposition from local groups, left-wing politicians and a wide range of campaigners who hoped for an altogether more socially oriented regeneration vision for the area, Travelstead and his group submitted and obtained planning permission for the scheme (now 10 million square feet of offices, plus retail) in one month in 1985. Soon after, he was forced to pull out in favour of Olympia and York (O&Y) when his financing for the deal fell through. The deal was finally sealed in a Master Building Agreement signed in July 1987 between the LDDC and O&Y, with the first phase of the scheme beginning on site shortly after, and completing (up to One Canada Square, but not Canada Square itself) in 1992. History tells us, however, that O&Y had seriously over-stretched themselves, and in the property crash of the early 1990s soon went out of business.

The construction of Canada Square had to wait until the revival of Canary Wharf (now owned by the banks) spearheaded by rising demand for deep-floor-plate grade A office accommodation (not being provided in sufficient quantity in the City). But when market conditions were right, the developers had an effective free hand to carry on where they had left off, including the right to vary significant aspects of the masterplan within the flexible confines of the Master Building Agreement. In effect, Canary Wharf Group (CWG) (as they had become), could play the role of planning authority within their estate, and from 1997 to 2002 they built out phase two of the project, including Canada Square, which had by then been redesigned by Koetter Kim Architects reflecting the changed market context. When it opened in 1998, this single space was framed by the three tallest buildings in the UK (One Canada Place and the World and European headquarters of respectively HSBC and Citigroup). It finally delivered Travelstead's and O&Y's vision based on the idea that the creation of place through design was the basis for successful development in such a sub-prime location.

The sequence of squares at the centre of the scheme were designed to contribute to establishing this place in an otherwise barren landscape, and each square was to have its own character and function, with Canada Square designed for sitting out and events. The space itself took the form of a large (6,200 m²) rectangular sward of grass, surrounded by trees and roads, i.e. a twenty-first-century garden square (see Chapter 2).

Designing corporate space
Defining, or being defined, by place?

Both Paternoster Square and Canada Square followed initial development processes in which design had been the subject of considerable scrutiny. In the case of Paternoster Square, the need for consensus had driven a safe design solution that would neither offend (too much) the classicists nor alienate (too greatly) the Modernists. The resulting classically inspired design remained a source of contention during the detailed design phase, with the most hotly debated element being the loggia that defines the northern edge of the space, the presence of which along the edge of his building caused Modernist architect, Michael Hopkins, to resign from the design of 10 Paternoster Square. By contrast, at Canada Square, the formal and pseudo-classical spaces and colonnaded buildings of the first phase of Canary Wharf (e.g. Cabot Square), which had been criticised as soulless and pastiche, were replaced with a universal modern/corporate architecture around a public space that harked back to the garden squares of London's past.

Following an original concept by Sir Roy Strong (English art historian and landscape designer) who had advised O&Y, Koetter Kim had analysed the Georgian squares of London and attempted to bring this analysis to bear at Canada Square (**5.9**). In this case, the scale of the space ensures that it is experienced as a park as well as a square, a characteristic shared by some of the largest of London's historic garden squares, such as Russell Square (see **4.13d**). The key concept at Canary Wharf had always been scale, and Canada Square was part of this. The project drew from the American experience of thinking big and using design and public realm to establish place identity, and, 'As the development was built out and its true scale became apparent, a greater confidence was achieved in the role of the spaces as "addresses" for the properties and venues for relaxation for the tenants and employees of the estate' (developer). Reflecting this confidence, during its second phase, the formality of the masterplan concept (and its key spaces) was eased somewhat, although Canada

5.9   Canada Square – contemporary garden square, a swath of grass with entrances and vehicle circulation around the space

Square retained its symmetry. The combination of scale and greenery created a new type of place in the Canary Wharf lexicon, and a unique space in London, although surrounded by internationally ubiquitous flat curtain-walled facades.

At Paternoster Square, by contrast, 'The site had always been recognised as a space of huge importance and St Paul's had to remain the star of the show' (planner), with views to it protected in the City's own development plans. To exploit this historical character, the design reinstated the view of the north transept of St Paul's, and the City brought back (at a cost of £3 million) Temple Bar (built to mark one of the original gateways in the ancient City) from Hertfordshire, where it had been moved in 1880 to ease traffic congestion. The space itself was designed as a picturesque townscape composition (5.10), whilst the location adjacent to St Paul's dramatically restricted the scale of the new buildings (in stark contrast to the buildings around

5.10 Paternoster Square – the decision to retain the low-rise Chapter House to the south of the scheme dictated the need for a continuous wall between St Paul's Cathedral and the new space, and thereby the position of the square. This also creates a physical space between the cathedral and the development, whilst the cathedral visually forms the southern side of the square, increasing the perception of space

Canada Square) and effectively determined the position of the space, key routes to and from it, and, thereby, of the key buildings. For their part, the City managed to retain the same quantum of open space as the 1950s scheme, but were never sold on the detailed design of the new project.

Establishing value through design
Whilst the constraints of place dictated the nature of the Paternoster

Square scheme, the desire to create place had dictated Canada Square. At Canary Wharf, this represented a continuation of the strategy to maximise unit amenity (and thereby value) through design that had been pursued since the mid 1980s: 'The critical concern was always "quality", and through a proper strategy it was possible to maximise utility out of small urban areas' (developer). Like the previous spaces at Canary Wharf, huge attention was paid to detail, but unlike them, new attention was now paid to how the space would actually be used and enjoyed by the occupiers of the surrounding buildings. For example, the aim was to keep the grass open and clear of obstructions to allow people to move around following the sun. The spaces were no longer seen as simply attractive settings for the buildings, but had an intrinsic value in themselves.

This was not entirely altruistic, since, emerging from the experience of going into administration, the developer recognised that the spaces of phase one had contributed to negative perceptions about the development as a whole. As such, there was a strong desire to see more life in phase two, and that this should take the form of an adaptable space able to host a programme of activities to support the growing emphasis on retail at Canary Wharf. Thus the design of Canada Square 'was as much a function of the implications of the retail as it was of the idea of making a public space; in other words as a means to attract more customers to the shops' (masterplanner). Indeed, the space itself had been moved westwards in the masterplan in order to allow the shopping centre below it to expand.

Paternoster Square exhibited a similar concern for 'quality'. However, the hard landscape strongly favoured by Whitfield (in the face of some opposition from the planners, who would have preferred a softer space), was not designed with user comfort in mind, but instead as a set-piece composition. Seating, for example, was only introduced as an afterthought. Nevertheless, the radial floorscape treatment, public art and non-axial foci on a column reclaimed from the 1630s Inigo Jones portico for St Paul's are designed to enhance distinctiveness. Here, it was the very fact of competition with Canary Wharf that was driving the City to encourage the development of deep-plan developments. This, and the desire at long last to secure a viable development on the site, perhaps explains some of the timidity of the planning authority when faced with a design solution that they were not wholly in favour of. Instead, the economics of competition won through.

The compromises of commercial public space design

A challenge for the urban designers at Canada Square was to handle the relationship between the retail and parking below and the buildings and space above, and to try and allow movement between all four. However, despite the aspiration of the designer to improve vertical connectivity, for example through installation of the flying saucer skylight (**5.11**), the connections to the retail mall below the space are not obvious and the retail fails to inform the character of

5.11 Canada Square – flying saucer skylight, a suggestion of something significant below

5.12 Paternoster Square – loggia running along the north of the space

5.13   Left-over space around Swiss Re, City of London

the space above. At Paternoster Square, the planners laid down the necessity to retain at least the quantum of ground level retail space that had been included in the 1950s scheme, the result being that the space features semi-active edges on three of its four sides, although the loggia to the north obscures some of this activity (**5.12**).

In both schemes, the surrounding buildings now have their main entrances from the space rather than from the car parking below (a characteristic of the phase one spaces at Canary Wharf and of the Holford masterplan at Paternoster Square), and this ensures that even during inclement weather, the squares remain animated by the comings and goings of workers from the surrounding buildings. However, the scale of the buildings and the control enacted through the requirements of occupiers for single secured entrances to their commercial office buildings ensures an abundance of continuous inactive facades at ground level and concentrated activity in just a few places. In both schemes, the buildings were designed to be architecturally restrained in order not to compete for the visual dominance of the spaces. In this, they show a marked contrast from some of London's more recent corporate developments such as Swiss Re (**5.13**) or The Shard, which are designed instead as architectural statements with spaces below that are simply what is left over after development.

Developing corporate space
Who is in control?

The delivery models were quite different at Canada Square and Paternoster Square. At Canada Square, the public sector role was negligible. During their stewardship, the LDDC were interested in achieving a quality scheme overall, but largely left the detail and delivery to the developer. Thus, once the Master Building Agreement had been signed, regulation of the estate, including the whole of the second phase, was largely an internal matter, with the LDDC (and later the London Borough of Tower Hamlets) simply kept informed on planning matters, whilst the privately owned and managed roads and footpaths of the estate were altogether outside of the borough's purview. Because the masterplan allowed flexibility for interpretation, expansion and contraction, Canada Square was also able to change during its detailed design, reflecting new ideas about how it could be used. For their part, the community were nowhere to be seen in the design decision-making process, whilst the developer's desire to make and retain a long-term investment with a scheme that would hold its value was enough to ensure careful control against their own, self-imposed, Canary Wharf Design Guidelines.

At Paternoster Square, by comparison, the development was shaped by a partnership of interests between the investor (led day-to-day by Stanhope) and the City, with the latter involved in detailed discussions about the Whitfield masterplan for four years and playing a critical role in facilitating the development by resolving tensions between the various parties. Extensive consultation and a public exhibition focused on the masterplan, with discussion of individual buildings following after once the basic urban design principles had been established. In this case, the City carefully controlled everything down to the individual shopfront designs, with officers retaining tight control over the process in order to avoid the uncertainty that the involvement of political members might have caused. Alongside the planning permission, a (Section 106) Planning Agreement was signed to ensure that the public space was delivered before any other part of the scheme was occupied, and to establish that the space would remain an open square in perpetuity. The agreement also covered the return of Temple Bar and the provision of public toilets on the square.

Two further critical roles decisively shaped these corporate development processes – one explicit and the other, hidden.

5.14   2009 new intervention within Canada Square, animating the edge

5.15   Commercial appropriation of Paternoster Square

The power of design

Over the years, both developments had been the focus of a surfeit of design talent, largely from the USA in the case of Canary Wharf and from the UK in the case of Paternoster Square. In each case, a single designer was to prove pivotal in facilitating the move from aspirational to viable development. In the case of Canada Square, O&Y (and then CWG) firmly led the process, employing a wide range of urban designers, including their own in-house team, who over the years prepared multiple schemes for the site. In this process, 'They invested in the very best talent but only worked with those they respected and who spoke the same language' (planner), namely those able to combine financial thinking with a very clear three-dimensional vision. For Canada Square, this was Fred Koetter, who 'was able to inject the necessary urban design rigour into the decision-making processes' in order to move the design decisively on from the more staid phase one scheme (planner).

For very different reasons, William Whitfield had been appointed masterplanner at Paternoster Square, in his case as seemingly one of the few people able to steer the 'political' path between the competing views on how to redevelop the site, and achieve the necessary permissions and a viable development option. This put him in a powerful position to ensure that the Square was delivered as he envisaged, even facing down the City planners on a number of key issues. To facilitate the process of coordinating the design, a single

planning application for the development was to be made, including the massing, form and appearance of all the buildings, with their architects briefed in regular seminars about how they should work within the masterplan. For Whitfield, however, the process of bringing the designers of the individual buildings (five other teams) along with the masterplan was problematic as 'some of the architects wanted to go their own way' (masterplanner), arguably, undermining the coherence of the final result. Thus even the strongest of designers can be compromised by the pragmatics of the development process.

Tenants, the hidden hand

To fill the spaces they created, the developers of Paternoster Square and Canary Wharf (phase two), were fishing in the same pond for corporate tenants, most notably that of international financial services. Both developers had learnt the lessons of the property crash of the early 1990s, and CWG in particular had abandoned the speculative build model in favour of the custom building of pre-let space, a model that places greater power in the hands of occupiers. Significantly, both schemes demonstrated a move away from the use of integrated mega-structures. At Paternoster Square, this had the advantage of allowing the site to be developed (and in the future to be redeveloped) incrementally as and when tenants could be found. At Canada Square, although the space sits on top of the retail, the foundations of the surrounding buildings are independent, reflecting both the need for a cheaper solution to be found to the underground

5.16   Canada Square observational analysis of user patterns – typical local movement patterns (a), density of activity (b) and typical activities (c)

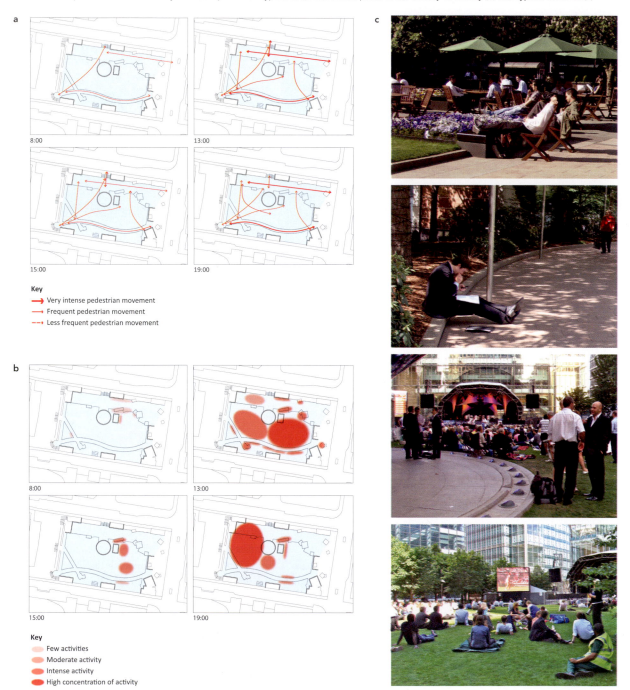

a

8:00

13:00

15:00

19:00

Key

→ Very intense pedestrian movement

→ Frequent pedestrian movement

--→ Less frequent pedestrian movement

b

8:00

13:00

15:00

19:00

Key

Few activities

Moderate activity

Intense activity

High concentration of activity

c

5.17 Paternoster Square observational analysis of user patterns – typical local movement patterns (a), density of activity (b) and typical activities (c)

a

8:00

13:00

15:00

19:00

Key

→ Very intense pedestrian movement

→ Frequent pedestrian movement

--→ Less frequent pedestrian movement

b

8:00

13:00

15:00

19:00

Key

Few activities

Moderate activity

Intense activity

High concentration of activity

c

parking and also the security concerns of occupiers unwilling to allow retail uses directly beneath their blocks or at ground level.

The particular needs of financial service tenants were therefore the driving hand in the way that both spaces were shaped, for example impacting on such fundamentals as the depth of plan (and associated building bulk), the location and control of entrances, and the mix of uses at ground floor. It explains why, even in such contrasting locations, a similar corporate ambience shines through.

Using corporate space
Learning to successfully animate corporate space
At Canary Wharf, 'As the estate has matured, the understanding of how people use the space and what the space could be has changed' (developer). This willingness to learn from the first phase of Canary Wharf has been vindicated, since Canada Square is now a well-used space – the heart of the Canary Wharf development – with a concentration of users around the space to fill it with activity. Conflicts are few and far between, since the space is open, well overlooked and heavily policed and 'Users feel relaxed and safe, for example, people putting prayer mats out to pray, mums breast feeding, and so on' (developer). Patterns of use depend upon the time of year. Thus in good weather people opt to walk across the space and in bad weather they go underneath (via the retail mall), whilst the types of commercial tenants that are targeted give a particular mix across the estate, 'retaining a level of quality overall' (developer). At Canada Square, this has recently been reinforced by the attraction of high-end restaurants to a new low-rise development situated between One Canada Square and the space itself, creating a more active edge to the west end of the space (**5.14**). The attraction of premium tenants (and users) is an explicit objective of the development model.

Paternoster Square was designed with both tourists and City workers in mind, whilst the mix of retail uses was largely dictated by the market. Indeed, it proved difficult to attract 'high-end' designer shops (as was the original aspiration), and instead chain food and drink and a few high street retailers have taken the space. Despite the take-up, shortly after the development was launched in 2005, the poor use of the space led to the commissioning of Townshend Landscape Architects to evaluate it with a view to making recommendations for its better animation (e.g. signage, lighting and events). In fact, as the economy improved, the ground-floor uses took off and the square

has become more animated of its own accord. The space is now heavily used during the week in daytime, and particularly at lunchtime on sunny days, when it quickly fills up. The bars and restaurants stay open into the evening and at weekends, and although the majority of users are the office occupiers, tourists also use the space heavily, in the main by simply passing through. Today, the City even report some concern over the extent to which some of the surrounding uses have appropriated the space outside their units (**5.15**), whilst complaints have been received from some of the office tenants about the noisy nature of the ground-floor uses. Corporate ambience has clearly not been a barrier to filling either space with life and activity.

Comfortable can mean corporate
Detailed observation of both squares revealed them to be distinct places for social exchange activities, as well as critical spaces within the local movement frameworks of the wider Canary Wharf and Paternoster developments (**5.16, 5.17**). In this, there were very clear and active attempts to nurture activity, with, at the time of observation, Canada Square acting as a venue for some significant events – a big screen, bar and stage – that in turn supported a wide range of relaxed informal activities. The clientele for the space was far more narrowly focused on local office workers than was the case at Paternoster Square, where activities (with the exception of a street piano) were generally more formal in nature.

Together, the two cases revealed a remarkable satisfaction amongst users with their experiences of the spaces, albeit from a very narrow group of users in the case of Canada Square (**5.18, 5.19**). Although far from uncritical, particularly over their corporate ubiquity – 'mundane and monotonous for its location and just like any other place in London' (user of Paternoster Square) – most users applauded the respective designs of these spaces and felt at home and comfortable within them, appreciating, in particular, the active nature of their management – that removed any 'sense of danger' (user of Canada Square). At the same time, users were realistic, in both cases, that the spaces would not feel equally welcoming to all potential users of London's public spaces.

Managing corporate space
Taking a long-term view
Both CWG and MEC took a long-term view of their developments, investing on the basis of retaining a stake in the profit-generating

5.18   Canada Square – user perceptions

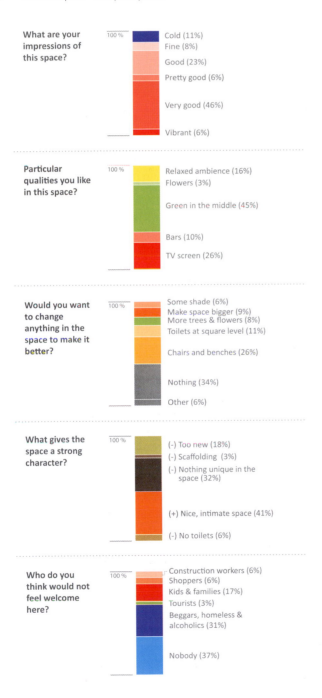

What are your impressions of this space?

100 %
- Cold (11%)
- Fine (8%)
- Good (23%)
- Pretty good (6%)
- Very good (46%)
- Vibrant (6%)

Particular qualities you like in this space?

100 %
- Relaxed ambience (16%)
- Flowers (3%)
- Green in the middle (45%)
- Bars (10%)
- TV screen (26%)

Would you want to change anything in the space to make it better?

100 %
- Some shade (6%)
- Make space bigger (9%)
- More trees & flowers (8%)
- Toilets at square level (11%)
- Chairs and benches (26%)
- Nothing (34%)
- Other (6%)

What gives the space a strong character?

100 %
- (-) Too new (18%)
- (-) Scaffolding (3%)
- (-) Nothing unique in the space (32%)
- (+) Nice, intimate space (41%)
- (-) No toilets (6%)

Who do you think would not feel welcome here?

100 %
- Construction workers (6%)
- Shoppers (6%)
- Kids & families (17%)
- Tourists (3%)
- Beggars, homeless & alcoholics (31%)
- Nobody (37%)

5.19   Paternoster Square – user perceptions

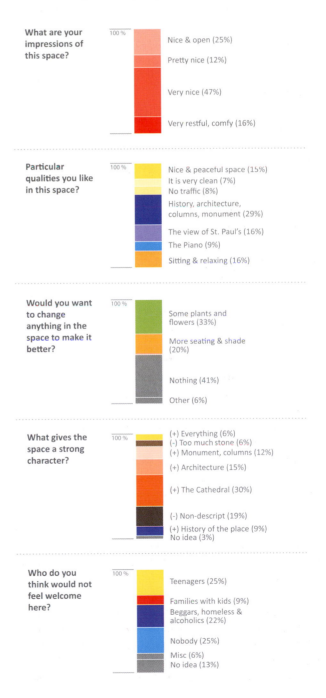

What are your impressions of this space?

100 %
- Nice & open (25%)
- Pretty nice (12%)
- Very nice (47%)
- Very restful, comfy (16%)

Particular qualities you like in this space?

100 %
- Nice & peaceful space (15%)
- It is very clean (7%)
- No traffic (8%)
- History, architecture, columns, monument (29%)
- The view of St. Paul's (16%)
- The Piano (9%)
- Sitting & relaxing (16%)

Would you want to change anything in the space to make it better?

100 %
- Some plants and flowers (33%)
- More seating & shade (20%)
- Nothing (41%)
- Other (6%)

What gives the space a strong character?

100 %
- (+) Everything (6%)
- (-) Too much stone (6%)
- (+) Monument, columns (12%)
- (+) Architecture (15%)
- (+) The Cathedral (30%)
- (-) Non-descript (19%)
- (+) History of the place (9%)
- No idea (3%)

Who do you think would not feel welcome here?

100 %
- Teenagers (25%)
- Families with kids (9%)
- Beggars, homeless & alcoholics (22%)
- Nobody (25%)
- Misc (6%)
- No idea (13%)

5.20   Paternoster Square – ongoing cleaning

5.21   Events in Canada Square – 2011 Motor Show

potential of their respective schemes into the future. The approach, similar to that taken by London's landed estates in the eighteenth century (see Chapter 2), ensures their heightened interest in both the in-built resilience of the design and the quality of the ongoing stewardship. CWG have total responsibility for Canada Square and aim to achieve a high and continuous quality of management to keep their tenants happy, all paid for through a service charge. This, they argue, is a key selling point for the estate.

Paternoster Square Management Ltd manage their square with the brief of maintaining the assets in the same condition as they were upon completion of the development, thereby maintaining the asset value. They employ two full-time and two part-time estate management staff on site, plus nine cleaners and nine security guards, all paid for by a service charge that raises £1.5 million per annum (**5.20**). A Fabric Manager inspects the square once a month and reports on any necessary repairs.

Balancing corporate and civic needs

An arts and events team at CWG have responsibility for the planned activities that take place at Canada Square (the prime events space at Canary Wharf), although sometimes tenants and external parties also come forward with ideas for events. The space has been used, for example, to host a winter ice rink, concerts, motor show (**5.21**), big-screen TV, the London Marathon, and charity events, all of which give an informality to the estate and have a wider social role. Some events with a wider civic significance are also housed in the space, such as a three minutes' silence on the anniversary of the 7/7 bombings, a vigil marking the 2008 Mumbai bombings, and religious events hosted by local groups to celebrate key religious days. In this, CWG remain acutely aware that their first responsibility is to their tenants, and that a balance needs to be struck between office tenants, who do not like activities that restrict their access to the estate, and retail tenants, who welcome all activities that attract users to the site. To help achieve this tenants are involved through a regular forum organised by CWG and are kept informed on all management issues.

At Paternoster Square, events are considered valuable to attract visitors and to moderate the otherwise overwhelmingly corporate feel of the development, although the formal layout of the space and positioning of fixed elements such as seating make the space difficult to use for events requiring a marquee or auditorium. The management company has nevertheless learnt to work around these physical constraints and put on a wide range of planned activities. Events are organised on Fridays during the summer and there is a high

5.22   Canada Square – highly visible security presence

5.23   Paternoster Square – closed against anti-capitalist protestors and in the process closed to all

demand to use the square from third parties (e.g. to launch products), although only about 10 per cent of such external requests are granted. Stakeholders are clear that the management of the space is primarily for the benefit of the occupiers who pay for the service, and not for other users of the space, but despite this there is a civic dimension to some activities. The City of London Festival uses the square, for example, and it is regularly used for charity events such as the Lord Mayor's fun run.

Security ... an imperative

Both schemes showed a heightened concern for security issues – a concern bordering on excessive in the case of Canary Wharf, although a response based on tenant demands within the context of the potential for the development to be a high-profile target for terrorist action, as testified by the attempted and actual bombings in 1992 and 1996, respectively. Security is deliberately kept at a very high level, with more than 1,600 CCTV cameras across the estate. As a result, problems are dealt with very quickly, whilst crime is virtually negligible: 'If you wish to cause trouble you go elsewhere – part of that is about the feeling of the place, its quality and upkeep, the lack of litter and graffiti, the fact that it is well lit and maintained, plus the knowledge that there is a security presence that will step in if necessary' (manager) (**5.22**).

At Paternoster Square, high levels of security are also required by the security-aware high-profile occupiers of the scheme, including Goldman Sachs and the London Stock Exchange. Thus, although the space and routes to it are designed to maximise visibility and are fully covered and actively monitored by CCTV, the concerns of occupiers also translate into a highly visible uniformed security presence, patrolling 24 hours a day. In 2011, the 'defensive' nature of the design was put to the test when anti-capitalist protesters attempted to occupy the space. The protesters were frustrated and occupied St Paul's Churchyard next door (see **12.11**), but only at the expense of the complete closure of the space and its occupation instead by security and City of London Police for several months (**5.23**). The experience revealed how such spaces are targets in more ways than one.

To ban or not to ban, that is the question

Estate managers have a very clear sense of the activities that are encouraged and those that are proscribed in the two spaces. At Canada Square, these were summarised as follows: 'activities that don't interfere with others are not discouraged, but activities that do are stopped' (manager). On this basis, begging, selling the *Big Issue* magazine by the homeless, selling any other items or demonstrating, are not allowed. Charities are allowed to collect, if permission is

5.24   Canada Square – smoking is carefully controlled around the estate

obtained first, and photography is allowed, 'unless suspicious or for professional purposes' (developer). This leaves some activities as borderline issues. For example, when the grass is used by office workers for a kickabout, as long as it is not causing harm to neighbouring users, it is tolerated, although never encouraged. Smoking is also limited to prescribed zones (**5.24**).

At Paternoster Square, the planners argue that 'people are not encouraged to linger' (planner). Nevertheless, seating is provided in the square and around its edges, associated with its surrounding restaurants and cafes. The Inigo Jones column also provides a natural meeting place. The space is heavily managed to discourage 'undesirable' uses, with skateboarders in particular seen as a key undesirable group about which meetings have been held with the Police to discuss how to discourage them, leading, amongst other measures, to the insertion of studs in the benches. Cycling is also banned in the space, as is photography (without a permit).

EVALUATION

The completion of Paternoster Square and Canada Square just five years apart demonstrate the huge complexities and compromises involved in constructing public spaces at the heart of immensely valuable corporate real estate. Although profoundly different in many respects – one is a hard piazza, the other a green garden square; one is built in a very historic setting with hands-on planning control to match, the other sited within a cleared landscape with little or no detailed public sector control; one is fully pedestrian, the other a shared space, etc. – both have in common an intention to serve the prestige corporate market, a hugely complex set of above- and below-ground constraints, a drive to deliver high-quality public space (albeit of a particular type and for a particular audience), and both featured a complex design/development process to rival even that of the highly serviced buildings to which they play host.

In general, the stakeholders involved in their realisation proclaim a broad satisfaction with what has been achieved, although they are noticeably more critical at Paternoster Square than Canada Square. External commentators, by contrast, have been generally unkind to both schemes. Thus, with the completion of phase two, with Canada Square at its heart, Canary Wharf came of age, as did its new role as the focus for critiques of privatised public space in the UK (e.g. Imrie & Sakai 2007; Minton 2009). For the developers, however, 'What has been created is a place that looks like a piece of London, but which is privately owned and managed and could technically be closed to anyone. In reality, it is a 24 hour open space and kept open because that is what the tenants demand.' They observe 'It seems to annoy some commentators in principle, that an open patch of grass is privately owned. But this contrasts strongly with an earlier tradition in London where spaces were and still are literally private and a key is needed to enter' (developer). Just as the Georgians went through a learning process (followed by the gradual transformation of their original hard residential squares into softer garden squares), so has the design of public space at Canary Wharf, where a key lesson from the first phase was the need to understand how people use and animate the public realm.

Looking back on the scheme, the head of urban design at the former LDDC commented that Canada Square 'is a highly successful piece of square building, the level of detail and quality goes all the way through. There was an English way of doing things, but one has to say that the Americans have given us a model which in some ways is now being repeated around London. As a result of the development, the City of London was forced to up-grade its attitude to public realm, as has latterly the West End. It would not be unfair to compare it to some of the great Georgian squares in terms of its impact' (planner).

At Paternoster Square, although a general contentment reigns amongst stakeholders who were involved, this is tinged with regret that more could have been achieved. The City planners, for example, are broadly pleased with the outcomes, although they feel that the space is a little bleak and would benefit from softening. For the developer, although the end result is good, it is a little bland, including the architecture, 'as everyone worried too much about being respectful to the master plan' (developer), no doubt wishing to avoid a continuation of the stalemate that had bedevilled previous incarnations of the scheme. The City are also concerned about what they see as obtrusive security, and an over-sensitivity to the likes and dislikes of the scheme's tenants, which, for example, are blamed for putting a break on the types of active uses that feature in the space. The City has let it be known that they wish to negotiate greater control of the scheme's public realm and intend that the square and routes within the development should be designated as 'city walkways' (as they were in the 1950s scheme). The possibility of these spaces reverting to public control is therefore under discussion, aided by the fact that a designation of 'city walkway' was a condition to the planning permission. Such a designation would allow the City to control aspects such as tables and chairs in the public space and overcome what, for them, has been the overly assertive nature of the space's management, such as the no-photography policy.

The result of the design and development process at Paternoster Square is certainly a compromise between competing interests, creating what the designers describe as 'timeless common sense – identify the site's constraints and respond to these and be concerned with the needs of the client' (masterplanner). Others have been less kind, with Jay Merrick of *The Independent* describing it as 'a fudge dictated by the requirements of the developer package' (Merrick 2003), whilst Jonathan Glancey of *The Guardian* described the ensemble as 'kitsch', asking why 'It is not half as good as it should be' (Glancey 2003).

5.25   Relative stakeholder influences

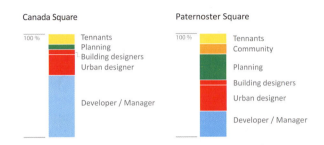

Canada Square

Paternoster Square

Carmona & Freeman (2005: 329) argued that many of the repeated problems associated with commercial developments are not so much inherent in the development type, but rather are to do with how such developments are designed and subsequently managed to meet market expectations. For Michael Cassidy (2010: 72), former Chairman of the Planning Committee at the City Corporation, this is highly appropriate, since, for him, in all the debate about design, it is too easy to loose sight of what should be uppermost in minds: 'Does anyone want to occupy this building?' He argues, 'The customer knows best. Without them the project is toast.' Arguably, it was forgetting this that was the cause behind the decade-long delay at Paternoster Square, whilst schemes such as Canary Wharf and Broadgate changed the game through their awareness of the new and unstoppable market forces touching down in London from the mid 1980s onwards: 'If we had taken the view that all of this energy had to be restrained whilst well-meaning but naive planners delved into broad questions of balance and design, the boat would have sailed' (Cassidy 2010: 71).

Yet, despite the history of deregulation in the City, large-scale development in that historic environment inevitably remains open to challenge and controversy, as the intervention of Prince Charles at Paternoster demonstrated. Such pressures continue to shape what is produced in a manner that long ceased to have any impact in the Docklands. The result is a very different set of power relationships between the constituent teams in these cases. Thus, whilst relying on external design assistance to interpret and deliver their vision, the overriding power at Canary Wharf lay with the developer. In the case of Paternoster Square, this was severely tempered by that of the public sector (the City), albeit a public sector amenable to the commercial imperatives facing City developers. There, also, the relationships were carefully negotiated and aspirations skilfully reconciled by a consequentially powerful masterplanner able to walk the tightrope of competing public and private interests. The relative influences of key stakeholders on the resulting developments are represented (unscientifically) in **5.25**.

Addressing the critiques

Clearly, the examples of Canada Square and Paternoster Square represent classic cases of corporate privatisation of the public realm. In the former case, these processes have moved space that was formerly publicly owned but not generally publicly accessible wholly into private hands. In the latter, the development has retained a post-war situation where this part of the city was privately owned, although where the City had negotiated some rights (now extinguished although being re-negotiated) to control the resulting spaces. In both cases, the logic of the corporations that developed and now own the spaces were clear and rational, namely to use the public spaces of their schemes to add as much value as possible to the real estate portfolio represented by their investments, and in so doing to meet a clear tenant demand in the prestige market for corporate headquarters to be situated within high-quality space, and to benefit from cleanliness/maintenance thresholds that the public sector is unable to match and from a high-profile and active security regime.

Yet, whilst the imperative of the developers in each case is first and foremost to meet the narrow corporate needs of their occupiers, it is also to create developments that will carry on delivering a healthy economic return to them over the long term. In this respect, although representing the ultimate in footloose international capital, both investors remain concerned with the local realisation of their schemes and with the sorts of tenants that they serve. They have been footloose, but not fancy-free.

The analysis revealed a relatively narrow clientele for these spaces, particularly in the case of Canada Square, but also a tacit understanding amongst users that their relative comfort within, and contentment with, these spaces may not be shared by all groups, some of whom would be implicitly and others explicitly discouraged from becoming users of the spaces. For the users, the fact that the spaces were well maintained and attractive, offered opportunities for relaxation and engagement, and were, above all, safe, were the key

factors in determining their use, whilst debates about the inevitable limits on access, heightened control, and potential reductions in freedoms and accountability remained non-issues.

In securing such positive reviews from their users, the designers and developers of both schemes had clearly understood the lessons of both areas' recent histories, namely, that life and activity at ground level and the design of flexible spaces (particularly at Canada Square) that are part of the continuous movement network in themselves are the key determinants of the sense of publicness, whilst stylistic concerns (although seemingly hot potatoes amongst some elite groups) are of little consequence to most users. As such, the design/development teams in both cases were clearly happy to engage with the process of invention (and reinvention) in order to shape particular narratives around their spaces.

In this respect, Canary Wharf is an entirely invented place, master-planned from scratch on an almost blank canvas. It contains within it a range of public spaces, each based on a clear concept that differentiates it from the others, with Canada Square clearly referencing London's historic garden squares. Paternoster Square is also invented, or more precisely reinvented, as a return (partially) to something that existed on the site previously, a corporate space replete with imported historic references, whilst introducing some-thing that is new to the area, namely a classically inspired pictur-esque piazza. Both exhibit a desire to create distinct place, whilst, perversely, the constraints of the existing place in the case of Paternoster Square have arguably greatly constrained this potential, limiting the development options through a process of negotiation and compromise whilst also raising the value and significance of design as the currency through which these negotiations were played out. The result is two spaces that, although in many respects unique in a London context, are nevertheless also the result of conscious attempts to design-in place-derived meaning, whilst also grappling with the formulae-driven limitations of commercial developments. For users, although they criticise aspects of the designs, their authenticity remains unquestioned, as does the desire to engage in the carefully managed and programmed spectacle that each space offers.

6 SPACES OF THE CIVIC CITY

CIVIC LONDON

Formerly capital of the British Empire, today London remains the capital of the UK and one of the planet's undoubted 'world cities' in commerce, culture, communications, influence and influences, and in the diversity of its inhabitants. It is the centre of Government and the economic powerhouse of the UK. At the same time, it is home to 7.5 million people for whom it sustains their everyday lives. At times in its history, a tension between local and national needs has come to the fore, for example the debates in the 1980s over Canary Wharf and Docklands (expansion of the City of London and attractor of international investment for UK plc, or site of reinvigorated industry and social housing for the local disadvantaged and dispossessed community?). Sometimes national need has seemed to win out, as in the Docklands. At other times, plans for nationally significant projects such as the part-pedestrianisation of Parliament Square have been sunk on the back of local opposition (see Chapter 3).

In a city where almost every locality is having to cater for many overlapping functions, with, for example, residential populations living side by side with commercial, entertainment and civic ones throughout central London, and within its numerous outer town centres, these tensions are perhaps inevitable. However, in periods when London had no city-wide government of its own, national need could too easily override local concerns with regard to the larger decisions, whilst decisions at the next level down (out of the purview of national government) could too easily be hijacked by the lobbying of unrepresentative local groups or simply for short-term pragmatic or economic purposes. In the Docklands, for example, the unwillingness during the 1980s of the LDDC to safeguard a riverside walk in its territory continues to compromise the River Thames as London's great civic space, undermining a hugely successful policy elsewhere across London with its roots in the 1970s and the policies of the GLC.

6.1   Barking Town Hall Square – the civic centre of the town, but not the heart of the community, a role taken by the East Street market next door

The coming of the Mayor of London (and the GLA) brought with it a new and powerful voice for the city, which, through the energy and enthusiasm of the first two incumbents, has delivered 'the feeling that city life in the twenty-first century is capable of making London a more integrated and better-managed place' (Farrell 2010: 260). Although not immune from local lobbying (e.g. with regard to the decision at Parliament Square), in the key decisions impacting on the capital as a whole, the Mayor has the authority to oppose national decisions seen as detrimental to the capital when required, for example the opposition of Boris Johnson to the expansion of Heathrow Airport, and to override local views and interests when a wider benefit is envisaged, such as Ken Livingstone's support for high buildings.

These tensions between national and local and between one local view and another have often come to the fore in debates about a comparatively rare form of space, the civic square. Taking as a departure point the definition of 'civic' from the *Oxford English Dictionary*, such spaces are 'of the city' and 'of its citizens'; in other words, designed to cater for the civil life and well-being of the city and its inhabitants (perhaps alongside other wider functions). In contrast to the corporate spaces discussed in the previous chapter, civic spaces are the most inherently 'public' of the types of spaces examined in this book, being clearly the responsibility of the state that will own and manage them as a form of public good. Such spaces might be most directly associated with the types of formal public spaces in front of and setting off key civic buildings – such as the regenerated space in front of Barking Town Hall (**6.1**) – but will range from the grandest of public spaces designed to represent the essence and pretentions of society, to modest spaces for rest and contemplation.

This chapter examines a key critique of public space, that spaces are increasingly invaded by traffic. Civic spaces seem particularly prone to such problems for two reasons:

- First, because of the location of many at key strategic points in the city's movement framework. These locations are considered to be civically significant precisely because of the presence that such great accessibility gives them.

- Second, because their public ownership has made them susceptible to the whims and priorities of municipal authorities who can change the nature of such spaces without recourse to complex private interests. Thus, if the free flow of traffic is seen to be a priority, then traffic will get precedence even if that undermines the environment for pedestrians.

The consequence of a decline in the city's civic spaces may be that other types of spaces are sought out for gathering and exchange opportunities.

THE CRITIQUE

Invaded space

The most basic, most pervasive, and perhaps the most insidious influence on the character and quality of public space in industrial and post-industrial cities over the last hundred years has been the growth and impact of private cars. Universal derision is apparent in the urban literature for these bastions of private free will and choice, yet public policies rarely curb their growth and often indirectly encourage them to the extent that some have described them as invading public space. They argue that in old cities and urban areas where car traffic has gained the upper hand, public space has inevitably changed dramatically with traffic and parking gradually usurping pedestrian space in streets and squares. 'Not much physical space is left, and when other restrictions and irritants such as dirt, noise and visual pollution are added, it doesn't take long to impoverish city life' (Gehl & Gemzoe 2001: 14). This 'tragedy of the commons' (Webser 2007) exists because the absence of a pricing mechanism for roads (London's Congestion Charge zone being an obvious exception) or a mechanism for car-based users to gauge their own negative impact on the space, results in (if unchecked) the overuse and degradation of the space itself, for all users.

The invasion critique is nothing new, and manifests itself in a number of primary problems:

- Lefebvre (1991: 359) describes how urban space is often 'sliced up, degraded, and eventually destroyed by the proliferation of fast roads' so that 'Movement between the fragments becomes a purely movement experience rather than a movement and social experience' (Carmona *et al.* 2003: 75).

- Buchanan (1988: 32) argues that the remaining public space itself is too often dominated by traffic and has lost its social function as a result. Thus, even when the number of car users is greatly exceeded by the numbers of pedestrians using a street, the space given over to road space far exceeds that dedicated to footpaths. Farrell (2010: 202), for example, comments how perverse it is that in London 'the money spent on the most primary of human transport methods [walking] is quite derisory compared with the money spent on wheels'.

- A related problem stems from the impact of parking on public space, which Shoup (2005) argues carries an indirect and unseen cost. For him, amongst other impacts, free parking encourages unnecessary congestion, distorts urban form, creates unsightly expanses of cars, and removes the opportunity for public space to be used for other functions, such as walking or social activities.

● A further problem relates to the ease with which car owners can move from one unrelated place or event to another. In such a context, physically distant places can be compressed into a single space, whilst others (in between) can be ostracised and allowed to deteriorate because of their perceived reputation or absence of attractors. Hajer & Reijndorp (2001: 53–61) characterise this as an 'archipelago of enclaves' and argue that unless the in-between parts of the city also develop an attraction value, the new network city will ensure that they continue to be ignored.

● A final impact can be seen in the range of exclusively car-reliant environments where external public space does not exist at all, at least not in any traditional form, but is instead replaced by a series of disconnected roads and car parks.

In London, large parts of the city have long suffered the types of characteristics described above, most notably areas outside the more urban cores of central London and between the historic town centres of outer London (**6.2**). Thus Richard Rogers (1992: xix–xx) has long bemoaned the impact of and manner in which the 'ghettos of poverty and affluence are segregated and disrupted by traffic noise and pollution' as successive governments have subsidised cars through huge investment in the road network. For him, as well as the social and ecological impact, the 'tyranny' of the car (as he refers to it) has undermined key London civic set pieces, such as the composition of Brixton's town hall, church and public library (all now brutally separated by major roads), whilst everyday spaces are 'paved with scarred tarmac', 'planted with lines of cars' and 'adorned with the paraphernalia of traffic control'.

Gehl and Gemzoe (2001: 14) argue that invaded space is generally impoverished space, and that most of the social and recreational activities that did or would exist disappear, leaving only the remnants of the most necessary, utilitarian functions. In such places, people walk only when they have to, not because they want to, whilst collectively the invasion of private cars has led to a dramatic reduction in the space available to pedestrians, a reduction in the quality of that space, significant restrictions on the freedom of movement for pedestrians both within and between spaces, and the filling of spaces with the clutter and paraphernalia that conventional wisdom has determined the safe coexistence of cars and people requires: 'This panoply is generally owned and managed by different bodies. At worst, there is no co-ordination and the only functional considerations are engineering-

6.2   North Finchley – public space reduced to a protected island for pedestrians

led and car-oriented. The pedestrian is ignored or marginalised. Some of these items are introduced on the grounds of "pedestrian improvements", yet the "sheep-pen" staggered pedestrian crossings and guard rails impede pedestrian movement while allowing a free run for the car' (Llewelyn-Davies 2000: 102).

Campaigners such as David Engwicht have written about the need to reclaim such street space from cars to once again make it available as social space and to the full range of users. He argues that 'the more space a city devotes to movement, the more exchange space becomes diluted and scattered. The more diluted and scattered the exchange opportunities, the more the city begins to lose the very thing that makes a city: a concentration of exchange opportunities' (Engwicht 1999: 19).

Non-traditional spaces

An alternative view is that the invasion of traditional space by traffic (or indeed its commercialisation – see Chapter 7) is simply a sign of life, reflecting the changing nature of cities as contemporary lifestyles change. Indeed, some authors have argued that the reported decline in public space is much exaggerated. Lees (1994: 448–9), for example, concedes that contemporary public spaces still contain important aspects of urban life, and although many new primarily commercial public spaces lack wider civic functions, we should remember that

6.3 Kingsland – informal street corner gathering for singing and worship

6.4 Woolwich – Plumstead Road supercrossing, designed to re-balance this busy truck road in favour of pedestrians

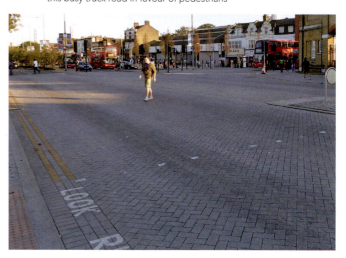

commercial space has always been built into public space and vice versa. 'The core of city life – exchanges of goods, information, and ideas – still has a strong grounding in space, the design, accessibility, and the quality of such urban space can and ought to be criticised, but its existence must be recognised.'

Worpole and Knox (2007: 4) argue that 'Contrary to conventional assumptions, public space in neighbourhoods, towns and cities is not in decline but is instead expanding'. So, whilst critiques abound about a decline in public space, for them this results from a tendency for commentators to confine their notions of public space to traditional outdoor space in public ownership. Instead, it is important to reframe debates to reflect how people actually use spaces, and the fact that to members of the public, ownership and appearance do not define the value of space, rather the opportunities it provides for shared use and activity. For them, 'Gatherings at the school gate, activities in community facilities, shopping malls, cafes and car boot sales are all arenas where people meet and create places of exchange' (**6.3**).

Carr *et al.* (1992: 343) suggest that new forms of public space are only to be expected as cultures and societies develop and new uses need to be housed, whilst for Hajer and Reijndorp (2001: 15), the pessimism of many commentators is founded on an artificial dichotomy

between the centre and periphery (the suburbs) that is established in many writings, the latter being seen as replacing the former with impoverished forms of space. Instead, they suggest, 'if we regard city and periphery as a single urban field then we discover countless places that form the new domains that we are seeking'. For them, however, 'The urban field is no longer the domain of a civic openness, as the traditional city was, but the territory of a middle-class culture, characterised by increasing mobility, mass consumption and mass recreation' (Hajer & Reijndorp 2001: 28). The consequence is that we should no longer associate public space solely with the streets and squares of the historic city core, but should instead embrace the new urban network of dissociated places.

Despite such views, some have noted an improvement and re-investment or return to the traditional forms of space, with a consequential improvement in the quality of public space and a resurgence in public life. Gehl and Gemzoe (2001: 20), for example, examine 39 public space exemplar projects from across the world, and conclude that 'In a society in which increasingly more of daily life takes place in the private sphere – private homes, at private computers, in private cars, at private workplaces and in strictly controlled and privatised shopping centres – there are clear signs that the city and city spaces have been given a new and influential

6.5   The Scoop amphitheatre – despite being next to and part of the City Hall complex (the home of the Mayor of London) on London's Southbank, this space (and City Hall itself) is part of the privately owned and managed estate – More London – with restrictions imposed on users by its owners

role as public space and forum'. They argue that examples of such reconquered cities can be found across the world, not least as ideas of reclaiming space from the car have taken hold. In London, this is exemplified by the streetscape scheme at Kensington High Street (see **3.10**), by a small number of shared (or semi-shared) surface schemes (**6.4**), and by more grandiose schemes, such as the implementation of a shared surface scheme along London's busy Exhibition Road, also in Kensington.

CIVIC SPACES

The research revealed relatively few civic-type spaces, and almost no entirely new civic spaces. In other words, civic spaces in London tend to be long-established, and recent civic space projects largely focus on their renewal, rather than provision. The London-wide analysis (Chapter 4) showed that 13 per cent of new and regenerated spaces are of this type.

Civic spaces cater for a range of functions but typically have a representational value reflecting a formal civic role, be that for formal gatherings, for historic celebration and remembrance, or for simply representing the 'public' civic values of the state through, for example, the presence of public art, facilities (e.g. public toilets or places to rest) and events. Their design tends to be permeated with this sense of publicness, and in almost all cases these spaces are owned (and typically managed) by the public sector or by pseudo-public organisations such as the church or cultural organisations; although in London there is at least one major high-profile exception to this rule (**6.5**). Their edges are typically active, the spaces themselves are filled with everyday life of people moving through, meeting and relaxing, and their architecture is imbued with historic meaning and sense of place. The choice of civic-type case studies reflects, first, a nationally (indeed internationally) significant civic space – Trafalgar Square – where the government, and subsequently the Mayor, took the key role in recognising and driving through the project in the face of local opposition, and second, a locally significant space – Sloane Square – where different local interests battled for supremacy, the result being that the scheme stalled and the space remains a largely un-regenerated traffic gyratory.

Trafalgar Square – a political game

Trafalgar Square is the symbolic centre of London today, and in the past was the symbolic centre of the British Empire. The origins of the square lie in the commissioning by the Prince Regent of John Nash in the 1820s to redevelop the area around Charing Cross. For Nash, a formal civic space quickly became an integral part of his wider vision for central London (see Chapter 2), although its detailed design was later undertaken by Sir Charles Barry, who completed the space in 1845 (**6.6**). 'Trafalgar Square occupies a politically charged spot at the heart of London' demonstrating 'the primary importance of location, and also of getting the dimensions of the open space right. Although the buildings around the square have often been redeveloped, the public space has continued to serve in its role as the main square of London and the UK for almost two hundred years' (Corbett 2004: 64).

When designed and built, Trafalgar Square was the only purpose-built civic square in central London (Carmona *et al.* 2008: 30). Adorned with civic monuments and statues from the start, the scale of the space and its location ensured it took on a prominent role in the life of the nation from day one, not least as a focus for demonstration and celebration.

6.6   Site of Trafalgar Square

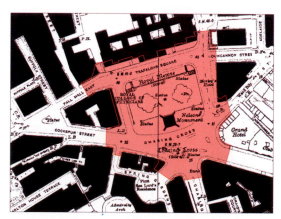
1910s

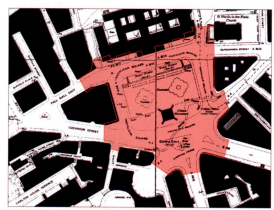
1950s

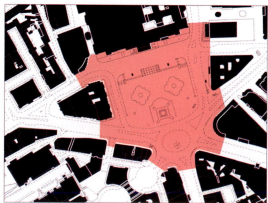
2010

In fact, the square needed to respond to a complex brief that sought to reconcile the Nelson naval memorial (Nelson's Column), with traffic route improvements and crowd management. This led, in effect, to it becoming a huge traffic gyratory. In time, as traffic increased on its surrounding roads, a slow strangulation of pedestrian movement across the space occurred as users increasingly chose to avoid the centre of the space and walk around its edges on narrow footways, despite facing long delays at multiple pedestrian crossings. By the late twentieth century, only tourists ventured into the centre and would congregate on the lower level in the southeast corner, often attempting a range of dangerous crossings of the fast-moving traffic around the space.

Although Heath (1998: 14) recounts how the space had been studied by a variety of consultants over the years, including Richard Rogers, Ove Arup, Halcrow Fox and W.S. Atkins, for him the preconditions for success – the right expertise, a proper budget and sustained political will – were never in place. By the mid 1990s, however, with the renewed interest of government in questions of design (see Chapter 2), a determination gradually grew to do something about this national embarrassment. Stemming from this concern, Trafalgar Square became part of the 'World Squares for All' initiative discussed in Chapter 3, fronted by a powerful but diverse steering group with representatives from the Government Office for London (who – pre-Mayor – took on its leadership), English Heritage, London Transport (prior to TfL), the City of Westminster and the National Gallery (located on the square). The main role of the steering group was to build a coalition of interests, often in the face of local opposition, in favour of a significant intervention in the area. Thus, faced with competing interests and objections and the sheer diversity of stakeholders needed to be brought on-board, the unwritten tactic of the group was simply to repeatedly commission new studies into the project's viability in order to keep the project alive and eventually appease the critics. This was until a London-wide mayor could be elected, for whom, they knew, such a project would be a highly visible and early win. 'Every time there was another onslaught we did another piece of work, this was the most over researched project ever' (steering group).

As part of this effort, Foster and Partners were appointed as masterplanners and over the years proposed a range of more or less radical interventions, from very minor changes to the existing layout, to complete pedestrianisation of the entire area. In the process,

they used their international profile to add gravitas to the project and to lend it the oxygen of publicity through the media and debates that followed. Space Syntax, Atkins (traffic engineers) and other consultancies supported the design technically, whilst the analytical studies were funded by the government, with the City of Westminster, the local borough, commissioning the technical work. This, because of continuing opposition to the project from their local residents, Westminster had to undertake in a semi-detached manner. However, whilst publicly distancing themselves from the project for most of its duration, behind the scenes Westminster became an integral part of the team.

In 2000, the new Labour government was looking for schemes to go with their new transport plan and found Trafalgar Square 'ready to go', making funds available in the process. From this point on, strong ministerial support followed by strong mayoral support (under Ken Livingstone) drove the project forward to construction and completion in 2003. The steering group, through the astute and highly political leadership of its Chair – Joyce Bridges – had done its job in the face of hugely complex traffic issues, hostile opposition from residents and no public support from Westminster. For visitors today, the result – closing the north side of the square to traffic, and using a new roundabout at the southern end to handle the new two-way traffic flows – might, on the face of it, seem a rather limited intervention for such a protracted process.

Sloane Square – the battle for public space

Sloane Square dates back even further than Trafalgar Square, to 1771, when it was developed as part of the Georgian Hans Town extension to London, but its recent development history has been far less successful. Both the town and square were named after Sir Hans Sloane, whose heirs owned the area at that time. Rather than a garden square, the space was essentially a road junction containing an important crossroads at its west end and later separate islands in the space (**6.7**). 'This created an angled crossing around which a fine oblong of buildings was established in the 18th century to enclose a junction within a square' (Moylan 2010: 66). In the 1930s, the then borough council (Chelsea) proposed changes to the road system based on two alternatives: a gyratory around the square, or a roundabout. The gyratory was implemented, with traffic flowing around the four sides of the space with a First World War memorial relocated and a fountain introduced (**6.7**). In the face of huge opposition from local

6.7 Site of Sloane Square

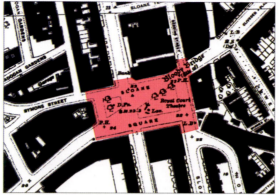

1910s

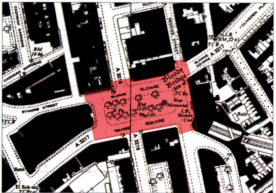

1950s

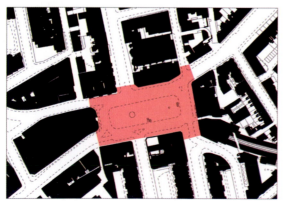

2010

residents, the scheme was implemented as a traffic management proposal, although the traffic was light by modern standards.

Reflecting the huge increase in traffic in the intervening period, and working for the ancestral firm of the original developers of the area – the Cadogan Estate – JMP Consultants proposed a 'crossroads concept' in the early 2000s, a scheme that was supported by Richard Rogers in his new role as advisor to the Mayor and promoter of the 100 Squares initiative, of which this space was part (see Chapter 3). The council, now the Royal Borough of Kensington & Chelsea, agreed to a local consultation on a number of alternative schemes, although it expected little support for the most radical, the crossroads plan, which, in essence, drew heavily on the original layout for its inspiration. In fact, there was considerable support for the proposal and it was taken forward with the support of local amenity groups, such as the Chelsea Society. Stanton Williams subsequently won a limited competition to design this square, and developed their proposals with help from the borough traffic engineers, subjecting the result to a second round of consultation that gave 75 per cent approval to the proposals.

However, local groups, supported by a number of local celebrities (including Rupert Everett and Bryan Ferry), organised in opposition and launched a high-profile and vocal campaign. This resulted from a gradual welling-up of opinion driven by an increasing concern that the proposed scheme was not being properly represented to the public: 'The illustrations gave the impression that the square would become traffic free and fully pedestrian, and there were errors and omissions in the data' (Save Sloane Square). The council co-opted representatives from the opposition onto the Sloane Square Management Group set up to progress the design (until then consisting of council officers and councillors, English Heritage and TfL), and agreed to fund an alternative scheme. As a result, the campaigning residents group, Save Sloane Square, commissioned Atkins (also traffic engineers at Trafalgar Square) to produce a scheme that retained and improved the gyratory system – although, in the view of some, it proposed 'no real change, just prettification of the existing square' (councillor). The schemes were subjected to a third round of public consultation carried out by ICM in early 2007, this time with 67 per cent favouring the Atkins proposals and 26 per cent the Stanton Williams plan. Work continued for a short time afterwards in an attempt to address some of the concerns, but both schemes were abandoned amidst acrimony in 2007 (Lazell 2007).

6.8   Trafalgar Square – a light but significant touch

Designing civic space
Rebalancing the public realm

In both Trafalgar Square and Sloane Square, the overriding intention was to re-balance the public realm away from vehicles towards pedestrians. The vision for Trafalgar Square was for a public civic space that would be given back to the public whilst also opening up and showing off the National Gallery, with which the space has a symbiotic relationship. It did not resort to major new visual interventions, but instead adopted 'a light touch in terms of physical works and changes' (traffic engineer), promoting the heritage and spatial assets of the space, removing traffic and improving connections, adopting high-quality materials, and upgrading seating, disabled access and facilities (a coffee house and toilets) (**6.8**). The scheme, as realised, was refined through public consultation and working with the client, and although the original aspiration was for a more radical approach, the transport implications were such that this would be very difficult to deliver. 'In reality the whole scheme was driven by traffic models and forecasts' (steering group), and assisted by the modelling of

6.9   Sloane Square – the crossroads scheme

6.10   Sloane Square – the alternative scheme

Space Syntax, which helped to convince stakeholders of the potential benefits of the scheme.

For Kensington & Chelsea, the aspiration was to improve Sloane Square as a gateway to Chelsea. The proposals followed on the heels of the changes to Kensington High Street (see above) and reflected a wider ambition of the borough to better balance the needs of pedestrians and traffic. This, the crossroads scheme would have achieved, by creating two pedestrian spaces, a 50 per cent increase in pedestrian space overall and lower traffic noise, whilst allowing the same traffic capacity through the square (**6.9**). For English Heritage, however, the promised improved connectivity across the new space (a major proposed benefit) was never fully resolved because of the proposed water features, planters and elements required to guide vehicles and prevent cyclists cutting through the space; therefore also undermining the freedom with which pedestrians could use it. On this issue, the borough's own highways department remained concerned about traffic safety and proposed to retain the option to add other bollards at key points around the space if it should prove necessary.

The heritage question – is it recognisably London?
Heritage arguments were writ large in both schemes, although the pragmatic approach of the key public guardian on this count – English Heritage – ensured that the issue never became the barrier that

it might easily have done. At Sloane Square, arguments were often framed in the context of what is or isn't appropriate for London. There, TfL undertook extensive modelling on the Stanton Williams scheme, with the whole area being seen as a shared surface (although still with distinct carriageways, signs, lights, etc.) and featuring a unified treatment of paving across the square. English Heritage opposed this aspect of the scheme, feeling that such a treatment would not provide a proper setting for the area's listed buildings, and would remove the kerbs that those with visual impairments rely upon to guide them. They argued that 'the approach resulted in a design that could have been in Barcelona or any other city and had little reference to London street character' (English Heritage). The Atkins (Save Sloane Square) alternative (**6.10**) suggested raised tables at the junctions, wider pavements, a café in the square, and an exhibition space in the centre for use during the Chelsea Flower Show or London Fashion Week, but also retention of the traditional kerbs and paving, and what the Save Sloane Square Group characterise as 'A recognisable welcome to Chelsea, not a place that could be anywhere else in the world' (Save Sloane Square).

By contrast, the crossroads proposal deliberately envisaged a more continental informal feel to the space, with flexible seating that could be removed, open-air cafes outside the Royal Court Theatre, careful differentiation between carriageway and walkways to guide disabled

6.11   Sloane Square – proposed continental-type space with informal seating and piazza-style paving

access, and the removal of some trees and replacement with others to give a more informal feel (**6.11**). Lighting was planned to enhance the square at night and to make the trees a feature, whilst the fountain, statue of Hans Sloane and war memorial were to be repositioned (again). The intention was to create a lively but flexible space, with the centre connecting to the activities at its periphery, with the adaptability required for special events, such as Remembrance Day. The scheme would also restore historic north/south views across the space – a feature that won over the grudging support of English Heritage for the proposals, despite their reservations.

At Trafalgar Square, the need to respect the original design concept of the Square was a concern, in particular its nautical references.

Thus Sir Charles Barry had envisaged the space as replicating a naval dockyard, with a continuous (dock-like) wall along its north side that had remained unchanged over time. English Heritage were particularly concerned to retain the 'heroic feeling' this gave the square and were initially critical of the idea of linking the top-level National Gallery Terrace to the space below through the new central staircase, although they were later persuaded that the benefits of pedestrianisation and the central staircase outweighed the costs in terms of compromising the original design (**6.12**). The idea of more extensive interventions under the National Gallery Terrace was also discussed, but on this issue the view was that the single café was all that could be achieved without detracting from the importance of the National Gallery façade and the ambiance of the square.

6.12   Trafalgar Square – as well opening up the possibility for diagonal movements through the space, the central steps offer seating opportunities and enhance the view of the space and surrounding historic buildings

6.13   Trafalgar Square – lift enclosures, a negotiated compromise

cabinets. Despite this, English Heritage believe 'the design has made the space more distinctive, as it reinforced the qualities that made it special'.

Whose space is it anyway?

A critical tension in both schemes was how to reconcile local with wider needs. In the case of Trafalgar Square, the refurbishment of the space was arguably a long-term investment in the economic future of Britain through improving a key tourist destination that was, for many years, a disappointment. Hugely more people can now enjoy the space, including those with disabilities, making a more inclusive public space. Yet, despite the potential gains, a vocal and articulate local community remained opposed to the proposals, largely because of the potential for displacing traffic into surrounding areas.

The choice of materials was carefully chosen to integrate with the existing scheme – Yorkstone and granite – whilst the transparent glass boxes Fosters and Partners had designed around the lifts for people with disabilities proved more controversial and involved considerable discussion with Westminster, who required some convincing that more solid construction would not be appropriate. The result was something of a compromise (**6.13**), whilst other detailed elements of the project were abandoned for pragmatic or cost reasons. These included a coordinated signage strategy, street tree planting, improvements to the underground station access, coordinated floodlighting of surrounding buildings, and the burying of above-ground utilities

For the designers at Sloane Square, local views and local realities often suffered a disconnect. Thus, they argued, although a much loved space, it is significantly underused, with a reality that is far from local perceptions: 'traffic circles the square and by night it is a rather hostile environment so that pedestrian movement is low at the best of times' (urban designer). Observing how the proposals became hugely political, they conclude that 'people did not want a square that would attract the wrong sort of people', an accusation repeated by Daniel Moylan, the Deputy Leader of the borough, and responsible for driving the project forward. For him, 'the underlying cause of objection was in fact a tribute to the proposal: that the new layout would draw people into the area. One opponent even claimed that the new square would be so attractive that drunks would migrate from Victoria to sleep in it!' (Moylan 2010: 67). As at Trafalgar Square, many others were simply concerned that the scheme would displace traffic into surrounding streets (the main source of objections from local Belgravia residents). Although the potential for this was largely disproved through the transport modelling, it remained a powerful source of residual concern amongst residents, who, in one view, 'were simply interested in the value of their properties' (urban designer).

Developing civic space
Capturing and managing the agenda
At Sloane Square, the whole project was shaped by 'the relationships between the council and the Save Sloane Square Group which soon became poisonous' (councillor), with the residents' group believing that Daniel Moylan 'was motivated solely by vanity'. This came to a head when they threatened to put up four candidates in the local elections, despite the fact that the existing ward councillors were evenly split on the proposals. The move nevertheless persuaded the council leader at the time to sanction the third round of consultation, with the stated intention to 'implement the scheme that had most support' (Save Sloane Square); although in so doing effectively loosing control of the agenda.

The experience showed the potential impact that an articulate and determined local group can have; even, as in this case, with just 12–15 people actively involved: 'They would stop people on the space and tell them that the council wants to drive a motorway through the square' (urban designer), whilst those in favour (e.g. the Chelsea Society and many of the local residents' associations) were far less vocal, and were not easy to mobilise. In effect, Save Sloane Square usurped the project leadership, promoting their own scheme until it received public endorsement and sunk the 'approved' proposals. The group, however, saw themselves 'in a David vs. Goliath relationship, opposing a scheme that they felt was weak and being imposed on locals' (Save Sloane Square), despite the fact they were never entirely unified around any set of proposals, with some favouring aspects of the crossroads scheme and opposing others. In essence, most felt that the existing space was OK, had important symbolic value for the neighbourhood and that a lighter touch set of interventions would be preferable. They

learnt to work together, overcame their disagreements, and quickly identified the key powerbrokers that they needed to influence. The organisation of the group and their ability to capture the agenda and influence the processes ensured that they eventually carried the day.

By contrast, the national significance of Trafalgar Square helped to overcome local objections and avoided the scheme suffering the same fate as Sloane Square (and in a different way, Paternoster Square – see Chapter 5). Although local groups continued to cause Westminster difficulties throughout, the potential range of interested parties was far wider. Thus, at the start of the project, there was a list of 50 key stakeholder organisations needing to be persuaded; by 1998, the list had grown to 150 groups; and by 2001, it had grown to over 180. 'There was an excellent communication strategy in place which actively sought maximum numbers for public consultation. It helped obtain over 80% of support at key times, from very large numbers of residents/businesses as well as visitors' (traffic engineer), contributing in the process to drown out the negative voices such as the taxi trade, bus companies, the motoring lobby and local residents' groups, the most vocal of which was the Smith Square Association, despite their location over half a mile away.

Harnessing the key players
Helping to sustain the Trafalgar Square project were a number of factors:

- The project was well publicised by a specialist communications agency.

- The steering group got all the key parties involved early in the process, avoiding unresolved issues rearing their heads later on (despite the occasional friction between disciplines and one or two egos).

- The high-profile nature of the project helped to sustain enthusiasm despite the huge amount of time and effort that went into explaining the scheme over five years.

- Norman Foster's personal standing was particularly useful at points when the project became political; 'One had to be a bit macho about the project, and that was easier for an established firm, than for a smaller talented office' (urban designer).

- There was an element of luck: 'It was about doing the right things at the right time, getting the momentum going, which was about managing the politics and the media, there was a huge amount of behind the scenes plotting' (steering group).

Throughout this process, the role of the steering group was critical, which only stepped back once a mayor was elected and after they had taken the project from concept to detailed design. Through the auspices of TfL, the Mayor funded the £19 million (with an additional £1 million contribution from the national Heritage Lottery Fund to raise the specification) and managed the construction process: 'Livingstone really saw the point of the space and was determined to use it. Any venture is only as good as your client, and he was excellent and saw the point immediately' (urban designer).

Westminster, by contrast, were in a difficult position; acting for their residents and at the same time acting as the guardians for the public face of one of the most important cities in the world. Because of this, they were more cautious than other parties, protective of their constituents, and from time to time 'needed a bit of encouragement from the Government Office for London' (urban designer): 'The politics were very very difficult, so a huge amount of clandestine work was carried out' (steering group). For example, a re-launch of the scheme not long after the election of Labour, with John Prescott (the Deputy Prime Minister) and Norman Foster on the stage, received coverage in every national newspaper and helped to demonstrate the huge political buy-in from the government, giving the scheme an unstoppable momentum. This, along with an unrealised proposal to transfer ownership of the roads surrounding the space (alongside the interior of the space itself) from the City of Westminster to the (ex-Labour) Mayor encouraged the Conservative borough to carry on commissioning the technical studies whilst refusing to support the scheme financially. In fact, Westminster gradually went 'from a promoter of the brief, to an unwilling and sceptical partner, and later-on, when reconciled to the implementation, to an advocate for higher standards' (traffic engineer).

At Sloane Square, the crossroads scheme received wholehearted backing from CABE, TfL, Design for London and Kensington & Chelsea, although the reservations of English Heritage meant that they were never fully onboard. English Heritage believed that their conservation concerns were sidelined and that it was only the request by Save Sloane Square to spot-list the existing fountain in the space (in an

attempt to block progress on the scheme) that meant their views were taken more seriously. Although English Heritage supported the idea of reinstating the crossroads, seeing it as a return to the original form of the space, their opposition to the shared surface effectively undermined any potential for a united front amongst the key public sector agencies involved in the project and, perhaps unwittingly, ended up helping the case of the objectors in opposing the crossroads. Their focus on the details (albeit important) in effect helped to sink the bigger picture.

A straightforward delivering process

As primarily landscape and highways schemes, both projects benefited from an uncomplicated regulatory process. Thus, with the exception of the need to move the listed fountain and war memorial (proposals that in fact received consent without delay), the proposal was to implement Sloane Square under a Highways Order with a cost of £5.5 million, paid for on a 50/50 basis from the deep coffers of Kensington & Chelsea and TfL.

At Trafalgar Square, since all the relevant organisations were involved on the Steering Group, the necessary permissions – listed building consents, planning permission (for the café and toilets) and the relevant traffic orders – all went through without a hitch. As the implementing organisation, TfL (on behalf of the Mayor) took over control of the highways temporarily for the duration of the works, although with the perverse implication that as the money was notionally allocated through their budget for a traffic scheme, and not for moving statues, restoration, etc., every element needed to be justified on the basis of traffic benefits. In fact keeping the city on the move during the 20 months or so whilst the works were ongoing represented one of the greatest challenges, whilst the construction work itself went largely without a hitch, with the majority of the expenditure actually spent on the traffic scheme rather than the public realm elements.

Using civic space
Making way for people ... or not

At the heart of the failure to realise the Sloane Square project were two fundamentally different views about how the square should be used. On the one hand, a passionate and vocal element of the community primarily saw the space as a local amenity, and for them the fact that it was underutilised (except by traffic) was not a

6.14   Sloane Square – today an overloaded gyratory

6.15   Trafalgar Square – the café, discreetly located so that users often do not realise it is there

major concern. Of greater importance was that traffic should not be displaced into their roads, that the space should retain the character that they associated with it, and that 'undesirable' users should not be attracted to the locale. For example, reflecting local concerns, benches in the crossroads scheme were to be vagrant-proof, despite the fact that there is no real vagrant problem in the Sloane Square area. The aspirations of the borough, designers and others to give the space a new role beyond a traffic gyratory (**6.14**), to open the space up to Londoners and visitors, and to fill the space with people (not cars), was fundamentally at odds with this.

Although local issues raised their heads at Trafalgar Square, the vision of the space as a 'World Square for All' carried the day. Today, it continues to be used as a square for protest and celebrations, now added to by a very full cultural and social events agenda that was impossible before. Commuters grab a coffee on their way to work, in the middle of the day the space is primarily occupied by tourists, and at night it is populated by a diverse range of groups, with the lighting scheme making it a comfortable and safe place to be. The introduction of the new central steps, in particular, have changed the way the space is used, and, as well as opening up new routes through the square, have provided a seating place and a natural meeting place from where events in the lower levels can be observed. Despite this, operators of

the café on the square have not faired well, as the discreet design and the ban on advertising the presence of the café within the space have led to a high turnover of tenants (**6.15**).

At Trafalgar Square, pedestrians have clearly come out on top at the expense of traffic capacity. Those involved in its realisation observe that users of the space generally enjoy it, sometimes a little too much, with bathing in the fountains and climbing on the lions damaging both users (on occasions) and monuments. On four occasions, drunk drivers in sports cars have also spun off the road, causing much more expensive and extensive damage to the listed features of the square.

Compromised or convivial public space?

Because the crossroads scheme remained unrealised, no systematic observations were conducted at Sloane Square. Cursory observations nevertheless reveal that although the space continues to be an important local landmark, its role as a social space and as a node within the local movement framework is compromised (**6.16**). Thus whilst the centre of the square remains largely underutilised, through much of the year on sunny days people do gather around the fountain. By contrast, the road space and pavement on the south side of the space are heavily overloaded all of the time, with shoppers moving to and from King's Road (beginning at the south-west corner of the

6.16   Sloane Square – typical activities

space) and Sloane Square tube station (in the south-east corner). By contrast, observations at Trafalgar Square revealed how a once highly compromised space has been given two new and important roles within the city fabric as a social and movement space (**6.17**). Thus, at the time of observing during the summer of 2009, the square was home to Antony Gormley's 'One & Other' concept for the fourth plinth in which 2,400 members of the public from across the UK were occupying the plinth over a period of 100 days (see **6.24**). The concept was clearly alien to the formal and serious side of the space, but along with other

events drew huge crowds and demonstrated how a lighter and more active engagement with the space can exist side by side with its other roles, in the process bringing new users to appreciate the space.

It is impossible to know how the Sloane Square scheme would have performed had the crossroads scheme been implemented, although a postscript to the story may be relevant here. In 2009, a small 13 by 13 metre portion of the square at Holbein Place in the south-east corner leading from Sloane Square Underground Station was redesigned to incorporate a flat shared surface without kerbs (**6.18**). This continuous floor treatment reflects what would have been secured, on a much larger scale, if the crossroads scheme had gone ahead. Once complete, this small intervention was immediately attacked by an alliance of groups coordinated by the national Guide Dogs for the Blind charity, who argued 'We believe strongly that all road users, including pedestrians, must be considered in any new street design. It is surely wrong to think that a new street which cannot be used by some pedestrians because of the lack of key navigation cues, can be a success' (Guide Dogs 2009). By contrast, the largest residents' group in the area – the Chelsea Society (2010: 4) – report that the thousands who go in and out of the station seem to find it convenient to be able to walk on the flat, even if they sometimes encounter cars and vans. To allay fears, the borough's traffic engineers have inserted rows of warning studs in the paviours on either side of the route taken by

6.17 Trafalgar Square observational analysis of user patterns – typical local movement patterns (a), density of activity (b) and typical activities (c)

a

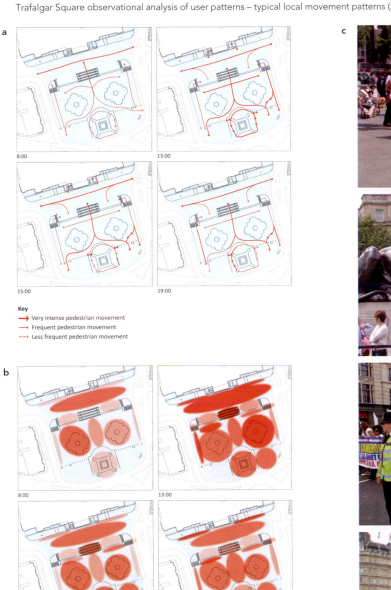

8:00

13:00

15:00

19:00

Key

⟶ Very intense pedestrian movement

⟶ Frequent pedestrian movement

⇢ Less frequent pedestrian movement

b

8:00

13:00

15:00

19:00

Key

Few activities

Moderate activity

Intense activity

High concentration of activity

c

6.18   Sloane Square – Holbein Place, shared surface

6.19   Trafalgar Square – user perceptions

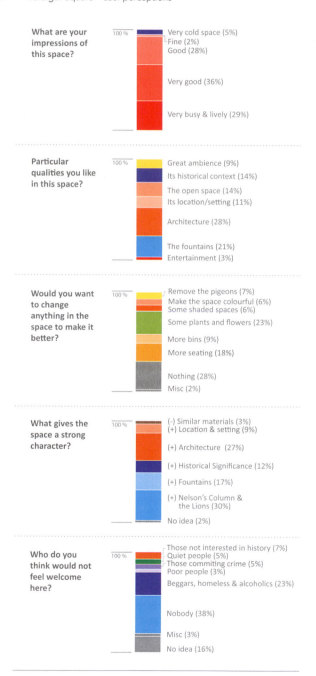

vehicles, 'SLOW' has been inscribed on the tarmac at the threshold to the shared surface, and two road signs saying 'pedestrians' have been put up to warn drivers. These, to some degree, defeat the object of creating a shared clutterless space, but may portend what would have been in store if the crossroads scheme had gone ahead.

The hugely successful intervention at Trafalgar Square, by contrast, demonstrates what can be achieved through what amount to relatively straightforward urbanistic interventions that work with the grain of an established historic context. For example, when asked what undermines the character of the space, just 5 per cent cited heavy traffic, suggesting that the changes to the layout had re-balanced the space to such a degree that, despite heavy traffic remaining along three sides of the space, this was no longer seen as a problem. The result is a scheme that users in large part agree is 'truly interesting, shared by all, and inspires a sense of belonging in its users' (user of Trafalgar Square) (**6.19**).

Managing civic space
Public (but private) management
The management of both Trafalgar Square and Sloane Square remain a public responsibility, and had the remodelling of Sloane Square gone ahead, Kensington & Chelsea Council would have retained the role, alongside their ownership of the space. In both cases, however,

6.20 Sloane Square – subject to standard management arrangements

6.21 Trafalgar Square – safety first (signs in the fountains)

the contracting out of day-to-day management responsibilities is the norm. Thus Sloane Square is subject to a seven-day-a-week cleansing regime (one clean a day and bins emptied three times a day), currently contracted out to Sita UK Ltd, as are the Council's graffiti cleaning and other specialist stewardship roles. In addition, they offer residents a Charter with certain guarantees about performance, whilst a detailed contract sets out performance expectations against an aspiration to achieve 'Grade A' standards across the borough (not always achieved – **6.20**), whilst the council's role is reduced to managing the contract, monitoring performance, interfacing with the public on management matters, and collecting fees from the council-owned and/or licensed trading pitches and public toilet along the busy south side of the Square.

As a strategic authority, the GLA provides few direct services to London, although the management of the central areas of Trafalgar Square and Parliament Square are amongst the few they do. Responsibilities include by-laws, maintenance, licensing and events management, whilst the highways and footpaths around, including the National Gallery Terrace, are managed by Westminster Council. Thus, when in 2005 Ken Livingstone wished to put a statue of Nelson Mandela in the newly created paved area, opposition from Westminster and English Heritage, who wished to prevent the newly created space from becoming cluttered, won the day. The statue was eventually

located within the GLA-controlled central garden area of Parliament Square. All services, most notably security, maintenance of the fabric and cleaning – although not events management – are performed by external contractors, whilst the GLA invites public comments within its annual squares review documents. Management is paid for through core GLA funds, supplemented in small part by the £90,000 or so received each year as income from the café, promotional activities and filming. The baseline is to protect the fabric and to ensure the safety of the public (**6.21**).

Secure spaces – actively, and not

Whilst Kensington & Chelsea sponsor the employment of additional Police Community Support Officers by the Metropolitan Police for deploying across the borough and maintain a network of 60 CCTV cameras, no special arrangements are made for Sloane Square, which also has no public CCTV. With the exception of discouraging pigeon feeding (also discouraged at Trafalgar Square, where pigeons are actively dispersed), and the control of traders through local by-laws, no other legal activities are specifically proscribed (or for that matter encouraged). The crossroads proposals would not have changed these basic arrangements.

By contrast, Trafalgar Square is more actively managed, with a philosophy of making the space available to all. Security is seen as an

6.22   Sloane Square – remembrance at the Sloane Square war memorial

6.23   Sloane Square – The Caravan, the 2009 performance in a caravan on Sloane Square for an audience of just eight

important part of this, with 24-hour 'Heritage Wardens' employed in the space to provide assistance to people and information about the square, and to prevent antisocial behaviour. The public highways and National Gallery Terrace also have Enforcement Officers contracted by Westminster Council, whilst major events security is managed by the Metropolitan Police. The square is surveyed through discreet CCTV, which, along with the on-ground 24-hour security presence, has dramatically cut crime in the space. Other behaviours, including sliding down the central staircase handrails and skateboarding, are prevented though design interventions.

Civic space or space of fun?

The absence of activity in the island of Sloane Square for much of the time and the nature of the types of events that do take place there give the Square a sober and civic feel, which the dissenters to the crossroads proposal aimed to preserve (**6.22**). Despite this, occasional events sanctioned by the council demonstrate a possible alternative vision for how the space could be used (**6.23**).

The GLA run the programme of events at Trafalgar Square and through their events management team determine what are and are not appropriate activities. Under this regime, the space has become a major London venue (see Chapter 3), with all necessary services

built into the space during its refurbishment to support this new purpose. Generally regarded as a major success, the programme illustrates 'how desperately London lacked a social civic space; the equivalent of the space outside of the Pompidou Centre in Paris or Bryant Park in New York' (steering group), and how this key function of city government had been missed. Two streams of events are managed in this fashion. First, there are those organised by the GLA with the support of the Mayor's Office. These tend to be large-scale cultural events such as St Patrick´s Day, Diwali, Vaisakhi, Pride, or the management of arts installations, including of the fourth plinth (see Chapter 3) (**6.24**). Second, an open application process exists for public gatherings, promotional events, and commercial filming or photography. There is no charge, but all have to be applied for in advance.

The very success of the square as an event space has bred some concern over the degree to which temporary events diminish the site's civic dignity. English Heritage, in particular, feel that the number of events (about 40 per year), the nature of some of them (e.g. letting of the space for commercial events) and the regular construction of a stage in the piazza (**6.25**) are unsympathetic to the formal and historic character of the Square, leading to surface damage in the process. Some argue that because the events are temporary, the essence of the space remains untouched, others that 'Optimising and balancing the utilisation of such a public space – rather than its constant overuse – is the real key to success' (traffic engineer). The nature of civic use and who defines it clearly goes to the heart of ongoing difficulties with the design and management of this sort of space.

EVALUATION

In essence, the projects at Trafalgar Square and Sloane Square were similar. Both involved already historic and well-loved spaces in the city, both involved dealing with thorny traffic issues, and both involved an attempt to reclaim space for pedestrians. Whilst Trafalgar Square seemed to be a relatively minor intervention on paper, although one with significant traffic impacts, the changes at Sloane Square from the start always seemed more radical. In effect, local residents saw a 'grand design' that, for them, removed a square and inserted a junction (the crossroads) – a perception that confused how traffic moved through the space with the nature of that space itself. In other words, instead of a space containing traffic, it became, in the minds of some local users, a road around which some leftover space remained.

Fundamentally, this reflected how the project was communicated, rather than its content. By contrast, communication at Trafalgar Square was always very carefully handled, and, despite the involvement of some big reputations (and egos) in the project, these were used positively to promote the scheme, and were never allowed to dominate the process: 'There are some places where you need something radical and innovative, and other places where you need something restrained and subservient to what you have already got' (steering group). The result is that 'Trafalgar Square is re-established as a world class square on the local, national and international scale' (traffic engineer), whilst Sloane Square is still an invaded place.

The stakeholders involved in the Trafalgar Square project are generally very positive about the outcomes: 'It has been made connected, safer, more attractive and more convenient, with better facilities, attractions, events, resources and management and security' (traffic engineer). Moreover, this positive assessment has been fairly universally shared

6.24 Trafalgar Square – Antony Gormley's 'One & Other'

by external reviewers of the scheme, including CABE (CABE, Trafalgar Square [n.d.]), the RIBA and English Heritage (2006: 19).

For those involved, key process lessons include the need for a powerful patron to champion the scheme: 'You need to have somebody driving such a complex project, if you don't have a strong local authority you need something else' (steering group). In this case, government ministers and then the Mayor gave the project its momentum. A strong steering group to bring together all the players with a part to play, early on, was also important – not least to solve likely problems in advance. The genius of the project, though, was in thinking through who the stakeholders were and how relationships could be handled politically to achieve the desired ends, all carefully backed up with thorough analytical work, which 'gave a lot of credibility to the proposals' (steering group) and helped to deflect a sometimes emotional local public. Delivery was then dependent on having a clear brief in place, with a budget confirmed at the onset, good project management, and, of course, the right design in which long-term management and maintenance had been thought through with adaptability and longevity in mind.

At Sloane Square, the final assessment of the two sides is as far apart as ever, as captured in the sentiments of the Deputy Leader of Kensington

6.25   Trafalgar Square – formal or informal space?

& Chelsea Council: 'the Council should have emulated the behaviour of the Metropolitan Borough of Chelsea in the 1930s and simply gone ahead with the proposals in the face of massive opposition'. For him the irony is that the scheme that was opposed so forcefully in the 1930s by the then local community is being defended tooth and nail today, whilst the crossroads plan envisaged a return (of sorts) to the pre-1930s situation. For the designers, this was a scheme of London-wide importance, for a London (not local) audience, but one that was hijacked by very local concerns. Whilst recognising that civic spaces

have to be held up to scrutiny by a far wider range of stakeholders than other forms of space, they argue that this also makes controversy more likely, and in such cases, letting schemes drag on only undermines momentum, and opens the door to derailing perfectly good schemes that would otherwise serve a wider interest.

English Heritage conclude that, in its detail rather than its broad concept, the scheme at Sloane Square threatened to undermine London's character, continuing a trend towards more continental-type spaces that say little about London. These trends continue to be a concern for them, and in this case were shared by the protesters who argued 'change should be rooted in tradition and the history of the locality' (Save Sloane Square). English Heritage argue that the borough and its designers should have been more amenable to criticism, and less dogmatic in sticking rigidly to their plan, whilst the Save Sloane Square group argue that the priority should be the 'repair' of existing streets and squares, rather than the creation of 'new ones' that should only be considered when support exists from all stakeholders. For them, it has been a massive effort to turn the situation around, and they feel let down that their alternative scheme has still not been implemented (as the council leader originally promised).

The perceptions reflect a wider concern around a tendency to over-design new public spaces, and to emphasise the grand design vision rather than the social needs that are being met (Worpole & Knox 2007: 13). Some have argued that this represents a potential fault with the urban renaissance agenda that dominated national (and London) policy since 2000 (see Chapter 4) and through which innovative design was sometimes seen as an end in itself, whether schemes required it or not (Worpole & Knox 2007: 3). This emphasis on the 'design solution' separated the two schemes. So whilst in Belgravia 'crossroads' became a dirty word, CABE conclude that 'To those hoping for "Barcelona Style" modernist interventions the results of the Trafalgar Square improvements will come as something of a disappointment. ... the success of the scheme lies in what is not visible or apparent. The traffic management in particular has enabled pedestrianisation ... [and] the extensive use of natural materials ... assist in achieving a seamless integration between old and new' (CABE, Trafalgar Square [n.d.]). For those new to Trafalgar Square, the changes might always have been there.

These two cases demonstrate that schemes involving civic space, by their very nature, invite the interest of a wider range of civil society than is otherwise the case in public space projects. In particular, because such schemes (in London) largely relate to existing historic spaces, the involvement of local communities and how that involvement is managed is critical. It was the ability of the local groups in wealthy Belgravia to organise themselves and project their case (and the inability of the promoters of the scheme to manage this) that gave them such power in the process, and it was this decisive factor

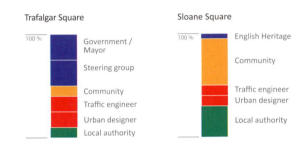

6.26   Relative stakeholder influences

that determined the variation in relative influence of key stakeholders in the resulting processes. These are represented (unscientifically) in **6.26**, which shows the driving hand at Trafalgar Square of the steering group, who where able to gain authority via careful analysis, high-profile design support and the political weight of their masters. At Sloane Square, the authority of the council and their designers and engineers was quickly undermined by the insurgent community.

Addressing the critique

From its origins as a consciously planned civic space, Trafalgar Square has had a clear public remit, both a representational one (of the city/state/empire) and a socio-political one, as the nation's gathering place. Sloane Square happened more by accident, as a space formed around a key junction that has gradually accrued civic meaning and a strong sense of local ownership. Although very different in history, scale and purpose, both spaces represent classic examples of the gradual subversion of public space by traffic, so much so that, by the end of the twentieth century, Trafalgar Square could be characterised as a splintered and fragmented environment in its own right, containing at its centre its own dissociated and neglected urban enclave. To a lesser degree, given the scale of the roads circumventing it, Sloane Square still is.

At their most basic therefore, both schemes first and foremost were traffic management schemes, aiming to re-balance the available space in favour of the pedestrian; at least in terms of the space available to those on foot, if not the capacity of vehicles to move through these areas. In fact, whilst Sloane Square would have maintained the same vehicle capacity, Trafalgar Square removed capacity, an effect re-balanced by the imposition of the Congestion Charge in central London, which reduced (to some degree) demand: 'The net effect for the public was that the traffic was about the same and the buses moved slightly more freely, a key requirement of the original masterplan' (urban designer). Nevertheless, it was traffic issues that dominated the opposition to development of both schemes, reflecting the complex relationships property-owning Londoners have with traffic (and their cars). Thus, whilst few wish to be inconvenienced by the closure of roads when they step into their own cars, even fewer would vote for more traffic outside their own front doors. This fear of displacement (and the inevitable but unspoken impact on property prices) represented a powerful source of opposition in both schemes, which, in the Sloane Square proposal, found succour in related criticisms around the loss of character that the detailed design of the crossroads scheme threatened (in the objectors' view) to impose.

Without this additional ammunition, it may be that the crossroads scheme might have survived to fruition. For their part Kensington & Chelsea seemed to have learnt from the process, and during the re-design of Exhibition Road (the next major public realm scheme in the borough), emphasised the nature of the project as a public space proposal, rather than a traffic scheme, in order to better steer the debate. Unfortunately, their determination to deliver a shared surface (or as near to one as possible) again courted controversy, and in a re-run of the Holbein Place dispute (see above), the council ended up battling an alliance of 28 disability groups led by Guide Dogs for the Blind in order to deliver this aspect of their proposals. Whilst the problem was eventually resolved with the installation of a strip of textured 'corduroy' paving along the road to replace the kerbs, a key lesson from Trafalgar Square seems to have been missed, namely that more important than any particular design of kerbs, surfaces, or street furniture is the relative distribution of space to pedestrians and traffic. Thus once pedestrians are given enough space to thrive, and are freed from the overpowering effects of traffic-dominant environments, they can quite happily exist alongside busy traffic. Indeed, as the experience at Holbein Place demonstrates, even if subjugated, traffic has a nasty way of re-asserting itself (in that case through studs in the paving and renewed signage). For its part, Trafalgar Square is still a busy junction, but is a renewed social, cultural and civic one as well.

If the re-unification of the centre of Trafalgar Square with its immediate hinterland has given a new social meaning and purpose to the space, this has been strongly encouraged by the very active management of the square; setting standards that users are quick to criticise if they see them slipping. Thus, through a combination of physical and management changes, Trafalgar Square has been re-interpreted, giving in the process this most traditional of civic spaces a new lease of life. The result is a space with particular appeal (it seems) to younger audiences and to audiences that at the time of survey were also heavily skewed to the middle classes, who (in common with some local residents around Sloane Square) were not always entirely generous in their views about less fortunate potential users; one user describing the homeless as 'nothing but a nuisance'. Civic space may be explicitly public, and therefore for all, but, in the view of some users, 'all' did not mean everyone.

Traditional civic-type space clearly does still have a role. Indeed, if the success of Trafalgar Square is anything to go by, there is a pent-up demand for this type of public space – no doubt alongside the other types of non-traditional spaces that some of the literature argues are so important. 'London now has a major outdoor civic space which it never had before. That is quite an achievement given that it was always in the context of an operating city and a square that had been designed 150 years previously. The project raised the bar in terms of what could be achieved' (urban designer), not least in making civic space fun.

7 SPACES OF THE CONSUMER CITY

CONSUMER LONDON

London owes its origins around AD50 to its strategic position on the River Thames in the most accessible (from Continental Europe) southeast corner of the country. There it was established as a largely civilian (as opposed to military) city that quickly became the capital of Roman Britain. Its strategic location leant itself to movement (by land and sea) and, importantly, to trade, which has been the mainstay of the city ever since.

Today, with an internal market of 7.5 million, a huge wider catchment across southeast England and beyond, and international visitor numbers in excess of any other city worldwide – 15.5 million in 2006 (Bremner 2007) – London has become a global centre for retailing, with consumer habits to match. The 2006 figures demonstrate the vital importance of retailing to London's economy. Of every £10 spent by Londoners, almost £4 went to the retail sector, whilst in that year around 9 per cent of Londoners worked in retail. The capital is home to 40,000 shops, many in its numerous high streets, at which Londoners spend more per head than any other part of the UK (GLA Economics 2006: 4–7, 15, 31).

Despite the 2008–09 recession, retail has been a section of London's economy that has powered ahead, with major shopping centres opening up in 2008 (Westfield at Shepherd's Bush), 2010 (One New Change in the City), and 2011 (Westfield at Stratford). Moreover, this growth is at both ends of the retail investment market, with central London shops continuing to see rising rents as strong retailer demand, notably from high-brand international chains, is focused on a finite stock (CBRE 2010: 13), whilst at the other end of the market pound stores have also thrived in London, reflecting something of the divided nature of the city. In 2009, London hosted 25 per cent of the country's 1,423 discount stores, reflecting a move of this type of retailing into more affluent areas where it helps to drive up footfall (Morris 2009).

From a business perspective, the London First Retail Commission (2009: 12) argue that a viable and diverse retail sector is critical to London's long-term success. For them, no one size fits all, and not every high street should try and emulate Marylebone High Street with its careful mix of small independent stores. The report argues that some of London's town centres have only remained strong during the 2008–09 downturn and beyond because of the pull of the national and international brands, although strength should not be linked solely to the representation of multiple retailers. What is clear is that the cost of conducting retail in London is generally high, for example in servicing costs (GLA Economics 2006: 36), whilst London comes top of retail rental league tables, with costs in prime locations at least twice those of equivalent locations in other UK cities (Jones Lang LaSalle 2008). Despite this, the consumer habits of Londoners and visitors to the city remain prime drivers for development in the city.

Retail has not just been the driver of major new shopping centres, it is also the oil that smoothes the wheels of much new and regenerated space in London, particularly schemes with major social/civic elements, effectively cross-funding them. It is the mainstay of the sorts of active ground floor uses that urban design theory and planning policy requires developers to provide. Thus DTZ (2008: 27) in their research for the British Council of Shopping Centres highlight as good practice the case of The Centre in Feltham, west London. There, a redevelopment of 60 retail units with active frontage onto the existing high street and residential development on top has helped to cross-fund affordable housing, public transport improvements, a library and a community health centre. The development, like many others across London, demonstrates how physical regeneration can clearly be achieved and public goods delivered through retail development, although in this case without any significant investment in the public realm (**7.1**). The scheme demonstrates how retail (even in large quantities) can only fund so much, and if it is libraries and health centres, it is unlikely at the same time to be public space. In essence,

7.1   The Centre, Feltham – the public space elements amount to little more than an enclave (a) off a major new 1,000 space car park on to which much of the new active frontage faces (b)

a

b

these and similar spaces are wholly consumption spaces as they have no other purpose than parking and transit in order to consume.

Through a focus on the consumer city, this chapter examines two closely related critiques concerned with the problematic of space dedicated to consumption and the phenomenon of homogenisation that this (and other trends) give rise to.

THE CRITIQUES

Consumption space

The notion of consumption space might be viewed in two separate lights:

1 as space in which the activity of consumption takes place, be that purchase of goods (retail), of food (restaurants, cafes, etc.) or services (corporate hospitality, advertising, etc.)

2 as the consumption of space itself, in which the space (and what goes on there) becomes the spectacle to be consumed just like any other product.

Each potentially gives rise to pressures for homogenisation.

Consumption of space

Sorkin (1992: xiii–xv) describes a world dominated by multinational companies, producing a standard urbanism where public space is for consumption. For him, this is a type of global space where economic phenomena cross over to society and culture, and where public space is at the forefront in creating a city of simulation with spaces defined by pseudo-historic links to the past. His arguments cross over with those already discussed (see Chapter 5) relating to the notion of invented space, although, to be consumed, spaces do not have to be invented from scratch or even reinvented. The phenomena of global mass tourism, for example, can quickly turn formerly historic and meaningful places into just another photo-opportunity on the tourist trail. Some of London's prime and emerging attractions have something of this quality (**7.2**).

Hajer and Reijndorp (2001: 49–50) note an unprecedented increase in the deliberate consumption of places and events as a consequence of the dramatic expansion and domination of the middle classes in developed countries: 'A phenomenon that has mushroomed in recent years concerns the desire of the ordinary citizen to have "interesting" experiences. Leisure experts talk about an "experience market".

7.2 Borough Market – gentrified market space, now firmly on the tourist trail

7.3 Burlington Arcade – the original 'exclusive' shopping mall, replete, then as now, with its own private security or Beadles

Where all kinds of events are offered that can excite people for a short time, from factory sales to art biennials.' Thus cities compete with each other by producing experiences.

For them, this is a worrying trend, since producers and managers of public space have to continually revise and update their formulae to keep in tune with consumer (meaning public) preferences and expectations for something new. Boyer (1994: 408) explores the question of simulation further, and how postmodern cities contain layers of history and symbolism that can be manipulated and exploited as an instrument of late capitalism. For Knox (2005: 5), neo-traditional new urbanist space 'represents the design community's best-articulated response' to the cult of 'fast' consumerism; although its overriding concern for physical form leaves it with little to say about the social construction of place. Boyer (1994), on the other hand, sees the postmodern return to history and the evocation of the past as an overt attempt by political and social authorities to recreate a familiar and cherished local scene in which visual memories are manipulated to combat social tensions and the impact of uneven urban and economic development. She observes, however, that whilst some districts in cities may be carefully designed in this manner, they are unlikely to cater for all in society, not least because to fully engage will usually require consumption in, as well as consumption of, space.

Consumption in space

Exchange of goods and services has always been a core function of public space, and cities have long possessed consumption opportunities for every taste and wallet. Nevertheless, a significant body of literature argues that the pervasiveness of retail in public space can, through design and management strategies, act to explicitly exclude certain groups and encourage others through financial means.

This might be overt, for example by charging an entry fee, tied to a series of codified rules and regulations often specified on the ticket. In London with its free parks, museums and art galleries, this is rare within the public realm, although to enter and ride the London Underground and other transport infrastructure does incur a charge, as does entry to some otherwise publicly owned facilities such as the Royal Botanic Gardens at Kew. A more subtle practice involves establishing visual cues which communicate that only those with the ability to pay are welcome, and that those who fall outside this category will be treated with suspicion, or even physically barred (actively or less actively filtered out – Németh 2008: 2479). For those who enter, it is necessary to advertise their right of entry through a separate set of visual cues, for example the clothes they wear (Carmona *et al.* 2003: 127). Exclusive shopping arcades fall into this category, outwardly welcoming all – at least all with the ability to consume. In London, these date back to at least 1819 and the opening of Burlington Arcade between Bond Street and Piccadilly as the forerunner to Europe's nineteenth-century grand arcades, which led, in time, to the now ubiquitous covered shopping mall (**7.3**).

By the same token, Loukaitou-Sideris & Banerjee (1998: 291) argue that although public space in traditional cities serves as a venue for political debate, this is explicitly discouraged in the consumption space that characterises such privately owned places where 'Owners and developers want their space to be "apolitical". [Instead] they separate users from unnecessary social or political distractions, and put users into the mood consistent with their purposes' – to consume.

Mattson (1999: 135–6) discusses this trend in the context of American suburban shopping malls and argues that many are examples of what sociologists call a 'total institution' in which the outside world is intentionally locked out so as not to divert shoppers' attention from their primary responsibility, to shop. However, as malls have increasingly become the only central gathering place in many communities, 'the activities of regular citizens who leaflet, protest, or otherwise use malls as public space have resulted in a number of contentious court cases'. In the USA, many states have come down on the side of protecting private property rights over the constitutional rights to free speech, with only a minority validating a view that malls are in fact public spaces. 'Citizens have made clear that they need places where they can interact with fellow citizens and try to persuade others of their viewpoints. Malls, they have argued, must serve as these places, simply because they focus public interaction within a defined arena. In making the argument, these citizens have recognised a key weakness in the contemporary suburban landscape – a lack of public space and the insidious impact of that lack on democracy' (Mattson 1999: 136–7).

In London, most shopping centres have been associated with existing traditional high streets such as the Bentall Centre in Kingston upon Thames or Ealing's Broadway Shopping Centre. By contrast, free-standing mega-shopping malls have tended to be relegated to the very edge of suburban London, notably Brent Cross, Bluewater, and Lakeside. However, with the move of this type to Inner London, notably the two Westfields (Stratford and Shepherd's Bush), the critique now has greater resonance, although the structure of London is still distinguished by over 600 lengths of traditional high street (outside the central area – Carmona *et al.* 2010a: 32), from the affluent King's Road in Chelsea, to the down-at-heel Commercial Road in Stepney. As such, the impact on democracy and citizen freedom, if present, is likely to be relatively small on a London-wide basis, although the knock-on impact of such developments on the types of spaces used by less affluent and less mobile sections in society, such as London's traditional high streets, and the wider narrative associated with the gentrification of less affluent consumption spaces – including London's markets (see the discussion of Queen's Market in Chapter 4) – may be more significant.

The homogenisation of public space?

For Minton (2009: 31), however, the management of London's private shopping complexes remains a significant concern, not least because of the rather vague and non-specific assurances about public access and the rights of owners to exclude users that are typically written into otherwise voluminous planning applications. Equally significant is what for her is the anonymous nature of the resulting spaces. Speaking about her experience of visiting the new Westfield at Shepherd's Bush, she complains: 'There were lots and lots of shops and acres of pristine marble floors, but little to distinguish this place from any other or to remind me that I was in west London, with Television Centre outside the doors and down-at-heel Shepherd's Bush Green down the road. ... I didn't feel as if I was in Shepherd's Bush, but ... more as if I was in an airport, behind the departure gates, in that transnational shopping area, a place which is neither home nor abroad' (Minton 2009: 17–18).

Minton's critique represents a dimension of a much wider set of concerns around 'placelessness' and the consequential loss of attachment to place (Carmona *et al.* 2010b: 123–5). Many have argued that global economic changes have meant that urban public space is now recognised as a valuable commercial commodity, and global business in partnership with city governments has re-ordered the historic functions of public space through the production of new forms of space that bring together those in society who can afford to consume. As cities increasingly compete for investment at a national and international level, they need to create environments that are seen as safe and attractive and that offer the range of amenities and facilities that their (increasingly white collar) workers, and the tourists that they hope to attract, expect (Madanipour 2003: 224). Elsewhere, where global investment is sparse (e.g. in parts of East London), abandonment and neglect may be the order of the day. Hajer and Reijndorp (2001) conclude, 'The consumption of space in the urban field is thus on the one hand focussed on the massive increase in "events" and positive places, and on the other, the equally massive avoidance of all kinds of negative aspects of social progress.'

New forms of public space are linked to the move to late capitalism and mass consumption, which is significantly different from previous historic periods or the economic systems in place at the start of Modernism, and can be generically described as globalisation. These forms of contemporary public spaces use symbolism in design as described by Boyer (1994) as a wider part of postmodernism's referencing to history and culture (see above) – symbolism when combined with entertainment that can be viewed as populist (Light and Smith 1998) or lacking the public sphere nature of public space (Sennett 1990). Together, these trends act, it is argued, to sanitise the built environment and create a homogenised form of urbanism that is replicated across the globe – to what Sorkin (1992) describes as departicularised urbanism.

Such investment and management trends may be exacerbated by a further impact of globalisation, namely the speeding up of ideas and influences around the globe. Today, designers, developers and clients in both the public and private sectors are no longer tied to particular localities, but operate across regions and states, and increasingly on an international stage. The result is that design formulae are repeated from place to place with little thought to context. Thus London's new Westfield shopping centres are built by an Australian property company that also owns similar 'Westfield' malls in Australia, New Zealand and the USA, designed with the assistance of transnational retail design specialists such as Benoy and Gabellini Sheppard. For

Zukin (1998: 837), it is the very competition amongst cities and corporations that 'has led to a multiplicity of standardised attractions that reduce the uniqueness of urban identities even while claims of uniqueness grow more intense'.

Locally, also, development processes may assist in trends towards the homogenisation of public space. These are likely to be many and various, but might include:

● the adopted guidelines and control practices that parrot generic globalised design principles which may or may not be appropriate locally

● de-skilling in local governments with consequential pressures to adopt standards-based regulatory processes for assessing design

● the marketisation of property, with pressures to standardise real estate types in order that they can be exchanged just like other commodities

● the perceived 'compensation culture', as a result of which public authorities have been attempting to design out risks in public space as a means to manage their liabilities in case of accidents and other dangers

● the power and spread of national multiples and global brands with the power to drive development processes and shape local environments in their image.

The notion of brands contributing to the 'cloning' of British high streets and the loss of identity and local character that goes with it represents the central charge of work undertaken by the New Economics Foundation (2004: 2). In a highly charged polemic, they argue 'In place of real local shops has come a near-identical package of chain stores replicating the nation's high streets. ... Many town centres that have undergone substantial regeneration lost the distinctive facades of their high streets, as local building materials have been swapped in favour of identical glass, steel and concrete storefronts that provide the ideal degree of sterility to house a string of big, clone town retailers.' They quote Nick Foulkes, who, writing in the *Evening Standard* and commenting on the London scene, observed that 'The homogenisation of our high streets is a crime against our culture. The smart ones get the international clones – Ralph Lauren, DKNY, Starbucks and Gap; while those lower

7.4   Covent Garden – a spectacle for all, now being 'value-engineered' upwards

down the socio-economic hierarchy end up with Nando's, McDonalds, Blockbuster and Ladbrokes' (New Economics Foundation 2004: 2). Of these, only Ladbrokes (the betting chain) is originally a British brand.

In London, Covent Garden represents a case in point. The area has become an international tourist phenomenon since being saved from demolition in the 1970s (see Chapter 2), but the mix of off-the-wall and affordable chic outlets it once housed is being driven upmarket by the explicit strategy of owners Capital & Counties Properties as part of their strategy to 'unlock latent value' from their estates (CAPCO 2010: 1). This may simply continue a pattern already well established through which Covent Garden was 'cleansed of undesirables and its inveterate

working class so as to make way for "higher order" and more profitable future activities' (Merrifield 1996: 65). Whilst tourists may continue to consume the carefully curated spectacle (**7.4**), in the future, the average middle-class Londoner may not be able to afford the goods on offer. A by-product of the strategy being adopted at Covent Garden is also, potentially, the homogenisation of the place, with independent and home-grown brands increasingly swapped for the international upmarket brands that frequent 'exclusive' (meaning expensive) retail locations around the world – Armani, Burberry, Apple, etc. These offer the same image and products, everywhere.

CONSUMPTION SPACES

The notion of consumption space is perhaps a difficult one given that many of the case studies examined in this book include consumption elements of one type or another, from the café in Trafalgar Square (Chapter 6) to the retail elements that dominate the spaces of the domestic sphere as discussed in Chapter 9. Yet spaces whose *raison d'être* is consumption were less frequently found. The London-wide analysis (Chapter 4) showed that less than a tenth of new or regenerated squares are of this kind.

Spaces in this category vary hugely – from the types of space found within the retail mega-malls discussed above, to the more sedate spaces of London's burgeoning café culture (**7.5**). They are highly animated, with active edges, and often feature obvious homogenisation through branding and the design of standardised retail units. Typically, these spaces are in private ownership and range from the flashy to the utilitarian, although increasingly facilities and institutions in public and pseudo-public ownership see such spaces as opportunities to cross-subsidise their core business. This chapter focuses on this latter type of space and deliberately does not examine the spaces associated with London's large retail developments, a type that have been extensively researched and written about in the literature and that, in the main, are internalised environments that fall outside the scope of the types of traditional public spaces examined in this book. Instead, three smaller developments with consumption space at their heart form the focus of the case studies, each in their way using retail to subsidise the core functions of the wider developments within which they sit: respectively infrastructure

7.5   Duke of York Square – upmarket retail, restaurants and cafés adjacent to Sloane Square, Chelsea

(Euston Station Piazza), community building (Gabriel's Wharf) and cultural amenities (Festival Square).

Euston Station Piazza – for 'operational purposes'

The history of what is today known as Euston Station Piazza is irrevocably linked to one of the critical moments in the evolution of British urban policy, namely the decision in the early 1960s to demolish the Victorian Euston Station, the first inner-city station in London complete with its grand hall and the imposing classical Euston Arch (**7.6**). This caused a huge stir, and the resulting campaign to save the arch followed by the eventual decision of the then Prime Minister (Harold Macmillan) not to intervene in the matter was a key building block in the establishment of a strong conservation movement in Britain and the eventual discrediting of clean-sweep Modernism. For Euston, however, this came too late and the Victorian buildings were replaced in 1968 by a largely unremarkable Modernist station, replete with external forecourt over the station car park.

The space was completed by the construction of an office development around its other three sides designed by the commercial architect

7.6 Site of Euston Station Piazza

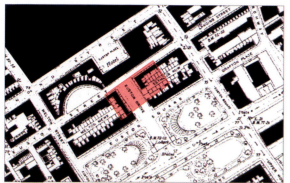

1910s

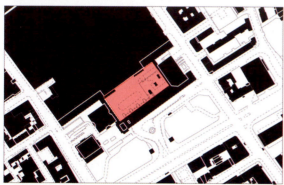

1970s

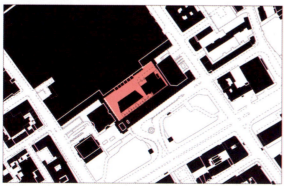

2010

7.7 Euston Station Piazza – retail pods added from 2005 onwards

Richard Seifert (**7.6**). This constituted three high-rise towers and a horizontal block using air rights over a new bus station to enclose the south side of the forecourt. The space itself included little more than hard concrete landscaping, although over the years various attempts

to humanise it with greenery, benches and public art were made. The space was broadly 'civic' in nature, intended to set-off the new station as a monument to the coming in the 1960s of the electric age (to rail), whilst also celebrating the glory days of the past with the inclusion of a statue of Robert Stephenson that had previously stood in the old ticket hall. The forecourt was windswept (the high buildings and undercrofts creating unfortunate wind-tunnel effects), drab and without real function. It was echoed to the south of the Seifert towers by another space, this time 'green' and owned and managed by the London Borough of Camden, namely the carved-up and unloved remnants of the once grand Euston Square (built 1813 – see Chapter 10).

Despite plans by Network Rail (the publicly owned operators of the station) to comprehensively redevelop the station in the future, in 2009 a number of interim projects were undertaken to improve the operation of the station. In line with a strategy pursued since the 1980s to commercialise Britain's railway stations to take advantage of the revenue-generating opportunities of so many users passing through these spaces (in 2005–06, approximately 24.6 million passengers journeyed through Euston Station, a figure expected to rise to 70 million by 2013). Typically, such schemes have involved shops, cafes and restaurants, and from 2005 Network Rail began to experiment with the siting of temporary free-standing fast food units (**7.7**) within the forecourt, which was quickly re-named Euston Station

7.8 Site of Festival Riverside

1910s

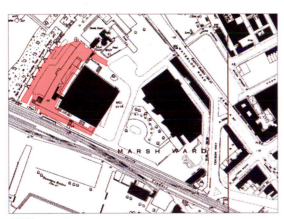

1950s

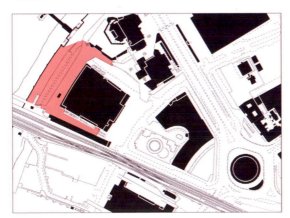

2010

Piazza. Not only did this bring in a new revenue stream, but effectively extended the interior station concourse outside, replete with its own departure board.

The success of this venture led to the more comprehensive (although still temporary) attempt to remodel the piazza in 2009. This time the work involved the construction of lightweight restaurant units along the south side of the space, its re-paving, extensive new seating, and the repositioning of the free-standing units along the north side next to the station itself. The aim was to maximise commercial income whilst alleviating the congestion of people in and out of the station. Network Rail undertook the piazza refurbishment through their commercial property arm Spacia, who identified the type and number of retail spaces. The train operating companies that use Euston were consulted, whilst the station management looked at the operational implications of the proposals. Camden, by contrast, had only minimal involvement in the project, since Network Rail argued that the works were for 'operational purposes', for which no permission is required under the Railways Acts. Other interested but sidelined parties included TfL (who operate the tube station under the concourse and the bus station), British Land (freeholder of the Seifert office buildings) and Sydney and London Properties (leaseholders of the Seifert office buildings). In 2010, three separate plans existed for the long-term re-development of the station prepared separately by Sydney & London, Network Rail with development partner British Land, and Camden. Camden's Framework Plan includes the requirement for additional public urban space in front of a new station and enhanced visual and physical permeability from Euston Road. That, and the other plans, are for the future.

Festival Riverside – culture commercialised

The south bank of the Thames has had a history as a subsidiary and service centre to the activities occurring on the north bank, with (until the Second World War) the riverfront being devoted to wharves and warehouses and functions of ill repute (**7.8**). Bombing during the war and clearance for the 1951 Festival of Britain swept all that away, at which time the Royal Festival Hall was built by the London County Council, with Leslie Martin, Peter Moro and Robert Matthew leading the architects team. The building, along with a new riverside walkway, was the only element of the exhibition to survive after the Festival of Britain closed. The hall subsequently became part of the larger Southbank Centre complex, when, in 1964, foyers and an upper

Festival Terrace were added to its riverside. The terrace was later joined to the network of raised concrete walkways to serve neighbouring buildings of the complex.

The building, housing one of the world's premier performance venues, was listed Grade I in 1988 but by 2000 was deteriorating whilst the Southbank Centre (which was always considered ugly and alienating by the public) remained isolated, often deserted and threatening, and generally in need of regeneration. In fact, there had been several masterplans for the site. The first, by Terry Farrell in 1986, was abandoned in 1991 following the commercial property collapse. The second, by Richard Rogers in 1994, involved roofing over much of the Southbank Centre, but became highly politicised and failed to get Lottery Funding. Finally, in 2000, Rick Mather Architects were appointed to be the masterplanners for the whole site, having gained their commission via an international competition set by the Southbank Employers Group (an alliance of about 20 employer organisations in the area). They proposed the refurbishment of the Royal Festival Hall as the key element in the regeneration of the Southbank area, but, as part of the masterplannng process, had also been tasked to identify commercial opportunities to cross-fund the scheme. Foremost amongst these were a proposed row of seven shop/catering units on the riverside frontage of the hall and under the Festival Terrace. These opened in 2005, displacing office space into a new building at the higher level running along the west side of the hall, which also had retail space underneath. The hall reopened in 2007.

The design strategy to regenerate the Southbank was funded by the Southbank Employers Group, match-funded by the government, although the initiator and lead stakeholder at the Royal Festival Hall was the Southbank Centre itself, the charity in charge of the 21-acre Southbank complex and all of its venues. For their part, the London Borough of Lambeth supported the Southbank in the refurbishment and regeneration of the public spaces around the Royal Festival Hall, although they took a facilitating rather than a controlling role. Rick Mather continued to supervise implementation of the overall masterplan and the way the building interfaces with the public realm, whilst Allies and Morrison undertook the detailed design of the refurbished Festival Hall, including landscaping the upper Festival Terrace. Gross Max landscaped the lower Festival Riverside adjacent to the river walk, and other spaces around the building.

Gabriel's Wharf – temporary place with staying power

Further east along the river from the Southbank Centre is the estate of Coin Street Community Builders. This area had not been touched by the Festival of Britain and in the immediate post-war period retained the warehouses and wharfs that had historically been the mainstay of the area (**7.9**). By 1970, however, the area was largely derelict and ripe for redevelopment. After fighting off plans for a huge office development (designed by Richard Rogers) on the Southbank in the 1970s and early 1980s, local residents set up a development trust and social enterprise, Coin Street Community Builders, which in 1984 bought the 13-acre Southbank site from the GLC in its dying days. The knockdown price was just £1 million, on the understanding that the site would be used for provision of social housing and other supporting uses (Coin Street Community Builders 2002). The case was all the more remarkable for occurring at a time when social housing elsewhere was being sold off, rather than renewed, and when big business rather than community was resurgent (Baeten 2009).

Because this was a long-term endeavour, in the short run, Coin Street Community Builders were left with large areas of cleared derelict site. At the time, Urban Space Management (USM) were involved in running Thames Days in the area and opened discussions with Coin Street Community Builders about the use of Gabriel's Wharf for a temporary market and venue for arts and crafts units based on the 'alternative development' strategy discussed in Chapter 2 and first trialled by USM at Camden Lock. A 50/50 joint venture partnership was signed for the development of a temporary four-year project on a site designated in the Coin Street Masterplan as housing for the elderly. Gabriel's Wharf was opened in 1988, together with the completed riverside walkway and a new park adjacent to the retained OXO building. At the time, the Southbank was a deserted and unloved place and the aim was to prove that the area could be a viable and desirable place, and that commercial uses could be used to support social housing. The intention was to overcome the sense of dereliction and to animate the area seven days a week through shopping and restaurants at Gabriel's Wharf (and later in the OXO building).

USM acted as the developer, designer and manager of the scheme, borrowing the money to deliver the project whilst Coin Street Community Builders put in the land. The joint venture partnership was disbanded in 1993 when Coin Street took the wharf and its management

7.9   Site of Gabriel's Wharf

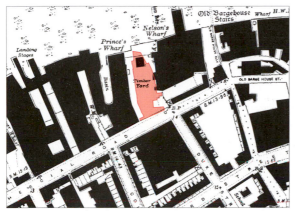

1910s

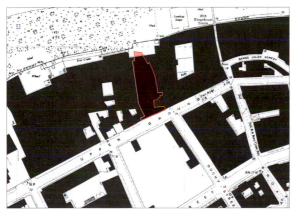

1950s

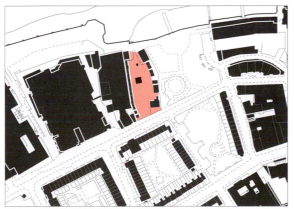

2010

7.10   Festival Terrace: an integral part of the new space, linking and connecting east and west / north and south / above and below

in-house. According to the Coin Street Community Builders, at that time the attention of USM had been diverted elsewhere and Gabriel's Wharf was 'half un-let and looking a bit sorry for itself' (manager). Today, 24 years after its creation, the site is still operating in its temporary use, at the heart of which is an informal space around which low-cost small temporary retail units sit. Initially, the space contained a market but in 2011 the wharf hosts 13 independent design and art shops, a complementary therapy studio, bicycle hire, six restaurant/café outlets and a resident sculptor – Freidel Bueckling – who fills the space with his work.

Designing consumer space
Meeting wider design objectives ... or not

The three cases showed very different approaches to the potential of design to address issues beyond those of the immediate site. At Southbank, the masterplan sought to address head-on one of the critical flaws in the area, namely to improve the legibility and permeability of the site, making it a safer and a more enjoyable place. The Festival Riverside and redesigned terrace (to which it links) were critical components of this scheme, allowing better connection to the Golden Jubilee Bridges (and from there across the river), southwards to Waterloo and east to the rest of the Southbank complex (**7.10**). The scheme aimed to remove the ambiguity of the previous spaces

7.11   Euston Station Piazza – route to the bus station, tenuous and illegible

7.12   Gabriel's Wharf – the bandstand is the only part of the temporary construction that has been replaced after the original bandstand fell down

and enhance connection between the ground plane and the raised walkways.

By contrast, at Euston, the aspirations for more commercial and commuter space were pragmatic and short-term, and the wider design aspirations limited. Thus, although the insertion of new retail units in the space and removal of the random landscape and street furniture features that had been added in the past helped to establish a more coherent and contained space (and seating area), this was at the expense of the retail units turning their backs on the bus station and undermining, rather than improving, connectivity and way-finding (**7.11**). The temporary nature of Gabriel's Wharf also meant that a wider potential urbanistic role was never considered. Thus, although the space links the river walk through to Upper Ground (which runs parallel to the river to the south), creating a route through the site, the scheme has never been linked to the new park that sits immediately adjacent to the site, and retains instead a continuous wall along its eastern boundary. Gates also exist to the north and south so that the space is technically lockable to avoid a right of way being established across the site.

Creating an event
The idea at Gabriel's Wharf was instead to create a destination on the

river, an event that nearly quarter of a century later still works, despite appearing a little down at heel (*Time Out* magazine christened it 'the last frontier town' – Coin Street Community Builders 2008: 21). The large mural that was initially painted along the western wall of the site (above the retail units) adds to this impression – a visually distinctive element that is now faded whilst the space itself has gradually been allowed to fill with wooden sculptures and other objects, adding to a slightly chaotic feel. A bandstand was constructed as part of the original scheme at the centre of the space and provides a visual heart to the space and an image that has been used to market it (**7.12**).

The design of the Festival Riverside was inspired by the playfulness of the Festival of Britain, for example its nautical theme, including boat masts acting as lightning poles. The landscape design sought to enhance the linearity of the riverside walk and people's movement through whilst at the same time establishing a distinct pause with an amphitheatre following the curve of the river, 'pulling the curve of the river back in' (landscape designer) and offering a sense of a beach and seaside (**7.13**). People can sit on the steps, around the trees (on benches) or at the cafes, or look down from the terrace above at the activities below. Although originally conceived in the 1960s to be a lively space in contrast to the quieter river walk

7.13   Festival Riverside – an event on the riverside

7.14   Robert Stephenson – relocated to reinforce the historic pedigree of the station

below, Festival Terrace is now a quieter (although on sunny days still busy) space where it is possible to get away from the crowds that throng the riverside. The relationship between higher and lower spaces aims to draw people in to the site and away from the river establishing a place to pause, take-in and engage with the spectacle of the riverside walk.

Commercial distinctiveness, important or not?

The Southbank Centre and Network Rail both took advantage of already huge local footfalls to commercialise their estates, whilst, in its early days, Gabriel's Wharf had to use commercial development to draw a clientele, and needed a distinctive offer to achieve that. At Festival Riverside, the location, architecture and quality of design, together with regular installations and events, were seen by stakeholders as the distinctive elements, whilst the type of tenants and any homogenisation they cause was a much less significant concern: 'There were issues of balancing the commercial uses with the listed building status and the need to ensure appropriate open space. These were considered during the planning process, but in general the commercial units were seen as positive, and the commercialisation a price worth paying for the greater benefits' (planner). Not least, these establish active frontage (day and night), helping to overcome the previous perception of the area as hostile.

At Euston, commercialisation provided the *raison d'être* for the whole scheme, with 2,000 square feet of retail space inside the station swapped for 10,000 outside. Thus, with the exception of moving the Robert Stephenson statue to a more prominent location (**7.14**), neither the distinctiveness of the design nor the commercial mix were considered important factors, although in the future, with the possible redevelopment of the whole station (including the potential to reinstate the Euston Arch), these factors will be greater concerns.

For Gabriel's Wharf, the mix of attractions was the sole draw: 'Gabriel's Wharf was the first scheme of quality in the area to cater for this market'

7.15   Gabriel's Wharf – needed to be commercially distinctive to attract an audience

(manager) (**7.15**). As such, the scheme was not directed at the Coin Street residents, but instead targeted to attract more affluent users from across London and tourists from further afield. The restaurants and cafes were also seen as facilities for local workers who, at the time, were largely without provision in the area. The tenants were carefully chosen to give a particular feel and to establish a distinctive community of occupiers and sense of place.

Developing consumer space
Avoiding public scrutiny …
A curious characteristic of each of the schemes examined in this chapter is the absence – in large part – of public scrutiny during the development process. Euston Station Piazza was perhaps the most extreme in this respect, where the nature of the space changed entirely for 'operational purposes' (see above), despite the space

itself sitting outside the curtilage of what most observers might regard as the station proper. In fact it sits on 'operational land', in connection with which Network Rail needs only to inform the local borough, Camden, about its plans. The only regulatory process was the formal 'Station Change' procedure, requiring sign-off by the train operating companies and the Rail Regulator. Beyond that, the entire process, including the construction of the new buildings, was handled within Network Rail, which, for example, checked and approved the plans of each retailer. Gabriel's Wharf, by contrast, was subject to formal planning requirements, but sits on the boundary of the London Boroughs of Lambeth and Southwark, neither of which had a significant role in the scheme, being far more interested in the housing elements at Coin Street rather than in what was seen as the temporary installation at Gabriel's Wharf. Planning permission was therefore obtained very quickly, in just three months, for a part of the wider masterplan that has provided an important public interface to the development ever since.

At the Royal Festival Hall, the regulatory processes relating to this Grade I listed building were of a different order, although the urbanistic implications of commercialising the waterfront were not a major factor, and, despite the prominence of this part of its territory, Lambeth was happy for the Southbank Centre to take the lead and instead took on a largely enabling and supportive role whilst firmly tying down the social and public benefits of the scheme in a (Section 106) planning agreement. In part, this is explained by the preoccupation of the council with the more deprived parts of their borough, but also by their confidence in the Southbank Centre and Southbank Employers Group who had demonstrated themselves more than capable of dealing with the riverside in the broad public interest.

... whilst involving others

For the Southbank Centre, relationships with other stakeholders have been carefully nurtured over time through establishing a steering committee consisting of Lambeth, the GLA, English Heritage and themselves, and to which each stage of the project has been presented. Over time, this has established a coalition of interests and ensured a strong sense of ownership for the project, helping also to secure funding from the Heritage Lottery Fund and other sources. Ken Livingstone, for example, was an active supporter of the regeneration plan, persuading TfL under its walking budget and the London Development Agency (LDA) to contribute to making the public realm

elements happen. Extensive consultation focused on the masterplan, with most public attention (and concern) expressed around the future fate of Jubilee Gardens (a designated area of Metropolitan Open Land to the west of the scheme), rather than on the details of the space around the Royal Festival Hall.

Stemming from their origins as local community activists, Coin Street Community Builders have nurtured a similarly inclusive process to advancing their aspirations with a board that still consists of local people. Even at Euston, and despite the avoidance of regulatory scrutiny, the plans were subjected to views of potential users in order to help frame aspirations for the site. Thus Network Rail met with Camden, representatives from the Department for Transport, and a range of passenger, disability and cycling groups. However, the absence of stakeholders with formal power in the process (beyond Network Rail) ensured that any potential wider benefits of the scheme were not considered, with the entire project based around the needs of commuters and maximisation of commercial value to re-invest in the station. Indeed an early proposal to build a covered sitting area was rejected for fear that it might attract users from the surrounding area, adding to an already congested station.

Doing it slowly

All three schemes reflected a similar dilemma, how to address short-term imperatives whilst at the same time striving towards long-term goals. Both the Euston and Gabriel's Wharf schemes adopted temporary solutions to their sites, although of quite different orders, with the Euston scheme estimated to cost £3–4 million for the piazza as part of a wider package of alterations to the station costing £11 million and expected to have a five- to six-year lifespan. By contrast, Gabriel's Wharf took an investment of just £140,000 (in 1988) to get the development up and running, with the development still making a return on the initial investment in 2012, although for how much longer it is unclear. For Network Rail, the huge numbers of passengers through Euston and the commercial potential they represent made the scheme both viable and necessary whilst much more complex and time-consuming redevelopment plans are worked on for the station as a whole, and its surrounds. Even there, however, funding problems meant that initial design aspirations had to be compromised, with, for example, the initial choice of pavement material being replaced by a cheaper one that is difficult to clean (it cannot be steam- or jet-washed and has to be scrubbed), and cheaper benches.

7.19   Euston Station Piazza observational analysis of user patterns – typical local movement patterns (a), density of activity (b) and typical activities (c)

7.20   Festival Riverside observational analysis of user patterns – typical local movement patterns (a), density of activity (b) and typical activities (c)

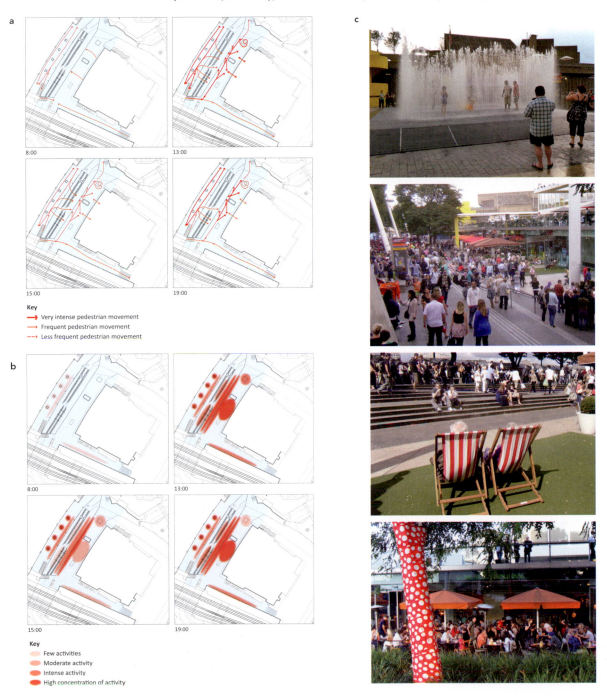

a

8:00

13:00

15:00

19:00

Key
→ Very intense pedestrian movement
→ Frequent pedestrian movement
--→ Less frequent pedestrian movement

b

8:00

13:00

15:00

19:00

Key
Few activities
Moderate activity
Intense activity
High concentration of activity

c

7.21   Gabriel's Wharf observational analysis of user patterns – typical local movement patterns (a), density of activity (b) and typical activities (c)

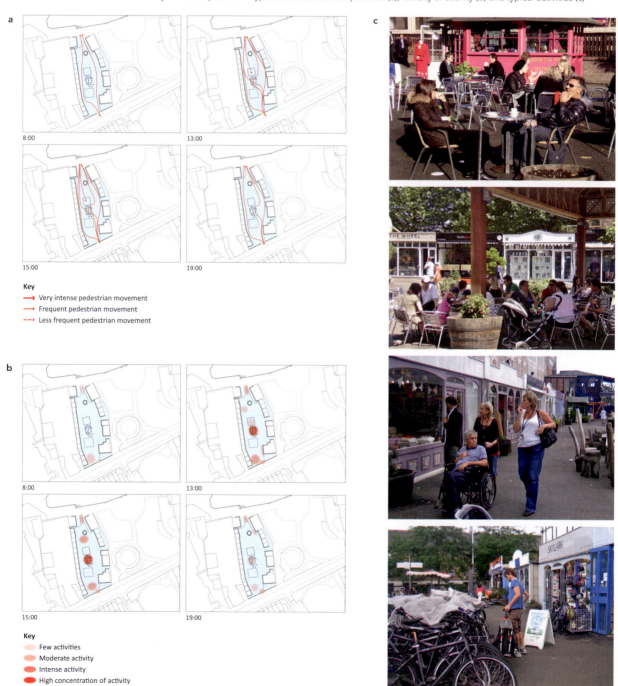

a

8:00

13:00

15:00

19:00

Key

→ Very intense pedestrian movement

→ Frequent pedestrian movement

--→ Less frequent pedestrian movement

b

8:00

13:00

15:00

19:00

Key

Few activities

Moderate activity

Intense activity

High concentration of activity

c

locally as 'the quirky little bit in the middle, between the flashy tax payer funded stuff' (designer/developer).

Consumption and more

The observational analysis showed that Euston Station Piazza and Festival Riverside both benefit from the critical fuel for most retail/hospitality activities, namely an almost continual flow of ready customers through each space, a proportion of which are diverted into the spaces themselves to engage directly with the consumer opportunities on offer (**7.19, 7.20**). The final space – Gabriel's Wharf – is situated perpendicular to the main flow of pedestrian traffic and, through the manner in which it contrasts with its surroundings and the promise it offers of something interesting and different, is able to attract enough customers into the space to support the types of small-scale commercial activities that exist there (**7.21**). In each space, the consumption opportunities provided the main draw, but whilst the majority of the seating at Festival Riverside was reserved for customers only, at Euston and Gabriel's Wharf, many users did not choose to consume, but, respectively, to rest, smoke and work; or, window shop, rest and play.

A general satisfaction across the three spaces was obvious from the interviewees, but also a sense that each space had its particular role and character that would, in turn, appeal to particular audiences: the transient and functional nature of Euston – 'not one to spend a lot of time in, there is nothing uniquely Eustonish' (user of Euston Station Piazza); the buzz of Festival Riverside – 'vibrant, trendy and happening' (user of Festival Riverside); and the quirky relaxed nature of Gabriel's Wharf – 'a different shopping experience' (user of Gabriel's Wharf) (**7.22–7.24**). The evidence from the user interviews suggested that each was deemed appropriate to its function, even though, when asked to criticise, users were clear that improvements could be made. Critically, these place characters were defined as much by the physical setting and by the way the spaces were used as by the consumption opportunities on offer, and it was the total experience of the space, rather than simply an assessment of the retail opportunities, that defined perceptions – positively or negatively – of each.

Managing consumer space
Encouraging versus discouraging behaviours

The question of security was handled very differently in the three spaces. When it first opened, young boys from the local area saw Gabriel's

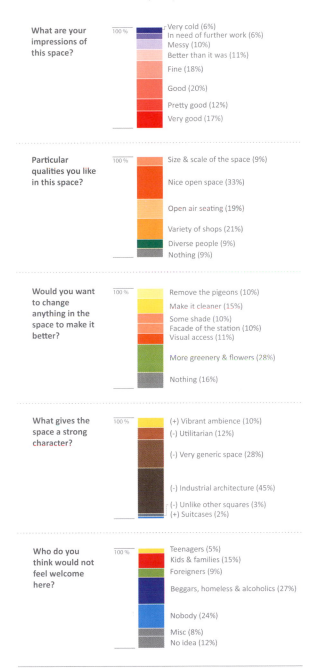

7.22   Euston Station Piazza – user perceptions

What are your impressions of this space? 100 %
- Very cold (6%)
- In need of further work (6%)
- Messy (10%)
- Better than it was (11%)
- Fine (18%)
- Good (20%)
- Pretty good (12%)
- Very good (17%)

Particular qualities you like in this space? 100 %
- Size & scale of the space (9%)
- Nice open space (33%)
- Open air seating (19%)
- Variety of shops (21%)
- Diverse people (9%)
- Nothing (9%)

Would you want to change anything in the space to make it better? 100 %
- Remove the pigeons (10%)
- Make it cleaner (15%)
- Some shade (10%)
- Facade of the station (10%)
- Visual access (11%)
- More greenery & flowers (28%)
- Nothing (16%)

What gives the space a strong character? 100 %
- (+) Vibrant ambience (10%)
- (-) Utilitarian (12%)
- (-) Very generic space (28%)
- (-) Industrial architecture (45%)
- (-) Unlike other squares (3%)
- (+) Suitcases (2%)

Who do you think would not feel welcome here? 100 %
- Teenagers (5%)
- Kids & families (15%)
- Foreigners (9%)
- Beggars, homeless & alcoholics (27%)
- Nobody (24%)
- Misc (8%)
- No idea (12%)

7.23   Festival Riverside – user perceptions

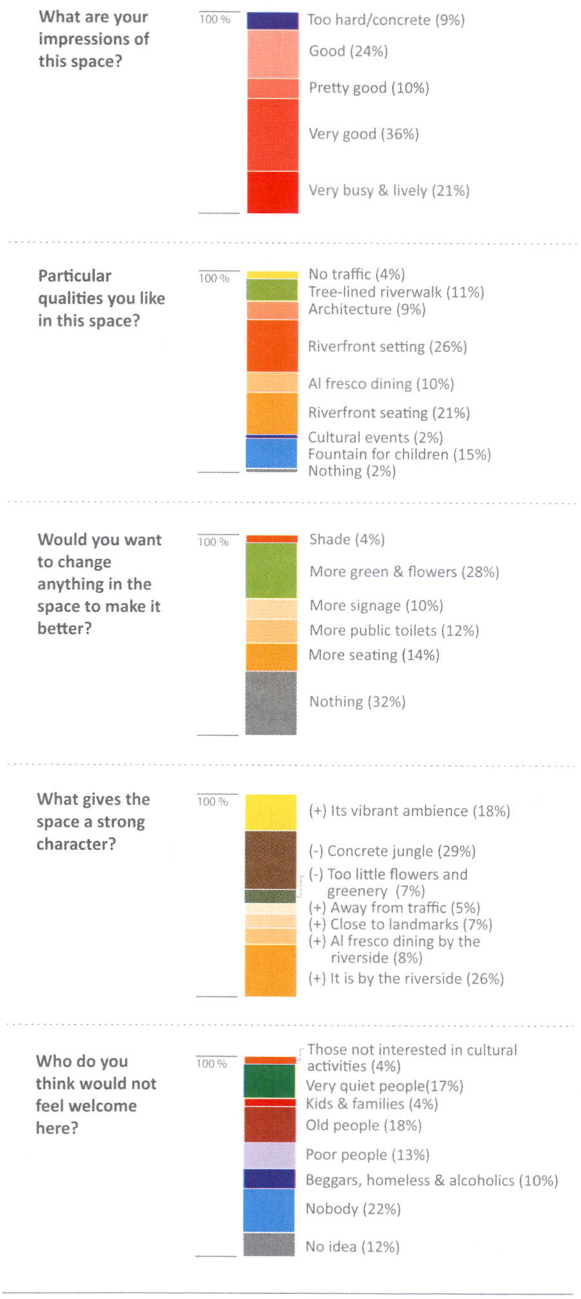

What are your impressions of this space?

100 %
- Too hard/concrete (9%)
- Good (24%)
- Pretty good (10%)
- Very good (36%)
- Very busy & lively (21%)

Particular qualities you like in this space?

100 %
- No traffic (4%)
- Tree-lined riverwalk (11%)
- Architecture (9%)
- Riverfront setting (26%)
- Al fresco dining (10%)
- Riverfront seating (21%)
- Cultural events (2%)
- Fountain for children (15%)
- Nothing (2%)

Would you want to change anything in the space to make it better?

100 %
- Shade (4%)
- More green & flowers (28%)
- More signage (10%)
- More public toilets (12%)
- More seating (14%)
- Nothing (32%)

What gives the space a strong character?

100 %
- (+) Its vibrant ambience (18%)
- (-) Concrete jungle (29%)
- (-) Too little flowers and greenery (7%)
- (+) Away from traffic (5%)
- (+) Close to landmarks (7%)
- (+) Al fresco dining by the riverside (8%)
- (+) It is by the riverside (26%)

Who do you think would not feel welcome here?

100 %
- Those not interested in cultural activities (4%)
- Very quiet people (17%)
- Kids & families (4%)
- Old people (18%)
- Poor people (13%)
- Beggars, homeless & alcoholics (10%)
- Nobody (22%)
- No idea (12%)

7.24   Gabriel's Wharf – user perceptions

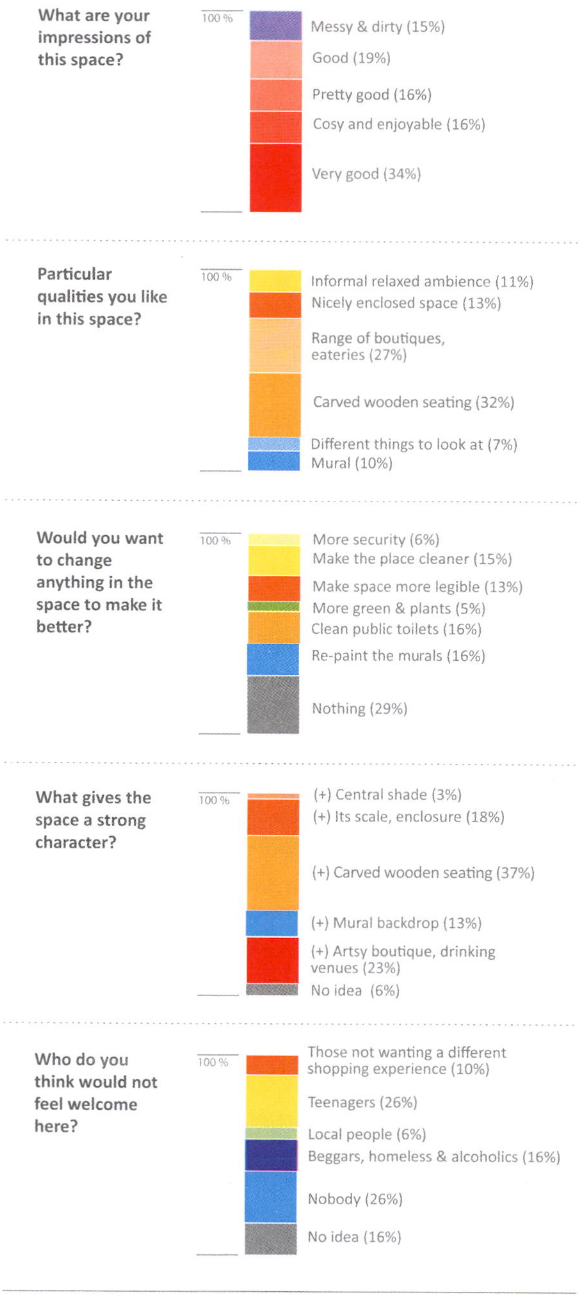

What are your impressions of this space?

100 %
- Messy & dirty (15%)
- Good (19%)
- Pretty good (16%)
- Cosy and enjoyable (16%)
- Very good (34%)

Particular qualities you like in this space?

100 %
- Informal relaxed ambience (11%)
- Nicely enclosed space (13%)
- Range of boutiques, eateries (27%)
- Carved wooden seating (32%)
- Different things to look at (7%)
- Mural (10%)

Would you want to change anything in the space to make it better?

100 %
- More security (6%)
- Make the place cleaner (15%)
- Make space more legible (13%)
- More green & plants (5%)
- Clean public toilets (16%)
- Re-paint the murals (16%)
- Nothing (29%)

What gives the space a strong character?

100 %
- (+) Central shade (3%)
- (+) Its scale, enclosure (18%)
- (+) Carved wooden seating (37%)
- (+) Mural backdrop (13%)
- (+) Artsy boutique, drinking venues (23%)
- No idea (6%)

Who do you think would not feel welcome here?

100 %
- Those not wanting a different shopping experience (10%)
- Teenagers (26%)
- Local people (6%)
- Beggars, homeless & alcoholics (16%)
- Nobody (26%)
- No idea (16%)

Wharf as a target to attack, to break in and steal from. Reflecting these problems, initially the space was secured at night and patrolled by a dedicated security guard, but after a few years the presence of the scheme was accepted and the need for security declined to such a degree that the Wharf is no longer secured at night; although CCTV is monitored from a control room and a security team patrols the wider estate of which the Wharf is a part. 'There was a deliberate attempt to create a non-confrontational, relaxed environment, avoiding people in uniforms and a sense of securitisation, so that people felt at home in the space, [Coin Street] focuses entirely on encouraging things, rather than discouraging things' (manager). For example, as long as it is safe, tenants are allowed to use and fill the space as they see fit and there is no signage restricting behaviour. Tenants quickly report infrequent problems when they occur.

The Southbank Centre has had a similar encouraging attitude to some behaviours. The area, for example, has had a long history as a magnet for skateboarders, which the centre does not want to encourage in their newly refurbished spaces; indeed, Festival Riverside includes subtle design features to discourage them. More positively, the Southbank Centre provides dedicated space to skaters adjacent to Festival Riverside, in exchange for which the skaters leave other spaces intact (**7.25**). Security in the wider area has been a problem, a function that is outsourced to the Southbank Employers Group (funded through Planning Gain – Section 106 – monies from the London Eye), who organise general site and events security and who monitor the site through CCTV.

At Euston, the security imperative takes precedence, as it has done since 1973, when the station was bombed by the IRA. More recently, the fourth of the 7/7 bombs was detonated in nearby Tavistock Square, bomber Hasid Hussain having been forced off a previous bus at the bus station on Euston Station Piazza. As such, no bins are allowed in the square and bins within retail units have to be locked, whilst the refurbishment of the piazza enabled a new CCTV system to be installed. Security checks are done hourly by station management and all staff wear IDs. Security is largely paid for by the train operating companies (including in the piazza), although tenants also contribute. The station has also long been the venue for a begging community, many of whom are attracted by Boots (the chemists on the station forecourt), who operate a methadone clinic that brings drug addicts into the area. Such pursuits are actively controlled by the station's security

7.25 Festival Riverside – adjacent skate / cycle area

staff with the assistance of the British Transport Police, who maintain a heavy presence on the station and in the piazza. Other occasional problems include the use of the station by football fans on match days, in connection with which the British Transport Police identify problem teams and/or problem matches well in advance, and carefully plan for the consequences.

The nature of the threats at Euston are thus of a different order to those faced in the other spaces, on occasions in recent years even meriting the patrolling of the station by armed police, a rare sight on London's streets. Stemming from external sources, the management team have no opportunity to influence such factors. Security is thereby in the main overt and active, rather than relaxed and non-confrontational as is the case at Gabriel's Wharf and Festival Riverside.

Generating custom (and income) through adaptable space

Despite its security imperative, the management goals for Euston Station are to make the area more inviting, cleaner and brighter, and the piazza plays a part in this. Thus Network Rail manages events at the space in periods of high impact. Mostly these take the form of revenue-generating promotional activities as an extension of its wider effort to commercialise the space (**7.26**), but have included a range of music activities and, particularly at Christmas, performance and collections for charity (manager). Generally, these types of activities

7.26 Euston Station Piazza – commercialising the space, in this case selling artificial cigarettes to the ready audience of smokers who continually use the space

7.27 Gabriel's Wharf – Thames Festival weekend

are relatively discrete, since the layout of the space with its new fixed retail outlets onto the space and benches arranged in rows has created an inflexible space more akin to a shopping centre food court than a relaxing piazza.

Both Gabriel's Wharf and Festival Riverside were designed very differently, to be flexible spaces. Festival Riverside and the terrace above are adaptable spaces with infrastructure that allows for events simply to plug in, including for regular art installations, performances and seasonal markets. Lambeth welcome such activities, although they remain concerned that these should be carefully curated in order that spaces avoid becoming tacky. For this reason, they carefully regulate events such as the Christmas Market that has happened on the riverside walk since 2008.

Over the years, Gabriel's Wharf has hosted events as diverse as city farms, history days, bands and concerts, craft demonstrations, and the Coin Street Festival (**7.27**): 'Creating adaptable space means avoiding filling spaces with fixed features that prevent them being adapted for different functions, but also avoiding over-specification in a manner that stifles adaptability' (designer/developer). Recently, these events have declined, the resource-intensive Friday, Saturday and Sunday market being an early casualty of this trend. Originally, the Wharf had an on-site manager whose role was to curate the space and manage it from day to day, but this role ceased when Coin Street Community Builders parted company with USM. As a result, the Wharf no longer has the same focused attention, but 'the general buzz in the area means that neither does it have to try quite so hard' (designer/developer).

Supporting arts through managing space

Today, Gabriel's Wharf is serviced by the Coin Street estates team, who have responsibility for security and public realm, and by a separate technical service team responsible for maintenance. Reflecting its temporary status (at any one time, it only has a guaranteed two-year lifespan), expensive maintenance is avoided and the units and mural look faded, although this does not seem to disturb the visitors. The tenants pay a service charge, but this is discounted for the designers in order to support their work and encourage the idea of Coin Street as a creative space. In effect, the more commercial elements on site (particularly the restaurants) cross-subsidise the more marginal.

The Southbank Centre has a long lease for the area from the Arts Council and are responsible for day-to-day management through their Operations Department, which maintains the space, undertakes repairs and outsources its cleaning. The management regime is paid for by a general grant received through the Arts Council, which also funds the public-realm-related work of the Learning and Participation and Literature, Music, Dance and Visual Arts Teams, with whom

7.28   The riverside walk – part of the Southbank experience

Operations works to stage arts installations. Thus, since 2005, the intention has been that the external spaces will showcase something of what goes on within, as part of the artistic experience (**7.28**). By contrast, the aspirations of Network Rail, the train operating companies and the retailers at Euston (who collectively pay for the management regime) are very different and focused on quickly and efficiently moving customers through their spaces whilst, preferably, relieving them of some money on the way. The station management is responsible for the cleaning, security, lighting and CCTV, whilst

Network Rail's Commercial Property section manages the retail units and the tenancies.

EVALUATION

Festival Riverside and Euston Station Piazza were completed just two years apart, but 20 years or so after Gabriel's Wharf (the latter being completed at the height of Thatcherism and the drive towards private

8.1   County of London Plan: Social and Functional Analysis – the communities of London in 1943

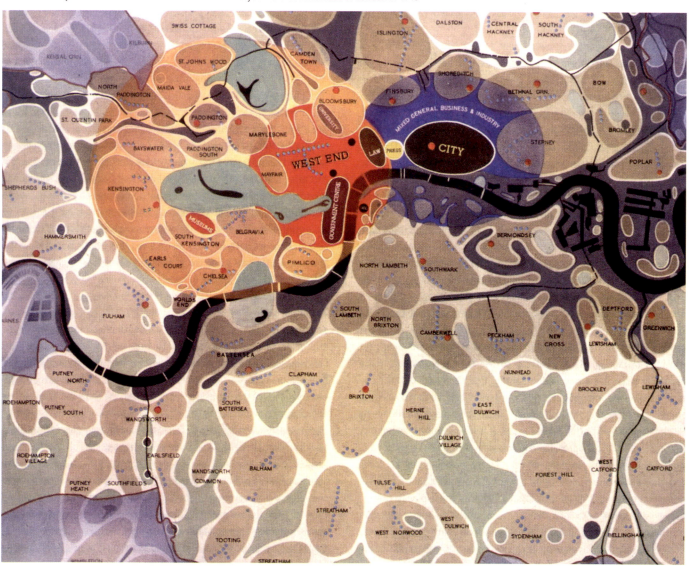

features in the regeneration aspirations of public agencies, with the underpinning aim of delivering a more socially equitable city. The scale of aspiration is therefore above and beyond that seen in the sorts of domestic space associated with individual large private developments (see Chapter 9), but well below the scale of the types

of civic spaces with a city-wide relevance discussed in Chapter 6. This chapter explores two critiques of public space related directly to this notion that the city should be shared and equitable, namely that space is becoming more threatening (scary) for its users and, in different ways, more exclusionary to key groups.

THE CRITIQUES

Exclusionary space

Previous chapters have already discussed certain forms of potential exclusion from public space, most notably those relating to the privatisation of public space, exclusion through the invasion of space by traffic, and financial exclusion through the real or perceived barrier of consumption as the passport to participation in public space. At its most basic, the use that public space receives is likely to be related to a wide range of 'quality' factors associated with its original design, the opportunities it offers to users and the ongoing processes of management. Therefore, if space is poorly managed and declines either physically or in the opportunities and activities it offers, then a vicious cycle of decline may all too easily set in. 'If people use space less, then there is less incentive to provide new spaces and maintain existing ones. With a decline in their maintenance and quality, public spaces are less likely to be used' (Carmona *et al.* 2003: 111). Arguably, many of London's traditional 'community' spaces – its high streets – have suffered in this way – overloaded with traffic, undermined by the impact of private shopping malls, and robbed of public and private sector investment to fill the gap. In part this may explain why newly created spaces – typically squares – have become so prized, many with an identified community role.

Disabling spaces

Although the physical quality of public space will be important to all who choose to use it, for some it will be more important than others. For some, particularly the disabled, those with young children in pushchairs or the elderly, simple physical barriers can present major obstacles to their use of public space, often completely excluding them from certain areas as a result (**8.3**). Hall & Imrie (1999: 409) argue, for example, that the disabled tend to experience the built environment as a series of obstacle courses, whilst most built-environment professionals have little awareness of their needs. The result is that public space is disabling when it need not be (Imrie & Hall 2001: 10).

In the developed world, as populations live longer, disability is no longer the exception and is increasingly the expectation as ageing takes its toll on the physical and mental faculties of even the healthiest individuals. For most, at some point, ageing will leave them less able to cope with the physical demands of using the built environment,

8.2   Watney Market – consciously designed community space

8.3   Access to Hyde Park Corner from the southeast – until 2002 the system of pedestrian underpasses provided the only access across the six lanes of highway to the centre of Hyde Park Corner, making access to its war memorials and monuments impossible for many disabled users. A grade-level processional route now links Hyde Park to Green Park across the space

typically from a combination of minor impairments to hearing, eyesight, dexterity, mobility, bladder control and memory (Burton & Mitchell 2006: 5–7). In reality, however, simply designing the built environment so that it is good for those with disabilities will result in outcomes that are better for everyone, making the environment more accessible and easier for all to use, either now or in the future (Nasar & Evans-Cowley 2007).

Parochial space

Although the exclusionary impacts associated with the creation of disabling environments have been longstanding and universal, other potentially exclusionary practices reflect more recent trends in contemporary urbanism. Loukaitou-Sideris (1996: 100) bleakly describes how 'the fragmentation of the public realm has been accompanied by fear, suspicion, tension and conflict between different social groups'. This fear, it is argued, results in the spatial segregation of activities in terms of class, ethnicity, race, age or occupation – for example, city centres filled at night with youthful revellers to the exclusion of all else (see Chapter 10). Lofland (1998) describes such spaces as 'parochial' because they are appropriated by particular groups, so whoever wanders in feels either like a stranger or a guest, depending on how they fit in.

Loukaitou-Sideris (1996: 100) describes users of contemporary public space as having suspicion of the stranger; so, instead of creating the idealistic undifferentiated 'community' spaces of Modernism, there is now a move to segregate into distinct spatial types and users (**8.4**). Key determinants of this (the argument goes) are physical barriers and concerns for safety and well-being, in particular of the old and the young, so that life-cycle stage is now amongst the most significant determinants of environmental accessibility (Lang 1994: 269). For example, the reluctance of parents to let their children play in the street or walk to school has been widely reported, and has been linked to associated health and obesity problems amongst children unable to get enough exercise, as well as to a decline of the overseeing role of children by adult strangers, and to a growing tendency to see the presence of children in public space as a threat to public order (Shonfield 1998: 11).

Beunderman *et al.* (2007: 3) conclude that 'children and young people suffer from a mix of invisibility, segregation and exclusion'. The development of car-dominated urban forms may be partly to blame

8.4   Tabard Gardens, Southwark – here unaccompanied adults are actively excluded, a practice most famously pursued in Coram's Fields in Holborn where since the mid-1920s the site has been gated and preserved for the well-being of Central London's children, with dogs, glass containers, alcohol and adults (unless accompanied by a child) all excluded; many might argue justifiably in the interests of safety and child development

and has been extensively criticised, not least by 'New Urbanists', who argue that suburban environments too often dictate that only one lifestyle is possible – to own a car and to use it for everything (Duany *et al.* 2000: 25). But the way that existing environments are managed is likely to be just as culpable, not least in the way that space for the pedestrian has increasingly been starved of investment, although with the notable exception of dedicated children's play spaces. For some, however, the resources lavished on such spaces owe more to the lobbying of the industry now built up around manufacturing playground equipment and to the angst among adults no longer willing to allow their children to play freely within the wider built environment (Cunningham & Jones 1999: 12).

Other heavy users of public space have been very actively denied access to it, or to parts of it, prominent amongst whom are the homeless (see below) and teenagers. Exclusion because of fear or an inability to consume are key amongst the reasons that teenagers may feel excluded (Rogers 2010: 67), but teenagers are also excluded because of their pastimes, the most high profile of which is skateboarding, regarded by some as anti-social because of the (often illusory) conflict it creates with other groups and the damage it does to street furniture

(Johns 2001). Rather than positively designing for and managing such activities, which, seen positively, build social skills and physical strength in teenagers, and can help to animate public spaces (Woolley & Johns 2001: 227–8), the strategy is more often to design or police them out of shared spaces or to banish such uses to dedicated places. On the latter, Malone (2002: 165) has argued that 'skate ramps and other youth-specific spaces on the margins of city centres are less than appealing places for young people (especially for young women)'. In such places, teenagers experience problems of safety and security and feelings of exclusion, whilst what they desire in a public space is 'social integration, safety and freedom of movement'.

Scary space

Concerns about the ability to move safely through the environment, free from crime or a debilitating fear of crime, are likely to be amongst the most serious causes of externally and self-imposed exclusion from public space. For Minton (2006: 24), it is fear of crime (rather than actual levels of crime) that is often the driver of moves to privatise parts of the public realm, segregating communities in the process. She argues, however, that whilst ubiquitous reporting of crime in the media undoubtedly drives increased fear (even when, in London, actual crime has been consistently reducing – Metropolitan Police, Crime Figures [n.d.]), processes of polarisation and the associated atomisation of communities also drive a heightened fear of 'the other' (strangers), and a further withdrawal of those with choice from public space. Research in the USA, for example, has revealed that the perception of crime is linked to the presence of visibly different groups with mutual suspicions of each other sharing the same space, such as the presence of homeless people in public space (Mitchell 1995). This group more than any other challenges the limits to the concept of 'public' – a group forced to live much of their private life in public and for whom public space is their primary venue for acquiring money in order to survive, but against whom other citizens and merchants can be especially hostile (Crawford 1995: 7–8). For Mean & Tims (2005), however, fear is frequently a consequence of ignorance and hearsay as much as anything else, with neighbourhoods developing a 'reputation' (often undeserved) that once gained becomes difficult to shake off, turning certain spaces into no-go-areas for little apparent reason.

Being an important investment commodity, for their part the owners and/or managers of urban public space ensure that visitors to public space perceive and interpret it as being safe. Thus, it is argued, the multicultural and pluralistic nature of public space today means that fear of the stranger needs to be dispelled through techniques of design, management and surveillance. As Madanipour (2003: 217) notes, 'A combination of the need for safe investment returns and safe public environments has lead to the demand for total management of space, hence undermining its public dimension'. Moreover, Goldsteen and Elliott (1994) contend that in order that visitors interpret public spaces as safe, strangers are increasingly being removed through the use of semiotic codes in space.

Excluding behaviours

Minton (2006: 2) describes the potential for social exclusion in terms of 'hot spots' of affluence and 'cold spots' of exclusion. 'Hot spots' – such as urban regeneration areas or Business Improvement Districts (BIDs) – are characterised by having clean and safe policies that displace social problems. On the other hand, 'cold spots' are characterised by the socially excluded who are unwelcome in the hot spots. By this analysis, public space management is actively creating socially polarised urban public spaces. Minton (2006: 21) also identifies the slow creep of the private security industry in the UK, effectively supplanting the role of the publicly funded police force in those areas that can afford it. For her, 'private security does not equate with safety' but represents a further degree of privatisation of public space, and a further withdrawal of the state from this, its traditional territory, typically in the cause of improving business and therefore the bottom line (Minton 2009: 42).

Murphy (2001: 24) highlights how exclusion practices are not always the work of the private sector through processes of privatisation, but are increasingly supported in public policy aiming to counter undesirable social activities. The 'exclusion zones' that result vary, but typically control factors such as smoking, skateboarding, alcohol consumption, begging and the use of mobile phones (**8.5**). This raises concerns about personal freedom versus personal and collective responsibilities. Citing the banning of alcohol on public transport in London by Mayor Boris Johnson as a prime example, the Manifesto Club argue that such restrictions are not the result of public demand but of the over-zealous actions of the police and local politicians: they are 'infantilising, treating citizens like irresponsible wards of the state' (Manifesto Club 2008: 3) and a symptom of the hyper-regulation of public places. This brings to the fore two very different

8.5   Emma Cons Gardens, Waterloo – a favourite hangout for vagrants
where conflicting signs attempt to control undesirable behaviours (a)
whilst passively accepting that it happens (b)

8.6   Blackwall, Mulberry Place – the authors being asked by private
security to desist from taking photographs outside the Town Hall of
the London Borough of Tower Hamlets, located on a private estate

a   b

views of public space: one a communitarian vision that emphasises the responsibilities of individuals to the wider community good and the other a libertarian view that stresses the rights and freedoms of individuals in space (Madanipour 2003: 182–6). In reality, a balance needs to be struck between the two, and in a city like London that balance will vary across ownerships, municipalities and time.

Jane Jacobs (1961: 39) famously asserted that society acts together to establish and police norms of behaviour, in doing so controlling what she described as 'street barbarism'. Therefore, are the various control zones any more than the codification of these rules in areas where the voluntary controls have broken down? Put another way, are they a delimitation of personal freedoms, or simply a statement of the freedom of others to use public space in a manner that reflects societal expectations? Reacting to the stated intention of Design for London that all human life and activity should be allowed in London's squares as long as it is legal, Walker (2007) concludes that this 'admirable goal' does not allow for the complexity of the issue: 'There are activities which are not in themselves illegal, but which in public spaces need to be managed if the enjoyment and liberties of others are not to be compromised. At some stage, depending on the size of the bass bins and the numbers in the crowd, a group of kids listening to music ceases to be desirable socialising and

becomes noisy irritant. Someone has to be charged with making this judgement.'

Carr et al. (1992: 152) argue that freedom with responsibility necessitates 'the ability to carry out the activities that one desires, to use a place as one wishes but with the recognition that a public space is a shared space'. The question of management, and what is appropriate and what is not, may therefore be simply a matter of local judgement and negotiation.

Controlled space

Loukaitou-Sideris & Banerjee (1998: 183–5) identify two basic options: hard or soft controls. Hard controls are active and use a variety of private security, CCTV systems and regulations, the latter either prohibiting certain activities or allowing them subject to control (permits, scheduling or leasing) (8.6). At the extremes, they may involve the construction of actual security zones around key buildings, a post-9/11 phenomenon that in certain districts in New York has rendered nearly a third of non-building area in such zones (Németh & Hollander 2010). Although far less common in London, such zones are apparent around some key Government buildings (most famously the gating of Downing Street in the 1980s in response to IRA attacks in London), and in subtle ways are built into the landscaping schemes of key commercial office

8.7 General Gordon Square, Woolwich – refurbished along with neighbouring Beresford Square to give the town its heart back once again and to help deliver a wider regeneration

developments, such as the space at the base of the Swiss Re tower in the City (see **5.13**). They also feature in the reluctance of some commercial occupiers to see active uses in the base of their buildings (see Chapter 5), whilst the 'ring of steel' around the City of London (see Chapter 3) might be seen as the demonstrable sign of what Sorkin (2004: 258) describes as the 'landscape of fear'.

Elsewhere, more prosaically, the London-wide analysis (Chapter 4) revealed a surfeit of signage attempting to restrict a range of different activities across all space types, signage that Worpole & Knox (2007: 9) argue is often ineffectual since it attempts to control activities that do not seem to disrupt public life – skateboarding, cycling, ball games, dog walking, and the like. Others have reported on how simple physical measures can prevent spaces being used in certain manners, most ubiquitous of which is the creation of seats carefully designed to be so uncomfortable that they prevent loitering or lying down – what Flusty (1997) aptly christens 'prickly space'.

A particular danger with hard controls is that their very presence, whilst aiming to help people feel more at ease in public space, may actually simply alert them to the possibilities of danger (Atkinson 2003: 1833). Soft controls, by contrast, are passive, using a range of symbolic restrictions that discourage undesirable activities or make others impossible through removing opportunities. The perceived loss of freedom and a resulting change in character of public space reflects a view that the former set of controls are increasingly favoured over the latter by those with responsibility for managing public space – both public and private. If this is the case, it represents a failure to appropriately manage shared public spaces in a manner that allows their equitable use by all groups without diminishing the welfare of others. Fyfe & Bannister (in Fyfe 1998: 256) conclude that 'Responses to the fortress impulse in urban design, and the broader "surveillance society" of which it is a part, range from optimism at the discovery of potential technological fixes to chronic urban problems, to despair at the creation of an Orwellian dystopia. Laying between these extremes, however, is a middle ground characterised by a profound ambivalence about the impact of increased surveillance.'

COMMUNITY SPACES

Despite the relatively recent notion of spaces specifically for community purposes, the research revealed large numbers of community squares, with 45 per cent of spaces featuring in this category, particularly in Camden, the City and Southwark (see Chapter 4). In reality, however, many of the spaces in this category were also counted in other categories, since community characteristics were common in spaces with a wide range of other primary functions. Around half of these were dedicated to community functions, and these spaces tended to be publicly financed projects, typically as outcomes from regeneration processes in which the creation of new or refurbished public space is seen as both a public good in its own right and/or a potential draw for further (non-public) investment (**8.7**). Often, although not always, these were associated with the provision of other public amenities.

The three spaces discussed in this chapter are of this type. Swiss Cottage Community Square in north London replaces a formerly neglected and dilapidated park as part of a huge reinvestment in sporting, cultural and learning facilities in the area. Peckham Square

8.8   Site of Swiss Cottage Community Square

1910s

1950s

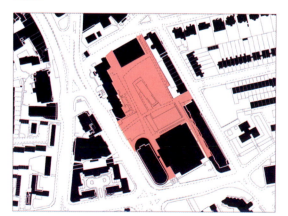

2010

in south London sits in one of the most deprived parts of London, created as a by-product of a huge regeneration of the area's housing stock and accommodating a famous Will Alsop designed library and a separate leisure centre. Royal Arsenal Gardens in southeast London was created as part of a vision to reinvigorate the Thames waterfront at Woolwich and to bring new life and activities into the area.

Swiss Cottage Community Square – re-centring Swiss Cottage

Swiss Cottage was built as a suburban expansion of London from the 1820s onwards, mainly with substantial detached and semi-detached houses, added to by mansion blocks from the 1930s, and large quantities of public housing after the Second World War, built by the London County Council. From 1892, this mix included the Friedenheim (later St Columba's Hospital) occupying a Victorian House opposite Swiss Cottage Station on Avenue Road (a major London arterial), with two acres of grounds for its patients – the terminally ill (**8.8**). Following the move of the hospital in 1957, the grounds became Swiss Cottage Park in the early 1960s, including (at its centre) the external pitches of the Swiss Cottage Leisure Centre (sports centre and library), built to the immediate south of the park to a design by Sir Basil Spence. By the 1990s, however, the park was in a very poor state – disconnected, graffitied, unattractive and unsafe – and the sports centre was condemned as structurally unfit.

After much negotiation, it was decided that a newly designed space was needed to bring together an ensemble of key public buildings of local significance that were to be built or refurbished around the site: a new leisure centre, refurbishment of the Grade II listed library, a new Hampstead Theatre, a new community centre, doctors' surgery, the Winchester Project youth centre, offices, affordable housing and a home for the elderly. Four teams were shortlisted for the project, with the winning team featuring a masterplan by Terry Farrell & Partners that aspired to redress the deficiency of open space in the area and create a new centre for Swiss Cottage that could bring its diverse communities together (the area having formerly lost its centre following the widening of the A41 in the 1960s). The space was designed by Gustafson Porter Landscape Architects and the scheme developed by Dawnay Day with Barratt Homes, who built 173 new homes (three-quarters luxury apartments) as part of the deal. It was completed in 2006 at a cost of £76 million, £4 million of which was the public space.

8.9   Site of Peckham Square

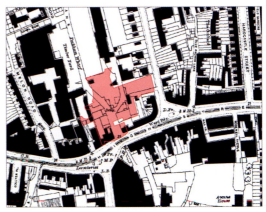

1910s

1950s

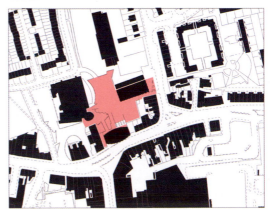

2010

Peckham Square – an incremental urban vision

The town of Peckham was originally one of London's outlying villages, since urbanised as part of the great Victorian expansion of London. In the twentieth century, much of the area was heavily redeveloped in order to replace the (by then) dilapidated housing with new high-rise flats in what became the North Peckham estate. The area was heavily populated by new immigrant communities, and by the late twentieth century housed one of the most ethnically diverse areas in London, with an especially large African-Caribbean community. It had also become synonymous with urban decay. Throughout, however, Rye Lane had remained a diverse and vibrant local high street, substituting for the actual High Street (A202) running east/west through the area, which had become an important radial traffic artery around London, effectively dividing the area. At the nexus of the two, land was assembled by the London Borough of Southwark in the 1980s for a new Town Hall and road by-pass scheme, a project that subsequently failed, leading to the sale of the site for housing. When this private venture also failed, the site (an old canal head and associated yards – **8.9**) was bought back by the council and became part of an initiative in the 1990s to regenerate Peckham's housing using national Single Regeneration Budget (SRB) funding.

As the funding required that a broader social agenda be addressed, an idea for a library and square originally mooted in the 1980s was resurrected (as a small part of the much larger regeneration proposals). The first phase of this, involving an SRB grant of £1 million, was completed in 1994 following a limited competition won by John McAslan, who proposed the Peckham Arch opening onto a new square behind (see **8.11**). The project opened up this hinterland space to the High Street in front. A subsequent SRB grant of £60 million to stimulate housing regeneration led to a further invited competition for the proposed new library, with Will Alsop winning, whilst the Council's own architects department designed the Peckham Pulse leisure/health centre. Completed in 1999, the intention was to redefine Peckham. The project was local authority led, with no private sector involvement at all, controlled in its entirety by the council's Department of Regeneration and Environment.

The motivation for the project was informed by the absence of any external social space in the locality, in contrast to other settlements nearby. The very contemporary design of the library aimed to establish a strong identity for the space, whilst the detailed landscape design was undertaken in part by Jennifer Coe Landscape Architects (brought in by Will Alsop), in part by Southwark's in-house architects, and in part by John McAslan, who had already landscaped the southern portion of the site under the arch. The result was an incremental accretion of elements, just like the buildings. The square cost around £2 million, the library £5.4 million and the leisure centre £12 million.

Royal Arsenal Gardens – Barcelona to Woolwich and bust!

Woolwich has a long history as a military town on the Thames, with the Royal Arsenal established in 1471 and the Royal Artillery Barracks still in the town today. It also hosts the Woolwich Ferry and a Foot Tunnel across the Thames, and between these and the old Royal Arsenal Site (closed as a military base in 1994) there existed a series of warehouses and wharves in the nineteenth century and later a coal power station (**8.10**). All of these, along with most of the rest of the town's industrial base, closed during the twentieth century, leaving by the 1990s a town in desperate need of regeneration, Woolwich having become run down and a centre of multiple deprivation. Into this context, Royal Arsenal Gardens was designed and delivered as a regeneration vehicle, a piece of publicly funded public realm that, it was hoped, would inspire the redevelopment of the vacant sites around it. The project was delivered in 2000 by the Woolwich Development Agency (WDA), an arm's-length regeneration agency of the London Borough of Greenwich, whose leaders had been inspired by the regeneration experience of Barcelona and by the design-led regeneration philosophy of the Urban Task Force. They wanted to bring a little of Barcelona to deprived Woolwich in south-east London on a site that just previously had been targeted by Tesco's for a 'big box' superstore.

The aspiration was for a high-quality, animated public space, suitable for events and markets, as well as for play and relaxation, a space designed to attract people from Woolwich town centre down to the Thames, helping in the process to overcome the disconnect between Woolwich and its previously industrial riverfront. The aim was to help address the chronic under-provision of open space in the town, set a quality benchmark that subsequent development would be inspired to match, and deliver a 'quick win' to demonstrate physically that 'Woolwich was not going to be left behind' (regenerator). The context for the project was provided by a loose and aspirational masterplan for the wider area, and a two-stage design competition was initiated and

8.10   Site of Royal Arsenal Gardens

1910s

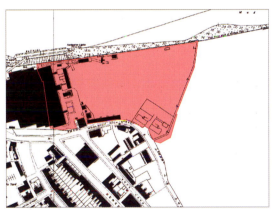

1950s

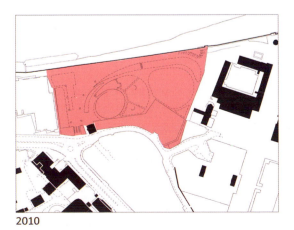

2010

won by Whitelaw Turkington Landscape Architects, who subsequently took the scheme from design to completion and eventual adoption by the London Borough of Greenwich, who manage the space today through their Parks and Open Spaces Department. The space was completed in 2000, well ahead of any actual development to go around it, and in 2012 still sits in glorious isolation over a decade later.

Designing community space
Repairing the fabric, making it safe

Each of the three case studies aimed to create a new space where none (or only degraded space) existed before, using formerly industrial or back lands to carve out a space and create new routes, the intention being (in each case) to knit the new square into its surrounds. At Swiss Cottage, for example, the key ingredients of Terry Farrell's masterplan were permeability, access and visual links through the site, with two new north–south axes and an east–west axis. In doing so, the new space draws people away from the divisive A41 road and into the protected centre of the block, creating a traditionally enclosed space and bringing more people into and across the site by connecting to the communities around and making the space feel safe and secure as a consequence.

At Peckham, the space and facilities were intended for all and particularly for children, with the designers consulting the police and disabled groups on the design in a locality known to be problematic. These concerns informed the eventual 'open' space, with good sight-lines to deter crime and anti-social behaviour; for example, a screen of trees proposed to enclose the north of the square was abandoned for safety reasons. The conception for the space itself was very different and essentially Modernist: 'The square was meant to be open-ended, stretching out to the outlying areas around it, rather than a traditional square defined by buildings and borders. Here the buildings [Peckham Library, Arch and Pulse] are just placed in space as objects – train crash architecture – and make big statements' (planner) (**8.11**). However, whilst the buildings depart decisively from the rules of traditional urbanism, and the landscape design is similarly fragmented, it is the landscape that holds the composition together. A downside is that the somewhat open nature of the square (a consequence of the object architecture), has delivered a poor microclimate, with northerly winds allowed to invade and chill the space.

If the space at Swiss Cottage created an enclosed traditional space,

8.11   Peckham Square – statement architecture held together with public space

and that at Peckham a more free-flowing set of relationships, then the approach taken at Royal Arsenal Gardens was different again, since the space itself was designed and created in advance of any real sense of what the final buildings around it might be, what they would contain and how they would relate to the space itself. A pragmatic approach was therefore adopted, with flexible edges designed to allow a wide range of development scenarios to follow, where necessary eating into the site. Even the space as originally conceived was never completed, because a site owned by the London Electricity

Board (LEB) to the immediate south, which was to be incorporated into the scheme along with an old substation building (intended to be a café and bicycle hire shop), was never purchased. The result was an unfinished space (some paths lead nowhere), isolated, difficult to access and without active uses.

Build it and they will come?

The landscape designers at Swiss Cottage aspired to create a multifunctional, vibrant but still 'poetic space', a space that would

8.12 Swiss Cottage Community Square – drawing people in and through the space

8.13 Peckham Square – space as social generator

8.14 Royal Arsenal Gardens – still surrounded by blank sites a decade after completion

naturally draw the community to it, becoming a new focus for the surrounding high-density urban area that otherwise lacked a centre. Place-making was the key, a new 'heart of a plural community' (masterplanner), but this amounted to more than the space itself, instead encompassing the full range of attractors around it – theatre, library, leisure centre, etc. – drawing people into and through the square (**8.12**). The concept at Peckham was similarly to create a lively space, mimicking the activity that once existed at the canal head, although now generated by community events rather than industrial activities. The square 'was meant to act as a social generator, where the community could interact' (landscape designer), and, like the Swiss Cottage space, had the immediate advantage of being surrounded by generators of activity (the library to the northeast, Peckham Pulse to the west and busy Rye Lane to the south) (**8.13**).

Royal Arsenal Gardens was also seen as a space for the whole community and for all ages, with a small amphitheatre space incorporated to encourage performance, and a kickabout and play area for younger users. Only 'outside drinkers' were viewed as potentially problematic, and therefore, despite the very exposed nature of the site, no covered seating spaces were included in the scheme (to discourage them). Despite the aspirations, however, the site was viewed largely in isolation, with little attempt to consider some of the larger issues that might impact on its success or failure in urban design terms as well as its attractiveness for market-led development. These include the presence of a 'big box' leisure centre to the west of the scheme, the divisive A206 to the south dividing the space from Woolwich town centre, and the high walls of the Royal Arsenal to the east. With these factors exacerbating the general low development pressure in

8.15   Swiss Cottage Community Square – design facilitating use

the area, the failure to develop the sites immediately surrounding the space has 'left the scheme high and dry' (regenerator) (**8.14**). Building the space did not attract the envisaged developers, nor, in the main, has it attracted the sorts of uses and users originally envisaged (see below).

Make it funky

The three spaces were each designed to stand out and through their designs create unique London spaces. The striking architecture of Will Alsop's library firmly set this direction at Peckham, an aspiration that came from the local authority in order to 'shift Peckham's pathetic image to a place with potential and respect' (planner). The 11-metre cantilever and 'playful' angled supports (see **8.30**), for example, met the client's brief that the library should be on one floor, although without the need for this to be the ground floor, something that would have 'killed the space' (architect). Originally, Will Alsop and Jennifer Coe proposed a more intricate response to the space itself, with more features in the square to encourage people to linger (e.g. fibre-optic lighting and public art), and a greater division into smaller more intimate communal spaces, including a water area and

8.16   Royal Arsenal Gardens – a beacon of regeneration (deserted, as usual)

green area for quiet enjoyment. This evolved into a hard urban space featuring a grid paving pattern meant to guide users to the library and leisure centre, all built from high-quality sustainable materials. The final more 'empty' design was chosen in order to be flexible for events (and for safety reasons – see above) although for the landscape designer the downside is a space that is somewhat bleak at certain times of the year, whilst, like the library, managing to 'avoid formality in its conception' (landscape designer). For her, the experience demonstrated how little power designers have in such circumstances.

The space at Swiss Cottage also had a strong design strategy at its heart, to give it 'soul'. The land is modelled into a new landform with undulating grass wrapping around a water feature to create an amphitheatre. The water feature has 15-metre-long jets to create a screen of water that slides down on a 40 x 11 metre fountain slab to a shallow paddling pool 6 inches deep – a popular feature with children that 'animates the space' (landscape designer) and gives it a clear identity (**8.15**). Around the green space are sun-and-shade gardens using British native plants that were popular in 1950s and 1960s gardens, helping to stimulate the collective memory. The sunken sports pitch is also evocative of the earlier pitch on the site, with walls clad by Portland stone salvaged from the former sports centre. The aim is to contrast with a traditional council park, creating instead the character of 'a garden' rich with detail and interest, including high-quality materials and bespoke furniture.

At Woolwich, the key (perhaps the only) strength of the site was its open character next to the Thames, a perspective rarely experienced in London, and providing a strong sense of sky and water. The designers aimed to use this by metaphorically bringing the river into the site through a series of organic forms, whilst contrasting these with a series of harder rectilinear and vertical elements, providing 'a metaphorical and literal beacon of regeneration' (landscape designer) (**8.16**). In doing so, the land was raised, establishing an innovative flood remediation solution that overcame the need for a concrete wall by the river and that accounted for much of the £1.3 million price tag. Sculptural seating and vertical lighting elements line a slipway-shaped hard space reflecting the shipbuilding history of the area, but to be used for markets and events and connecting backwards to the town in a southerly direction. However, whilst external design advisors appointed by the council to the competition panel had argued that the project was not nearly adventurous enough, internally the perceived difficulties in maintaining 'specials' led to fierce resistance to any innovative features by the council's own public space mangers. In the end, the political masters wanted a bit of Barcelona innovation in Woolwich, and strongly backed what they saw as a creative design solution.

Developing community space
A very public vision
Each project was conceived and led by the public sector, but relied on the private sector to different degrees. The core of the Swiss Cottage scheme was a public–private partnership between Camden Council and Barratt Homes, established to deliver Camden's vision as laid down in their development brief for the whole site and each of its elements. Camden took the lead in the process and also took advantage of the very favourable market context and location to deliver significant public gain (including the public space) as tied down through a series of complex Section 106 agreements. The clarity of vision resulted in large part from firm championship from within the local authority by two Directorates: Environment Services and Leisure and Community Services. Between them, they pushed through the vision whilst relying

on the private sector to generate enough profit to subsidise the public vision, the latter requiring that greater leeway was given to their commercial partners – Barratt Homes – in the commercial parts of the project than Camden would otherwise have liked.

At Woolwich, by contrast, the public elements were funded and delivered in advance of the anticipated private schemes, which then failed to materialise. However, the provision of a new open space had been enshrined in the delivery plan of the Woolwich Development Agency and had to be delivered in order to release monies for the wider remediation works. Despite strong political backing and a belief that public realm improvements could be used to drive regeneration, the public vision was far ahead, and therefore out of sync, with the market aspirations for the area. The general disconnect between the two pointed to a wider challenge in the need to synchronise public funding cycles with market opportunity if one is to benefit from the other.

At Southwark, a huge amount of power was vested at the time of the Peckham redevelopment in the hands of Fred Manson as Director of Regeneration and Environment, who was responsible for architecture, highways, planning, property, economic development, streets, environmental health and leisure. This arrangement greatly reduced the opportunity for internal dissent within the local authority and allowed Manson to effectively drive the project, resolving any internal conflicts as they arose. He faced down, for example, the wishes of the property section within his ambit, who argued for a commercial element on the square to bring in income. Thus, when the project came in over budget, Manson had the flexibility to divert monies from other budgets to ensure its successful completion. The project nevertheless demonstrates a comparatively rare example of a public vision, delivered entirely through public funds for entirely public purposes.

Building a coalition of interests – or not
Despite the objectives to meet community needs, only one of the three community spaces went through a process of serious engagement with local stakeholders. The need for change and renewal at Swiss Cottage Park was acknowledged 12 years before the project started, but for a long time the far larger King's Cross project took all the attention and resources of Camden. Gradually, however, political support built around the idea, culminating in a Citizens Jury in 1997. The jury included local stakeholders involved in the site and defined objectives to meet the various aspirations for it, namely (i) to facilitate Hampstead

Theatre's accommodation into a new building, (ii) to redevelop the sports centre, (iii) to refurbish the existing Library and (iv) to redesign the open space. Each were subsequently delivered as independent projects, with the council acting as 'umbrella motivator' (project manager). In 1999, following the organisation of the development package and an options appraisal, separate competitions were held for the Leisure Centre and square, with a community consultation exercise held on the submitted proposals. The winning projects were entered for planning in 2000 and approved in 2001, although a judicial review subsequently interrupted progress as disgruntled home owners in the Winchester Road conservation area challenged the decision to allow 15 storeys of housing at the southeast corner of the site. As the height was required to cross-subsidise the rest of the scheme, the project was held up until the dispute was resolved in the council's favour, raising pressure on the council to produce a space of the highest quality in order to justify their stance.

As the Peckham and Woolwich schemes were largely 'internal' to their respective councils, the nature of external engagement was rather different. Detailed internal stakeholder consultation processes with regard to the Royal Arsenal Gardens helped to maintain support and ensured that all necessary regulatory permissions were forthcoming without delay. The project was characterised by good relationships across the development team, with the exception of the contractor, who mispriced the project and tried to cut corners. The design brief specified a subtle design sympathetic to the landscape, and the winning scheme was seen as responding to that brief, with its relative simplicity securing strong backing at the public consultation exercise held on the short-listed competition entries from a conservative (with a small 'c') community that revealed during the process their own preference for traditional rose beds, fountains, play spaces and bandstands. These preferences were ignored in the completed scheme, and no private-sector partners were bought on board to either validate the proposed development solution or to help cross-fund the public works.

At Peckham, a very extensive public consultation was held on the wider regeneration plans for North Peckham, but it quickly became apparent that residents were mainly concerned with the housing, and that there was little interest locally in the social facilities and no interest in the proposed public space. 'As there was no interest in the design of the square and the buildings within it, the council could implement

Royal Arsenal Gardens – seating without backs, leading to the unintended exclusion of older users

their concept unchallenged' (planner), with no planning permission required for the square. The library building was subject to a separate more contentious consultation process, being approved by just one vote at the planning committee.

Using community space
The proof is in the using

Stakeholders are honest that Royal Arsenal Gardens has not performed as expected. Since its completion, the space has 'remained boxed in by hoardings, dereliction and blight; a space that has no reason to be there' (regenerator). Although office workers in the vicinity do sit out on the grass on summer days – in small numbers – and the thoroughfare along the riverfront is well used (independently of the space itself), in the winter the exposed position of the site means it is little used. This, along with the inappropriateness of the bespoke benching (**8.17**), means that older users in particular have shunned the space, as largely do families with young children (few of whom live close), and even residents from the neighbouring developments at Royal Arsenal. Reflecting the problems, two elements were added to the scheme post-completion: a public art scheme by the Groundwork Trust to aid interpretation and way-finding, and a skate-park. The latter was provided following observations made by managers that skate-boarders had appropriated parts of the space. For the skate-boarders, the relative isolation of the space and its hard landscaping

8.18   Peckham Square – a place to rest

8.19   Swiss Cottage Community Square – dancing in the pool

allows practice without hindrance and for personalisation through tagging, etc. The presence of skateboarders polarised political opinion in the council, although the decision to build a full-scale skate-park on part of the site followed when realisation dawned that the space had found perhaps its only viable constituency – which was better than none. It now attracts skaters from across London, who use the skate-park (although not the remainder of the space) heavily on summer evenings and at weekends.

The failure at Royal Arsenal Gardens is matched by the success at Peckham and Swiss Cottage. At Peckham, in direct contrast, the uses around the square generate activity and give life to the space, whilst the space is used as a through route to avoid the busy and over-crowded High Street. The space is deliberately adaptable – its architect Will Alsop describing it as 'a space pregnant with possibilities' – whilst the activities on the square (festivals, market, etc.) have become a natural point of gravity for Peckham. Informally, people sit on the benches in the space to eat lunch or to rest (**8.18**), although most users are simply passing through (particularly shoppers, commuters and children). The space really comes to life everyday about 3.30pm when schools end, but is well used into the evening. Some problems with antisocial behaviour do exist, particularly after dark, many related to the pub that backs onto and opens up to the square. At weekends, the space is quieter, although hosts a small but successful farmers' market.

Swiss Cottage is similarly well used across the day and into the night, with a single Japanese restaurant generating users until 2 or 3 o'clock in the morning, whilst the Leisure centre is open between 6am and 10.30pm, bringing people through the space between these times. Cafes in the leisure centre and Hampstead Theatre also open onto the square and contribute to its activity. During the week, local workers use the space during and after work, drama students from the nearby Central School of Speech and Drama use it to rehearse (**8.19**), and at the weekend the number of families increases significantly, whilst the Eton Avenue market (four days a week) also generates traffic. In summertime, the sculpted green area has become a favourite place to relax and watch others, with the playground and water feature proving particularly popular with children. The area is one of an eclectic mix of society and community, and stakeholders perceive that 'people of very low income and millionaires can be seen rubbing shoulders in the space' (developer), but also that most users are young, indeed older users have complained about the lack of seating in the quiet green areas. In 2007, the scheme received a Cape Silver Award for social integration and sustainability.

Community space, but different communities
Observations at the three spaces revealed three very different patterns of activity. The space at Swiss Cottage was primarily a space of leisure and relaxation for use by the local community, especially mothers, nannies and children, for whom it was a destination in its own right, as

8.20 Swiss Cottage Community Square observational analysis of user patterns – typical local movement patterns (a), density of activity (b) and typical activities (c)

a

8:00

13:00

15:00

19:00

Key

→ Very intense pedestrian movement

→ Frequent pedestrian movement

→ Less frequent pedestrian movement

b

8:00

13:00

15:00

19:00

Key

Few activities

Moderate activity

Intense activity

High concentration of activity

c

8.21 Peckham Square observational analysis of user patterns – typical local movement patterns (a), density of activity (b) and typical activities (c)

a

8:00

13:00

15:00

19:00

Key

→ Very intense pedestrian movement

→ Frequent pedestrian movement

--→ Less frequent pedestrian movement

b

8:00

13:00

15:00

19:00

Key

Few activities

Moderate activity

Intense activity

High concentration of activity

c

8.22 Royal Arsenal Gardens observational analysis of user patterns – typical local movement patterns (a), density of activity (b) and typical activities (c)

a

8:00

13:00

15:00

19:00

Key

→ Very intense pedestrian movement

→ Frequent pedestrian movement

--→ Less frequent pedestrian movement

b

8:00

13:00

15:00

19:00

Key

Few activities

Moderate activity

Intense activity

High concentration of activity

c

well as the location on which other community facilities were located. Peckham was a more utilitarian space, a space for movement, for hosting events that take advantage of the passing pedestrian traffic, although for most of the time it was not a destination itself and did not hold the attention of its users for long unless a specific event was being staged. There, the library and the Pulse were the events, not the space. Both spaces, however, bustled with life and were well populated by their diverse local communities (**8.20, 8.21**). By contrast, Royal Arsenal Gardens remained underutilised, and felt abandoned by all but the skateboard community, who used just part of the space (the retro-fitted skate-park) whilst making their presence felt elsewhere, rather ominously for some (**8.22**).

The very different nature of the three community spaces was confirmed in the user assessments (**8.23–8.25**). Thus the space at Swiss Cottage was first and foremost a family space, receiving very strongly positive views as a destination of choice from almost all users, many of whom (particularly women) appreciated its nature as a relaxing oasis in an otherwise busy urban context (although one that could be managed better) – a place that 'encouraged interaction amongst familiar faces' (user of Swiss Cottage Community Square). At Peckham, the space was seen as subservient to the architecture, whilst its hard landscape gave it a character as a pause in the urban fabric, a space to rest a while, then move on. It was nevertheless clearly seen as an important and overwhelmingly positive community space that had 'completely changed people's perceptions of this previously dark and unsafe area' (user of Peckham Square). Users were somewhat confused about the nature of the space in Woolwich, not quite understanding its purpose. They appreciated the potential of its setting, on the river, and skateboarders appreciated the skate-park, but, in general, this was not viewed as a space for the community (particularly not for women and families), rather a space to pass through and to avoid after dark. As one user put it, 'you would not be sure if anybody would come to your rescue if attacked' (user of Royal Arsenal Gardens).

Managing community space
Managing public space … publicly
Each of the community squares remain in public ownership and are managed internally by different council departments, although with day-to-day work typically contracted out, paid for from recurrent revenue budgets. At Swiss Cottage, management is well coordinated

8.23   Swiss Cottage Community Square – user perceptions

What are your impressions of this space?   100 %
- More green (2%)
- Relaxing space (10%)
- Nice & open (31%)
- Pretty good (12%)
- Very good (45%)

Particular qualities you like in this space?   100 %
- Relaxed ambience (17%)
- Openness (8%)
- The green grass to sit & relax (10%)
- The pool & play area (43%)
- Mix of activities (18%)
- Misc (2%)
- Nothing (2%)

Would you want to change anything in the space to make it better?   100 %
- Raise fence around football court (8%)
- More trees & flowers (31%)
- Some shaded seating spaces (16%)
- More activities (14%)
- Misc (15%)
- Nothing (16%)

What gives the space a strong character?   100 %
- (+) Relaxed feel (12%)
- (-) Nothing unique but the pool (21%)
- (+) Fountain (32%)
- (+) Varied range of activities (19%)
- No idea (8%)
- Misc (8%)

Who do you think would not feel welcome here?   100 %
- Teenagers (15%)
- Elderly people (17%)
- Beggars, homeless & alcoholics (15%)
- Nobody (33%)
- Misc (18%)
- No idea (2%)

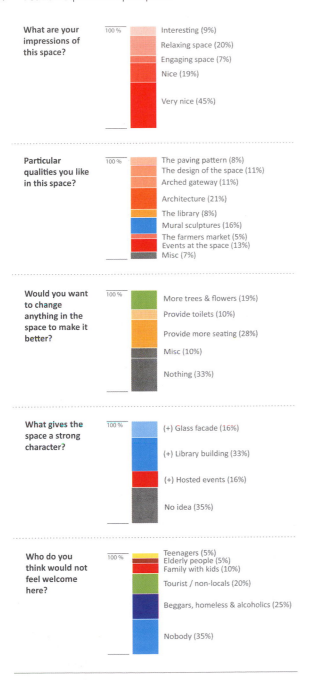

8.24   Peckham Square – user perceptions

What are your impressions of this space?
100 %
- Interesting (9%)
- Relaxing space (20%)
- Engaging space (7%)
- Nice (19%)
- Very nice (45%)

Particular qualities you like in this space?
100 %
- The paving pattern (8%)
- The design of the space (11%)
- Arched gateway (11%)
- Architecture (21%)
- The library (8%)
- Mural sculptures (16%)
- The farmers market (5%)
- Events at the space (13%)
- Misc (7%)

Would you want to change anything in the space to make it better?
100 %
- More trees & flowers (19%)
- Provide toilets (10%)
- Provide more seating (28%)
- Misc (10%)
- Nothing (33%)

What gives the space a strong character?
100 %
- (+) Glass facade (16%)
- (+) Library building (33%)
- (+) Hosted events (16%)
- No idea (35%)

Who do you think would not feel welcome here?
100 %
- Teenagers (5%)
- Elderly people (5%)
- Family with kids (10%)
- Tourist / non-locals (20%)
- Beggars, homeless & alcoholics (25%)
- Nobody (35%)

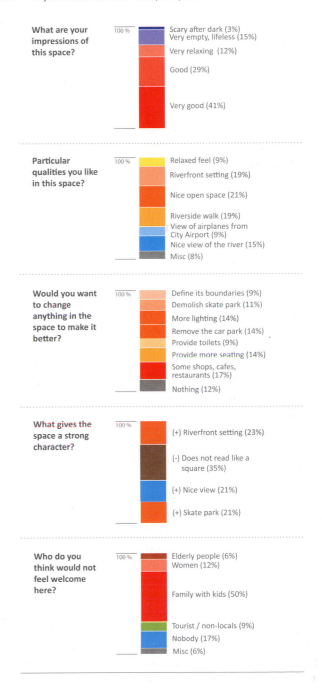

8.25   Royal Arsenal Gardens – user perceptions

What are your impressions of this space?
100 %
- Scary after dark (3%)
- Very empty, lifeless (15%)
- Very relaxing (12%)
- Good (29%)
- Very good (41%)

Particular qualities you like in this space?
100 %
- Relaxed feel (9%)
- Riverfront setting (19%)
- Nice open space (21%)
- Riverside walk (19%)
- View of airplanes from City Airport (9%)
- Nice view of the river (15%)
- Misc (8%)

Would you want to change anything in the space to make it better?
100 %
- Define its boundaries (9%)
- Demolish skate park (11%)
- More lighting (14%)
- Remove the car park (14%)
- Provide toilets (9%)
- Provide more seating (14%)
- Some shops, cafes, restaurants (17%)
- Nothing (12%)

What gives the space a strong character?
100 %
- (+) Riverfront setting (23%)
- (-) Does not read like a square (35%)
- (+) Nice view (21%)
- (+) Skate park (21%)

Who do you think would not feel welcome here?
100 %
- Elderly people (6%)
- Women (12%)
- Family with kids (50%)
- Tourist / non-locals (9%)
- Nobody (17%)
- Misc (6%)

8.26   Peckham Square – Sunday crafts and farmers' market

by an on-site estate manager for the whole estate, with the power to intervene as and when necessary. The manager inspects the space once a month and monitors the work of three contractors: one for maintenance works, one for pavement cleaning (the pavement is swept and litter removed daily) and a third for soft landscaping. The site manager is also responsible for the rolling programme of events, often held in the pool (with the water turned off), which is equipped as a stage. The Hampstead Theatre, for example, regularly uses the space for events and the Library for toddler poetry sessions.

Peckham Square is also fully serviced with electricity and water, and hosts a programme of activities strongly focused on the local community: job fairs, dog shows, fire brigade displays, police and military recruitment events, Christmas carols, story telling, consultation events, and a Sunday market (8.26). Responsibility for managing the space at Peckham is somewhat chaotic, by comparison, being split between the council's Events Manager and its Public Realm Assets Manager, whilst the buildings are the responsibility of the Department of Culture, Libraries and Learning, with agents (Fusion) managing the Pulse. Despite the surfeit of council actors, there is no coordination, and the only attempt to create an Area Management Plan fell through.

At the Royal Arsenal Gardens, a plan was incorporated into the original funding proposals for a part-time warden to manage the space, but

despite money being put aside for the purpose, this arrangement soon ceased as financial pressures elsewhere in the council squeezed resources. Instead, a standard mobile regime is maintained, with parks officers in the space two or three times a week to clear litter, of which the skaters leave 'lorry loads' (manager) and graffiti, which is rarely cleared. 'If you are able to put a Rolls Royce service in to somewhere, the place will be maintained to a high standard. We are not able to do that' (manager). The original aspiration for an adaptable space able to accommodate community events was also quickly abandoned, although, in its early years, the space was occasional host to themed markets and events (the last being in 2008). Today, it has been abandoned for such purposes in favour of the newly regenerated and centrally located spaces in the heart of Woolwich town centre – General Gordon (see 8.7) and Beresford Squares.

Capital aspirations / revenue realities

In all three spaces, the rush to make the large capital investments led to design decisions that backfired when faced with maintenance budgets based on standard revenue streams. The soft landscape at Swiss Cottage, for example, is particularly badly maintained: 'It's actually very sad, to design a very beautiful place and see it go to bits because the money isn't there to upkeep it to the required standard' (landscape designer). The designers requested that an on-site gardener be employed to properly care for the planting (particularly the turf, where problems have predominated – 8.27) and that an automatic irrigation system be installed, but neither have yet been put into place, and the council blames the contractor and the contractor the council. For the council, much fault also lies with the designers, who specified too many materials on the site and plants and features (e.g. glass signage) that were unable to stand up to the context, and which have since been replaced. Here, the scope of the maintenance aspirations were simply beyond the ability of Camden to deliver, with the Head of Parks and Open Spaces only involved in the scheme relatively late in the design process.

At Peckham, the council's Public Realm Asset Manager was also involved too late, and was not able to inform the design. The result is that there remains concern that not enough thought was given to maintenance issues, despite most of the square being redesigned in-house reflecting a concern that Jenny Coe's ideas were too complex and not amenable to a standard maintenance regime. In common with the other case studies in this chapter, some expensive

8.27   Swiss Cottage Community Square – a lack of turf maintenance following handover has left the grass in a poor state

materials that featured in the original design (e.g. wooden block paving) had to be replaced with cheaper alternatives, whilst the fibre-optic lighting never worked and the heavily trafficked (for deliveries) paving near the Library is extensively cracked. The maintenance regime is based on Southwark's standard model, based in turn on level of use, but this seems inadequate for what has become a high-profile heavily used space.

At Woolwich, although issues of management were extensively discussed during the design phases of the scheme, the critical views of managers about the bespoke nature of much of the scheme were consistently overruled after political pressure was brought to bear, for example to get the lighting scheme adopted. For them, the scheme 'was never fit for purpose' and although 'it looked nice, it was impractical in the long-term' (manager) and a greater degree of standardisation would have been preferred for a scheme that quickly had to fall in to line with the council's standard management regime. Indeed, a standard approach was to some degree retrofitted through the addition of traditional park benches to supplement the sculptural but uncomfortable bespoke ones and the removal of the 'architecturally nice' (manager) litter bins in favour of larger standard municipal ones. For others, the problem was a lack of institutional memory and in particular 'a problem passing on knowledge from the design/ implementation phase to those responsible for management' (regen-

erator). The designers look back with sadness that 'the place now looks scruffy and unloved' (landscape designers). It seems that, despite the original enthusiasm for the space and for excellence, this enthusiasm quickly waned as attention shifted to other projects and as the implications for maintenance budgets were felt.

Security: passive, active and abandoned

If maintenance problems were similar, then security responses at the three community squares were very different. Swiss Cottage is a 24-hour space, but security is deliberately passive. During the day (until 4pm), security is informally covered by the landscape operatives, after which a mobile patrol is employed by the council, to whom users may report incidents up until 10.30pm. From then until 3am, the space is surveyed by a CCTV system monitored in the control room, with a patrol being sent out in the case of an incident. Behaviour signage on site is kept to a minimum and problems such as skaters in the water pool (when it is not working) are dealt with on a daily basis by the site-manager (elsewhere, they are discouraged by the design of the street furniture). Generally, the square is well respected by users, and vandalism (which was a feature of Swiss Cottage Park and which was expected in the square) has hardly been a problem.

By comparison, vandalism and antisocial behaviour was more pronounced in Woolwich and Peckham. In Peckham Square, for example, the extensive CCTV system has picked up intimidation by groups of youths and cars driving into the space and knocking down bollards and then having parties with heavy drinking and loud music. Such problems are actively addressed in a space that is regularly patrolled by the borough-wide community wardens and by the police. The space is also well lit to 'discourage drinkers and rough sleepers' (architect), although there are demands to further enhance the lighting and CCTV. During the observations of Peckham Square, the researcher was stopped by the community wardens and asked for security reasons to discontinue photography until a permit was obtained. The local authority later advised that a permit was not necessary and the work was completed, but the episode illustrated the active nature of the security response in this clearly public space.

At the Royal Arsenal Gardens, because the surrounding developments never happened, the aspirations for the space have largely remained un-met, the space has no natural surveillance and, despite the initial project brief calling for a space that would resist vandalism

8.28 Royal Arsenal Gardens – a sense of abandonment and decay, multiplied by the failure to remove graffiti and to resist vandalism

low-level but persistent problems remain.

EVALUATION

The three community squares were marked out by the aspirations of their initiators to use public space both as a means to regenerate otherwise difficult environments for their communities and to provide a venue where community activities and interaction could occur. In two of the spaces, this vision extended from the space itself to the uses surrounding them, which also had a very clear community (public) focus, whilst in the third, the space was seen as the incentive for a market-led regeneration. The first two (Swiss Cottage and Peckham) have become the respective brands for these locations, whilst Royal Arsenal Gardens has been all but abandoned as a focus for either local pride or investment, and looks likely to be swept away altogether in the future as new opportunities driven by the expected arrival of Crossrail (see Chapter 2) in Woolwich look set to transform the town. In 2010, new proposals were brought forward by Berkeley Homes (developers of the neighbouring Royal Arsenal – see **9.6**) to redevelop the area (including Royal Arsenal Gardens) in a comprehensive fashion.

Since its completion, Swiss Cottage Community Square has won many plaudits, and although stakeholders are critical about some aspects of the surrounding architecture (most notably the new residential blocks), there is a strong sense that this has become 'a hub gear in the community's sense of itself' (developer). Those involved recognise, nevertheless, that the project demonstrates the need for a much fuller consideration of how management issues should be dealt with during the process of handover from those responsible for its development, to those with long-term stewardship roles. In this, the space is not alone, although the project manager comments, 'Whilst it is important to tap into the creativity of designers, creative personalities are often not interested in the budget.' All three community spaces demonstrated that the enthusiasm to commit capital funds to achieve something 'special' may not accord with the standard routines, fragmented responsibilities and limited revenue-based funding streams of municipal management, potentially undermining carefully conceived design solutions in the process: 'the management expectations of the client will be a good indicator for

and graffiti, it has suffered from such activities from day one. The children's play area, for example, never attracted users, and its expensive Scandinavian equipment was soon torn out and thrown into the river. The vertical elements on the site, particularly the bespoke lighting features, are particularly susceptible to graffiti (**8.28**). Moreover, although the skateboarders have given the space a purpose, an unfortunate side effect is that the area has become a hot-spot of petty crime in the form of thieving from the skateboarders themselves – 'kids having their phones, iPods, and bikes nicked, rather than serious crime' (manager). Police community support officers intermittently patrol the space and three CCTV cameras link the space to the council's CCTV control room, but the disconnect of the space from any activity ensures that it remains a low security priority and

8.29   Relative stakeholder influences

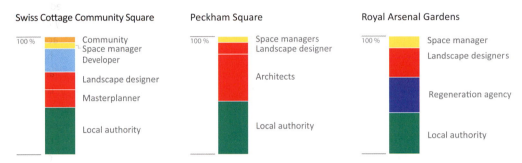

what you can achieve and what you can't with a piece of design work' (landscape designer).

The three projects were each driven forward by strong champions, both political and executive. At Swiss Cottage, there was strong political support to create a new focus for the area, and individuals in the local authority with the leadership skills, continuity of responsibility and vision to deliver it. This was situated within the context of a buoyant local market able to cross-subsidise the scheme and a realistic masterplan through which the separate projects could be coordinated. At Peckham, 'It was a brave decision to have a public square in such a deprived location, as there were concerns about social behaviour and previous public spaces in the borough had been a disaster' (planner). The resulting development has been very well received by external audiences, although with the library winning most acclaim, including the 2001 Stirling Prize. Today, it is the focus of a new leisure and cultural offer for Peckham that has played a large part in regenerating the wider area. For Fred Manson (the project champion), the key to success has been in thinking bold, but also thinking about the context and what is right there – in other words avoiding importing standard models from elsewhere. In a very real way, the power he held was critical to getting the scheme delivered, as long as he could convince the politicians, who themselves knew that they 'could always blame the officers if things went wrong' (planner).

Those involved firmly believe in an incremental approach to space design (rather than a masterplanned one). For them, the square should be allowed to adapt and change organically over time, and in this sense it is still not a completed space (e.g. the existing uses onto the high street could open onto the square, and new uses could be created under the arch, such as a proposed new art gallery). In such circumstances 'when there is no structure and the boundaries of the space are disparate, the uses make the space. It would not work with an office or hotel, it is the cultural and social programme that animates the square' (landscape designer). 'The space performs better and better as time goes on.'

At Woolwich, the key lesson has been the need to deliver regeneration in a more holistic manner in a way that does not rely on a single element – the public space – to drive it forward. There is also a need to carefully research and understand likely users in the context of location and the type of space being proposed: 'putting play equipment for small children on the site, for example, was never going to work as no children lived within easy reach, instead the key user group turned out to be much older children' (regenerator). Stakeholders agreed that it may have been better to pursue a more temporary solution for the space, something that was flexible and usable and that generated activity but that could be quickly replaced when more permanent development came forward. Looking at development in another way, however, although the space has been problematic, the area has been safeguarded for a future more suitable development, and in the meantime remains in public ownership, rather than as a big-box private supermarket. The space has certainly provided a better environment than the derelict site it replaces, and by chance has also tapped into a previously un-met demand from the skateboarder community. As the Swiss Cottage masterplanner concluded: 'A square needs to have a purpose, a reason for its existence; its design needs to be integrated with all the needs of its community.'

The relative stakeholder influences in these projects varied, but all had in common a strong local authority role, either at political or executive level and for better or for worse (**8.29**). In all cases, this role powerfully shaped the resulting schemes, carving out an opportunity space (Tiesdell & Adams 2004) within which designers were able to operate, which, in the case of Peckham Square strongly influenced the nature of most other aspects of the resulting square (**8.30**).

Addressing the critiques

The intention of the public authorities in creating each of the squares reviewed in this chapter has been to assist in the regeneration of the neighbourhoods in which each is located through creating a new locus for public life. As the communities concerned were amongst the most diverse in London, these were clearly lofty aspirations and difficult to achieve. Despite this, two of the three spaces, in different ways, have been overwhelming successes. The third has failed as an inclusive space for the wider community, but in this failure has found its own (more narrowly constituted) community of users, London's skate community.

Yet despite the success at Swiss Cottage and Peckham and their use by a diverse constituency of users, these spaces (and Royal Arsenal

8.30   Peckham Square – a large opportunity space was given to, and exploited by, the designers

Gardens) have demonstrated an absence of concern for one group of potentially heavy users, the elderly. Although each space (in common with all those studied in this book) is physically highly accessible, featuring no evidence of attempts to be deliberately disabling, a general lack of appropriate seating, shading/shelter and public toilets is ubiquitous – factors that unduly impact on older users. The absence of formal seating around the pool at Swiss Cottage and the provision of seating without backs at Peckham and in Woolwich, for example, say much about the desire amongst designers to see clean sculptural lines and uncluttered spaces, but also about their ignorance of the needs of this important constituency. The dominance of these (and other) spaces by younger user groups provides some evidence of the impact.

At Royal Arsenal Gardens, the heavy skew in the use of the space by male users demonstrates how parochial the space has become – a space in which young male skaters have found a home, but to which other users (particularly women) feel alienated. The space confirms the view in the literature that the creation of dedicated 'teen' spaces may not be as attractive to young women as to men, and, graphically, the observation made long ago by William Whyte (1980) in his studies of New York's public spaces, that the absence of female users is a strong indicator that something is wrong with the design of the space. Indeed, the skaters at Woolwich have been particularly vulnerable to petty crime. By inference, the strong female presence at Swiss Cottage suggests that this space is particularly welcoming for its users, something reinforced by the successful integration of play elements (the pool and play area) into the design, avoiding the isolation of children into a separate dedicated play space (although a fenced play area also exists on the site). The playful public art at Peckham has a similar effect.

Case studies across the last three chapters have already shown how design, development and management processes in London have sometimes been shaped by security concerns (e.g. Canada Square and Euston Station Piazza), and, arguably, by fear of 'the other' (Sloane Square). The spaces discussed in this chapter revealed a widespread fear of teenage groups and the various indigent communities, whether justified or not, but little sign that London's communities are being atomised through decisions made about public space; thus, when high-quality community spaces are provided, they are used with relish by a diverse range of users, including the young. Far from

withdrawing, those with the greatest choice actively embrace such spaces, although all users remain concerned with issues of safety (not least relating to children), and are generally appreciative of design and management measures that help to reassure them. Rather than undermining the 'public' dimension of space provision, the provision of high-quality community space is enhancing through encouraging users to participate. The exception is when all goes wrong, as it did at Royal Arsenal Gardens. Even there, however, there was no deliberate attempt to exclude. Instead, the failure of the private sector to embrace the public vision for the area led to its isolation with consequential fear of crime and eventual decline.

Today, almost no new public spaces are created without ubiquitous CCTV coverage, whilst, as the attempt to limit the researcher's freedom to photograph at Peckham demonstrated (see above), over-enthusiastic policing is not limited to privately owned 'public' spaces. But it was the presence of others that made users feel safe and comfortable in the community spaces. In general, the spaces demonstrated that the creation of high-quality well-used space is largely self-policing, with users overwhelmingly adopting the voluntary societal codes of behaviour without the need for additional rules or delimitation of freedoms. In general, these were public spaces that are designed to be used (not to exclude) and in the main they share this with most of the public spaces examined in this book.

9 SPACES OF THE DOMESTIC CITY

DOMESTIC LONDON

The domestic sphere in London, like any city, constitutes the vast majority of the urban realm. But unlike many British cities, which by 1980 had largely hollowed out their central areas as locations for residential living, London had retained a large and heterogeneous residential population in its central boroughs (the exception being large parts of the City of London). The wealthy preserved their strong predilection for living centrally, most notably in the highly exclusive and expensive Georgian and Victorian expansions to the immediate west and north of the centre. The working classes also maintained a strong presence in the public housing estates, most notably to the immediate south and east of the centre. By contrast, for a long time during the twentieth century, the expanding middle classes were being squeezed out through a combination of high housing costs, poor-quality schooling (perceived or real) and an environment seen to be unsuitable for children (Edwards 2010: 192).

By the late 1980s, the population of London (including in its inner and central areas) was on the rise again as London boomed on the back of a decline in its traditional manufacturing sector accompanied by an equally dramatic rise in its financial and business services (Clark 2002; Pratt 1994). New areas of formerly working-class London were being gentrified (see Chapter 3), international investors poured huge quantities of capital into the London residential property market, and London increasingly becoming a venue for international migration (particularly after 2004 from the European Union accession countries). Thus Butler & Lees (2006) note that whereas in 1981 inner London had a lower proportion of the population in higher professional managerial positions than outer London, in 2001 the situation had reversed. Initially, these gentrification pressures focused on large period properties in multiple occupation, and when these opportunities dried up, developers turned to smaller properties or converted flats, and more recently to old warehouses, factories and even offices

(Hamnett & Whitelegg 2007). These activities have hugely driven up property prices, particularly as wealthy 'super-gentrifiers' (Butler & Lees 2006) brought increasingly higher wealth to the central and inner London property markets, with the housing markets leading the economic recovery and later the boom that stoked up from the mid 1990s onwards.

For Edwards (2010: 193–4), this influx of capital into London's housing markets resulted in surprisingly little actual new build, with new money acting to drive up prices in the existing stock. For him, 'London had become a tremendous wealth machine for established owner-occupiers and investors, and simultaneously a poverty machine for the rest of the population: tenants and new purchasers'. This failure to build enough new homes was a national problem, but the London situation was particularly acute, and preoccupied the plans of the first two mayors. Ken Livingstone presided over an increase in completions, with, for example, 24,000 completions in the 2005/06 annual returns, 18,600 of which were new-build. Planning permissions in the same year amounted to some 51,000 new homes, a figure well in excess of the 29,400 achieved in the year before his election (1999/2000) (GLA 2007).

Arguably, this was a relatively straightforward achievement in a booming housing market where demand far exceeded supply, a situation that changed somewhat following the 2008 banking crisis and the recession that ensued. Moreover, in the main, the units being produced were very small, 34 per cent studio or single-bedroom and 49 per cent two-bedroom flats, with just 5 per cent of units four bedrooms and above (GLA 2007). The rising completion rates were being achieved at the cost of space standards, the needs of families and a huge rise in densities, the latter taking advantage of the 'renaissance'-inspired policies of Livingstone (see Chapter 4). Concurrently, policies also delivered a third of units in 'affordable' categories (GLA 2007), some by grant-aided registered social

9.1   Seaton Square, Barnet – buildings defining suburban space, even if little more than a roundabout

landlords, but many as a direct result of planning obligations (Section 106 agreements) entered into by private developers to deliver a proportion of affordable stock in exchange for planning permission. In 2005/06, the boroughs estimated that planning obligations raised £230 million across the capital, of which the largest proportion (29 per cent) was spent on transport improvements, 24 per cent on public realm schemes (including new streetscape and public/open-space projects) and 14 per cent on affordable housing (DCLG 2006: 19–21). The figures do not include in-kind benefits (the provision

of a public good directly by the developer rather than through a financial contribution to the authority). London receives more in-kind benefits than any other part of the country, with 70 per cent of planning obligations containing such provisions.

These benefits, like the housing completions to which they relate, are not distributed evenly across London. Thus in 2005/06 over a third of completions were delivered in just five inner London Boroughs (Tower Hamlets, Greenwich, Wandsworth, Southwark and Westminster – GLA

2007), who, with the exception of Wandsworth, also benefited from very substantial Section 106 monies (in excess of £8 million each), alongside Islington, the City and Brent (the success of the latter outer London borough largely relating to the redevelopment of Wembley Stadium). The figures demonstrate the ability of inner and central London to raise substantial funds through such means to cross-fund public goods, including public space, whilst many outer London boroughs lag some way behind (DCLG 2006: 19). In outer London, development has often followed the roads-dominated model that characterised much private residential development across the country, although more recently schemes have adopted the sorts of neo-traditional layouts that since 1998 have been promoted through Government guidance (**9.1**).

This chapter examines two related critiques, the first concerning explicit strategies of segregation in the domestic sphere and the second, the knock-on implications of a withdrawal from public space into the more insular and private worlds of the domestic sphere.

THE CRITIQUES

Segregated space

The first critique in this chapter relates closely to those of privatisation as discussed in Chapter 5 and to the fear of crime leading to exclusion as discussed in Chapter 8. As argued previously, crime, or often, more correctly, the fear of crime, remains a major reason why those with choice may seek to avoid public space (Miethe 1995). This may manifest itself in the avoidance of perceived hot spots of crime, typically shying away from urban locations into suburban ones, and can result in the deliberate segregation of space, behind gates. Boddy (1992), for example, contends that people feel exposed and vulnerable when outdoors, and, conversely, safe and protected when inside, a fear that can result in the increasing spatial segregation of activities by class, age, ethnicity and occupation – communities for the elderly, ethnic areas, skid row, etc. However, rather than a fear of crime or a sense of exclusion, the primary drivers of such trends are likely to be (i) economic realities – the rich gravitate to high-value areas and the poor group together in low-cost or subsidised housing – and (ii) social preferences – those with choice gravitate to the catchments of good state schools, whilst cultural groups concentrate in areas where

family/friendship ties are strong and where institutions and facilities are available to meet their needs.

Ethnic tensions are often rife within parts of London's poorest communities, particularly between newcomers (who often benefit from vibrant religious and other support networks) and the indigenous poor (whose social networks have often broken down and who feel under siege) (Norman & Ali 2010: 7). However, areas strongly characterised by particular ethnic groups, such as Brick Lane in the East End (the focus of the capital's Bangladeshi community) or Green Lanes in north London (the focus for London's Cypriot community, both Greek and Turkish) have become popular destinations in their own right for others wishing to sample something of these cultures. More disturbing are the pressures in the housing market referred to above deriving from cost, scarcity and gentrification that have led to a highly segregated market, divided between well-off owner-occupiers and comparatively impoverished social renters, with the middle squeezed out of large parts of the London property scene. Geographically, this distributes itself across London into zones of relative affluence such as much of the Borough of Richmond upon Thames in West London, zones of relative poverty such as much of the Borough of Newham in the East End, and large zones of mixed communities where gentrified homes or new housing schemes sit alongside local authority estates or housing association properties. The last of these include the Isle of Dogs, where some of London's poorest housing estates now sit within a stone's throw of Canary Wharf and in the shadows of gleaming residential blocks that increasingly house some of the richest of London's residents.

The response in places where such stark contrasts are apparent has sometimes been gating (**9.2**) (Carmona 2009a: 118), the most famous and one of the largest such sites being the Bow Quarter a mile north of Canary Wharf. At Bow Quarter, 733 one- or two-bedroomed apartments and a range of luxury resident-only facilities occupy the buildings and land of the former Bryant and May match factory, and gates and security separate the compound from its traditional East End hinterland, whilst studies have shown that the occupiers lead very different and separate lives to the surrounding communities. Without gating, however, some have argued that the relatively affluent residents would not have chosen to live in such an area at all, and that the restricted area is no larger than that previously occupied by the enclosed factory premises (Rice 2004). Although still relatively rare

9.2   Isle of Dogs – gated estates sprung up in the Docklands area in the 1980s and 1990s, although typically these are relatively small, no larger than a block in size, and do not disrupt any established rights of way

in London, contemporary trends to physically gate communities have been well documented (Blakely & Snyder 1997; Low 2006; Webster 2001) and reflect the long established desire of affluent groups in many societies to separate themselves from the rest of society, arguably reflecting a fear of crime, but also a desire to be, and to be seen to be, exclusive (e.g. the eighteenth-century gating of the garden squares and streets of Bloomsbury – see Chapter 2). In essence, the gates turn the space inside into a private space, accessed on the basis

of ownership rights, whilst the residents turn their backs (the walls and gates) on the communities around.

Undoubtedly crime and uncivil behaviour can quickly undermine the quality and experience of public space, encouraging users to manage the perceived risk by avoiding using places and in turn contributing to their further decline. In this respect, fear of victimisation is real and a significant factor in how the contemporary urban environment

9.3   Hampstead Garden Suburb – private security patrols

is both designed and managed (Oc & Tiesdell 1997), not least in pressures for segregation. A huge literature exists around approaches to crime reduction, with arguments focusing on the extent to which environments can be made safer through various combinations of defensive design, surveillance, street animation, active control, and social and educational approaches to crime reduction – approaches that, at their most extreme, lead to accusations of over-management (see Chapter 8). Although prescriptions vary, most commentators would agree with Jane Jacobs's (1961: 45) basic prescription that public peace is kept primarily by the network of voluntary controls that most individuals in society subscribe to and that are (typically) codified in law. By its very nature, this requires users to be actively engaged in the process of civility, and a perverse consequence of the privatisation of residential environments may simply be the withdrawal (behind their gates) of many law-abiding participants from this role (Bentley 1999: 163).

In the USA and elsewhere, such practices extend to large neighbourhoods that are responsible for their own policing, waste collection, local planning, local taxation, and so forth, effectively declaring unilateral independence from wider civic society (Mattson 1999: 134). Although such arrangements based on the US Residential Community Associations model were briefly advocated in the UK as part of the 1980s privatisation agenda (Punter 1990: 13), they came to nothing,

and in London such practices are not possible with the curious historic exceptions of Middle and Inner Temples (home to a good part of the English barrister profession). As Liberties within the City of London, these enclaves are effectively run as independent municipalities and have been so since the fourteenth century. Elsewhere, a small number of affluent neighbourhoods, including Hampstead Garden Suburb (**9.3**), employ their own private security on the basis of a group or individual subscription as an 'additional' private arrangement within their boundaries, whilst remaining public in all other respects. Larger private estates, some with a very long providence, also exist in suburban outer London and the surrounding home counties. Some of these estates own, manage and maintain their 'public realm' whilst remaining physically open to all (e.g. the 280-acre Cator Estate in Blackheath), whilst others are fully gated (e.g. the 360 acres of Burwood Park in Walton-on-Thames). However, even in such locations, developments tend to be small by international standards (Compton 2002).

Moreover, it is overstating the case to argue that all forms of gating are inevitably destructive or just for the 'benefit' of the affluent. Just as the private gardens of suburban London have long been fenced and gated to preserve the privacy of their inhabitants, so, in recent years, have many larger communal gardens associated with apartment buildings and other residential complexes where the garden space is held in common. Atkinson (2003: 1834) also praises the installation of concierge schemes and security doors on previously open public housing estates as a means to exclude unwanted guests and improve the quality of life of inhabitants. Indeed, a long-time criticism of many Modernist housing estates has been the presence of no-man's-lands that no-one seems to own or care for. Although criticised for over-claiming about the impact of her prescriptions, Alice Coleman's (1985) study of housing estates in Southwark and Tower Hamlets led to the enclosing of much previously 'communal' land on estates such as Lisson Green (in Lisson Grove), whilst estate redevelopments since, including that of Angell Town in Brixton (**9.4**), have made great efforts to avoid the creation of undefined shared spaces. Instead, spaces are defined as clearly public and therefore open to all, communal but with restricted access, or wholly private. Arguably, therefore, gating may only be a problem when the spaces being gated are those that might reasonably, in most circumstances, be considered part of the public realm by dint of their extent, location, and/or significance.

9.4   Angell Town, Brixton – previously undefined space, now new garden square

Insular space

Some have extrapolated the trends they see in public space design and management into an extension of what Sennett (1977: 5–15) has described as a decline in public life brought on by an increasing emphasis on the private relations of individuals, their families and intimate friends, driven by the rise of secularism and capitalism. He argues that public life has increasingly been seen as a matter of dry formal relations, whilst the introspective obsession with private life has become a trap, absorbing the attention of individuals rather than liberating them. The consequence is a retreat to insular domestic

space whilst the venues of public life, the streets and squares, have increasingly been replaced by the suburban living room.

Supporting this view are arguments that identify the spread of new technologies and new private venues for social exchange as a key threat to the very notion of a public life. Ellin (1996: 149), amongst others, notes how many social and civic functions that were previously – by necessity – conducted in the public realm have increasingly transferred to the private. Entertainment, access to information, shopping, financial services and even voting can increasingly be undertaken from the home using modern technologies, potentially undermining the viability of traditional public space. This, on top of increasingly dramatic rises in personal mobility, has, in many places, led to a decline in the 'local', 'small-scale' and 'public' and to a growth in the 'regional', 'large-scale' and 'private' as venues for public life. In London, the increasing dominance of regional shopping centres and their impact on local high streets represents a case in point (see Chapter 7). Thus Sennet (1977) and others have long argued that individual lives are increasingly private and that, as a result, public culture has declined.

Third spaces

This tendency may simply necessitate a broadening of the definition of public space to incorporate some of the new forms of semi-public space that have been emerging. Banerjee (2001: 19–20), for example, has suggested that urban designers should concern themselves with broader notions of public life rather than just physical public space, reflecting the new reality that much public life exists in private spaces, 'not just in corporate theme parks, but also in small businesses such as coffee shops, bookstores and other such third places'. For him, these spaces support and enable social interaction, regardless of their ownership.

This notion of 'third places' was originally advanced by Oldenburg (1989), who argued that because contemporary domestic life often takes place in isolated nuclear families, and work life, with the spread of new technologies, is increasingly a solitary activity, people need other social realms to live a fulfilled life. For him, this 'informal' public life, although seemingly more scattered than it was in the past, is in fact highly focused in a number of third-place settings – cafes, bookstores, coffee shops, bars, hair salons and other small private hangouts. These places host the encounters from the accidental to the organised and regular, and have become fundamental institutions of mediation between the individual and society, possessing a number of common features. They are neutral, inclusive, open, comfortable and social.

One might argue that these features also (or should) characterise public space, and that these spaces are nothing new – the British pub, French café or American bar provide examples from the past that remain significant third places in the present. Today, these have been supplemented with other forms of third place – the shopping centre,

9.5   Dalston Eastern Curve Garden – a place of escape

health club and a surfeit of new leisure spaces – although empirical evidence examining the social life of public spaces in London suggests that traditional public spaces are far from dead (Dines & Cattell 2006: 29). In east London, researchers found that not only were traditional public spaces still valued as important social venues, but, rather than their users seeing domestic space as an escape from the hustle of the city, public spaces were viewed as opportunities to escape from the pressures of domestic life (**9.5**), to be together with friends (in particular the young) and, on occasions, to be alone with their thoughts.

Virtual space

What is new is the growth of virtual spaces – chat rooms, virtual worlds, social networks, and the like – that some have argued will supplant our need to meet and interact in traditional public space, and will eventually lead to new forms of urbanism (Aurigi 2005: 17–31). Leaving on one side the most extreme predictions from the 'techno-determinists' of the obsolescence of public space, or from the 'techno-romantics' who see the Internet as the new democratic realm, some of the most thoughtful writers in the field have concluded that the nature of cities as we understand them today will be challenged and must eventually be reconceived as 'Computer networks become as fundamental to urban life as street systems' (Mitchell 1996: 107).

Others have argued that, rather than undermining traditional cities, the new technologies actually act to reinforce their role since they are most advanced in metropolitan areas, whilst those who work in these fields increasingly wish to live and work in places that bring them into contact with others in the field and that meet their quality of life aspirations (Graham & Marvin 1999: 97). As a result, the quality of public space may become more rather than less important.

In reality, the long-term impact of the new technologies on city form and public space is still to be played out, but the fact that face-to-face communication remains the preferred mode of interaction for business as well as for private activities suggests that public space may not be as threatened by the new technologies as was once thought (Castells 1996; Sassen 1994). The expanded role of third places seems to confirm this, as, in London, does the relentless growth in the office market, even following the 2008 crash (PropertyWire 2010), reconfirming the attraction of physically doing business in London. Critically, however, whether private domestic, third, or virtual spaces, all these worlds are effectively beyond the normal realm of civic society to manage, as is their impact upon 'traditional' public space.

DOMESTIC SPACES

The London-wide analysis (Chapter 4) showed that approaching a fifth of new London squares are of a domestic type, with unexpectedly few found in suburban outer London. In part, this may simply reflect the difficulties faced by many outer London Boroughs in making a significant new contribution to housing provision in London (GLA 2007). Underpinning this are a variety of historic factors relating to:

- The presence since 1947 of a greenbelt around London, constraining growth on greenfield land both within the boundaries of Greater London and immediately beyond and ensuring that most other developable greenfield land has long since been built upon.

- The low-density nature of much of outer London, with borough population densities on average less than half and often less than a quarter that of central London (below 2,500 people per square kilometre), and with pressure from local populations to keep it that way (UK National Statistics, London [n.d]).

- The absence of significant quantities of brownfield land in large areas of outer London, particularly to the west of the metropolitan area.

- The acceptance, even in Ken Livingstone's renaissance-inspired London Plan, of a density range from 1,100 habitable rooms per hectare in central London to as low as 150 on the periphery, reinforcing the trend for fewer larger homes on London's periphery and more smaller homes towards the centre.

Together, these factors have ensured that much of the new housing in London over the period covered by this research has been of a high-density nature, typically in the inner/central London areas, often featuring large numbers of small units for individuals and/or couples to occupy, many of which were purchased by investors seeking to ride the property market upwards and benefit from a burgeoning buy-to-let market (until the bubble burst in 2008). Thus, whilst Hamnett (2003: 218–23) adds high-density typologies born of the post-war local authority housing estates and the later conversion of industrial buildings into luxury residential apartments (**9.6**) to Rasmussen's pre-war depiction of the low-density terraced and semi-detached 'Unique City', a more recent assessment should also include the high-density, sometimes high-rise, and decidedly continental sorts of purpose-built apartment blocks that have sprung up with increasingly frequency as the renaissance policies took hold. A quid pro quo for the permissions that gave rise to these developments has often been the provision of public space as part of the planning obligation that accompanied it, or in order to add value to the developer's offer. The two case studies featured in this chapter are of this type: the 'village' square of the high-profile Greenwich Millennium Village (GMV) and the internal residential court of the Empire Square development in Southwark.

GMV Village Square – when aspirations and realities diverge

Before the nineteenth century, much of Greenwich Peninsula (to the east of historic Maritime Greenwich) was pasture, although from the early nineteenth century onwards, the area became increasingly industrial in character, with chemical and gas works being situated there as well as a range of other heavy engineering activities (**9.7**). When the gas works (the largest in Europe) closed following the

9.6   Royal Arsenal Riverside, Woolwich – redevelopment of the historic Royal Arsenal by Berkeley Homes, including a network of public spaces

discovery of North Sea gas, the area was left as a contaminated wasteland. In 1990, the decision was made to extend the Jubilee Line eastwards, including a new stop (North Greenwich) and associated bus station to the north of the Peninsula. The intention was to open the area up for housing development, and British Gas (who then owned much of the Peninsula) contributed £25 million to the scheme. They sold their holdings to English Partnerships (the national regeneration agency) in 1997, and not long after the decision was taken to locate the Millennium Dome (today the O2) to the far north

of the Peninsula and to launch a competition for the design and development of a showcase 'Millennium Village' on the southeastern portion of the site.

The competition was won by a joint venture between Taylor Wimpey and Countryside Properties (as Greenwich Millennium Village Ltd, GMVL) with their designers Ralph Erskine (later Erskine Tovatt Arkitekter) and EPR Architects, with a masterplan that featured a village square along its northern edge. GMVL subsequently took a lease for the site of 999

9.7   Site of GMV Village Square

1910s

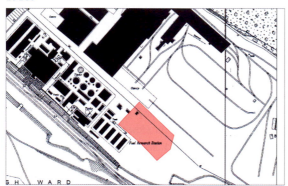

1950s

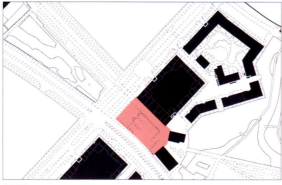

2010

years, whilst English Partnerships (today the Homes and Communities Agency, HCA) remain the freeholder. Since Ralph Erskine's death in 2005, Tovatt Architects have retained an advisory role as overall masterplanners, although each phase is designed by a separate design team. The village square was designed by Randle Siddeley Associates (RDA, landscape designers).

The Village Square was completed in 2009 as part of Phase 2 of GMV and designed to link into the progression of spaces on Greenwich Peninsula from the O2 southwards through the Peninsula's Central Park to its Southern Park, with the square acting as the bridge between the two parks. The aspiration was for a space for the new community to use, a space with 'a real buzz about it' (regenerator) stemming from its mix of ground-floor activities and hard and soft landscaping. It was seen as 'the centre-piece of the development' (planner) with buses and the proposed Greenwich Waterfront Transit (cancelled in 2009) running through it. The intention was to create a space to be, rather than just to pass through, a multifunctional space that could house events and other activities. The construction cost of the square (excluding the buildings) was £0.5 million.

Empire Square – when commercial realities bite

Empire Square is situated at the end of Borough High Street in a historic part of Southwark, occupying a large urban block. Before redevelopment, the site had been derelict for some time, and before that had been in industrial uses, including a goods depot (**9.8**). The London Borough of Southwark were keen to see development happen, but also that this should be a high-quality development. Initial permission had been granted for 270 residential units as part of a gated development with no public space; however, the developer (Berkeley Homes) wanted to significantly increase the density to 576 (mixed-tenure) units and saw a new public square and affordable units as a quid pro quo, effectively giving a third of the site back in public benefits through the new space. For them, making the new square publicly accessible was a price well worth paying for the extra units achieved, many of which were to be housed in a new 22-storey tower.

The revised scheme largely failed to fit in with the Borough's strategic objectives for the area, which envisaged a lower-rise solution, and today, despite its architectural qualities, the tower is still considered 'arguably quite harmful' (planner) by some in the authority. Nevertheless, planning permission was given in 2001, with the planners being swayed by the major benefit that the public space was seen to offer: creating additional linkages and movement through the site, as well as practically allowing day and sunlight into the residential units surrounding it, and offering amenity space.

9.8 Site of Empire Square

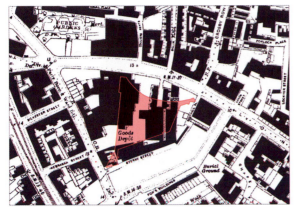

1910s

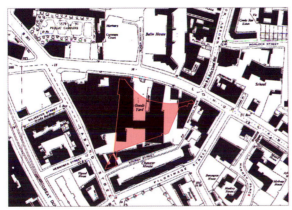

1950s

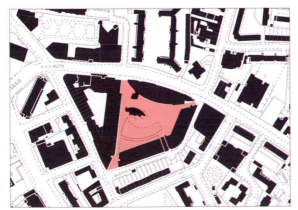

2010

For their part, the architects – Rolf Judd – analysed how new linkages through the site could fit in with a series of connected green spaces all the way to London Bridge Station (to the north) along a key desire line. The aspiration was to 'give something back to the community in terms of a piece of public realm' (planner), whilst boosting the local area through a range of commercial uses at ground level, including a large supermarket. For the local authority, the idea was to have active frontages, with retail and restaurant uses spilling out into the space, whilst the designers sought to create a relaxing and peaceful space. Both the local authority and the Mayor's office (to which it was referred because of the height of the tower) were keen to see greater permeability and a good mix of uses. Since completion in 2007, the scheme has been sold to Fairhold Athena Ltd, who have appointed managing agents to manage the development on their behalf.

Designing domestic space
Residential or community space?

The Village Square at GMV evolved through the design process as one of a number of focal points within the wider development. The morphology of the GMV consists of blocks of residential apartments surrounding inner private courtyard (garden) spaces with controlled access for residents only. The Village Square, by contrast, was designed to be an open and publicly accessible version of these private courtyard spaces, a key arrival point at a strategic location where the Central Park meets the development's circulation spine. 'It was envisaged from the beginning that this would be a gathering place, with commercial uses and cafes that would spill out on to the street, and a space for informal market stalls and social events' (planner). Yet the space was also seen by stakeholders as primarily a local space for the GMV residents and other passers-by, and not for the wider community of Greenwich and beyond. To some degree, this revealed a tension from the start over the nature of the space – quiet residential or vibrant community space – particularly given the types of residents likely to be attracted to GMV, many of whom, research suggests (Butler 2004: 278), will be transient and live at GMV for short-term convenience and not in order to make a long-term commitment to the community (**9.9**).

At Empire Square, similar tensions were apparent. The planners, for example, advocated opening up one side of the square to the road (and to the surrounding community), but this was opposed by the

9.9   GMV Village Square – what type of space?

9.10   Empire Square – sculptural gates and tight enclosure reduces visual permeability into the space

developer, who was concerned that such a solution would be noisier and less attractive to potential residents. The planners quickly backed down and the resulting buildings tightly enclose the space, with just 6-metre entrances at the four corners of the block (one a tunnel under the building), heightening the sense of enclosure. For the designers, 'this provides a strong contrast between the street and the space and a sense of surprise on entering the square, replicating the historic pattern of tight lanes off Borough High Street' (designer) whilst preserving the permeability through the new space, for all. The continuous perimeter block form also allows a greater volume of

development to be housed on the site, but makes the presence of the space (and routes through it) less obvious to those not already in the know. Gates at the entrances utilise sculptural designs so as not to convey the idea of a private space, but in obscuring lines of sight they act to further mask the public nature of the routes (**9.10**).

Unintentionally introspective and subservient, or purposefully low-key?

Planners at Southwark were particularly keen to see active uses on Long Lane (to the north of Empire Square), a major regeneration corridor. The designers were also keen to provide active frontages, wherever possible, onto the surrounding streets. The original mix of uses envisaged a large supermarket facing Long Lane and into the space and a restaurant in a pavilion building that sits within the square, with the majority of the scheme dominated by its residential uses, including serviced apartments. The final mix includes a small Tesco convenience store, a nursery school, a gym, a facility for Guy's Hospital Renal Unit, and some other small-scale commercial elements, including offices in the pavilion. For the planners, the changes are disappointing, since their hope had been for a more active space. Instead, most of the more active uses have no relationship with the space (for example, the small supermarket faces onto Long lane and not onto the space) leaving a more introspective and quiet space than had been envisaged (**9.11**)

9.11 Empire Square – a failure to animate

9.12 GMV Village Square – easy to miss Core 10 bridges

By contrast, the space at Greenwich was designed to open up to its surroundings, and is itself surrounded on two sides by retail, café and restaurant uses (with apartments over). On a third it opens up to Central Park and on a fourth to the peninsular spine road and more apartment blocks. The space is brightly lit in order to look vibrant (surrounding residents complain that it is too bright), yet it is the architecture, rather than the space, that is visually dominant, whilst the landscape was deliberately designed to be 'simple and crisp' (landscape designer), with a number of subtle contemporary features (**9.12**). Bolder elements, including a proposed water feature and central public art element, never materialised (owing to cost and procurement issues). Moreover, the original design, which featured an innovative oval shape with a shared surface road passing through its middle, was quickly abandoned following a process of 'value engineering' and concerns from TfL that buses would be passing through a pedestrianised area. The final scheme adopts a more conventional rectilinear shape with the spine road along its western edge. Here the road is block-paved to indicate that it is entering the space and in order to encourage buses to slow down. However, the line of the Greenwich Waterfront Transit on which buses move is private (leased to TfL from the HCA), and its 20 mph speed limit is not enforced, so that the speed of buses passing through the space has become a problem. The combined result is a large but low-key

space in a clearly subservient role to both its architecture and traffic function.

Green or urban?

The domestic, residential, nature of both spaces reveals itself in their green qualities, reflecting the long London tradition for residential squares. Yet the split personality of both spaces also features in their landscape treatments, which are neither fully green nor fully urban. This is most obvious at GMV, where the Village Square is half soft green space and half hard landscape. The design is rationalised on the basis of a role as a transition from the Peninsula's Central Park to the hard urban spaces of the GMV, with fingers of landscape and trees on a grid projecting into it. This sits alongside a hard landscape, fully serviced with pop-up power supply and watering points in order to cater for markets and other such functions, although little thought was given to whether enough users would be available to support such uses in an essentially local domestic space.

At Empire Square, the landscape design by Lovejoys was carefully considered to introduce a range of treatments into the space, with hard treatments contrasting with the grass and trees, the latter reflecting the idea of an orchard, looking back to the time when fruit was imported into London from Kent via Borough (**9.13**). Again, the

9.13   Empire Square – the pavilion

space is evenly divided between hard and soft treatments, although the partition is less stark, with elements further separated by the presence of the pavilion in the space.

Developing domestic space
Internalising versus externalising decision-making (and spaces)
The decision-making at Empire Square was relatively tight-knit. For

Berkeley Homes, the scheme was breaking new ground for the company and represented a significant innovation in their development model, one that used public space to add value to the scheme as a whole. Berkeley held the purse strings and therefore the leadership role, but gave the architects a very loose brief beyond the number of units they were to achieve on the site. They relied on the professional expertise of the architects to resolve the problem, the key to which was the square and tower. The planners, after backing down on their preferred open square scheme, were happy to accept a space within the block. This internalisation of the space on entirely private land led to a simplified regulatory process with no direct impact of the space upon surrounding public roads or buildings.

At GMV, by contrast, a rather complex structure of decision-making has sometimes led to a lack of clarity. The key decisions are made by a three-way partnership constituting the two developers (GMVL) and public sector partner, English Partnerships (now HCA), who together lead the development with advice from Tovatt Architects to ensure that at each stage of the overall development, the original design intentions are being correctly interpreted. At the Village Square, this cocktail was added to by the relatively benign role of the London Borough of Greenwich and by the less benign contributions of TfL, who were involved because of the public transport routes running along the western side of the square. The result has been a large number of design iterations, including abandoning the original oval scheme and later, on the insistence of English Partnerships (supported by Greenwich), the substitution of a new brief and landscape designers for the space in an attempt to create a square that is more than a purely transient place. The result is a 'square that has been subject to a series of compromises because no one has been in overall charge of the design' (developer).

Design (and compromise) is in the detail

Although both schemes delivered on their broad intentions to establish new squares at the heart of their respective developments, in both cases the short-term pragmatics of the development process undermined the realisation. At GMV, these changes were physical, most notably the demand from TfL to move the bus stops out of the space, undermining its potential as a key arrival space for the development. This overriding concern for the efficient flow of buses extended to a failure to sanction a pedestrian crossing from the square over West Parkside (the spine road), in order not to slow the buses down. As a consequence, the west side of the space remains disconnected from its interior, and 'dangerous' informal crossing is encouraged. The proposed public art also proved problematic, with the favoured scheme (following a competition) going well over the £30,000 budget and being cancelled. Two years after completion, this element remains undelivered despite being part of the Section 106 agreement, with decision-makers paralysed on how to proceed. The speed of the design process and some corner-cutting by the contractor

also led to unresolved problems that have further compromised the design concept, including a failure to fully consider drainage requirements, which now clash (e.g. the manholes) with the lighting grid that extends across the new square.

At Empire Square, the failures were land-use related. These included a failure to lease both the large supermarket space and the pavilion restaurant space, despite almost three years of marketing. The restaurant location was seen to be too far off the beaten track, and its demise (and that of the large supermarket – failed through lack of parking) ensured that the space now lacks active uses directly on to it. Planners at Southwark confess to being bemused as to why the restaurant failed, given the range of successful models to emulate in the area, but believe that 'the space was never designed suitably for a restaurant' (planner). However, given the body of evidence presented that the pavilion had been adequately marketed, they reluctantly agreed to a change of use, concluding that 'it was better to have something in the space than nothing' (planner). The developer argues that only uses such as a bookmaker, takeaway establishment or pub were explicitly ruled out by them, and that the scheme has proven itself to be very adaptable, with the possibility that the mix could change again sometime in the future as and when circumstances allow.

Planning, by regulation

At Greenwich, the borough regard GMV as a flagship development and have been very cooperative in making it happen. The local planners had clear aspirations for the space that it be accessible, vibrant, open to a range of community uses and well connected to the Southern Park, but only played a very minor role (one pre-application meeting) in discussions about its design. They were content that as long as a space was delivered – its provision was tied down in the Section 106 agreement, as was its opening before the completion of the 228th unit – its exact nature was beyond their remit : 'I don't think we had a view one way or another' (planner). Therefore, apart from tying down the ground-floor uses on the space, 'Overall the role of the council was reactive' (planner), with the detailed planning consent being granted in three months.

For Southwark, Empire Square was seen as innovative, not least in the promised mix of uses it aimed to deliver and the public routes through the scheme. These, along with the hours of opening, are guaranteed as a condition to the planning consent. For the planners, however, the failure to attract a large supermarket reflected a clash of development models: the retail model at the time demanded extensive parking, whilst the renaissance-inspired central London planning model denied it. The result was that the developers eventually sought to change uses in order to get the spaces let – despite the fact that they had constructed (at great cost) a large basement car park beneath the square in the hope that permission would be given for its use in connection with the commercial elements of the scheme, something the planners have consistently refused. Today, 40 parking spaces remain unlet.

In both schemes, the planning processes tied a number of clear public benefits down, not least the right to access. They failed, however, to positively shape the resulting spaces, or to offer answers when faced with contrary market indications or other regulatory factors (e.g. the requirement of TfL) that dictated against achieving the original aspirations.

Using domestic space
Active but not animated
Despite aspirations that both spaces be active and animated foci for life, in reality both are quiet spaces for passing by in which few choose to linger long. GMV Village Square had only just opened when the fieldwork began in the summer of 2009. This period, during the 2008–09 recession was marked by significant difficulties in letting the retail, restaurant and café units around the space. As a result, all agree that 'the space has been a little dead. The shops need to open to bring the space to life' (developer). For the designer, however, the large hard landscaped area with no seating does not help, making the 'The space feel deserted and empty' even if there is some movement around its edges. 'In the main it is a transient space' (regenerator) and quiet, even on sunny days, although small numbers of people do sit in the space, for example on the grass after school. The aspiration was nevertheless for a good mix of uses, with provisional lets secured and then lost for a café, two restaurants and a range of retail uses. In fact, by Spring 2012, only two units remained to be filled, with the space housing, by then, a café (**9.14**), health and beauty spa, laundry, pharmacy, lettings agent, and convenience shop.

Stakeholder perceptions at Empire Square were similar: 'Generally it is pretty quiet' (developer). Southwark Planners put this down to

9.14 GMV Village Square – Café Pura, starting to animate the space

two factors: that the surrounding uses do not fill the space with life and that the design does not naturally invite users in – 'newcomers may at first feel apprehensive' (planner). In this, it contrasts strongly with Bermondsey Square (at the opposite end of Long Lane), where active uses, including a Sainsbury's supermarket and hotel, front onto the square, with a dual aspect onto the street behind (**9.15**). Empire Square is used by the nursery school for their children to come out and sing songs and occasionally by people from the gym to do exercises. Office workers from the development (but not from the surrounding area) also sit out and eat their sandwiches on the benches. For their part, although residents comment on the pleasant green nature of the space, few choose to actively use it, although children from the surrounding flats sometimes play in it after school, and, when sunny, some residents use the space for sunbathing. The space very rarely has more than 10–20 people in it at once.

Functional space, but that's OK
Observations at the two spaces revealed a similar picture, that, despite the intentions of stakeholders involved in their development, what has been created are two largely transient spaces in which static activities are rare (**9.16, 9.17**). Instead, the spaces are used as shortcuts, places for a smoke, to access the surrounding buildings and, just occasionally, to sit out in. These are not social spaces (as currently used) and although the potential may still exist in the future to change the nature of their use, this seems unlikely to happen without a more

9.15 Bermondsey Square – built at roughly the same time as Empire Square, the square opens up to the streets around, is animated by active edges and fills with life on Fridays as host to the Bermondsey Antiques Market and at weekends with a farmers' market

permissive and encouraging management regime in place in order to give users a reason to linger (see below).

Notwithstanding their rather functional nature, the two residential squares revealed a general sense of satisfaction amongst the users of the spaces, many of whom (particularly at GMV) were residents of the respective developments (**9.18, 9.19**). Notably, although a minority of interviewees (particularly at GMV) identified the need for

greater activity in and surrounding the spaces – 'a dead square with practically nobody around' (user of GMV Village Square) – in general, users were happy with the quiet, domestic, green, qualities of the squares, with little obvious appetite for the types of active animated spaces envisaged by some stakeholders at the start of the process. Despite this, a sense existed that the spaces should be more public and better used, particularly in the case of Empire Square – 'the square, sitting amongst these huge residential blocks and closed off

9.16   GMV Village Square observational analysis of user patterns – typical local movement patterns (a) and typical activities (b)

a

8:00

13:00

15:00

19:00

Key

→ Very intense pedestrian movement

→ Frequent pedestrian movement

--→ Less frequent pedestrian movement

Note: At the time of analysis, the low level of activity in GMV Village Square ensured that it was impossible to meaningfully measure density of activity.

b

9.17   Empire Square observational analysis of user patterns – typical local movement patterns (a), density of activity (b) and typical activities (c)

a

8:00

13:00

15:00

19:00

Key
→ Very intense pedestrian movement
→ Frequent pedestrian movement
--→ Less frequent pedestrian movement

b

8:00

13:00

15:00

19:00

Key
Few activities
Moderate activity
Intense activity
High concentration of activity

c

by the metal gates, remains completely invisible to people walking on the streets proving that the space is more private than public' (user of Empire Square). Users agreed that addressing the needs of families and children would be critical in this.

Managing domestic space

Management, in the residents' interests

At Empire Square the managing agents (Rendall and Rittner) have responsibility for management policy, devolved from the freeholder. The on-site manager describes the regime as 'tightly run in the interests of the private residents', not the wider public (manager). A Residents Association was set up in 2009 to better involve residents in managing Empire Square, although this is organised, run and controlled by the managing agent and in reality the agent has almost complete autonomy to manage the space in the manner they see fit within the limits of available resources.

At GMV, arrangements are more complicated, with four separate organisations involved in managing the space. The day-to-day management of GMV, including the interior of the square, has been passed over to GMV Management Ltd (GMVML), although their managing agents (Pinnacle) do the actual work on their behalf – cleaning, security, gardening, etc. – all paid for through the service charge. Local politicians are represented on the Board of GMVML, as are representatives of the resident community. In addition, the council have adopted the paths and road, although they do not coordinate with GMVML and, in the view of the managing agent, do a poor job, for example letting weeds grow. Further complicating arrangements has been the retention of the route of the now abandoned Greenwich Waterfront Transit (today a bus lane – **9.20**) in the ownership of the Homes and Communities Agency. Although the estate is managed in the interests of the developers (who are still building there) and the residents, the open nature of the space gives a more public feel, and GMVML are keen to encourage a market in the square. So far, despite discussions with an operator, this has not happened, perhaps because of the 'isolated' feel of the development and the lack of critical local capacity to support such an activity. The adaptability of the space means, however, that in the future it can be used for such purposes or for one-off events.

'Don't play on the grass'

At GMV, the space feels relaxed and safe, with excellent natural surveillance and no obvious security presence. It is monitored by

9.18   GMV Village Square – user perceptions

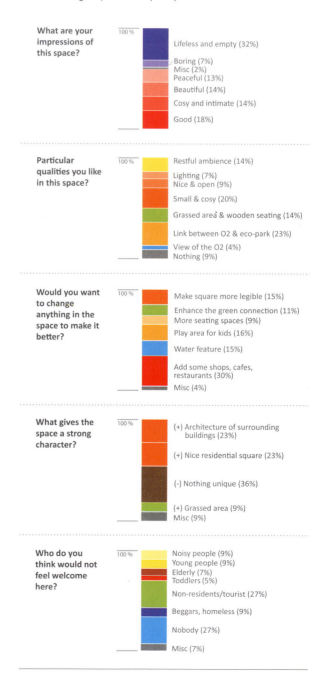

9.19   Empire Square – user perceptions

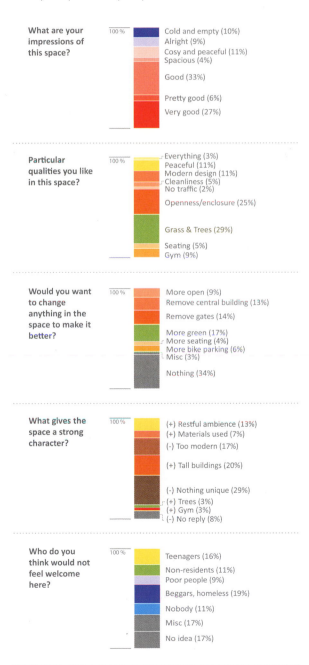

What are your impressions of this space?
100 %
Cold and empty (10%)
Alright (9%)
Cosy and peaceful (11%)
Spacious (4%)
Good (33%)
Pretty good (6%)
Very good (27%)

Particular qualities you like in this space?
100 %
Everything (3%)
Peaceful (11%)
Modern design (11%)
Cleanliness (5%)
No traffic (2%)
Openness/enclosure (25%)
Grass & Trees (29%)
Seating (5%)
Gym (9%)

Would you want to change anything in the space to make it better?
100 %
More open (9%)
Remove central building (13%)
Remove gates (14%)
More green (17%)
More seating (4%)
More bike parking (6%)
Misc (3%)
Nothing (34%)

What gives the space a strong character?
100 %
(+) Restful ambience (13%)
(+) Materials used (7%)
(-) Too modern (17%)
(+) Tall buildings (20%)
(-) Nothing unique (29%)
(+) Trees (3%)
(+) Gym (3%)
(-) No reply (8%)

Who do you think would not feel welcome here?
100 %
Teenagers (16%)
Non-residents (11%)
Poor people (9%)
Beggars, homeless (19%)
Nobody (11%)
Misc (17%)
No idea (17%)

9.20   Former Greenwich Waterfront Transit – alignment still owned and managed by the Homes and Communities Agency

CCTV from the concierge, and (in common with the rest of the estate) is patrolled at night. The design aims to reduce anti-social behaviour by omitting vertical features (**9.21**), placing bollards to prevent joy-riding, and designing simple robust lighting and street furniture. In its first two years, these measures have been successful, with the exception of some early damage by skateboarders. Significantly, despite the 'public' and non-securitised feel of the space, children are not encouraged to play there, whilst pursuits such as ball games and skateboarding are actively discouraged when observed.

At Empire Square, control was starker. For the manager, even some of the activities that do go on in the space are not really allowed – commenting about the use of the space by the nursery: 'We turn a blind eye to it as it is not really the done thing'. For her, 'the space is basically a courtyard and not to be used for ball games or having picnics with children. Once you have allowed it and people can see it then where do you stop, then we are losing control' (manager). At the time of analysis, signs were being put up to control ball games in order to prevent damage to the planting and the associated expense to residents keen to keep their service charges low (**9.22**). In this regard, the management regime clearly favoured the owner-occupiers (typically singles or mature couples) and occupiers of the serviced apartments over the social renters (typically families with children). Children, for example, are discouraged from playing in the space after 6pm, when many residents come home from work, in order to guarantee their peace and quiet.

In some circumstances, the use of the square by non-residents was also viewed as a problem, in particular youths coming into the estate from the surrounding area. 'On such occasions the police are called to remove them from the premises' (manager), whilst 'anyone who looks like they are up to no good is challenged and asked to leave'. Thus, she argues 'It is not fair on people who live here who have bought into the estate, if other people start to use it as a local park' (manager). This view was in stark contrast to that of the designers, who, for example, aimed to create a blank canvas with the hope that residents could use the space for events and activities. The fact that this has not happened is explained largely by management policy, which does not encourage such uses. For example, a request from one of the residents to use the space for a birthday party was turned down: 'If we grant it to one resident we will have to grant it to everyone else, and the control of the space will then become harder and may attract people from the outside' (manager). For the manager, the function of the space was as a green oasis for residents, as a pleasant outlook from their flats and little more.

Residents themselves seem unconcerned, and place their own emphasis on security concerns relating to the apartment blocks, with issues concerning the space itself not featuring in the early meetings of the Empire Square Residents Association. In fact, the design of the development means that it is largely safe and self-policing, with every part well overlooked and little crime reported. On Police advice, however, the space closes between 11pm and 6am to prevent antisocial behaviour: 'The Police would have preferred to have the area gated up at all times, but saw the benefits of the routes created through the space' (designer). There is also a monitored CCTV system, a permanent concierge and security patrols of the estate. Thus the managing agent confirms 'The security is as tight as we can get it, and control of the space is quite strict' (manager).

'easyManage'
The managing agents were appointed early in the process so that they could engage with the designers of Empire Square on management issues. For example, the idea of an orchard of fruiting trees was quickly squashed because of concerns that any fruit would also be, creating a maintenance headache (**9.23**). Despite early engagement, details still

9.21   GMV Village Square – largely vandal-proof space

9.22   Empire Square – a controlling regime

cause problems, including the lack of bins (leading to a build-up of litter) and the use of paving that is difficult to walk on in high heels. Today, the space is kept clean and well maintained and management is proactive, with a caretaker on hand seven days a week. But there is also pressure to keep costs down. The emphasis is firmly on what causes the least problems from a management perspective and is therefore easiest to manage, whether or not this conflicts with realising the full potential of the space.

9.23   Empire Square – the non-fruiting orchard at night

Pinnacle at GMV also work seven days a week with a staff of 15 across the whole estate. Although the management regime has never been an issue for Greenwich Council, a stipulation exists within the planning obligation that the borough retains the right to adopt the space if they so wish in the future. The developer concludes: 'it is unlikely that this will ever be taken up given the costs involved' (developer), although the stipulation was made out of a concern that the service charges might one day become unacceptably high, imposing an undue burden on the affordable housing tenants. Formal adoption is therefore reserved as a last resort for such an eventuality.

EVALUATION

The spaces at GMV and Empire Square represent one outcome of a particular view of urbanism, namely the renaissance-inspired urbanism that came to dominate thinking in London from the late 1990s onwards. The emphasis on bringing people back into the city (although in much of London, arguably, they never left) led to an emphasis on building at higher densities and in ways that clearly defined streets and traditional squares as the foci for public life. In this regard, the sorts of domestic spaces being created in the two case study developments were justified on the basis of their function

as spaces in which community life would flourish and that would be animated by activities both in and surrounding the squares. To some extent this vision overshadowed the other function of the spaces as local amenities within what are largely residential developments. The potential desires of residents for greenery, for quiet relaxation, and for play and family facilities were therefore never fully considered. This tension can be seen in the split personality of the squares: they are trying to be one thing (a vibrant hub for community life) and failing, and are only partially succeeding at another (an oasis and amenity for local residents).

At Empire Square, external assessments have generally been kind and the scheme won the national Housing Design Awards on its completion in 2007. CABE, for example, whilst questioning the need for a separate pavilion in the space – 'Traditionally spaces acquire vitality from uses at their edges, and siting the restaurant on one edge might have contributed more to animating the space' (CABE, Empire Square [n.d.]) – were positive about the scheme, arguing that a public space that closes at night is entirely appropriate in a busy inner city context in order to preserve the tranquillity for residents. In *Architecture Today*, Marshall (2007: 24) is also positive, whilst stressing the tension between the desire for mixed-use vitality and the detail of the central space: 'The tree layout with grass lawns and curved path seems restrictive, and too residential.   Somehow you feel the central space has been overdesigned', perhaps reflecting uncertainly about exactly what the space needed to be.

For the stakeholders involved, feelings are more mixed. Whilst the developer and designers are pleased with the outcomes, planners at Southwark regret that the original mix of uses was not achieved. All three of these stakeholders have a very different view to the managing agents about the nature of the space and for whom and what it was intended, the agent maintaining a firmly private-resident- and easy-management-focused vision as opposed to a public one. For the designer, the space was intended to have a wider public function and to be welcoming, not private. The planners, however, are realistic that this was never going to be an entirely public space, but feel it should be more of 'an obviously shared space' than it has turned out to be (planner). For them, it has beneficially created new routes through the area, but its primary role has been in raising value for the developer by enhancing the scheme and allowing them to build more units. Lessons have been learnt that both interior and exterior space (within and around the block) needs to be well animated, and this requires space that is clearly lettable. By contrast, the managing agent sees only problems and none of the benefits with such approaches: 'In theory it sounds wonderful to give something back to the community and open the space up for public use, but then not everyone will use it constructively which puts the residents and people who work there in a difficult position as it becomes confrontational' (manager). For her, more, not less, management is required to act as a permanent deterrent to users.

The different phases of GMV have received mixed, if generally positive, external reviews, although the Village Square has passed most reviewers by. For the stakeholders involved in creating it, early assessments are generally downbeat: 'Its OK rather than very good and hasn't really fulfilled our aspirations for having a vibrant space. It looks a bit barren, a bit open, with too much predominance of grey' (regenerator). The designers argue that a freer design process might have delivered more. They argue that 'public space designs in London are very conservative and all the same. There is a need to move beyond the English garden to produce more innovative design that will give a greater identity to spaces, but there is an in-built tendency for innovative design to become watered down and standardised' (designer). Their experience at GMV was of a rushed design process (because of the late decision to abandon the previous design), whilst what was required was time for consideration and to get the design right. For the developer, however, there is a need to 'consult and compromise ... things have evolved, and the square is an example of that. We shouldn't expect to get it right overnight' (developer). Like the developer at Empire Square, they argue that the basis is now there for a high-quality space, and that, whilst the future is unknown, there is always scope to build on what has been achieved in order to get closer to the original aspirations as and when the market and other opportunities allow.

In both cases, a key issue is the need to get the mix of uses correct – both those surrounding the space and the functions within – and this requires a proactive curatorial process. It is not enough to require that a space be provided and hope it will become the vibrant public realm of the renaissance ideal. There is also a need to recognise the value of spaces as simply of local amenity value for residents, much like private gardens in suburbia, as spaces to be valued even if sedate or simply transitory in function.

9.24   Relative stakeholder influences

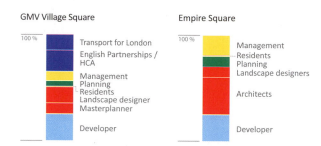

In both schemes the power to shape the resulting space was broadly distributed (**9.24**), most notably at GMV, where a wide range of stakeholders played (and continue to play) a significant role in how the space is experienced today, not all of whom have their impact on the space as an overriding objective in their decision-making (notably TfL). The result was certainly a dilution in the power of the designers involved and perhaps some confusion concerning the potential of such a space in such a location. At Empire Square, the architects had considerable power stemming from the freedom they were given to develop the concept within the confines of a loose brief from the developer. However, market circumstances and management practices have conspired to muddy the original vision that the planners also came to share, but which turned out to be unachievable. In both schemes, the residents wielded almost no power in how the spaces are continuing to be shaped.

Addressing the critiques

The spaces at GMV and Empire Square each sit at the heart of sizable new (predominantly) residential developments, but were each negotiated and sanctioned on the basis of visions that were more communitarian in their essence. In both cases, however, the domestic nature of the surrounding contexts re-asserted themselves to deliver spaces that are anything other than vibrant and outwardly social in nature, although still valuable as green spaces for low-key domestic and ancillary uses and as spaces along key routes through their localities. Although some regret was evident amongst stakeholders, the cases demonstrate the relatively straightforward needs of many residential users (particularly families) who are not necessarily looking for 'exciting' designs or social interaction and entertainment, but instead for grass, a safe and secure setting, and comfort in which to relax and play. They also demonstrated how an insensitive management regime can quickly kill off any demand that may exist to use spaces for more social purposes, for example the birthday parties proposed by residents to be held in the space at Empire Square.

London-wide, if the numbers of new public spaces are anything to go by (see Chapter 4), there seems to be little obvious pressure to gate new public spaces, which are instead increasingly seen as adding value to developments, not least in the additional density they help to justify. Empire Square, for example, was to be a fully gated development without a space at its centre until its re-design and the incorporation of the square demonstrated an alternative more open vision for the development. The two case studies also demonstrate, arguably, appropriate uses for gating: at Empire Square to secure the development late at night in order to safeguard the peace and quiet of residents (albeit partially obscuring the entrances to the development and emphasising the controlled nature of the space beyond – **9.10**); and at GMV to secure the private shared garden spaces at the centre of many of the GMV blocks, including those that front onto the Village Square itself (**9.25**).

Arguably, even if open and accessible, both schemes could be accused of complicity in spreading gentrification pressures into formerly industrial landscapes with surrounding, mainly working-class, communities. Yet, instead of creating enclaves of privilege (a.k.a. the Bow Quarter model, see above), both schemes offer mixed-tenure accommodation that attempts (as far as possible) to be tenure-blind through the design. In this, the schemes reflect the then-Mayor's drive to achieve 50 per cent affordable housing in all schemes over 10 units, a target that typically resulted in around 30 per cent actual affordable units being constructed (as was the case here). The reality, of course, remains a starkly divided 'community' in a context where the smallest one-bedroom flats in both locations sell in excess of £300,000 (in 2011), prices well above the affordability of most social renters. Evidence from the research also suggested a different reality on the ground in the experience of Empire Square between the families in the social rented units and the professionals in the private units – tension revealed in the competing claims on the space that the managing agent sought to resolve in favour of the owner-occupiers. At GMV, no such tensions were revealed during the research, although reports elsewhere suggest that for some residents the tensions are no less real (GMVSucks [n.d.]).

9.25   GMV – shared private garden spaces gated for privacy and security

In both cases, the lack of users in the spaces might be construed as evidence of a withdrawal from public space, but, seen against the evidence of use in other types of spaces discussed in this book, that seems an unlikely inference. More likely, it supports a thesis that cities need spaces of all types, and quiet domestic spaces are as valuable, in different ways, as vibrant social ones. Moreover, the demand, even if delayed by recession, for the retail units on GMV Village Square demonstrates a viable demand for small-scale and local facilities, if positioned to take advantage of a captive population and through routes. The creation of the units themselves, however, if not in the right place, will not by themselves create demand. The same goes for planned activities in public spaces, which, as the experience of trying to attract a market to GMV has shown, need the right location and population to sustain them. At GMV it is still early days and further persistence may yet pay off, particularly as the development grows. In the meantime, the types of third-space venues that have situated themselves around the edge of the Village Square – the café, convenience store, laundry, and health and beauty spa – are helping to gently animate the space, whilst providing important new social venues for the growing community.

10 SPACES FROM THE IN-BETWEEN

IN-BETWEEN LONDON

Chapters 2 and 3 explored the development of London from its Roman origins to its governance today, a period of almost 2,000 years in which the city has been built and rebuilt many times over. If the morphology of London is analysed today, one could certainly recognise Roman traces, medieval and Tudor/Elizabethan patterns, the more dramatic Baroque and Georgian interventions and the great Victorian/Edwardian, inter-war, modernist and postmodern expansions. During this history, much has been lost and much repeatedly built, swept away and then reinvented. Today, much of London is a hotchpotch of patterns and buildings that gives the city a hugely diverse and ever-changing character.

Within this melange, once created, public space is likely to be more robust than most buildings, it will also change and adapt over time, and will sometimes be lost altogether. Euston Square, for example, once one of the largest and grandest of the Georgian garden squares, is today only a remnant of its former self following the misfortune of being built with the New Road (London's first Northern bypass) bisecting its centre in an east/west direction, a road that was to become, first, the termini of the great Victorian railways (Paddington, Euston, St Pancras and King's Cross), and later the route of London's increasingly busy inner ring road (Farrell 2010: 135–8; 180). The southern half of the square was first built over, whilst the northern half became the stepping-off point for Euston Station, later to be joined by a bus station directly onto the remnants of the square and further bisecting it (north/south) with busy bus lanes. Today, the space is little more than two disconnected, noisy, often dirty and little-used green spaces with its own indigenous population of the homeless and *Big Issue* sellers, bypassed but ignored by many thousands of commuters and visitors each day (**10.1**).

Whole areas and features of London have been transformed over time. The Thames, for example, perhaps London's greatest public space

today, was not always so. Initially, as the major communications artery into London, it was the logical location for the houses and palaces of the rich and powerful who also owned and controlled large swathes of its banks. These included Hampton Court Palace, Syon, Ham and Marble Hill Houses, Kew Palace, the former Richmond Palace, Lambeth Palace, Westminster Palace, Somerset House, The Tower of London, and the former Palace of Placentia (Greenwich). The river was also an important trading artery into London, with much of the remaining space of the urban Thames lined with warehouses and associated industries, facilities that became larger and larger in scale through history until the modern era, when technology rendered this aspect of the Thames redundant. From that point on, the river has become increasingly a leisure and domestic space, with three of the squares explored in this book (Gabriel's Wharf, Festival Riverside and Royal Arsenal Gardens) each benefiting from this transformation in the river's function and the release of large swathes of land for other purposes. Today, much of the riverfront is safeguarded to allow direct public access, and so although one type of river has been lost forever, in the process the space has been reclaimed and reinvented. This is the pattern across London.

Although transformations of whole areas, whether through bombing, obsolescence, social good or in order to make a quick profit, are more dramatic than the stories of individual spaces, it is the approach to individual spaces that collectively and over time is likely to have a more dramatic impact on the whole. Thus, in the 1980s, it was the lack of attention to public space across London that incrementally led to decline in London's environmental quality and to the sense of neglect described in Chapter 2. Many would share the assessment of Richard Rogers (2011: 18) that the period since has seen London 'make faltering but persistent progress towards creating a public realm worthy of the 21st Century', although he, for one, concludes that 'there is still an enormous distance to cover before we have a public realm truly worthy of our city and our citizens'. These types of concerns provide the context for this chapter, which examines a final critique that space is being neglected by those with responsibility for its stewardship, and that as a result much public space is increasingly of a residual nature, with little inherent quality or function.

THE CRITIQUE

Neglected space

The final critique in this book is perhaps also the most prosaic – that we are simply failing to take good care of the spaces we have. Writing in the 1980s and commenting on the state of the urban environment as he saw it, Francis Tibbalds's now classic polemic *Making People-Friendly Towns* bemoaned the decline of public space across the world. Using the UK as an example of where a once-rich public realm was, at the time, declining, Tibbalds (2001: 1) argued that public space is too often 'littered, piled with rotting rubbish, covered in graffiti, polluted, congested and choked by traffic, full of mediocre and ugly poorly maintained buildings, unsafe, populated at night by homeless people living in cardboard boxes, doorways and subways and during the day by many of the same people begging in the streets'.

Tibbalds quoted Douglas Adams's *Hitchhiker's Guide to the Galaxy* when he said that the public realm is a 'SEP' (someone else's problem).

Not only, he suggested, do the general public expect someone else to clean up after them, but so do the numerous organisations with a formal role in the creation and management of public space. For Webster (2007) this is a classic 'tragedy of the commons'. He argues that, as a collectively consumed good, public space has a tendency to become over-used through unrestrained competition leading to degradation. Citizens each enjoy the benefits of public space, but individually they only bear a fraction of the costs and therefore over-consume an otherwise limited resource. Moreover, whilst re-investment and management can help avoid depletion of public space as a resource, this carries a cost that many administrations are only willing to shoulder for the most important and iconic of spaces. The remainder 'are not well tended' (Webster 2007: 82).

Through their influential 'broken windows' theory, Wilson & Kelling (1982) graphically demonstrated what a failure to deal with such signs of decay within an urban area could bring – a rapid spiral of decline. They argue that a failure to repair broken windows quickly, or to deal promptly with other signs of decay such as graffiti or kerb crawlers, can lead to the impression that no-one cares, and quickly propel an area into decline. Although some may argue that such arguments are environmentally determinist by giving undue weight to the impact of physical changes to the built environment, and that graffiti, kerb crawlers or even broken windows are signs of deeper socio-economic problems that need to be fixed before worrying about the windows, a more pragmatic view might see social and physical decay acting together, as two sides of the same coin. Thus, if signs of decay go unchecked, then the marginal additional impact of smashing a few more windows, trashing landscaping or burning derelict buildings may seem minimal to those bent on destruction – yet these are the very signs that will deter investment, encourage social flight, undermine the confidence of vulnerable groups in public space, attract crime and give the signal to all that nobody cares.

Like many urban designers, Tibbalds advocated the use of good design as a means to reverse the problems of a threatening and uncared-for public realm, although, unlike many others, he also recognised the vital role of public space management: 'Looking after towns and cities also includes aftercare – caring about litter, fly-posting, where cars are parked, street cleansing, maintaining paved surfaces, street furniture, building facades, and caring for trees and planting' (Tibbalds, 2001: 7). For him, aftercare mattered every bit as much as

10.2 Heart of London BID – highly visible continuous management

getting the design right in the first place. Evidence that backs claims that there had been a decline in the way the urban environment was managed in the UK was compiled by Carmona & de Magalhaes (2009) – neglect that from the early 2000s was accepted to be a problem, even in the highest policy circles – leading to significant attempts in London, and elsewhere, to address the issue, not least through the promotion of Business Improvement Districts (BIDs) (see Chapter 5).

Some have criticised the spread of BIDs on an ideological basis, arguing, for example, that it 'marks the beginning of private government and the decline of local democracy' (Minton 2009: 40). Others have used empirical evidence to demonstrate that, in fact, 'There is no moral or practical superiority of one model (state-, market-, or community-centred) over another, each, and different combinations of them, can provide the right solutions in particular circumstances' (Carmona *et al.* 2008: 209). One of the highest-profile BIDs has been the Heart of London BID, covering an area that includes Leicester Square and Piccadilly Circus and the roads between. Established in 2005 following an earlier pilot BID, the organisation aims to deliver a more targeted range of public services, especially those concerning safety and cleanliness, but extending to public-realm projects, branding and marketing, with an underlying belief in the perceived benefit of involving business in the management of the area. However, in common with all London BIDs, Heart of London maintains a close

relationship with the local council – Westminster – which it partners (DCLG 2007). The BID maintains its own team of wardens who act to deter petty crime, to report incidents and as ambassadors for the area, and a 'Clean Team' that operates in addition to the council's regular street cleaning services (**10.2**), but it is through Westminster that it derives much of its ability to act, and its effectiveness.

The emphasis on securing a 'Cleaner, Safer, Greener' environment became an increasingly major emphasis in national policy from 2001 onwards (see Chapter 3). In this remit, London was no better or worse that other parts of the UK, demonstrating a range of often poor but sometimes innovative practice, the latter, most notably (at the time) in the London Boroughs of Greenwich; Waltham Forest; Camden; and in the City of London (Carmona *et al.* 2008: 91–4).

Residual space

As well as neglect of space stemming from a simple failure to look after it, other contemporary spaces of the city are by their very nature difficult to manage and their concentration in certain urban areas can give a neglected, threatening and/or inhuman feel. Loukaitou-Sideris (1996: 91), for example, writes about 'Cracks in the City'. For her, cracks are defined as the 'in-between spaces, residual, under-utilised and often deteriorating'. She argues that poor management is also to blame for the state of many corporate plazas, car parks, parks and public housing estates, 'where abandonment and deterioration have filled vacant space with trash and human waste'.

Trancik (1986: 3–4) has used the term 'lost space' to make similar arguments. For him, lost space is a description of public spaces that are 'in need of redesign, antispaces, making no positive contribution to the surrounds or users'. Examples of lost spaces are wide-ranging and include 'the base of high-rise towers or unused sunken plazas, parking lots, the edges of freeways that nobody cares about maintaining, abandoned waterfronts, train yards, vacated military sites, and industrial complexes, deteriorated parks and marginal public-housing projects'. Trancik argues that the blame for creating lost spaces lies with a complex combination of an over-dominance of the car, insensitive urban renewal, the privatisation of public space, crude functional separation of uses, and the collected impact of the Modern Movement. For Madanipour (2004: 270–1), these spaces are all the more prevalent in the impoverished parts of cities inhabited by the poor, whether in the inner cities or in more marginal edge

10.3   Erith – a neglected landscape of residual and fragmented spaces

10.4   Paddington – liminal space under the Westway flyover, reclaimed as an occasional market space

locations. In such places, 'The cracks appear in the form of neglect and decline', whilst the competition to dominate the limited public space available can lead to tensions between groups, to a withdrawal from public space by some and to further decline. For Madanipour (2004: 277–8), it is the absence of shops, play facilities, benches and other facilities that makes them unattractive, combined with poor maintenance, and ubiquitous litter and graffiti giving a sense of abandonment and leading to a potential spiral of decline.

London, like any large city, suffers from a surfeit of residual and marginal spaces, often concentrated into particular locations. In classifying public space types in two Thames-side town centres in southeast London, Carmona (2010b: 171) demonstrates how the balance of space types varies from place to place and changes over time. In Greenwich, a World Heritage site, the historic urban grain remains largely intact, and although conflict exists between vehicles and people, space remains public and accessible. Erith, further east along the Thames out of London, by contrast, offers a fragmented landscape, where private stakeholders have been allowed to buy up and build large retail boxes and car parks in the town centre. Around these, Modernist public housing estates have imposed alien tower and open landscape forms on the traditional street pattern, and highways schemes have carved the town in two through the insertion of a new

trunk road and feeder system through the town. The result is that a traditional market town has become a car-dominated landscape where the former 'public' parts of Erith have been left to decline and are now eschewed by the local population. No public life of any significance remains in the traditional public spaces of the town, and these and many of the newer spaces are 'lost' and 'neglected' by those with responsibility for their management (**10.3**).

Liminal space

Not all writers are critical of these sorts of neglected spaces. Hajer & Reijndorp (2001: 128), for example, suggest that 'The new public domain does not only appear at the usual places in the city, but often develops in and around the in-between spaces. ... These places often have the character of "liminal spaces": they are border crossings, places where the different worlds of the inhabitants of the urban field touch each other.' Hajer & Reijndorp quote a broad group of supporters for the idea of 'liminality' (Zukin 1991; Shields 1991; Sennett 1990), each arguing in different ways that such spaces can also act to bring together disparate activities, occupiers and characters in a manner that creates valuable exchanges and connections. Worpole & Knox (2007: 14) have termed such spaces 'slack', arguing that they should be regulated with a light touch. For them, urban areas need places where certain behaviours are allowed that in other circumstances might be regarded as anti-social (**10.4**) or that are simply impromptu, unplanned and therefore unsanctioned by those in control (Frank & Stevens 2007). Others have shown that, far from being the carefully designed and expensive town square, such 'public spaces' can be found in the most incidental and unpromising places (Mean & Tims 2005) – places far removed from what Frank & Stevens (2007: 3) categorise as 'the aesthetically and behaviourally controlled and homogenous "themed" environments of leisure and consumption where nothing unpredictable must occur' (see Chapters 5 and 7).

Generally, however, the poor physical state of these types of public space seems to rest with the fact that it is rarely clear who should be managing them after they are built, or after they have declined. As a consequence, they are universally neglected, with Hajer & Reijndorp (2001: 129) arguing that much greater attention needs to be given to such transitional spaces.

Other forms of space are not neglected in the sense that 'lost' or 'slack' spaces are, but have nevertheless also taken on some of the characteristics of liminality. Roberts & Turner (2005) argue that the increasing emphasis on the evening economy and support for 24-hour-city policies has brought with it forms of behaviour that even the perpetrators would feel is unacceptable in their own neighbourhoods. In such places, the conflicts often revolve around the needs of local residents versus those of the revellers and local businesses serving the evening economy. Leisure and entertainment destinations such as London's Soho are of this type.

In the UK, a drive to invigorate the evening economy became a major trust in the regeneration efforts of towns and cities throughout the 1990s, and the government-led deregulation of the drinks industry that followed in the 2000s stoked this heady mix, turning many urban centres into what have come to be termed 'youthful playscapes' (Chatterton & Hollands 2002). These spaces may not have been neglected, but have nevertheless been abandoned to market forces and to a clientele of the young with disposable income to burn (Worpole 1999), in the process deterring other users from these previously shared spaces and perpetuating a further form of exclusion. For Roberts & Turner (2005: 190), the solution is the need for more active management and more sophisticated planning controls, without which the original ideals of a European 'continental ambience', so admired by the original proponents of the 24-hour city, will not be achieved. Some of London's BIDs, including Heart of London (see above) have been actively grappling with such issues in what remains perhaps the only true 24-hour city in the UK.

IN-BETWEEN SPACES

All spaces are in-between in the sense that they are the space between buildings, but this category relates solely to those spaces that have been carved from the forgotten, the incidental and the inconsequential in order to create something positive and new. The research revealed a wide range of spaces that might fall into this category, but these range across the sorts of functional and physical typologies identified in Chapter 4 and did not, therefore, feature as a type in the London-wide analysis.

Two broad types can be identified. The first are less frequent – 'internal spaces in-between' – spaces that were never in public use or that have been lost to the public through being hijacked by non-public uses and that are typically 'internal' to a larger estate. A dramatic example of this would be the Great Court of the British Museum. Although covered by Norman Foster's soaring glass roof and within the controlled confines of an august institution, the space has transformed a ramshackle and forgotten place into a major new meeting and cultural space for London (**10.5**). A similar, although un-roofed, example of such a space is the courtyard at Somerset House in the City of Westminster, which is explored in this chapter. The second type – 'external spaces in-between' – are more common. They are spaces that have remained public and are part of the continuous street/space network of cities, but have simply been neglected and perhaps forgotten and therefore

10.5   Queen Elizabeth II Great Court – originally a central garden space, then a series of ramshackle storage and workshop spaces around the famous Reading Room, and now revealed and reinvented

lost as positive people places – often because the space has been usurped for traffic. The second case study in this chapter – Monument Yard in the City of London – is of this type. A subset of this second type, and by far the most numerous in the category (18 per cent of spaces identified in the London-wide analysis), are the sorts of often very small incidental spaces that have been created in parts of London by simply extending the paving across the ends of side roads to cut them off from traffic and create an incidental space (**10.6**).

Somerset House Courtyard – car park to cultural space

On the site of an earlier royal palace in the seventeenth century, Sir William Chambers was commissioned to build a grand new Somerset House as the home of various public offices such as the Navy Office, Tax Office, Stamp Office and Salt Office in a building that addressed a growing concern that London lacked the sorts of great public buildings that other European capitals could boast. These departments were

10.6 Passey Place, Eltham – this incidental space creates a pause on the high street and a place to rest, meet and situate the community information boards

10.7 Site of Somerset House Courtyard

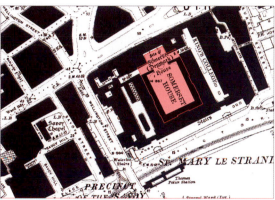

1910s

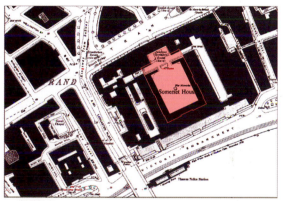

1950s

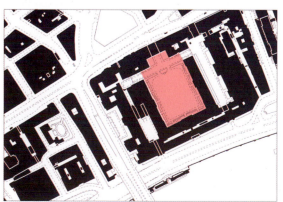

2010

housed around three sides of the courtyard. The building took a long time to complete, but eventually encompassed a northern frontage onto the Strand, a southern frontage overlooking the Thames and two wings, all enclosing a formal rectilinear courtyard complete with a bronze statue by John Bacon of George III. In the twentieth century, Somerset House was the home of the courts of the Lord Chancellor's Department (Family Division), the Principal Probate Registry, and the Registrar General of Births, Marriages and Deaths, with the Inland Revenue occupying most other buildings, whilst the courtyard was for most of the last century a car park for civil servants, a sea of tarmac and cars in which the Inland Revenue alone had 200 parking spaces around a central war memorial (**10.7**).

From the 1970s onwards, pressure gradually mounted (led initially by the *Evening Standard*) to give Somerset House and the courtyard a more public purpose, and in 1990 the Courtauld Institute and its gallery finally moved into the north building, the first key public attraction on site. With the help of funding from the Heritage Lottery Fund and the gradual vacating of the building by its various government tenants, the plan to open more of Somerset House could be pursued by the newly constituted Somerset House Trust, which has owned and run the building since 1997, leading eventually to the occupation of the south buildings (the Embankment Galleries) by the

Gilbert Collection (2001–08) and Hermitage exhibitions (2000–07), and now by a rotating programme of cultural events. Because the trust receives no state funding and relies instead on resources generated by its various commercial tenants and activities (e.g. the hire of venues), the refurbishment of the courtyard was only possible following a major donation by Mrs Lily Saffra in memory of her husband: one million pounds for refurbishing the space and constructing a fountain (the first major fountain in London since 1845) and another million for its maintenance. The Courtyard is now the Edmond J. Saffra Fountain Court.

The refurbishment of the courtyard was part of a wider regeneration plan that aimed to open Somerset House to the public and sustain it as a viable cultural venue. The space was therefore a critical part of a plan that involved the new cultural facilities and the restoration of other key historic features of the building, including a second public space, the riverside terrace. All this needed to be finished together in time for a grand launch in 2000, so that 'Somerset House could be appreciated as a major new visitor attraction' (Somerset House Trust). The Trust appointed Dixon Jones Architects as the masterplanners for the site and designers of the 'landmark' new design elements of the project, including the fountain, and Donald Insall Associates for the detailed restoration work to the courtyard and buildings and to provide facilities such as public toilets under the courtyard (enough to support major outdoor public events for audiences of over 3,000 people).

Monument Yard – rat-run to fitting monument

The story at Monument Yard is an equally historic one. The building of the Monument was sanctioned in the first Rebuilding Act of 1669 following the damage wrought by the Great Fire of London and the perceived need to preserve the memory of the Fire. As Surveyor General, the design fell to Sir Christopher Wren and his collaborator Robert Hooke, who built a 202-foot (the distance from the site of the Monument to where the fire began on Pudding Lane) fluted Doric column topped with a viewing platform and flaming gilt-bronze urn. At its base was a formal yard around and to the east of the Monument, completed to classical proportions along with the Monument itself in 1677, although subsequently destroyed when Monument Street was laid out in the 1880s. From that time onwards, the new street became increasingly a traffic rat-run from Thames Street (the east/west City bypass) up onto London Bridge (above),

10.8   Site of Monument Yard

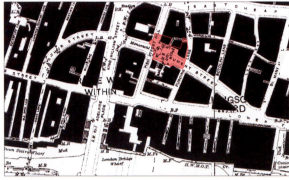

1910s

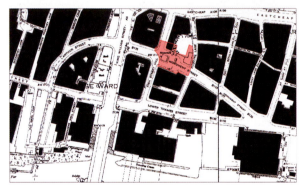

1950s

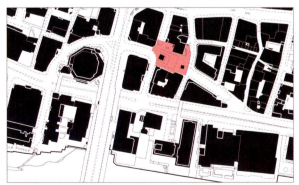

2010

with the Monument sitting in glorious isolation on an island in the centre of the road (**10.8**).

In 2003, Peter Rees, the City's Chief Planner, drew attention to the poor state of the environment around the Monument, which by then was used largely for traffic and parking, and which gave visitors a poor impression of the area. The project was therefore included in the wider Street Scene Challenge of the City Corporation, which started in 2003 and which by 2009 had completed over 50 projects across the City. Many of these were designed to reclaim bits of underused or degraded urban space and in so doing contribute to creating an environment to cement the City's competitive position as a leading financial centre. Most of these, including Monument Yard, have been funded directly by the City of London, although in this case with contributions towards a total budget of £1 million (including internal staff time and architects' fees) from the Pool of London Partnership and TfL.

The initial ideas envisaged a return to the classical scheme of Wren and Hooke, and although the size and shape of the space today is different from the original, the final scheme delineates the outline of the original in the new paving. An adjacent derelict site (on Pudding Lane) was also incorporated into the project as a temporary measure after a short-term lease was signed with its owners. A brief for the square was firmed up in consultation with the Environmental Services Department of the City Corporation, who manage the Monument, and who requested that staff facilities and toilets be included. Following a mini-competition, Bere Architects were chosen to design a new pavilion to hold these functions (**10.9**) and to design the temporary decking and street furniture of the leased site. The permanent floorscape of the Yard was designed in-house by the Department of Planning and Transportation's Street Scene Team, and, following a full-scale consultation, the development was completed in two phases: the Yard in 2005, and the decking and pavilion in 2006. A planning application has since been submitted for the temporary site, to replace this part of the scheme with a restaurant and outdoor seating as part of a larger redevelopment of the building to the north of the Yard.

Designing in-between space
Injecting some fun
In different ways, both spaces are designed with leisure users in mind.

10.9   Monument Yard – pavilion housing disabled toilets and facilities for the staff of the Monument

Although created to commemorate a serious event, the Monument quickly became a visitor attraction, offering from the top one of the best views of London. A key objective of the public-space scheme was thus to enhance this experience, providing an attractive space for visitors waiting to climb the monument and for small-scale events. The pavilion, for example, was designed to 'elevate a basic set of functions into a building that contributed to the overall space' (architect). Thus this tiny building is made from the same stone as the paving, surrounded by glass in order to give a smoother finish and to 'dematerialise it' (architect) when the glass reflects the light. Light effects were to be incorporated to mark the exact time of the Great Fire, but were omitted on cost grounds, although mirrors are included on top of the pavilion to reflect back the flaming urn of the Monument to those looking down from above.

At Somerset House, the instigators of the scheme were aware that the size and hard nature of the courtyard could create 'quite an austere environment' (Somerset House Trust). The fountain, inspired by one at Parc André Citroen (Paris), was therefore included in order to soften the hard paved character of the courtyard. When working, the fountain is designed to inject a playful element into the space, allow users to engage with it, and to have fun. It consists of 55 water jets rising to the height of 5 metres and lit with fibre optics. The jets are laid along a rectilinear grid of five by eleven, 3 metres from each other, whilst the

10.10   Somerset House – animating the courtyard

grid relates to the pattern of Somerset House elevations (**10.10**). They also help to cool down the courtyard on hot summer days, creating a feature that attracts people to stay and play.

Flexible space, flexible use

The flexibility of the space is also maintained when the fountain is turned off, allowing it to return to a multipurpose courtyard. During the winter, for example, the courtyard has become known as one of the best locations for outdoor skating, with a rink that fills the space from November for two months each year. The possibility of adding trees to the courtyard to further soften and cool the space was discussed and dismissed precisely in order to maintain this flexibility.

At Monument Yard, by contrast, a firm intention to plant trees to soften the space was frustrated by the highly complex service runs beneath the square and the lack of flexibility they implied for what

10.11   Monument Yard – temporary use for the Pudding Street site

10.12   Somerset House – 'a room without a ceiling' (architect)

went on above. For very different reasons, flexibility remained the key to the neighbouring Pudding Street site that was incorporated into the project (**10.11**). There, a temporary solution was required rather than full integration of the site with the new space, since under the terms of the lease the site will be required back when redevelopment occurs. A wooden deck over this derelict site represented the most economic and reversible solution, whilst elsewhere materials needed to be of high quality in order to comply with the City's maintenance standards.

Striking a balance

In both schemes, a careful balance needed to be struck between the historic (albeit degraded) settings and the aspiration to avoid pastiche and inject a contemporary feel. At Somerset House, this was complicated by the desire to give the space a new use through the capability to accommodate major events, requiring the use of robust materials and the discreet insertion of toilets and other facilities. The refurbishment consisted of five key elements: a buried plant room and toilets under the courtyard; a new pavement with granite cobbles laid with reference to the historic landscape pattern; restoring the York paving around the edge of the courtyard and insertion of light-wells to the facilities below; a new lighting scheme; and the installation of a contemporary fountain design. For the designers, this had to be achieved without compromise to the essential character of the space based on the *cour d'honneur* (grand court) concept of the original

design. In essence, the space was 'more of a Continental European square than a London square' (Somerset House Trust) of a type rare in London (**10.12**), although with surrounding building entrances arranged as a series of separate front doors from the courtyard, much like a garden square.

The presence of the Monument and the historic setting were likewise the driving influences for the Monument Yard scheme. The form of the square reflected a desire to stick as closely as possible to the original design for the Yard, although upgraded (without steps) in order to reflect modern accessibility needs. The intention was to keep the space simple, to avoid clutter and to stay true (as far as possible) to the original design principles. By removing traffic, safety has also been improved for tourists (especially children) and pedestrian movement encouraged through the space, with the main audience perceived to be both the visitors to the Monument and local workers, who now have a space to sit out in.

Developing in-between space
Single-minded and streamlined

A characteristic of in-between space is likely to be a relatively straightforward pattern of interested stakeholders, either because the space is internalised within a larger development, as at Somerset House, or because the space is downgraded and incidental, and therefore not valued by many. Once the Somerset House Trust was established by Act of Parliament with a long lease of 125 years from the government, Somerset House had a single-issue Trust as its advocate, determined to drive through positive change and create a major cultural destination for the wider public. For them, the major problems did not concern the vision for this transformation, but rather raising the funding to achieve it. In this, they were hugely successful in arranging financial support from the Heritage Lottery Fund, maximising the income from the estate through paid leisure and commercial ventures, and through attracting donations such as that which allowed the completion of the work to the courtyard. The single-minded determination to deliver the vision that they established for the project has ensured that the necessary doors have opened along the way, a vision driven forward by a clear project champion in the guise of the Director of the Trust.

Likewise, the ownership of the space around the Monument (and the Monument itself) resided exclusively with the City of London. In addition, they were the local planning authority, transport authority, designers and chief funder of the work, leading to a highly streamlined process at Monument Yard. The Street Scene Team led the project, obtaining planning permission for the pavilion and decking through, in effect, an internal application process that (unsurprisingly) went very smoothly, although TfL had to be involved in sanctioning the closure of Monument Street through a Highways Order. The work was managed in-house and carried out by external contractors, with whom good working relationships were maintained, helping to optimise outcomes from the process and delivering it on time and to budget.

Getting the ducks in a row

Despite the benefits of streamlined responsibilities, the complex nature of public realm schemes ensures that they are never entirely straightforward. At Monument Yard, two key inputs needed to be resolved. English Heritage were consulted because the Monument is a Grade I listed building and a Scheduled Ancient Monument. Their involvement led to a number of compromises, including to the moving of the pavilion from its original axial alignment with the Monument to an off-centre position where it was seen as more subservient to the memorial. The most difficult element of the project, however, was negotiating the lease for the derelict Pudding Lane site. Local ward members were particularly supportive of this aspect of the scheme,

seeing it as dealing with a long-term eyesore. However, the owners of the site, with their own redevelopment plans taking shape, needed significant reassurances and cajoling before they came on board and allowed the temporary lease to be signed. 'The success was getting all three elements [new square, pavilion and temporary decking] of the scheme to implementation stage as well as the associated road closure' (urban designer).

At Somerset House, the redevelopment was led by the Chief Executive to the Trust, Duncan Wilson, who worked hand in hand with the architect, Edward Jones. For both, the project became personally very important, and they invested huge time and effort in securing the right outcomes. Their key challenge was to keep the tenants involved and onboard during the process – these included King's College, the Inland Revenue, the Courtauld Institute and the Gilbert Collection, amongst others. At critical points, the relationship with some of the parties became difficult, threatening to derail the whole project in the process. At each stage, however, the difficulties were resolved through careful negotiation on a personal level. By contrast, strong political support for the project from Westminster and English Heritage – from whom planning and listed building consent was required (the building and courtyard is Grade I listed) – helped to drive the plan forward.

Using in-between space
Relaxed space

The courtyard at Somerset House is open daily until 6 o'clock in the evening, and in summertime until 11 o'clock, with people using it to access the House and its facilities, although with many others simply coming to relax and meet each other there. It is also enjoyed by people working in the various Somerset House buildings, and regularly by workers from the area around. Stakeholders observe that during the week the courtyard typically fills with tourists passing through, visitors to the Courtauld Gallery, and business people having their lunch and or a drink after work. At weekends, families with children come specifically to enjoy the fountains and curious shoppers wander in (**10.13**). On a hot summer day, the courtyard is so animated that 'it is like being at the beach' (manager) and children and families become the dominant group. Generally, however, user-groups are very varied and of all ages, with stakeholders viewing the courtyard as an inclusive and flexible space, allowing for a wide variety of behaviours and activities to happen all year around.

10.13   Somerset House Courtyard – children's play space

10.14   Monument Yard – The Britannia Pub, now engaging with the space

The space at Monument likewise caters for tourists and workers, and, stakeholders argue, has opened the area up to wheelchair users, who now have suitable toilet facilities. Office workers mainly use the decked area, whose raised level and different floor treatment encourages passers-by to walk around rather than through it, giving it a more relaxed feel. By contrast, the Yard proper is often filled with tourists waiting to ascend the Monument, particularly in the summer months. So far, no problem behaviours have been reported – in part, it is believed, reflecting the deliberate design of the street furniture to deter vagrants – although, unexpectedly, users can often be seen sitting on the kerb edges around the square, kerbs introduced to better facilitate drainage but now with a dual seating function. Completion of the scheme has also encouraged the pub on the south side of the space to apply for and obtain a licence for tables and chairs that spill into the space, a licence that is reviewed on an annual basis (**10.14**). Activity is mainly limited to the daytime and early evening, after which the City generally becomes quiet.

Places from mere spaces

Somerset House is many times the size of Monument Yard and, reflecting its nature as an 'internal space in-between' (and the Monument as 'external'), it is far less connected. Observations revealed, however, that both spaces are well and flexibly used, with Somerset House relying much more heavily on its own internal attractions to draw people in and animate the space, whilst Monument Yard naturally benefits from a high degree of background movement (**10.15, 10.16**). In both cases, however, real places have been made out of mere spaces, with the process of making the squares creating new (in the case of Somerset House) and releasing latent (in the case of Monument Yard) demand for places of relaxation and sociability where before there were none.

The user interviews revealed how two extremely positive places (in their collective view) had been carved from the in-between (**10.17, 10.18**). In both cases, the spaces had been created from amongst the historic fabric of London, and these associations played a large part in positively colouring user perceptions, as did the new uses that each space gave rise to in what were previously neglected locations – 'the fountain has done it all, not only does it allure the little kids and their parents to enjoy the cool showers under the hot sun, it also brings about different forms of interaction between them' (user of Somerset House Courtyard). In both cases, the primary benefits of the spaces were the opportunities they provided to relax, opportunities not helped (in the view of some) by the hardness of both spaces and the street furniture they contain – 'the chairs and benches are so hard and uncomfortable, it undermines the very purpose of providing a public space' (user, Monument Yard).

10.15 Somerset House Courtyard observational analysis of user patterns – typical local movement patterns (a), density of activity (b) and typical activities (c)

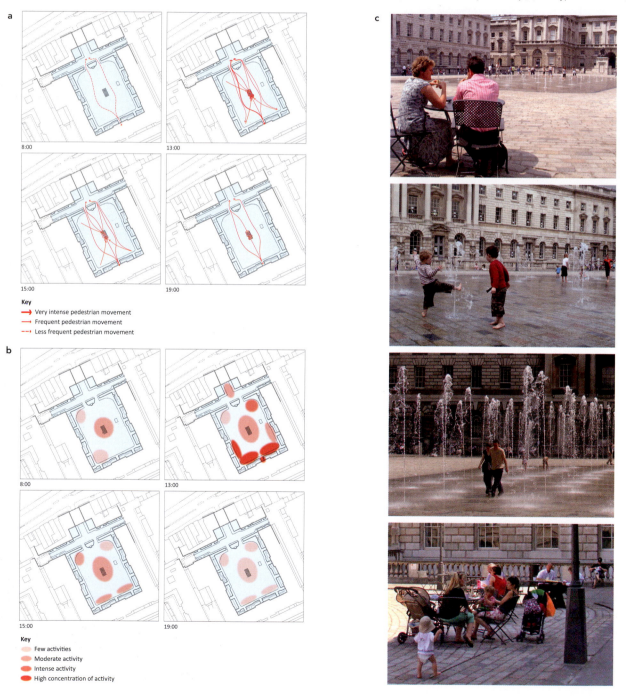

a

8:00

13:00

15:00

19:00

Key

→ Very intense pedestrian movement

→ Frequent pedestrian movement

--→ Less frequent pedestrian movement

b

8:00

13:00

15:00

19:00

Key

Few activities

Moderate activity

Intense activity

High concentration of activity

c

10.16   Monument Yard observational analysis of user patterns – typical local movement patterns (a), density of activity (b) and typical activities (c)

a

8:00

13:00

15:00

19:00

Key

→ Very intense pedestrian movement

→ Frequent pedestrian movement

--→ Less frequent pedestrian movement

b

8:00

13:00

15:00

19:00

Key

Few activities

Moderate activity

Intense activity

High concentration of activity

c

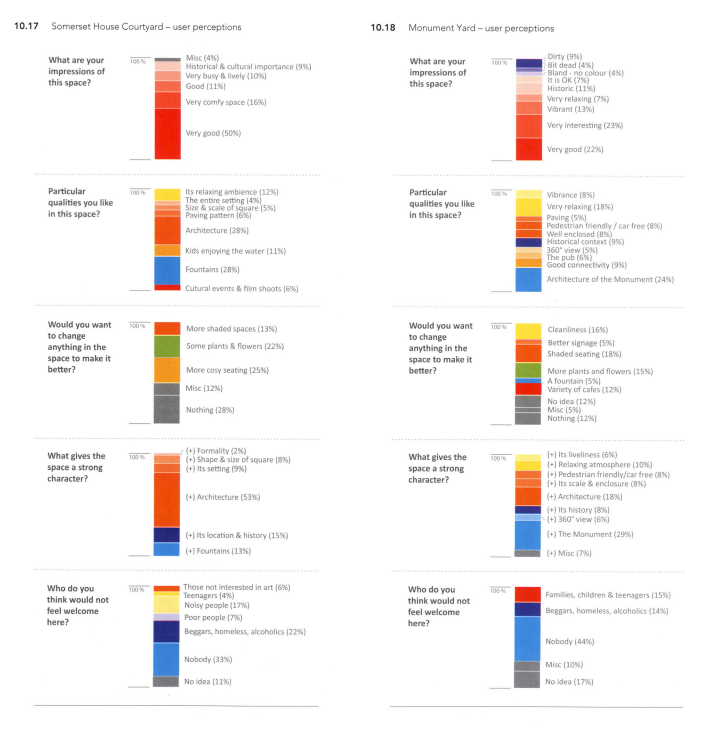

10.17   Somerset House Courtyard – user perceptions

What are your impressions of this space?

100 %

Misc (4%)
Historical & cultural importance (9%)
Very busy & lively (10%)
Good (11%)
Very comfy space (16%)
Very good (50%)

Particular qualities you like in this space?

100 %

Its relaxing ambience (12%)
The entire setting (4%)
Size & scale of square (5%)
Paving pattern (6%)
Architecture (28%)
Kids enjoying the water (11%)
Fountains (28%)
Cutural events & film shoots (6%)

Would you want to change anything in the space to make it better?

100 %

More shaded spaces (13%)
Some plants & flowers (22%)
More cosy seating (25%)
Misc (12%)
Nothing (28%)

What gives the space a strong character?

100 %

(+) Formality (2%)
(+) Shape & size of square (8%)
(+) Its setting (9%)
(+) Architecture (53%)
(+) Its location & history (15%)
(+) Fountains (13%)

Who do you think would not feel welcome here?

100 %

Those not interested in art (6%)
Teenagers (4%)
Noisy people (17%)
Poor people (7%)
Beggars, homeless, alcoholics (22%)
Nobody (33%)
No idea (11%)

10.18   Monument Yard – user perceptions

What are your impressions of this space?

100 %

Dirty (9%)
Bit dead (4%)
Bland - no colour (4%)
It is OK (7%)
Historic (11%)
Very relaxing (7%)
Vibrant (13%)
Very interesting (23%)
Very good (22%)

Particular qualities you like in this space?

100 %

Vibrance (8%)
Very relaxing (18%)
Paving (5%)
Pedestrian friendly / car free (8%)
Well enclosed (8%)
Historical context (9%)
360° view (5%)
The pub (6%)
Good connectivity (9%)
Architecture of the Monument (24%)

Would you want to change anything in the space to make it better?

100 %

Cleanliness (16%)
Better signage (5%)
Shaded seating (18%)
More plants and flowers (15%)
A fountain (5%)
Variety of cafes (12%)
No idea (12%)
Misc (5%)
Nothing (12%)

What gives the space a strong character?

100 %

(+) Its liveliness (6%)
(+) Relaxing atmosphere (10%)
(+) Pedestrian friendly/car free (8%)
(+) Its scale & enclosure (8%)
(+) Architecture (18%)
(+) Its history (8%)
(+) 360° view (6%)
(+) The Monument (29%)
(+) Misc (7%)

Who do you think would not feel welcome here?

100 %

Families, children & teenagers (15%)
Beggars, homeless, alcoholics (14%)
Nobody (44%)
Misc (10%)
No idea (17%)

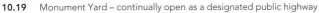
10.19   Monument Yard – continually open as a designated public highway

Managing in-between space
Self-contained versus continuous space management
Although similar in key respects, in management terms, the spaces at Monument and Somerset House are profoundly different, stemming from distinctions between the 'internal' and 'external space in-between' models identified above. Thus, whilst one represents a physically closed space and organisationally self-contained management system, the other is part of a larger continuous public realm and processes of public space governance. At Monument Yard, the space is designated as a public highway, with the exception of the

decked area, for which the City holds a lease (**10.19**). It is managed by the City's Environmental Services Department, who clean and maintain it, including the pavilion. The management regime follows the City's standards for maintenance, although the space has an extra sweep following lunchtime to collect any food wrappers. The space is also subject to the general concern of security across the Square Mile born of the ongoing terrorism threat. Although neither the space nor the Monument itself are considered at high risk and have no additional secrity, during the day there is a continuous official presence in the area via the Monument staff, and both

10.20   Somerset House Courtyard – a constrained and monitored entrance

10.21   Somerset House Courtyard – at Christmas

present and visible, with most visitors experiencing it as they come through the single direct, restricted and monitored entrance to the square, off the Strand (**10.20**).

Enabling events – large and small

With the reinvention of Monument Yard and the courtyard at Somerset House, London secured two events spaces at very different ends of the spectrum, the common thread being the flexibility of each space. Thus the Somerset House Trust run major events throughout the year that occupy the courtyard for at least 100 days each year and attract many thousands of people. These include the ice rink for two months in the Winter (attracting 200,000 people – **10.21**), London Fashion Week, Origin (the London Craft Fair), open-air concerts and a cinema: 'Somerset House regularly becomes a sort of mini-festival in the middle of town' (manager). Education programmes also regularly bring organised groups of children onto the site, such as the Sorrel Foundation's Young Design Centre and the Skate School in the winter offering free lessons to school children. In these endeavours, the space has been a huge asset, but relies on a very active committee of trustees and a dedicated Events Director who are constantly working to bring new events to the space. Those involved admit, however, that more time spent at the start understanding the infrastructure requirements of different types of events, could have saved resources in the ongoing management of the space.

private (on the buildings around) and public CCTV systems monitor the square.

At Somerset House, the terms of the lease require the Trust to maintain and manage the space and open it to the public. The estates department manages the courtyard along with the rest of the premises, with a remit that includes all issues of maintenance and security – work it contracts out. Thus Sykes & Son Ltd, a 'total facilities management' contractor, ensure the site is clean and the fountains are maintained. First Security (Guards) Ltd manages movement through the courtyard and monitors behaviour and security. The management regime is paid for by the rent received from tenants of Somerset House and by other commercial income and is considered light-touch, although ever-

By contrast, Monument Yard has no dedicated programme of events, but the flexibility of the space means that it is included as one of the venues for the *ad hoc* annual programme of activities of the City of London Festival. Thus the space has been used in the past for music, acrobats, a street piano and other street arts. Events generally take place in the centre of the space, with the surrounding raised paths retained for through movement. For the designer, the scale and intimacy of the space ensure that it is particularly appropriate for such small-scale activities and for buskers who can 'take possession of it' (urban designer).

EVALUATION

The spaces analysed in this chapter are very different in type. Whilst both are publicly owned spaces, Somerset House Courtyard is leased to a Charitable Trust and internalised within an institution. This makes its status ambiguous. Thus, whilst the architect was clear that the space 'is not public territory', for the Managing Director of the trust it is 'a managed space enjoyed by the public, a public space, occasionally privatised for big events'. For CABE, the space engenders a sense of being semi-private, whilst the events and activities inside help to draw people in and undermine this (CABE, Somerset House [n.d.]). In effect, the Trust has the autonomy to run the space as its sees fit within the public interest remit under which it was established in legislation. The courtyard now plays an important part in attracting users to Somerset House, but is also an attraction in its own right and a major venue, helping to sustain the wider Somerset House complex. Monument Yard, by comparison, is simply part of London's continuous public street network, but also an important historic location now suitably marked by the presence of a small incidental square reclaimed from the street space. The space is provided and managed in the interest of enhancing this previously rather unloved part of the City of London, but also as part of a wider effort of investing in the public realm of the City in order to retain its attractiveness as a business location.

Both spaces seem to have been successful in achieving their objectives, with, for example, Somerset House now receiving 1.2 million visitors a year, half of whom come solely to enjoy its spaces, particularly the courtyard. However, for every in-between space that has been reclaimed in London, many, many more have not, but possess a latent potential – great or modest – to be reclaimed at some point in the future.

For those involved in realising the Somerset House scheme, the project represents a significant success founded on a strong design concept that all parties signed up to, facilitated by the clear ownership of the space. The Trust had a clear incentive to grow the space culturally and to encourage new audiences to visit and do creative and imaginative things there. They were therefore open to new ideas about how the space could be used in a manner that a local authority may not have been, particularly to 'avoiding historical pastiche' (Somerset House Trust). They sought a design that would attract and be enjoyed by people and are very pleased that the results are of a high quality, relatively easy to maintain, flexible, and fit effortlessly into the historic space. For the architect, 'it was important not to be too prescriptive but instead to make something enigmatic that fostered appropriation and play. If you offer clues and props then things start to happen, instead of being deterministic' (architect). The refurbishment and new landmark design elements have helped Somerset House project a new identity. That, together with a robust events management plan, regularly attracts a great variety of visitors and sustains the institution as a cultural destination in the city of which the space is a crucial part. 'Somerset House is nowadays not only a visitor attraction, but a great urban oasis' (manager), a place to meet, relax and be inspired. In 2001, it won the Public Space category of the Royal Fine Art Commission Trust's Building of the Year Awards.

In a very different way, Monument Yard is also viewed as a success by those involved, not least in helping to bring forward the redevelopment of the site to the north of the Yard with an innovative 'MAKE' designed scheme, a redevelopment that includes the temporary leased site that had lain empty for 40 years. If the redevelopment goes ahead, that portion of the square will be permanently open, with new seating. Since the completion of the project, visitor numbers to the Monument have also increased by 30 per cent, reversing a previous decline that had dipped to around 125,000 visitors in 2005. For the City, the space remains clearly public, and people feel comfortable in it, including the Monument employees, who are now better accommodated in the new pavilion. For the designer, lessons include keeping the space simple: 'It is important that the designer does not get carried away with a design concept that may not work in the future;

10.22   Relative stakeholder influences

Somerset House Courtyard

100 %
- English Heritage
- Management
- Planning
- Architects
- Trust

Monument Yard

100 %
- Transport for London
- English Heritage
- Management
- Local authority

the design should be timeless, not dictated by the fashion of the moment' (urban designer) and materials should be robust and designed with ease of maintenance in mind.

External critics have similarly been kind to both schemes. Thus Glynn (2006: 30) concludes that Monument Yard demonstrates the 'continuing challenge faced by planners to strike a balance between old and new', and in this benefits from 'a limited selection of objects and materials that have been selected for their historical value and sustainability'. For the architectural critic of *The Observer*, the 'liberated courtyard' of 'Somerset House feels as if it is turning into a particularly upmarket village green, run by a committee of particularly altruistic squires bent on outdoing each other with ever more munificent entertainment' that have, for example, 'prompted such outbreaks of conspicuously un-British behaviour as fully clothed, apparently sober, commuters taking a dip' (Sudjic 2000).

In each case, the success was partly due to very clear lines of responsibility for the spaces, with direct accountability through a dominant stakeholder for the resulting solutions (**10.22**). Thus, at Somerset House Courtyard, the Trust were determined to make the space work for them, and along with their architects devised and drove through a clear vision that carried all before them. At Monument Yard, nearly all the powers, resources and responsibilities for the space were vested with the City of London (with some input from English Heritage), who internalised the process and were able to deliver a high-quality scheme quickly and efficiently in a similar manner (albeit at a very different scale) to that of a privately owned estate like Canary Wharf Group operating at Canada Square (see Chapter 5).

Addressing the critique

The case studies graphically demonstrate how public space in a city such as London is in a constant state of flux. Not only are new spaces created, but existing ones are removed or regenerated and some spaces that have long been neglected or even forgotten are reinvented. In this regard, the case studies demonstrate processes of loss and rediscovery even in and around some of London's great architectural set-pieces and monuments. In both cases, space had become degraded and residual in nature, dominated by parking, ancillary service functions, traffic and dereliction (part of the Monument site for 40 years). Moreover, these sorts of in-between spaces are both buried within and hidden by the urban structure (inside urban blocks and large set-piece developments), as was the case at Somerset House, and exposed as part of the continuous public street fabric, as at Monument. Each offers the potential to establish positive new places from formerly degraded spaces, although these opportunities will vary from the grand to the everyday and incidental – the latter being where most of the local opportunities are likely to lie.

Although projects such as Somerset House Courtyard will be relatively rare, the City of London's 'Street Scene Challenge' (see above) demonstrates how the urban fabric as a whole can be scoured for opportunities to shape new spaces from the in-between. Established in 2003, the initiative aims 'to manage the appearance of streets, enhance the public realm and street level environment and facilitate the flow of both pedestrian and motor traffic around the City of London' (City of London 2007). In this, it takes advantage of the fact that traffic in the City has decreased by 25 per cent overall and by 40 per cent in the central area, as a result of the City's introduction of its 'ring of steel' (see Chapter 3) and, later, the Congestion Charge by the Mayor of London. The result has been an opportunity to reclaim road space and turn it into pedestrian space, often in the form of small incidental public spaces (**10.23**). Challenge schemes are funded in the main by a partnership between the City and other interested parties such as private developers, building owners and occupiers, and Transport for London, with the City Corporation's contribution coming from a combination of parking income, contributions through Section 106 planning agreements and core funding.

The experience in the City demonstrates a view that public space matters to investors, workers and residents, and that degraded space actively counts against the competitive position of the City. The case

10.23   Basinghall Avenue, City of London – incidental space formed by turning part of the street into a pedestrianised space

studies demonstrated, however, that the enhancement of neglected space requires both an initial investment and a considerable ongoing commitment of resources in stewardship; for example, in the case of Monument Yard, the management regime needed upgrading, while at Somerset House it required complete reinvention together with resourcing (in part) through a large private donation. In both cases, these ongoing revenue commitments have been reduced through the adoption of simple, robust design solutions, whilst the fact that one regime is essentially private and the other public, and both are of a high quality, confirms arguments in the literature that it matters little who does the care, as long as it is done and done well.

In both cases, these stewardship roles extend to the programming of space for activities, whether large-scale income-generating events, in the case of Somerset House Courtyard, or simply allowing the local pub to put out seats and letting the space be used for occasional small-scale cultural activities, as at Monument Yard. Such organised activities, whether large or small, can play a critical part in giving residual space a new function, but, equally, the case studies showed how users are very capable of animating spaces themselves if the design is conducive to such activities. Somerset House Courtyard, like many spaces examined in this book, attracts a relatively homogenous clientele. There, the water feature acts to bring them together and

free up their actions through providing an intermediary with which people (particularly children) interact; effectively designing-in some of the qualities of liminality. The space is managed in order to encourage such free expression and engagement. At Monument Yard, the square brings two very different London populations – visitors and City workers – together in one relatively small space, in so doing undermining the tendency for space to be appropriated by one group or another. The experience of both places demonstrates that carefully designed public space can create the conditions for interaction and slackness, and one does not have to seek out the city's 'cracks' in order to create the right conditions for this to occur.

Thus both spaces have a key ingredient of slackness in the flexibility they provide, in the process avoiding the trap of over-design and allowing a wide range of activities to occur. In part, this recognises the value of creating spaces that are fun to be in – be that on a grand scale, as at Somerset House, or on a small scale, such as the design of the reflective pavilion at Monument Yard. The spaces in this chapter had the inherent advantages of excellent locations, ripe with latent demand and possibilities, as integral parts of profoundly historic contexts, benefits that many other residual spaces will not have and which will therefore be more challenging as a result, particularly in poorer areas of the city. On the other hand, both spaces also refused to be hamstrung by their locations (a potential danger in historic sites) and, instead of playing it safe, took advantage of the fact that anything is better than neglect in spaces from the in-between, and the opportunity this presents for thinking differently. Such an approach is likely to be all the more powerful in less advantageous surroundings.

11 CREATING AND RECREATING PUBLIC SPACE IN LONDON

BRINGING IT ALL TOGETHER

This, the first of two concluding chapters, looks across the different strands of work discussed in previous chapters to draw out overarching conclusions in order to gauge whether a better understanding of the nature of early twenty-first-century public space in London has been revealed. The focus here is on the processes of public space creation, use and management, both through history and today, whilst Chapter 12 relates these findings back to the critiques of public space discussed throughout the book.

Discussion begins through examining the complex nature of public space in London, drawing from three sources: a historical understanding as revealed in Chapter 2, a contemporary political and policy understanding as discussed in Chapter 3, and the wider context for the physical patterns of public space as presented in Chapter 4. The evidence base is developed in the second part of the chapter, which focuses on the design, development, use and management dimensions of public space by drawing on evidence from across the 14 case studies discussed in Chapters 5–10. There, overarching conclusions about the experience of public space creation and recreation in London are drawn out before, in a final part to the chapter, the power relationships that underpin public space development projects are discussed.

THE EVOLVING SPACES OF A GLOBAL CITY

London and its spaces evolve

Beyond its historic street network, London has always been a city of multiple complex spaces, many of which specialised early on, as exemplified by the market places of the City of London. As the city grew, so did the range of spaces London hosted, and the types of processes that gave rise to them. Thus, in common with most medieval cities, the first (post-Roman) spaces were not consciously designed and developed (e.g. London's market squares and village greens). From the 1630s onwards, spaces of a more consciously designed type began to appear, typically at the hands of private interests looking to enhance the value of their developments. In the process, the city invented the residential or (later) garden square for which London has become rightfully famous. This new form of space was, by its very nature, exclusive, gated, private and driven by clear commercial and design formulae, although over time many such spaces have changed their ownership (many are now public gardens) and even their function (Covent Garden, for example, quickly became a market space). Typically, they were also greened as the new elites imposed their rural landscape tastes on the new urban landscape, expressing in the process a preference for green that, arguably, continues in the English psyche through to today.

The purposeful design of truly 'public' spaces in London is a more recent, nineteenth-century, innovation, either appearing as the by-product of traffic schemes (e.g. Sloane Square) or as grand civic set pieces designed to impress and reflect London's growing significance as (even then) a world city. In these spaces (most notably in Trafalgar Square and Parliament Square), the idea of particular spaces for public gathering and expression first took hold and the notion of these places as spaces of democracy has persisted through to today – although so has another use, as a traffic locus. Thus, as garden squares gave way to the nineteenth- and twentieth-century suburbs and London spread out, the city was increasingly invaded by traffic that spaces at key strategic locations across the city were now expected to handle. This contrasted with the creation of a series of Modernist-inspired spaces in the post-war period, many, whether in residential, commercial or cultural schemes, designed with specific social purposes in mind: as places to meet, interact and share a common resource. These aspirations, along with the spaces themselves

11.1   Inigo Place, Covent Garden – former churchyard, now public space

and the developments of which they were part, have often failed, and in recent years many have been remodelled or replaced.

This history has left London with an immense heritage of public spaces across the city (**11.1**). A critical lesson, however, has been that the most successful spaces for 'public' uses (if judged by the fact that they still exist in largely their original form and are open and actively used by the public) were:

- created through largely unconscious design processes (e.g. London's historic market spaces)

- designed for private purposes (e.g. the garden squares) or

- have evolved into their present role from an initial far more staid and largely representational purpose (e.g. London's civic set-pieces).

Those (pre-1980) spaces designed with a specific social purpose in mind have, by contrast, not faired so well.

The London way; speculation and innovation

The development processes that shape London today are little changed from those that shaped it 350 years ago after the Great Fire. With the exception of the post-war rebuilding in which the public sector took an uncharacteristic (and largely ill-fated) lead in shaping London, the city has, and continues to be, shaped and re-shaped by an uncoordinated network of hands. In these processes, large landowners and powerful developers have typically taken the lead, guided by market opportunity, a light-touch regulatory process and a fragmented state that has often been reluctant or incapable of investing directly in public goods itself, including in the city's public spaces. The post-war period of 'heroic' reconstruction therefore represented a short-lived aberration, with normal business resuming once gain from the 1980s onwards, mediated now by a greatly enhanced conservation ethic.

In the mid 1980s, London's already-fragmented governance was further emasculated, allowing the city to once again fully engage with the speculative development model that had shaped so much of the city. The conflation delivered four key outcomes.

1 Large developers operating within such a deregulated environment attempted to safeguard their own huge investments by themselves investing directly in design and in new forms of private public space – like their Georgian predecessors, recognising the essential economic value that could be added through a high-quality public realm.

2 An 'alternative' privately driven model emerged in which low-value spaces have been regenerated through the insertion of imaginative although sometimes temporary retail, creative and community uses. Here, the model relies on the manufacture of a new social public realm that, by attracting people, also stimulates value, although of a very different (much smaller) order than the first model, at least initially.

3 Everywhere else, London's public realm deteriorated, with a decline in the sort of everyday public investment necessary to manage and maintain a reasonable quality public realm, whilst wider urban and social policy left London's streets as the *de facto*

receptors of a range of social problems and the consequences of spiralling car ownership.

4 In time, this led to a growing concern about the deterioration of London and its lack of strategic governance, and to the creation of policy approaches at the national level (although not in local planning) that portended a renewed civic concern with design quality, particularly that associated with London's urban environment. All this was dressed in an overarching concern that London would fail to compete internationally if the quality of its public realm did not improve.

In essence, the situation in the 1980s and 1990s simply reflected what had long been the London way, namely embracing the market, rejecting heavy-handed imposition of state-generated visions, and slowly innovating on the basis of what has come before. Thus, although the third and fourth outcomes from the period reflect a story of neglect and eventual retort, the first and second delivered new and innovative forms of public space not seen previously in London, each deriving from very different ends of the private investment spectrum that the city continually fosters.

Renaissance-max, let 100 spaces bloom

If the period up to 1997 and the coming of New Labour saw a return to normal business for London, then the period following was marked by subtle but nevertheless significant tweaks in the balance between the state and private enterprise, tweaks that in a resurgent market led to a flowering of new and regenerated public spaces across the capital. The prevailing politics both in London (from 2000) and beyond recognised that, to achieve real change, the state needed to work through the market in order to harness a proportion of its resources and capture an element of its growth for public ends, including enhanced public space. Also, there was a recognition that the state itself had a direct role in stimulating a context for better design (and therefore maintaining London's attractiveness to investors) through establishing encouraging policies, taking better care of that part of the built environment for which it was responsible, and setting standards through exemplar projects and proposals.

However, true to the London way (as opposed to the Third Way), this renewed interest in public space was *ad hoc* and uncoordinated, delivering only where market circumstance and happenstance allowed. Thus, as the first Mayor of London – Ken Livingstone – quickly discovered, the land ownership, development, funding and planning complexities of London ensured that fine aspirations were liable to remain just that unless direct (and considerable) public money could be invested in schemes, or the cost of public space was internalised within large and unified private development projects.

Fortunately for Livingstone, his urban-renaissance-inspired policies, by driving up the built densities across London, acted to make both schemes and spaces viable where they had not been before, and to upping the ante in terms of expected design quality. Thus, although Livingstone's own high-profile 100 Spaces programme quickly floundered amidst the complexities and extended time lags associated with delivering public spaces in London, across London, spaces were being delivered (see below). In part, this may simply reflect the fact that the drive towards higher-quality design as a precursor (some might argue a sop) for more development reflected developing national policy at the time – exhortations that eventually found their way into the local policies (although not always practices) of the London boroughs, and long before that into the practices of London's development community, which very quickly acclimatised to the opportunities presented by the new context. They also gradually infused the other constituent parts of the Mayor's empire, including, belatedly, parts of the huge streets budgets controlled by TfL. In this period, increasingly, London became associated with a renaissance in its public space.

Renaissance-light, the austerity years

If Livingstone's mayoralty had offered a continuation of London's historic embrace of the private developer to shape the city, then this had also been tinged with clear social goals that extended to the active involvement of the Mayor in the delivery of public space, where appropriate. The election of Boris Johnson quickly signalled a different emphasis on public space, with the cancellation of the Parliament Square Project and the 100 Spaces programme and its replacement with the Great Spaces initiative, demonstrating a greater desire to work through other organisations (including, of course, developers) to secure similar (on paper) public space aspirations. The programme represented, on the one hand, a less ambitious role for the Mayor, but, on the other, a greater sense of the reality of delivering public spaces, of the limits to the Mayor's powers, and a move (perhaps optimistically) to place the boroughs more in the hot seat. The move to lower-density requirements and encouragement of larger housing units in policy also presaged a possible move away from

higher-density 'renaissance' policies and towards medium-density solutions, and as a result back to the garden square, although long-term impacts are (at the time of writing) still to be seen.

More significant than differences between the two Mayors, however, was the fact that, despite being charged with strategic London-wide responsibilities, both incumbents (Johnson less enthusiastically at first) explicitly recognised the vital importance of public space to London's future. Thus, for example, when faced with the demise of the London Development Agency by early 2012, Boris Johnson chose to safeguard a non-statutory design service (although initially smaller than it had been) with the move of Design for London back to the GLA. Despite an ambivalent start, the decision reflected a Mayor who had become increasingly convinced about the importance of good design and of a public sector role in helping to deliver it, albeit a role more often than not in hock to the private sector. In this, however, both Mayors seemed to have honourable intentions, with design seen as a means to deliver clear social as well as economic goals, and not simply a mechanism (amongst others) through which to support a neo-liberal view of the state, as some critics have suggested. London's urbanism, just as its politics, embraced a third way, with the state taking a stronger role in the provision of high-quality public spaces, whilst typically looking to the market to deliver.

London 2012

In 2012, London remains:

- a permissive city, encouraging of growth and development, receptive to market opportunity, but resistant (as it always has been) to the grand plan

- largely reactive and fragmented in its public sector response to market opportunities (particularly beyond central London), but with a more sophisticated and proactive local policy framework emerging

- differentially sensitive to its extensive built heritage

- an economic powerhouse driving the UK economy, with its own diverse economy extending well beyond its important financial sector

- a socially diverse city with some of the richest and poorest of the UK's inhabitants mixed within a rich cultural soup

11.2 a & b London's contemporary public spaces

a

b

- a hugely expensive city in which inadequate house building, international investment and gentrification pressures have long driven (up) the property market

- a growing city with high birth rates and high immigration from elsewhere in the UK and overseas, stoking up development pressures

- a generally safe city, not, as some argue, obsessed by its own surveillance or safety, even though a continuing target for terrorist action

- unduly focused on its centre, with a declining interest and capacity to grapple with public space issues beyond the central London boroughs.

All these factors establish a context for the provision of public space and a diversity of approaches and engagement with public space issues across London. Despite this, the period from the mid 1990s onwards had represented a period of sustained growth and development in London, and from 1997 to 2010, a period of expanding public sector resources and interest in urban design. The combined result has been a flourishing of public space projects across London during the period covered by this study (1980 onwards), small and large, new and refurbished (**11.2**).

A manifestation in public spaces

Mapping these projects across London revealed 230 new or substantially regenerated public 'squares'. A 'quick and dirty' on-site visual analysis of 130 of these spaces across 10 London boroughs identified how this new phenomena manifests itself in a huge variety of new and regenerated square types, from reclaimed incidental spaces to grand piazzas, but also some evidence to support the dominant public space critiques of the period. At first sight, many squares exhibited a degree of homogenisation, dominance by single land uses, themes or functions, signs of control and exclusion, ubiquitous CCTV, and, in some spaces, an almost excessive sanitation, particularly in the half of the spaces that were privately owned and managed.

At the same time, this London-wide analysis revealed a generally high quality of space across the wide range of space types when measured by their physical qualities, functional purpose and rights of use. It also confirmed the strong resurgence in public and pseudo-public space types, alongside the privately owned squares. In summary, a new dominant type of London square has emerged: typically harder and more urban in nature, more clearly an extension of surrounding uses, but also, frequently well used as a result.

DESIGNING, DELIVERING, USING, MANAGING

The six faces of London's public spaces

From the 130 spaces examined in Chapter 4, the research moved on to a detailed examination of 14 public space projects reflecting the range

11.3 a-c   Space as event

a

b

c

of physical form and rights and responsibility categories revealed by the London-wide analysis. However, instead of the nine functions of public squares identified in Chapter 4, the focus in Chapters 5–10 was on just five of these: corporate, civic, consumption, community and domestic; representing, together, the dominant purposes of the city, for work, civil society, trade, social exchange and home life. A further category – in-between space – was also added to represent the residual spaces of the city and the yet-to-be-realised potential

between. In reality, the divisions are not anyway so stark as the categories might suggest. Consumer-type activities, for example, can be found in most of the other forms of space, as can community-oriented uses, whilst many spaces are surrounded by a mix of uses and a host of varied activities. The categories are nevertheless useful to reflect the 'dominant' activity in each case and because they suggest something about the processes that gave rise to them.

In general, however, commercial and residential developers create, respectively, corporate and domestic spaces. Civic, community and in-between spaces, by contrast, are instigated by the public sector and by pseudo-private agencies and organisations for 'public' purposes, although sometimes with cross-funding from private sources. The final category – consumption spaces – are being created in London by re-tail developers as part of large retail developments, but the case studies demonstrated that these sorts of spaces (on a smaller scale) are also created by a range of other stakeholders as a means to subsidise the wider objectives of their organisations, be those social, cultural or infrastructure-related. Reflecting these origins, corporate, domes-tic and consumption spaces are all generally private or private–public spaces, whilst civic and community spaces are unambiguously public in ownership. In-between spaces exhibit a range of ownerships, in-cluding exclusively private.

11.4 a & b Aesthetic value (a) vs. use value (b)

a

b

Whatever their function, all have been consciously designed and developed prior to their ongoing use and long-term management. The remainder of this section brings together evidence from across London's public space types to reveal the key process-related dimensions that shape London's public spaces and determine how we experience them today.

Designing London's spaces

A range of factors dictated design strategies for public spaces, design representing the process through which aspirations for public space were mediated and strategies defined.

Creating places, a shared endeavour

A characteristic of public space design processes, like the spaces they shape, is their infinite variety as informed by the very different contexts they mould, stakeholders they engage and aspirations they address. London is no different in this respect, with design processes that are often long and complex and informed by multiple overlapping factors. Fundamentally, whether designed for public or private sectors, the research demonstrated that the primary aim of creating new public spaces in London is to help forge a new place identity for the projects in which they sit. The regeneration of existing spaces will also involve a strong element of place-making, although typically involving a more careful balance between historic character and reinvention.

In doing so, there is no desire amongst any parties to create places that deliberately alienate or that are unattractive or soulless for users – quite the opposite. The aim (even if not always realised) is always to create an event, a place that is distinct, comfortable and attractive, something to draw users in and encourage them to partake in the space, even if just to momentarily pause. To this end, design strategies vary, but are broadly of three types:

- creation of a space that is remarkable in itself, attracting users through its physical design (**11.3a**)

- creation of a space that hosts a range of uses that provide the essential draw (**11.3b**).

- creation of a space that hosts 'fun' features and/or activities that encourage users to engage (**11.3c**).

Creating value, a necessary prerequisite

For private developers, an enhanced sense of place added to the intrinsic value of their developments by making them more attractive in the market. In the residential sector, this was often simply 'aesthetic value', but in the corporate sector, experience had shown that to maximise value, spaces needed to be 'put to work'. Thus above and beyond their aesthetic value, they had a 'use value' that it was important to optimise in order to increase the enjoyment of occupiers and to attract users (**11.4**). In this regard, simply creating a space and hoping that by itself it will create the demand necessary to attract further investment and/or users is not enough. The space needs an inherent purpose as defined by the activities (passive and active) it accommodates and 'attractors' (destination land-uses) around it.

The case studies consistently demonstrated that the commercialisation of space is the stuff of life: drawing people in, animating space, creating active frontages, giving space a purpose, helping to provide a return on investment, cross-subsidising other public goods, and so forth. Of the 13 delivered spaces examined in Chapter 5–10, only one (Royal Arsenal Gardens) has no commercial uses on or associated with the space – in that case because of the failure to attract such uses rather than because of a desire to keep commercial forces at bay. The other spaces varied from an almost exclusive focus on consumption activities at one extreme to, at the other, the sites of single cafe/ hostelry outlets, a market or paying events.

In such a context, the distinctiveness of any retail offer (including cafes/restaurants) seems far less important than that one is provided at all. Thus whether the offer is wholly distinctive or made up entirely of multiples (or something between) will be a market decision reflecting the purpose of the space and the commercial return required. It is also likely to change over time. Inevitably the choice and extent of retail will impact on the character of the place, but will not be the only, or necessarily the decisive, factor in generating the sense of place. It will, however, make the space more or less attractive to different sections of society (market segments), with greater distinctiveness actually reducing the attractiveness of schemes to society at large although making it more appealing to a smaller (perhaps more affluent) segment of society. In essence, this will be no different to other 'public' uses – cultural, sporting, leisure, educational – which will add social value, but appeal differentially to different groups.

Delivering long-term space quality

The range of spaces examined through the case studies were physically very different in their form, from very formal to entirely informal, from very enclosed to very open, from hard and urban to green and soft, and everything in-between. No evidence was found that any one form of space is necessarily superior to others, and all work well in the right circumstances. More important than the physical form, it

seems, are the uses in and around the spaces and the way they act to draw a clientele for the space and give it a purpose. Today's 'accepted wisdom' about what makes for a good space – active frontages, good connections, tamed traffic, opportunities to rest, responsiveness to setting, etc. – is, on the whole, informing contemporary public space design in London, although some design challenges remain. These include:

- security concerns that lead to a preference for single secured entrances/exits from large buildings and blank frontage elsewhere
- the reluctance of some corporate occupiers to allow active uses under their buildings
- the balance between privacy and physical/visual permeability in domestic projects, and consequently between peace and quiet and public openness
- a failure to design for older users of space, with seats and facilities that address their needs
- cutting corners and specifications during the procurement process, leading to less robust design solutions.

In making decisions about public space, design compromises and trade-offs are an inevitable part of what is typically a complex design process. The temporary nature of some schemes meant that compromising on long-term urban design objectives such as connectivity in order to achieve short-term benefits such as a more animated public realm was deemed worthwhile. Sometimes, however, sub-optimum design solutions were the result of two other key factors:

- the market not performing as expected, giving rise to a change in the balance of uses and therefore also in the performance of the space
- the impact of otherwise peripheral (in design terms) but powerful regulators such as TfL, for whom the quality of public space is not the primary concern.

In such cases, ensuring that the basic design is robust (despite the short-term changes) will be important in order that, over the long term, the initial aspirations may still be met as and when the market and/or regulatory priorities change.

11.5 a & b Innovation in use (a) vs. innovation in style (b)

a

b

Heritage versus innovation

Regulatory processes also impose pressures that some stakeholders perceive force them to play it safe, particularly in historically sensitive locations, creating design solutions that are not as ambitious as many designers would like. Equally, a danger in contemporary urban design (like architectural design) is that schemes can become mired in dogmatic arguments over semantics, for example on whether kerbs and shared surfaces are or are not appropriate, or in choosing between the continental European piazza model of public space and the greener English version, despite the fact that historically London has featured both models. In such cases, the danger is that the bigger picture and the wider aspirations are compromised.

In this regard, what is or is not recognisably London represented a reoccurring theme in discussions over schemes, often revealing tensions between more progressive designers and the guardians of London's historic street character (English Heritage) and local residents. In such places, these discussions often came down to the detailed choices between materials and to recognising and respecting the intentions of the original designers of historic spaces in refurbishment schemes.

In general, designers demonstrated a strong predilection for design innovation, as they have done as far back as Inigo Jones and the

emergence of the garden square – based on the argument that more interesting clearly contemporary spaces would attract users and contribute to other objectives, such as to wider regeneration. These preferences were indulged more often in the publicly funded and owned schemes than in the private ones. As a result, public schemes tended to be less 'traditional' in their physical design, although not necessarily in their use, with consequential challenges for their managers (see below). In general, however, the case studies demonstrated that design innovation of itself was not important, with some of the simplest design solutions delivering the greatest impact on the ground, whilst innovation, when it comes, should focus on innovation in use, rather than innovation in style, which overall was of little consequence to users (**11.5**).

Space, but for whom?

A final clear finding relating to design was that the way in which spaces deal with traffic can make or break schemes. Many of the opportunities for new public spaces in London have been provided by reclaiming space from traffic, helping in the process to rebalance the relationship between pedestrians and cars. But traffic remains controversial, not just to those who seek to drive and the pressure they put on politicians to allow them to do so, but also to local communities frightened by the perceived displacement effects of public space projects. In fact, nothing is likely to raise more concern amongst local communities than proposals to redirect traffic. Traffic modelling and forecasts effectively drive many urban design processes across London, as do the still-cautious instincts of traffic engineers. They represent the often hidden and poorly understood hand behind many public space projects.

The concern raises another important issue, namely that repeatedly space regeneration schemes raised issues about for whom proposals to re-model space were for in a national capital and world city such as London. In this balance of power, local communities and their more parochial concerns can have an unduly powerful voice through their direct line to local political decision-makers. In such a context, the needs of non-local beneficiaries of schemes – other Londoners, visitors and tourists – often have no such voice.

For new schemes, the voice of the local community was less obvious in its impact, in part because developers remained keen that community benefits should not be delivered at the expense of future resident/occupier amenity or the viability of their proposals. Whom space is for, however, is likely to remain an ongoing concern in the capital, particularly in central London, where local authorities are both representatives of their residents and guardians of the national built heritage of the city – a dual role through which tensions are bound to surface from time to time.

Developing London's spaces

The case studies had in common that there was no common development process. In each, the line-up of stakeholders, the leadership and the power relationships were different, but, despite this, common lessons were apparent.

Public space development processes are infinitely varied but always need leadership

A first critical lesson is that public space schemes in London can sometimes involve a bewildering array of stakeholders in development, regulatory, enabling and long-term stewardship functions. Moreover, these relationships are all the more complex in external-facing spaces (onto public highways or rights of way) than internal-facing schemes (within a block or development), which are typically in a single ownership.

Stakeholders include combinations of public sector client or private developer (one or more), investor, tenants, regeneration agencies, CABE, English Heritage, local planners, local transport planners, GLA (planning), Design for London, TfL, masterplanner, building designers, landscape designer, space managers, the community and other assorted interest groups. A critical role is to coordinate and actively manage these various interests in order to establish a common set of aspirations for each space in the face of contrasting views about how it should be shaped. At different times, and in different schemes, this leadership role was taken by the public sector client or developer, and occasionally by the designer. Indeed, where leadership was less than clear, the resulting delay and compromise resulted in solutions that rarely enhanced outcomes, revealing the importance of a clear vision and leadership focused on delivery.

In schemes focusing on the refurbishment of existing much-loved city spaces, the process is likely to become highly 'political', and leadership will require an understanding of the dynamics of the local stakeholder environment and how to steer it towards consensus. Communication will be key to ensure that aspirations are fully understood, that proposals do not become hijacked by narrow interests or arguments around single issues, but also that where legitimate objections are raised, these are taken seriously, with mechanisms in place to feed back into the design and development processes. Being able to listen and respond will be just as much part of the leadership role as creating and advancing a vision for change.

Market and non-market delivery

Of the 13 completed case studies, 6 were funded entirely through market mechanisms, 3 through entirely public funding from a combination of sources, 3 from a combination of heritage lottery fund and public, charitable or private sources, and 1 from a dedicated pot of Section 106 planning gain funds derived from neighbouring developments. Of the 13, just 3 were led and delivered by private developers acting in isolation, 1 by a state-owned private company, 1 by a private/public partnership, 1 by a private/social enterprise partnership, 5 by the public sector, and 2 by charitable trusts. Together, the case studies demonstrate the complex means and methods through which contemporary public space in London is delivered and how many spaces are delivered through a combination of private and public sources, requiring favourable market conditions for their delivery. Indeed, the danger of delivery without such conditions was demonstrated in Royal Arsenal Gardens, where private confidence in the area severely lagged behind public commitment (by at least 10 years) and revealed the difficulties in coordinating cycles of public funding and market opportunity in less advantageous locations.

As both market and non-market mechanisms are employed in funding and delivering spaces, both can also undermine outcomes. The case studies demonstrated, for example, how the failure to read the market and thereby lease key units with appropriately active or publicly oriented uses can quickly undermine intended outcomes, as can the prioritisation of narrow public transport objectives at the expense of local public space needs. Such examples demonstrate how seemingly minor variations, in these examples caused by unforeseen market incompatibility and regulatory inflexibility, can quickly undermine the best design intentions, resulting in spaces with a very different character and purpose than originally intended.

Regulatory responses are inconsistent (usually with good reason)

Three primary forms of regulatory process impacted on the public space schemes:

- planning controls to sanction new public space proposals or where changes of use or alterations to the (non-highways-related) built fabric occur in existing spaces

- highways orders, focusing on changes to highways themselves (including 'stopping up' existing rights of way)

- listed-building consent, for changes to the historic (listed) built fabric .

In general, the role of English Heritage in the last of these was benign, with the organisation taking a generally supportive attitude and being willing to trade off critical heritage aspirations for less critical concerns. The highways role of TfL was also generally benign when impacts on traffic and buses were seen as minor or had strong mayoral support, although more obstructive where it did not, instead prioritising their primary mission, to keep traffic moving.

The interest taken by planning authorities across London in the design of public space varies hugely, from no or almost no involvement, particularly in internally promoted schemes (those instigated and

delivered by local government itself) to a detailed involvement with all aspects of a design. In part, this variation was accounted for by the variation in context, with schemes in more historic settings receiving (generally) greater regulatory attention, although two other factors were also significant:

- the ability of boroughs to engage in such concerns, reflecting their own internal capacity and capabilities, which, for many, were limited

- the confidence of boroughs in the abilities of other stakeholders, reflecting a reduced pressure to intervene when those responsible for public space projects are seen as having the public interest at heart or are otherwise viewed as delivering a premium product.

Elsewhere, the peculiarities of the local regulatory process (e.g. at Euston) or a sense that what was being proposed was anyway temporary and therefore not worth too much consideration, resulted in minimal regulation, despite the fact that, as one case study (Gabriel's Wharf) demonstrated, temporary may become semi-permanent. Schemes wholly designed, delivered, regulated and managed within the same authority (e.g. Monument Yard) also benefited from a streamlined regulatory process, although, arguably, without the normal checks and balances of an open and truly public regulatory process.

Great outcomes stem from a great patron and designer (not regulation)

In almost all cases, the schemes had a clear promoter that acted as patron for the project, drawing together the coalition of interests and funding package and offering focused leadership in order to drive the project forward. No single approach to this role was apparent, and in different schemes it was undertaken by a range of individuals and organisations, including developers, a steering group, a masterplanner, council service heads, a local politician, charitable trust chief executives and an entrepreneur. Common to each was the determination needed to overcome the inevitable complexities and obstacles, a process that, with the exception of the temporary schemes, nearly always took many years to deliver.

The role of designers varied as much as the spaces they created, but in general two types of designer were found (sometimes wrapped up in the same individual or company):

- masterplanners, who worked on the larger development projects, with one or more integral spaces and who needed to combine financial thinking about development options with clear three-dimensional vision in order to maximise investment returns and space potential.

- public space designers (architects and landscape architects), who worked within the confines of spaces already defined by the masterplan or existing within the historic built fabric of the city and who designed or redesigned space in order to maximise space amenity: aesthetic, social and functional.

In both roles, the influence of designers varied. Their critical contribution was in dealing with the constraints imposed by site, context, client brief (aspirations), strict tenant requirements (in commercial schemes), regulatory requirements, cost and long-term maintenance needs, whilst still delivering a stimulating design. As these factors varied in their complexity, so did the impact of designers, with involvement ranging from 'fundamental' – through a creative design process establishing how to make a scheme viable by reconciling competing claims on the space – to 'peripheral' – largely concerned with applying a decorative sheen to spaces where all the key decisions had already been made by others. This they shared with planners, who, although not directly involved in the creative design process, had both fundamental roles in tying down (in many cases) key public benefits through planning gain agreements (e.g. the presence and position of public space and key routes through it), whilst also influencing final outcomes in less permanent ways through the development control function (e.g. the final balance of uses and landscape treatments).

Communities have a reactive and often negative role (but not by choice)

The diversity of London's communities (like its spaces) is a feature of development processes across the capital. These vary from largely apathetic communities who have to be coaxed through formal consultation processes into making any contribution at all, to highly active (generally well-off) communities highly capable of derailing projects if proposals are not in their interests. In the most sensitive locations, self-appointed (non-local) communities of the capital's aesthetes can also have a powerful impact, and, like the active middle-class communities, understand the levers of power and how to influence them. In the main, however, the role of communities is largely reactive or negative, reacting to proposals already made for spaces, sometimes voting on a beauty parade of options, or actively campaigning against projects.

Nowhere in the 14 case studies were communities positively engaged in the design processes, with the possible exception of Sloane Square, where the community effectively hijacked the agenda (after feeling aggrieved by the formal consultation processes) in order for their alternative scheme to be considered (and subsequently ignored). There and elsewhere, consultation exercises tended to reveal the conservative tastes of Londoners, in sharp contrast to that of most designers, and were consequently disregarded. Instead, the view amongst stakeholders was that local views and engagement needed to be managed (rather than positively captured), with success implicitly judged as engagement without impact. Thus sophisticated strategies were put in place in order that scheme promoters could claim to have involved the public, even if that influence was marginal and typically amounted to little more than endorsement for decisions already made.

Using London's spaces

Observing the 13 built spaces during the summer of 2009 revealed how they are actually used, whilst interviewing users revealed by whom and with what purpose. Findings were both generic, relating to all space types, and specific, relating to the six types identified in Chapters 5–10.

How are London's spaces used?

An initial set of findings relates to the success or otherwise of key design strategies, beginning with factors to draw users in and encourage them to linger:

- Movement in public space predominantly flows along dominant 'movement corridors' or desire lines passing through spaces, and from movement corridors to 'attractors' and vice versa.

- 'Amenities' – cafes/restaurants, shops, big screens, bandstands, kiosks, markets, sports facilities, toilets, seating, etc. – and 'features' around and in a space – fountains, paddling pools, street pianos, public art, sculptural furniture, play equipment, skating opportunities, etc. – encourage engagement with the space, learning through play and informal social exchange.

- In the majority of spaces that are well integrated into the movement network or that host major attractors, at any point in

11.6 Strategic integration maps for the 13 squares using space syntax analysis reveals the poor physical / visual integration of many of the case studies, despite which most were well (sometimes highly) animated

13 London Squares - Strategic integration maps

1.

2.

3.

4.

5.

6.

7.

8.

9.

10.

11.

12.

13.

1. Paternoster Square
2. Canada Square
3. Trafalgar Square
4. Euston Station Piazza
5. Festival Riverside
6. Gabriel's Wharf
7. Swiss Cottage Community Square
8. Peckham Square

9. Royal Arsenal Gardens
10. GMV Square
11. Empire Square
12. Monument Yard
13. Somerset House Courtyard

time only a small proportion of users stop in and engage directly with the space itself (situated activity), whilst the majority pass straight through (transient use). The exception are spaces off the movement framework in which the space itself, its amenities and features are the major draw (e.g. Gabriel's Wharf).

- Spaces with movement corridors/desire lines but without attractors, amenities or features are unlikely to become animated, but will benefit from a background level of movement and more or less continuous use.

- Spaces with attractors and /or amenities or features, but without movement corridors/desire lines still have the potential to become animated if the draw provided by the attractors/amenities/ features is significant enough.

- Spaces without attractors, amenities, features, or movement corridors/desire lines are doomed to failure, their lack of function and absence of users acting as further discouragement to others who may happen across them.

- Visual permeability into and through a space encourages through movement and a sense of 'publicness', but does not guarantee either. By itself, visual permeability has little to do with space animation, which is determined much more by the attractors, amenities and features of a space (**11.6**).

Once animated, certain factors helped to make the spaces comfortable:

- Users, on average, stay longer in soft spaces than in hard spaces (**11.7**).

- Grass is highly conducive to relaxation, play and social exchange; it is comfortable, flexible and allows users to position themselves to take advantage of microclimatic conditions.

- Hard spaces need to be designed with comfort in mind in order to encourage anything more than transient use. Careful consideration should be given to seating, both formal and informal (steps, kerbs, walls, etc.), and to its suitability to a range of users.

- Fixed seating is less flexible (and generally less comfortable) than movable seating, it constrains the formation of social groupings and it reduces the possibility of positioning to take advantage of the sun, shade and other microclimatic factors.

11.7 a & b   Comfort in space – soft (a) and hard (b)

a

b

- Different users are attracted by different microclimatic qualities: some seek shade and others sun; all seek shelter in inclement weather. Spaces that allow a degree of choice are more comfortable for a greater number of users across a greater part of the year.

Patterns of use varied hugely, but common patterns were revealed:

11.8 a–c Distinctive times – mum and toddler mornings (a) school's out (b) post-work wind-down (c)

a

b

c

of user groups at different times of day. Common times can be recognised in different spaces, although these temporal dynamics vary from space to space. Common distinctive times of the day include rush hours (07.30–09.30), mum and toddler mornings (09.30–12.00), lunchtime (12.00–14.00), peaceful afternoons (14.00–15.30), school's out (15.30–17.50), post-work wind-down (17.30–19.30) and night life (19.30–23.00), although these are not all apparent in every space (**11.8**).

- Space utilisation for situated activities is invariably maximised at lunchtime in London, when almost any space will find a constituency of users. Outside these times, use will depend on comfort, attractors, amenities and features, particularly in order to sustain use into the evening.

- Individual spaces (if large enough) can work successfully as a series of distinct and separate sub-spaces, each with a different character and purpose. Such strategies can also fail dramatically if poorly conceived in relation to a realistic assessment of user demand.

- Relaxing, drinking, eating, meeting friends, socialising with colleagues, play (for children), watching others, reading, smoking, skating and simply waiting, were the dominant situated activities.

- High levels of transient use generally stimulated high levels of situated activity, with the highest density of such activities occurring in the interstices between dominant lines of movement and around key features and amenities.

- Spaces have their own distinct patterns of use, which vary between the week and weekend and which see different flows

Spaces for all – not quite

Turning to who is using London's contemporary squares, spaces that mirror the social make-up of London in their user profiles do not generally exist as (unsurprisingly) spaces are dominated by the user groups that predominate in the areas in which they are located. Despite this, spaces can function equally well (in terms of being filled with life and purpose) with a narrow constituency of users as with a diverse range of user groups. Indeed, where space allows, users will further differentiate themselves, particularly by age, through the appropriation of different sub-areas by different groups; for example, teenagers will group in areas where they can be more boisterous and active, young families where children can explore whilst being supervised, and older users in quieter locations and where comfortable seating is available.

Most spaces were well used by both male and female users, although within a 10–25 per cent percent range more female users were found in spaces associated with being particularly family friendly (most notably at Swiss Cottage) and more male users in spaces associated with working life (close to commuting stations or corporate spaces). The outlier was Royal Arsenal Gardens in which female users were 42 per cent less likely to be seen than men, a consequence of being perceived to be the least family friendly and least safe of the 13 spaces analysed.

Users themselves are very clear about how they use space, what they like and do not like, who they prefer to associate with, and who not. Thus middle-class, young adult and white-collar users dominate the use of many contemporary public spaces in London and generally feel most comfortable in spaces in which other users have similar backgrounds to their own.

Users are also realistic about other groups who might or might not feel welcome in spaces. Down-and-out groups (beggars, homeless and street drinkers) were consistently identified as unlikely to feel welcome (apart from in Woolwich), particularly in spaces with highly visible security. Teenagers were identified as unlikely to fit-in in 8 of the 13 spaces and families also in 8 – teenagers because they were seen as noisy and in search of activities that most spaces did not cater for, and families where spaces were viewed as offering little to stimulate children. The poor were identified as likely to feel uncomfortable in six spaces, typically those associated with consumption or where

11.9   The presence of families with children, generally a sign of a safe space

activities were considered 'highbrow' (although not in the corporate spaces), and the elderly in four spaces, those perceived as less comfortable by users.

In making these assessments, a clear understanding is apparent amongst public space users that different spaces have different purposes, and need to be assessed in that light: some spaces are transient, others are for spending time in, some are relaxing, and others have a vibrant buzz. Users implicitly accept that not all spaces will be equally attractive to all, and should not be, but nevertheless reveal remarkable commonalities in what they like (the antithesis being what they do not like). Socially, London's contemporary public space users like:

- relaxed, comfortable, safe spaces in which they feel they can stay as long or as briefly as they want

- spaces that encourage a regular user community to emerge and that give rise to social interaction

- spaces with an urban buzz in busy locations, that are full of life and that offer a range of amenities (particularly consumption opportunities), such as al-fresco dining and markets

- family-friendly community spaces in which children can explore an interesting yet safe environment whilst under the watchful eye of parents who are able to relax and socialise (**11.9**)

- quieter green spaces in residential areas that are suitable for relaxation and play

- well-used and overlooked spaces, which thereby feel safe – the presence of CCTV and visible security is generally welcomed by users of public space.

Physically, London's contemporary public space users like:

- fun features, which are very popular for the relaxed and playful feel they can give a space and the interaction they stimulate, and which encourage users to linger for longer

- spaces that feel obviously open and encouraging to public use and that avoid ambiguity (e.g. the presence of gates)

- greenery (trees and grass), which represents a strong preference of Londoners, even in heavily used urban locations

- a distinctive setting with views, historic features, memorable landmarks or visually interesting (not austere or overly corporate) architecture – for users, building design rather than the design of the public space itself often determined whether a space felt distinctive or not

- clean and tidy and well-maintained spaces, which users associate with being safe and less threatening – most spaces met these benchmarks, although highly used public spaces with pigeons (Trafalgar Square, Monument Yard and Euston Piazza) attracted more criticism than others

- adequate, comfortable seating and toilets, particularly for older users

- spaces without traffic.

Fast and slow, high and lower-end spaces

For their part, corporate developers are generally very clear about the audience they aim to attract to their spaces, even if they do not always achieve this aim. At Canada Square, for example, the development model aimed to attract 'quality' tenants, and therefore, to match the expectations of these occupiers, highly managed and secured spaces were provided with high-end facilities. In turn, this gives a certain

11.10 a & b Fast (a) and slow space (b)

a

b

feel that is very comfortable for the targeted corporate users, who then provide a captive market for the consumption opportunities, particularly given the spatial isolation of Canary Wharf. A similar model was pursued at Paternoster Square, although with less immediate success. There, when high-end retailers could not be attracted, the chain establishments that took their place gave a less exclusive but more vibrant feel to the space than envisaged. This has resulted in some disquiet about the level and type of use amongst some corporate tenants, but a general satisfaction amongst stakeholders that, after a slow start, the space found its purpose.

In explicitly consumption-oriented spaces, promoters are equally focused on the market segment they wish to attract. In this regard, all three of the consumption spaces had been designed to make money in order to cross-subsidise the larger mission of their organisations: infrastructural, social and cultural. Nevertheless, the spaces were designed and the tenants selected to appeal to the different target markets. The mid market was the focus at Euston, where commuters and leisure travellers (not locals) were the intended audience for a fast-turnover space (**11.10**). By contrast, Gabriel's Wharf was designed to appeal to those seeking a more relaxed space in which to engage in a slower more idiosyncratic and therefore exclusive (high-end) retailing and leisure experience. At Festival Riverside, the mix is somewhere between, featuring chain outlets designed to maximise return by appealing to mid- and higher-end customers (workers and tourists) in search of quick (but not fast) food. There, the more leisurely linked space – Festival Terrace – serves those seeking a less frenetic and more relaxed environment.

Understanding and misunderstanding the potential of space

The experience with London's community and domestic spaces demonstrates how assumptions and aspirations of stakeholders regarding use can easily be misplaced. In each of the five spaces across these two categories, the intention of stakeholders was always to establish a vibrant new focus for, respectively, the existing communities of Swiss Cottage, Peckham and Woolwich, and for the new residents at Greenwich Millennium Village and at Empire Square. Yet stakeholders admit that these aspirations went awry in three of the five cases. Although the natures of Peckham Square and Swiss Cottage Community Square are very different – one a carefully defined green oasis and space for relaxation and the other a hard somewhat undefined but nevertheless flexible urban hub – both sit at the heart of their respective communities and are surrounded by attractors that give the spaces a natural constituency.

GMV Village Square, Empire Square and especially Royal Arsenal Gardens are, by contrast, somewhat isolated from existing foci of urban life, and from large-scale attractors. Despite this, stakeholders expected the spaces to establish enough draw on their own merits to

fill each space with vibrant life – something which did not happen. Nevertheless, the spaces were able to cater for a different range of uses than originally envisaged. Thus, whilst neither of the domestic spaces fill with animated life, both successfully cater for the lower-key more homely functions of visual amenity space, relaxation space, node on a pedestrian thoroughfare, and place around which local facilities are situated. Arguably, these low-key functions could have been perfectly appropriate aspirations from the start. At Royal Arsenal Gardens, by contrast, a very different type of community – the London-wide community of skateboarders – appropriated what had become an unwanted space and gave it a purpose that was later formalised with the construction of a skate-park. Stakeholders now admit that a more temporary range of functions of a similar nature would have been far preferable to the permanent space that was created in the blind hope that it would attract development.

Community spaces can work in many different ways and at one and the same time for the different communities in the same locality – teenagers, families, workers, elderly, etc. They can become attractors in themselves if the levels of comfort, amenities and features are conducive, but equally can simply be the incidental spaces on which larger attractions are located and occasional events occur. Location at the heart of the community (not on the periphery) seems key. Domestic spaces, despite the conflicting aspirations amongst those who create them, tend to be quiet and relaxed spaces, although the potential for greater activity is there if more active (or permissive) management allows it. In the main, however, these spaces should simply be allowed to act as oases of space, light and greenery for passers-by and for residents to look out on to and enjoy. This reflects the more peripheral locations of these spaces and the sedate uses with which they are surrounded. For residents, it is what they expect such places to be – not least a respite from traffic.

Gain with or without pain

Whilst the gradual invasion of London by traffic has been a slow incursion over many years such that few noticed the consequences until it was too late, the removal of vehicles provides a much greater challenge. The transformation of prominent civic spaces in London, for example, revealed significant tensions, bringing to the fore questions about who these spaces are for – locals or Londoners. At Sloane Square, the tensions were particularly marked, with a determination amongst locals that alterations to the space should not impact on the peace of their neighbourhoods, either by attracting 'undesirables' to the space or through displacing traffic. Their campaign was successful, revealing that an undue focus on the gain to non-local public space users can stem from a failure of decision-makers to understand and engage with the perceived pain to local residents (the voters). In complete contrast, at Trafalgar Square, the concerns of local residents failed to derail plans, in part because of the overwhelming gains of the project to London so that even the local authority could not ignore them, and increasingly gave its grudging, then tacit, support to the proposals.

By contrast, because the Somerset House and Monument schemes conjured space from the forgotten in-between in locations of traffic dominance but without significant local populations (of residents), these transformations were relatively smooth and seen as all gain for a new constituency of users without pain for an existing constituency (apart from a few civil servants who lost their parking privileges). The schemes are underpinned by the ideal of withdrawing space from the few (car drivers) and its gifting it to the many (Londoners).

Managing London's spaces

Moving from use to management, with the exception of Empire Square, where the original residential developer quickly sold on the freehold and long-term management responsibility for the project (the usual model in that sector), in all the remaining public spaces, the long-term freeholder was involved in the development process and still retains responsibility for stewardship. Whether public or private, the incentive was therefore there from the start to fully consider ongoing management costs and liabilities and to ensure that these issues were appropriately reflected in design solutions.

Economic versus public service rationales

Corporate developers are particularly sensitive to such issues – both to building in resilience to their projects in order that they will maintain their long-term asset value and to visibly demonstrating the quality and intensity of their management services, for which their tenants pay a premium. These services represent a key selling point for premium corporate space. At Gabriel's Wharf, by contrast, although cleaned daily, the 'temporary' nature of the development means that it has had very little maintenance in the quarter-century it has been standing. There, the somewhat scruffy and faded look of the space is part of its charm and plays into its own brand identity and business model as much as the pristine spaces of Canary Wharf do to its. The

nature of the space therefore dictates the nature of the management regime required.

The public sector, by contrast, does not operate on a business model and cannot compete with the obsessive cleaning regimes of the corporate sector. Instead, spaces are typically managed on the basis of specified performance expectations tied to:

- contracting out management services
- classifying spaces against the user load they receive, with more highly used spaces cleaned and cleared of rubbish more often
- set programmes for regular maintenance tasks (e.g. grass cutting and landscape maintenance)
- an 'as and when' regime for other and specialist services (e.g. repairs, graffiti removal, chewing gum cleared, etc.).

In a space like Trafalgar Square, this process is more or less continuous and designed (like its corporate counterparts) to maintain the integrity of the physical fabric. Elsewhere, cleaning and maintenance is more intermittent, for example three times a week in the Royal Arsenal Gardens, whatever the build-up of rubbish in-between. In essence, rather than operating as self-contained and closed management systems dedicated to the particular needs of a single space (e.g. Somerset House Courtyard) or small group of spaces (e.g. Gabriel's Wharf and its surrounds), the regimes of London's boroughs deal with the infinitely variable spaces of a continuous connected public realm. New public spaces have to fit as best as can be arranged within this regime, and in doing so their 'special' nature will not always be fully understood.

Encouraging and discouraging fun

In almost all the case studies, efforts were made to actively attract users through the coordination of arts, entertainment and charity events in the spaces (**11.11**). In the corporate world, this is part of the offer, helping to create a stimulating environment for workers, whilst attracting users to the associated retail opportunities. In general, the consumption spaces were located at such busy locations that they did not have to work too hard to attract users to their retail, and instead hosted events for wider social, cultural and educational purposes, the exception being Euston Piazza, whose events were mainly of a commercial nature (e.g. product launches), generating additional

11.11 a & b Encouraging (a) and discouraging (b) fun

a

b

income for National Rail. In corporate and consumption locations, the scale and type of events were dictated by the scale and nature of the space (for example, grass is more susceptible to damage but more versatile for temporary shelters – marquees, etc.) and by the resources available to programme such activities.

Civic and community spaces were subject to similar constraints, with the dedicated events management team at Trafalgar Square able to use the space to its full potential to put on a range of high-profile and large-scale events throughout the year, although not without some concern in some quarters that the number and type of events impacts negatively on the representational value and civic dignity of the space. Elsewhere, spaces hosted both regular small-scale activities and more occasional arts or community events focused on particular local needs. The farmers' market and jobs fairs at Peckham provide examples of each. In general, most spaces had been designed flexibly to allow events to just plug in, whether or not there was any actual demand, although the placement of fixed features in spaces can quickly stifle this adaptability.

The major exceptions were the domestic spaces, where the failure to encourage active pursuits at GMV Village Square and the active discouragement to almost any activities (even those requested by residents) at Empire Square contributed to the extremely sedate character of these spaces. This may or may not be appropriate for residential spaces, but certainly contrasts strongly with the original intentions for these spaces.

He who pays the piper

In corporate spaces, a balance needs to be struck in order that activities do not compromise the workings of businesses operating from these sites, in whose interests the management regime primarily operates, and who indirectly pay for it. Levels of maintenance, security and activities are all carefully negotiated with tenants, who see these spaces as an extension of their workspace – as their external public lobbies. This does not preclude contributing to the wider civic life of their localities, however, and the hosting of charity, religious and key memorial events are seen as part of a wider social mission of long-term investors, although this does not extend to tolerating begging, unauthorised selling (e.g. homeless magazines), unauthorised collecting (e.g. for charities) or demonstrating.

A similar situation pertains in the domestic spaces, which are run first and foremost in the interests of their resident communities, who, again, pay for the regimes. This is mollified, however, in the case of GMV by the presence of local political representatives on the board of GMV Management Ltd, the retained right held by the borough to adopt the space in the future if deemed necessary, and the more open nature of the space, all of which has created a more outward-looking regime than at Empire Square, where the regime is guided by the convenience of the management agent and the need to minimise service bills.

The regimes at the community squares, by comparison, are all paid for through the recurrent revenue budgets of their respective councils – budgets that compete year on year with services such as social services, education, libraries and housing, and which have to be justified to political masters. Typically, the pressure is on to reduce these costs and to deliver more for less. The result is that high-quality public realm schemes in each of the community spaces quickly deteriorated because the revenue realities were simply not up to the capital aspirations of the designers and original promoters of the schemes. As these actors left the scene, they also left their council public space managers a big headache, attempting to manage bespoke designs, planting and materials through standardised, inflexible and ultimately inappropriate management regimes.

In all the spaces, residents, tenants and occupiers generally wielded little direct power in the ongoing management processes and were little involved beyond basic consultation processes. Neither, it seemed, was there a significant unmet demand to be more involved, with users content to leave the day-to-day management of public spaces to the professionals who are paid to do the job.

Hard, soft and petty controls

A key dimension of the management systems across the spaces were the security regimes employed, adopting approaches that ranged from nothing (beyond that already provided by the everyday policing of London's streets), to the creation of über-secure environments with, variously, dedicated private and public security, extensive CCTV networks and night-time gating. As well as the detection of and deterrence to serious crime, these measures were deployed to enforce a range of petty controls, often denoted through on-site signage to ban 'offending' behaviours. These included:

- regular control of cycling and skateboarding

- control of smoking outside prescribed zones at Canada Square

- banning of pigeon feeding at Trafalgar Square and discouraging it at Sloane Square

- general control of unauthorised trading

- a ban on paddling in the fountains at Trafalgar Square

- alcohol restriction zones

- the control or outright banning of photography in corporate spaces (without a permit).

Increasingly, however, activities that are seen as undesirable were being designed out through 'soft controls' (see Chapter 8), and a range of strategies were revealed across the case study spaces to achieve this. Such strategies included the use of regular armrests on benches and high levels of lighting to stop rough sleeping, placing bollards to prevent joy riding, avoidance of vertical features to limit opportunities for graffiti, and the insertion of studs in the street furniture to discourage skateboarders. At Festival Riverside, a more positive solution was deployed to discourage skateboarders using parts of the scheme where their activities might do damage, the provision of alternative dedicated facilities elsewhere. Such proactive displacement strategies were rare.

THE POWER RELATIONSHIPS OF SPACE CREATION

This chapter has drawn out conclusions from the detailed examination across Chapters 2–10 of London's processes of public space creation and recreation. These both sum-marise the dom-inant models of design, development, use and management of public space in London and also offer guidance on how the potential of London's public space (and by implication that in other cities) can be maximised in the future.

The findings from this chapter are used to inform the discussion in Chapter 12, in which the more theoretical arguments contained in the international literature about the nature of contemporary public space are subjected to the empirical analysis from the London case. To conclude the present chapter, however, the issue of power relationships within the multiple complex public space development processes are briefly returned to, just as they were at the end of Chapters 5–10.

The case studies demonstrated that how public space is shaped and reshaped over time will depend on six factors, each of which derives from and represents a particular stakeholder group:

1   the aspirations, resources and determination of those who own the space, whether public or private

2   the aspirations, powers and skills of those with regulatory responsibilities and their willingness to intervene to secure particular ends

3   the aspirations, skills and sensibilities of designers, the scope given to them by the first two stakeholder groups (above), and their awareness of the needs and aspirations of the last three groups (below)

4   the aspirations of communities and their abilities and determination to engage with and influence the work of the first three stakeholder groups (above)

5   the aspirations, resources and abilities of those with management responsibility for the space

6   the manner with which public space users engage with spaces and, through their use, define and redefine the nature of each space over time.

The relationships between these groups vary hugely from space to space, as do the relative power they wield within the design and development process. A distinguishing feature of public space development and redevelopment projects seems to be that they involve a generally larger range of stakeholder groups than many building development projects and that the influence wielded by even the same stakeholder from one space to the next can vary significantly, whether intentionally or not. Ultimately, it is possible to conclude:

●   There is no ideal set of power relationships.

●   In local-authority-driven schemes, the concurrence of regulatory, development, funding and management powers in one place creates a powerful cocktail of influence able to deliver effective and positive change (and occasionally to conspire in the delivery of major public space blunders).

●   The influence of the community, through their elected representatives, can be significant and decisive, but is more often unengaged and seemingly unconcerned about public space projects.

●   Private and pseudo-private promoters of schemes are critical in establishing the funding package and set of alliances within which many schemes happen.

●   In market-driven schemes, the power of the masterplanner comes from their unique ability to creatively shape the development, contextual and regulatory constraints to create marketable solutions.

●   Landscape designers often feel frustrated that they are left 'decorating' a space already defined in its essentials by others.

●   Planning seems to have a relatively minor role in positively shaping the nature of London's public spaces beyond its crude land-use (zoning) and reactive regulatory responsibilities.

●   Heritage stakeholders wield significant influence on schemes situated in historic locations, but are generally responsive to innovation that respects its historic context.

●   Users and potential users typically have very little power in the formal processes of shaping and reshaping space.

●   Post-completion market circumstances and ongoing management practices have the power to make or break any design/development vision.

12 PUBLIC SPACE CRITIQUES, COUNTER-ARGUMENTS AND CONCLUSIONS

INTRODUCTION

This book has used the phenomenon of the 'new' London squares to explore the dominant critiques of public space by gauging if and how they relate to the design, development, use and management of contemporary public spaces in London. Drawing on the evidence provided by the scholarly and empirical work presented throughout the book and brought together in Chapter 11, this final chapter discusses what it reveals about the 'critiques' and 'counter-arguments' presented in Chapter 1.

Finally, to conclude, the chapter returns to the question with which the book began: 'Public space, is it really that bad?' In doing so, it looks to the future and reveals a seemingly obvious but (despite that) often forgotten essential truth concerning public spaces in London and other major cities across the globe – that the purposes for and permutations of, public spaces are almost infinite and that analysis does us a great disservice if it fails in its account to recognise the multiple complex nature of spaces in our cities today.

THE CRITIQUES

In Chapter 1, ten critiques of public space were identified in the international literature, whilst in Chapter 4, some evidence to support these was revealed in a 'quick and dirty' visual analysis of contemporary public spaces across London. In Chapters 5–10, fourteen case studies were used to drill down into the critiques a little further. Here, taking each critique in turn, conclusions are reached looking across the range of evidence discussed in the book.

So is London's public space neglected?
The history of London demonstrates a city in an almost-continuous process of development, decline and reinvention. Thus, as develop-

ment interest naturally or artificially moves from one place to another, investment follows, leaving other localities comparatively starved of funds. In such circumstances, resources for public spaces are limited, with day-to-day processes of management rationed, and areas of lower priority neglected in order that more resources can be devoted elsewhere. The natural state of much of London at any time is managed decline, at least until reinvestment occurs.

This process creates both problems and opportunities. There are problems in that from time to time during its history London has become stigmatised as a dirty, unkempt city with poor public governance. Equally, from time to time (roughly every 50 years) there is a reaction against this and a spate of reinvestment in order to address the concerns. One such episode was the production of the grand designs for London during the Regency period that gave rise to Trafalgar Square and other monumental civic set pieces. Another was the Victorian parks movement and another the post-war rebuilding efforts. Arguably, the 'urban renaissance' from the late 1990s onwards was such a period, itself building on an earlier more limited market-led renewal of interest in public space amidst widespread public sector neglect.

In a dynamic city such as London, opportunities are also generated as neglect and decline themselves selectively give rise to prospects for redevelopment, for example the sorts of spaces from the in-between explored in Chapter 10. There, both case studies demonstrated how processes of loss and rediscovery transformed two spaces that were previously given over to ancillary functions and neglect but that now play full and positive roles in the cultural and work life of the city. Thus, at very different scales (grand and incidental), these processes have created new flexible and social places from formerly degraded spaces, notwithstanding that both locations were advantaged by their historic contexts and relative attractiveness for investment (both public and private). Elsewhere, the challenge may be greater, or perhaps just

12.1   Royal Arsenal – with subsidy from the Home and Communities Agency, Berkeley Homes have created a network of new and refurbished spaces at the heart of this former military arsenal and barracks

different, requiring creative and open approaches to redevelopment in order to give new purpose (both traditional and non-traditional) to neglected space.

Typically, such processes have been led by the public sector, or by a range of pseudo-private trusts and agencies, although London's fragmented governance (and the London-wide analysis of spaces) reveals how interest in such processes varies hugely across the city. Increasingly, also, the private sector have become interested in parts of London's degraded historic fabric if a market opportunity (with

public subsidy) can be carved out. The redevelopment of the historic Royal Arsenal in Woolwich (adjacent to but separate from Royal Arsenal Gardens) with its network of new public squares represents such an example (**12.1**). In each case, it matters little whether the organisations owning, running and managing the newly created spaces are private or public, as long as the resulting spaces and their management regime are robust, broadly inclusive and of high quality.

Recent years have seen a renaissance in the approach to public space in London, with a greater awareness of the value of public space amongst public and private stakeholders alike, a renaissance that extends to design and development processes, as well as to the ongoing use and management of public space – at least when the spaces in question are new and high profile. In general, users seem very happy with the stewardship of London's public spaces, although there remains a tendency to abandon less high-profile everyday spaces to a far inferior management regime with negative knock-on impacts on how spaces are perceived and used. How, in a new age of austerity, London's public spaces will fare is still an open question, although past experience suggests that revenue budgets for the local environment are amongst the first and greatest casualties of stringent times.

So is London's public space invaded?

If selective but widespread neglect represents the 'natural' state of London as a city that throughout much of its history has had weak and fragmented governance, then perhaps the greatest single act of collective neglect was the manner in which the city was allowed to become overrun by traffic. Unfortunately, in that case, the local sacrifice of spaces to the tide of traffic was only partly an act of neglect, since from the rebuilding of London after the Second World War until the introduction of the Congestion Charge in 2003, much of the expansion of traffic in London was actively planned, or at least sanctioned and actively accommodated.

The impact was most dramatic in how it affected London's historic civic set-piece spaces, all of which became saturated by traffic and which have only gradually been reclaimed. In part, this may have been a natural consequence of the garden square typology that so dominates in central London, designed as they were as central swathes of green around which roads circulate. Thus, the fate of Parliament Square when first built in 1868 as Britain's first roundabout increasingly became the model elsewhere, including in the sorts of formal civic spaces discussed in Chapter 6. This gradual subversion by traffic most clearly resulted in a fragmented and splintered environment, with the centres of spaces dissociated from their edges and frequented by only the most intrepid tourists.

The reclaiming of space from traffic has been gradual, although the transformation at Trafalgar Square represents both the most dramatic example in terms of its scale and impact, if also one of the most (albeit deceptively) straightforward when measured by what actually occurred: the paving of one side of the space and the diversion of traffic

12.2 Brixton – rebalancing space, from gyratory to people place

around the other three sides. Thus these schemes are not generally attempts to move from a traffic model to a non-traffic one, but rather to strike a better balance between motorised traffic and other forms of movement in London. Indeed, attempts to reduce traffic capacity or to divert traffic from one location to another are typically met by storms of protest, making these types of projects amongst the most challenging of London's contemporary spaces to achieve. Yet, as interventions across London have shown, reclaiming invaded space does not have to involve major interventions, since even the most modest interventions can have dramatic local impacts, although for every space transformed there will be many many more with a latent potential yet to be realised.

Today, London is still invaded by traffic, and parts of the capital are dominated to an unacceptable degree by private cars, despite the negative local economic, social and health effects. These include spaces such as Parliament Square (Chapter 3) and Sloane Square (Chapter 6) that have been scheduled for change but that have failed amidst acrimony. These, as national embarrassments, are eventually likely to have their moment of transformation. Potentially more powerful (if transformed) will be the many local spaces across London with the latent promise to re-balance London's residential neighbourhoods, high streets and town centres. In this area, a lot more work needs to be done, and the City of London through its Street Scene Challenge has been showing the way. The lessons from London's contemporary public spaces are that, if the balance is right, pedestrians and traffic can co-exist quite happily side by side as long as those on foot or bike are given enough space to thrive. In other words, this is not an all-or-nothing agenda (**12.2**).

So is London's public space exclusionary?

An assertion can confidently be made that London is and always has been an exclusionary city in terms of the access it grants to its public spaces – in other words, there was no golden age in the past where all were somehow equal in their use and access to public space. This is simply a statement of fact, since for all of its history London has been a city divided by class and/or wealth, which, in every way, including access to public space, will dictate relative opportunity. Thus less economically advantaged inhabitants will generally find it more difficult to get around the city, and will tend to be concentrated in the environmentally less advantageous parts of the city. Despite this, the research detected no attempt on the part of those creating and recreating public space in London to actively exclude any users through the design process, although poor physical design and advertent and inadvertent exclusionary management practices sometimes had the effect of doing so. Quite the contrary, the attempt was often (sometimes quite unrealistically) to create spaces as a locus of public life where London's mixed communities could interact.

The community spaces examined in Chapter 8 demonstrated this aspiration most clearly, and in two of the three cases were successful in their aspirations in very diverse communities. The third was a failure, but created an opportunity for a narrowly focused body of users – London's (largely young male) skateboard community. In that case, this separation-off of what many might regard as a 'problem activity' was not an active strategy, but rather an act of appropriation that was later officially sanctioned. The fact that women (in particular) find the space threatening is not the fault of the skateboard community, but rather stems from its continued isolation and a failure to attract any wider purpose. The skate-park is not parochial (and thereby exclusionary in the sense of actively dividing this body of users from others), but instead opportunistic, with skateboarders willing to positively use the gaps in the city that others eschew.

Together, the case studies demonstrated that London's contemporary public spaces can be and very often are disabling, but often this is not for those groups one might expect. Thus building regulations

and planning standards take great care to ensure that new spaces are accessible for those with disabilities, whether on foot or in a wheelchair, for example, through the use of ramps and the removal of barriers. But almost no attention is paid to ensuring that spaces are comfortable and therefore useable for one of the largest potential (and increasing in size) groups of public space users, the active elderly, or simply those who are not as active and energetic as they once were. The observation may go some way to explaining the dominance of spaces across London by under-50s age groups. Minor physical oversights were generally at fault here. Thus, although spaces were highly accessible for most users, the preferences of designers for clean lines and sculpturally interesting forms led to the specification of functionally inappropriate seating (e.g. seats without backs) that discouraged older users from lingering in spaces. The absence of shade and shelter and clearly available public toilets were similar problems that impacted inequitably on older users.

At the other end of the age range, the creation of spaces for particular users, whether for skateboarders, children's play or consuming alcohol (**12.3**) seems to meet a clear demand by certain groups of users (as does the creation of spaces to shop or eat outdoors – see below). The fact that they will only appeal to certain groups (and not to others) is not of itself a sign of exclusion, but instead of a diverse society with different needs. The key may be that provision for one group should not diminish the welfare of others, and the provision of a diversity of actively managed space types is required.

So is London's public space segregated?

London is clearly a segregated city in that large areas (although not all) of the city are dominated by reasonably homogenous economic groups, only broken where gentrification or the provision of social housing have intervened. The question 'Is London's public space segregated?', however, needs breaking down further into two related questions: 'Is London's space intentionally segregated?' and 'Is London's public space unintentionally segregated?'

Taking the former first, London, like most cities, has a history of creating intentionally segregated ghettos. At one extreme, this encompassed the locking behind gates of society's unwanted and fallen in debtor prisons, lunatic asylums, and the like. At the other, it involved the gating of large parts of eighteenth-century London in exclusive neighbourhoods for the upper classes or *nouveau riche*.

12.3   Greenwich – reclaimed from the public highway, this space was paid for by the public house for their patrons to use

Today, whilst a few larger gated developments still exist in London (some of older pedigree and some more recent), in the main, the research revealed few attempts to segregate what might normally be regarded as public space, with truly public spaces instead viewed as 'value-adding' elements within development schemes. In this regard, a supplementary question arises: When should space normally be public and when might it legitimately be private? This question most often arises in connection with the types of domestic spaces discussed in Chapter 9.

The creation of communal (but not community) spaces in the centre of residential blocks, for example at Greenwich Millennium Village, perpetuates a dominant perimeter block model in which private space is captured in the centre of urban blocks and surrounded by private houses. This model has worked well since the founding of London and clearly divides public from private (even if shared) functions in the interests of privacy, security and amenity. Yet, as densities have been pushed up in London throughout the 2000s, apartment blocks have been built higher, with larger spaces between them that are more

12.4 Bermondsey Square – opening up an urban block to create a clearly public space

amenable to 'public' functions. At Empire Square, for example, early proposals for the site included a private gated courtyard space, whilst later proposals envisaged a public space enclosed in the centre of the block and gated only at night for security purposes. The space, as created, offers some benefits in the area, through breaking down and making permeable an otherwise sizable urban block, but arguably this is at the expense of the residents living there, who now have a space that is neither clearly public nor private (instead being reminiscent of failed attempts in the post-war period to give over more space to shared communal use).

Opening the centre of urban blocks to public use is still the exception rather than the rule in London, and the research suggested that their status seems somewhat ambiguous to users, and to managers. Thus, although not designed with segregation in mind, spaces can become segregated if management practices are unsympathetic to the original intentions of the designers, developers and regulators that gave rise to them. Turning therefore to the second question posed at the start of this section, spaces can become unintentionally segregated, and regulators need to pay particular attention to tying down their status and the rights of users (and to monitoring their ongoing use) if such pressures are to be avoided. Equally, stakeholders should avoid (if possible) confusing domestic space with vibrant community or consumption space. The research suggested that, whatever the

vision, the domestic nature of spaces is likely to assert itself in largely domestic environments, and spaces for safe and secure relaxation and play, or for simple aesthetic value, are just as legitimate and important in a city such as London as animated social places.

So whether London's space is segregated is a complex question that has at its heart the legitimate and desirable need to separate certain types of activities (public and private) from each other in distinct but related public and private realms. With changes to contemporary patterns of development, these realms can become muddied, and greater care needs to be taken in determining when segregation is legitimate and when it is not and subsequently in defining and guaranteeing the public and private spaces that result (**12.4**).

So is London's public space insular?

Little evidence was found for a general retreat from the public realm *per se*, or, more specifically, from traditional public space. Without exception, the 13 built (or rebuilt) schemes had found a (or greatly enlarged their) constituency of users, even if this was not always the constituency originally envisaged. In some respects, this simply echoes wider evidence about the nature of public space in London and how, over a period of 15 years or so, Londoners have increasingly embraced the city's public spaces – a trend most clearly exemplified through the appropriation of street space by cafes, restaurants and pubs across the capital, as well as by the more vibrant external events culture of the city. Moreover, this has been at exactly the same time that Internet use, and the virtual worlds it has given rise to, have spiralled beyond all predictions with London now situated as one of the global hubs for Internet traffic, as well as for people.

Thus 10 of the 13 spaces examined during the study had external beverage/food outlets and (a different) 10 a programme of planned external events/activities. Furthermore, whilst the traditional pub was a largely insular internal space in which people (particularly men) went to relax with like-minded associates, these new outlets are outward looking, each with a presence (seating) on the space itself and with a more inclusive and social countenance.

Not all the spaces were equally social, although in London this was always the way. The garden squares, for example, after their initial greening (see Chapter 2), remained functional arrival spaces but also became spaces for quiet perambulation, social exchange and aesthetic

12.5   Bankside Gardens – this new space in front of the Tate Modern acts as an external extension to the gallery

pleasure, an escape from the insular world of 'refined' domestic life. The domestic spaces discussed in Chapter 9 have similar roles as oases of green and places to situate (successfully or not) the sorts of local facilities that represent the new informal social venues of their communities – convenience stores, health clubs, etc.

Neither are all the users of public spaces equally social. The research demonstrated, for example, that families in the social housing units being created in London's new high-density developments have very

different, more active and gregarious, calls on public spaces to the professional singles and young couples who co-occupy many of the remainder of these developments and who seem to be more insular in their habits when at home. Tension can result from these different patterns of use in a manner that may not in a pure market situation (the social units having been provided via planning gain), although this problem seems minor when weighed against the benefits of the social provision. In sum, however, a thesis of a more insular London seems unfounded, and although spaces vary in their character and liveliness, there is certainly a return to building public spaces in the capital, and these are finding important new roles in the life of the city (**12.5**).

So is London's public space privatised?

The argument over privatisation of public space and the negative consequences that flow from this is perhaps the most pervasive amongst the critiques of public space. As was argued in Chapter 5, the idea of 'public' in public space is a somewhat slippery concept, since cities (including London) have always contained a wide range of spaces that are neither entirely public nor entirely private, yet still possess the essential characteristics of public space – namely open and broadly inclusive. Gabriel's Wharf, for example, is a space that despite its private ownership (by a social enterprise), nurtures a management approach based on openness and the active encouragement of positive behaviours (rather than the exclusion of negative ones). Even defining which spaces are and are not publicly owned and managed is challenging. The freehold of Somerset House, for example, is retained by the state, but the space and buildings are leased by a charitable trust who manage the space in the public interest but close it for 40 days of the year, in essence privatising it for paying functions. Euston Piazza, perhaps the most security-conscious of the spaces, is owned by a private company, albeit one now wholly owned by the state, with, in effect, its own planning powers. Other spaces amongst those examined are similarly ambiguous, with many passing formerly public land (ports, historic estates, industrial land, railway land, and cultural facilities) into private or pseudo-private hands in a form of state privatisation of existing and future public space.

Thus, along the continuum from purely public to purely private space, ownership and accessibility cannot by themselves explain 'publicness', which also needs some discussion of the types of encounters that a space facilitates, both in terms of the freedoms offered to users to pursue different activities (e.g. political activity, photography, etc.) and to act as participants in the life of the space. Processes of privatisation may or may not restrict such activities, but will not be the sole determinant of how a space feels and how it will be used – factors that will instead be determined by the management regime operated in each space. Begging, for example, is an illegal activity and is controlled across much of London, including in wholly public spaces, as are demonstrations, trading and a wide range of other activities. Nowhere is public space entirely 'free'.

The corporate spaces examined in Chapter 5 were amongst the most clearly private of the spaces examined. For the corporations that built, own and manage these developments, the very existence of the spaces themselves and their management represent clear commercial decisions: high-quality, highly managed public space is part of the package demanded by grade A occupiers of corporate space. For them, their corporate and retail tenants demand that these spaces be open, convivial, safe and accessible, and it is not in their economic interest to close them off or to design them in such a way that they are unattractive to users. In both corporate case studies, international money had settled on London and created these developments, but investors were making long-term commitments to the places they were creating and remain concerned for the economic sustainability of their investments. Public space represented a critical part of this strategy.

For users, the spaces were hugely valued, as was the active manner in which they were managed, although – reflecting the nature of the jobs supported in the surrounding corporate buildings – this clientele was drawn from a narrower group (particularly at Canary Wharf) than any other London spaces. As elsewhere across the built spaces, users were realistic about how these spaces and their management regimes might implicitly or explicitly exclude some potential users, but were content with the performance of each space in its own terms as comfortable, safe, attractive space, with appropriate opportunities for engagement and relaxation. Users remained unconcerned that the space was privately owned and managed. For them, it delivered what they expected and in the process helped to enrich their daily work lives. 'It did what it said on the tin.'

A wide range of significant spaces in London are privatised in one form or another. The research suggested that it is quite unimportant whether space is publicly or privately owned or is maintained in one of the myriad of in-between states that characterise so many of London's contemporary public spaces. What is important is how the space performs for its everyday users and as part of the wider city, and what rights users maintain. Arguably, the best private/public space should simply look and feel like part of the continuous fabric of the shared city, and if it does not, regulators have failed. This, however, may fail to understand the nature of London's differentiated public spaces, which typically look and feel the way they do for clear functional reasons. For the users of the privatised and semi-privatised spaces

12.6   Bishops Square, well-used, open and accessible private / public space

examined in the research, the spaces were typically performing well, and were at least equal (although often different) to those in public ownership. It is difficult to see how the city is poorer as a result (**12.6**).

So is London's public space consumption-oriented?

If one understands the origins of cities such as London in bringing together economic exchange opportunities and consumption potential in one place, then it is unsurprising that contemporary public spaces continue to offer both sorts of opportunity. The research indicated how these forces can be harnessed to positive ends, both through the life and character (positive or negative) they give to space and in their earning potential to cross-subsidise a range of public goods – infrastructure, housing, sports and cultural facilities. Indeed, every space (apart from Royal Arsenal Gardens, which failed to attract any such opportunities) was in some way associated with commercial activities, from London's great civic spaces to its incidental and transient spaces.

In places, the emphasis on consumption was more subtle, reflecting the nature of some spaces as more sensitive than others to the negative side effects of commercialisation, with some commentators arguing that London needs its spaces for contemplation away from the pressures to consume, as well as those for consumption. The case studies demonstrated some sensibility to such concerns, with consumption activities subtly or only periodically represented in many

of the spaces, and only dominant in the three explicitly consumption spaces discussed in Chapter 7. They demonstrated that consumption opportunities are quite simply part of the urban mix, and co-exist successfully alongside other functions of space.

Without exception, whether subtle or significant, unique or ubiquitous, the consumption opportunities enhanced the experience of the space in users' minds and were welcomed, for example giving colour and life to formerly unloved Modernist spaces. Equally, it was clear that in spaces with only subtle or periodic consumption opportunities, there was no obvious desire for more, suggesting that 'consumers *in* spaces' are content to see different types of space for different purposes. In the consumption-oriented spaces, this extended from spaces for quick, easy and predictable consumption, to more leisurely and exceptional consumption, each giving a particular flavour to the space that also manifested itself in user expectations.

'Consumers *of* spaces' were also evident during the research, with spaces such as Trafalgar Square, Monument Yard and along the Southbank now firmly on the tourist trail and 'consumed' by many thousands of visitors to the city each year. Yet, in consuming, these visitors also contributed to the buzz that they themselves were coming to experience, whilst the research confirmed that experience-hungry tourists did not unduly dominate any of the spaces. Instead, these remained 'real spaces', used predominantly by Londoners, particularly those working and living locally. The experience market is clearly just part of the mix in even the most overheated of London's public places.

In general, therefore, in even the most transient and 'cloned' of consumption spaces, the impact seems to be a largely positive one, although it is important to note that the research did not extend to the sorts of large internalised retail spaces so heavily criticised in the literature. Despite this, users were cognisant that, notwithstanding the open nature of the consumption spaces examined, certain mixes of outlets were likely to discourage the engagement of those with less ability to consume. The fact that in the relatively small spaces examined the units had (in each case) been carefully selected to appeal to certain target markets may have fuelled these perceptions and is a characteristic of modern retailing practice, which aims to maximise the potential of particular locations and create a coherent retail experience. Equally, this is nothing new, and unless consumption is somehow hidden from view or poverty eliminated, then its presence

12.7   Acton Town Square – big retail and small retail sharing this newly refurbished space

in public spaces will always run the risk that some users will feel financially excluded and others will be simply turned off by the mix on offer in any one location. Again, the key is diversity (**12.7**). A city the size of London should be able to offer something for everyone, whether that be spaces with little or no consumption dimension, or spaces with all manners and mixes of such opportunities.

So is London's public space invented?

The history of London demonstrates a city that has invented and reinvented itself and many of its constituent parts for almost 2,000 years. From the formal layout of Roman Londinium, to the urban expansions following the release of land around London after the dissolution of the monasteries in the sixteenth century, and up to the present day, each wave of development has followed a formal process of conscious design (some more considered than others), most of which have drawn inspiration from what has gone before (e.g. the replication of the garden square or the garden suburb model) or from new ideas imported from elsewhere (e.g. classical ideas from continental Europe). To this extent, almost the whole of London and the spaces within it are invented, including, without exception, each of the 14 case-study spaces.

Trafalgar Square, for example, was invented in the nineteenth century following imported classical principles, then reinvented in the twenty-first following urban renaissance ideals, both inspired by experiences elsewhere in Europe. In these processes of invention and reinvention, some spaces have more consciously imported a place image than others. In Peckham Square, for example, the space largely emerged out of what was left over after the set of development projects around it were complete, a space that was then given character of its own by a series of further design interventions. Gabriel's Wharf, by contrast, represents the classic invented space in the form of a temporary stage set for consumption, although also a unique, highly inventive and much loved piece of urbanism, rather than a sanitised and replicated one. It demonstrates a positive role for invention, creativity, fun and even pastiche in establishing place.

Fundamental to each episode of design was a conscious attempt to create or recreate place and (more or less successfully) to work within the constraints of the existing place to achieve that. In this regard, the research confirmed that some places require something radical and innovative to make a mark, whilst others require something restrained and subservient. A key strategy in a historic city such as London will be to restrain design egos to ensure that responses are appropriate in each location, whilst recognising that sensitivity to context does not mean rejecting welcome innovation.

Against this critique, the most criticised of the spaces (by reviewers rather than users) were the corporate spaces discussed in Chapter 5. In both cases, entirely new environments had been created, with the spaces used to provide a strong focus and sense of place – a garden square writ large at Canary Wharf and a continental piazza at Paternoster Square. In each, the essentials of urbanism had been generally understood by their designers – connectivity, comfort, activity, flexibility, visual interest, etc. – although the formulae-driven limitations of the international commercial property market infuse both with a strong corporate feel reminiscent of other such corporate campuses – large single entrance blocks, non-active side returns, pristine landscaping, etc. However, it was the international corporate (Canada Square) and modern classical (Paternoster Square) narratives in the architecture surrounding each space that drew the ire of professional critics. Analysis of user opinion, by contrast, demonstrated that such concerns largely passed their users by. Instead, they were more concerned with how each space functions

12.8 Bedford Square – this recently re-paved garden square now regularly exhibits work from the Architectural Association who are located on the space

and with the opportunities they present to engage with the carefully managed and programmed spectacle that the managers of the spaces continue to invent.

The research suggests that place invention does not necessarily equate to placelessness (often quite the opposite), and authenticity may be far less important to users than to design critics and other observers of the urban scene. What is more, despite the existence in a global city of the inevitable import (and occasional export) of globalised development formulae, the invention and reinvention processes that

occur in London continue to shape and reshape these trends in order to give them local meaning (**12.8**). Invention is thus an important part of normal space design processes that may or may not be successful in different circumstances. Quality of place, however, will depend on far more than the mythical 'authenticity' of a space.

So is London's public space scary?

With a higher average life expectancy than ever before (around 80 years), London is clearly a safer place to live in all sorts of ways than it has been in the past. Despite this, statistics suggest that fear of crime (particularly violent crime) amongst Londoner's far outstrip that elsewhere in the UK (see Chapter 3). This, however, was not the experience of the 650 or so users of public space interviewed during the research when asked about their perceptions of particular spaces. So, although some low-level fear existed in some places of teenage gangs and indigent groups, and a general concern about safety (not least that spaces should be safe from traffic), with the exception of users at Royal Arsenal Gardens, the vast majority of interviewees perceived few threats and generally felt safe in the case study spaces. As such, there was little sign that London's public spaces were suffering because of any perceived or real threats to user safety. Indeed, wherever provided, spaces are used with relish by a diverse range of user groups, and those with the greatest choice seem to embrace these spaces most completely.

Amongst managers, responses to security issues varied hugely across the spaces examined, with regimes varying from permissive to über-secured to reflect both the differential nature of the perceived threats, but also tenant expectations about such issues. At one extreme, the highly visible and comprehensive security infrastructures of London's corporate spaces reflect tenant demands stemming from the particular concern over possible terrorist threats, in connection with which London has both a long history and remains a target. These regimes are also used to maintain a highly ordered (some might argue unduly sanitised) environment in which crime, malicious damage and disorder are minimised in order to maintain the sense of safety that tenants demand. A similarly overt and active security presence at Euston Piazza aims to address head-on the challenges of a sizable local community of homeless and drug addicts and an ongoing terrorist threat, yet only one space – Empire Square – actually closes to protect against anti-social behaviours, and then only at night, when residents most value a peaceful environment.

At the other extreme, and at a far smaller scale, the non-confrontational, permissive and relaxed management at Gabriel's Wharf delivers a safe and secure space in a deprived area without the need for costly interventions or restrictive signage. Instead, the approach aims to encourage activities and behaviours as long as they are safe, whilst the broadly passive approach at Swiss Cottage has delivered equal success in a naturally well-surveilled space with a similarly relaxed atmosphere. By contrast, the hands-off security at the isolated and largely abandoned Royal Arsenal Gardens has merely facilitated the opportunity for anti-social behaviours, and created a space that women, in particular, avoid.

Despite the generally relaxed view, far from rejecting security regimes or viewing them as an indicator of threat, users are generally appreciative of management measures designed to reassure them, whether offered by the public or by the private sector, and including now-ubiquitous systems of CCTV. Fundamentally, however, it was the presence of other people in public spaces that most decisively reassured users – a factor most clearly demonstrated in the community spaces examined in Chapter 8, where use, rather than overt security, drove a sense of safety even in relatively high crime locations. In general, the contemporary public spaces examined in this book were successful in this regard with designs and management regimes that encouraged use, even if of a low background type, and thereby feelings of confidence and security.

So is London's public space homogenised?

Founded by a foreign occupying force, since its creation, London has been subject to international influences that have manifested themselves to varying degrees at varying times in its built fabric. This is as true today as it was in the past – for example the import from the Netherlands of the ill-fated shared surface ideas at Sloane Square, or of design-led commercial districts from North America. However, just as Inigo Jones adapted his design for an Italianate square at Covent Garden in 1630 to the London context, inventing the residential (later garden) square in the process, so – the research suggested – few new London spaces are homogenised. Instead, each is distinct and a product of a carefully conceived design process and response (to a greater or lesser degree) to: its context, the goals of its creators, and the forceful character of London.

Rather than homogenisation through the import of ideas, contemporary public space in London can be standardised to a greater degree through local development processes. Sometimes, this is planned and desirable, for example the common palate of materials, signage and street furniture used across the City of London. Elsewhere, it is a result of the compromise and indecision that sometimes manifests itself when key development stakeholders clash. Paternoster Square represents a case in point where over-compromise stemmed from a desire to secure a scheme that all were happy with and that was entirely respectful to all viewpoints. The result is a space that, whilst successful in many respects, none are entirely satisfied with. The Village Square at GMV offers a further example. The first of these flies in the face of London's dominant practice of allowing private interests a freer rein to pursue a vision, and sometimes to make mistakes. For example, the lessons learnt from the rather bland and underutilised phase one spaces at Canary Wharf were allowed to inform a more satisfactory design response in subsequent phases.

The danger of pale pastiche or bland compromise seems particularly potent in London's most historic environments, although not, it seems, at the insistence or intervention of regulators (local planners or English Heritage), who have generally been open to greater innovation than other influential and local voices. Yet despite their support for locally inspired innovations at Somerset House, Festival Riverside and Trafalgar Square, English Heritage have argued there is a London style rooted in the history and traditions of London, even though much of that 'tradition' is not that old, and arguably was radically redefined by the Georgians and again by the Victorians. For English Heritage, however, some forms of innovation are incompatible with these traditions (e.g. shared surfaces) and pander to an international design culture that prizes contrast and experimentation over historic tradition and repair.

The results from the research suggested that the public sector in its own schemes is easily seduced by the latest trends, but also that many such innovations seem quite unimportant when compared against a commonsense understanding of the basics of public space design – about how spaces are used and what their potential is. In this respect, over-design can far more easily undermine the potential of public space or lead to unintended management consequences than under-design – 'keep it simple' seems to be a sensible epithet for good public space design and helps to overcome homogenisation. When applied to a wider regulatory role, a permissive public sector framework that focuses more rigorously on securing a more limited range of public interest objectives (e.g. access for all, connectivity, active edges, etc.) whilst allowing the private sector to take the proactive lead in all other aspects of its developments might contribute to delivering better outcomes over the long term.

More than homogenisation by physical design, spaces in London feature homogenisation by use. Thus the spread of identikit coffee houses across parts of London (and the world) can be seen as reducing

12.9 Apple Market, Kingston upon Thames – complete with fake 'Irish' pub

distinctiveness and increasing homogenisation. The lesson from the research, however, was that these pressures are far from ubiquitous, and, in general, well-designed spaces are able to withstand a degree of homogenisation by use without detriment. Some consumption spaces are even characterised by the extent of the cloned uses they house (Euston Station Piazza) and still function on many different levels much better today with these elements than they did previously without them. Clearly, the impact of such uses will vary depending on the sensitivity of the context and their extent, but will also be fleeting in the sense that they will come and go over time. For public space users, homogenisation was rarely a concern, and when it was, tended to manifest itself as a critique of architectural styles rather than of uses (**12.9**).

To conclude, pressures for homogenisation are clearly present. In part, this is because pressures to maximise revenue from developments encourage the choice of safe, known and popular brands, and in part because architectural styles and trends in landscape design spread common design solutions from place to place. In London, however, the unique circumstances of each public space conspire to undermine these pressures, as do the activities (programmed or resultant) that go on there.

THE COUNTER-ARGUMENTS

Turning from the critiques to the counter-arguments presented in Chapter 1, it is possible to revisit these in the light of the research.

It is not as bad as many think and is anyway nothing new

An aspect of discussions around public space is that many assertions seem to be made on the basis of remarkably limited evidence. Even a broad (in terms of coverage) yet cursory (in terms of depth) analysis of the type undertaken during the London-wide analysis discussed in Chapter 4 can generate a skewed picture of public space, whilst a full understanding requires a more in-depth engagement with particular places in order to understand how they are actually created, used and perceived. Drawing on analysis of this kind from the case studies, it is possible to conclude that public space in London often leaves much to be desired, but the doom-laden assessments and predictions of many commentators seem far from the mark.

Many critiques of public space derive from an unwritten and entirely honourable concern that, as 'public goods', the benefits of public space should be distributed evenly amongst the populace – that they should be open, democratic and equitable spaces. Yet the benefits of public space (like any good – public or private) will not be evenly distributed, and never have been, and will certainly not be the same from place to place. A crude demonstration of this is that the vast majority of new and refurbished public spaces in London have been located within central London and parts of inner London (see **4.7**), arguably placing those on the periphery at a disadvantage in accessing this common resource. Despite this, most Londoners will benefit from the collective uplift their presence gives to the city as a whole, for example in making the inner neighbourhoods more attractive residential areas and reducing pressure on the outer suburbs.

In some cases, the benefits remain largely economic ones, with the space raising the value of development for developers and subsequent occupiers (whether or not the space is actually used). Elsewhere, the benefits flow disproportionately to a particular set of dominant users – stay-at-home mothers, office workers, 'culture vultures', shoppers, skateboarders, etc. Sometimes, the benefits accrue to locals, sometimes primarily to visitors, and often, it seems, to younger professional and middle-class audiences. In all cases, however, there are clear benefits of new or refurbished public space, and the fact that not everyone benefits equally all the time may not be an issue as long as the multiplicity of different spaces across the city (old and new, refurbished and not) are responsive to the range of citizen needs so that no law-abiding users are routinely excluded and all needs are catered for.

In this regard, spaces in London specialised from early in the city's history, and their functions have continued to evolve and fragment ever since. Building spaces that are deliberately exclusionary, uncomfortable, unattractive or unsafe will obviously be unwise, but, equally, attempts to impose an idealised notion of 'community' public space everywhere will be misplaced. Not every space will be characterised by democratic debate and a perfect cultural and societal mix of users, and, as the research demonstrated, attempts to impose inappropriate models of public space in inappropriate locations will surely backfire. Any location is likely to have a particular potential, and recognising what that is in each place will be the unique contribution of the public space builder, whether public or private.

Spaces today are not necessarily inferior and reflect a changing society

Of course, the fact that public space in London has not been ideal in the past is no reason to suppress aspirations today. But does this necessarily imply that every public space should be publicly provided and managed or does private provision also have a place? London's public spaces have always been linked to a profit motive, whether to create a collective place to trade, enhance property values, or show off to the world and thereby attract status and investment. Many (perhaps even most) spaces in London have also been designed, developed and, at least initially, managed by the private sector. To a greater or lesser degree, they have also always excluded, whether through the goods sold in them or the restrictions placed physically or, more usually, symbolically on access.

What is new in recent years is the seemingly successful emulation of the sorts of spaces produced by the private sector by a series of public, pseudo-private and partnership organisations/arrangements. On the whole, these spaces do not exist to foster democratic discourse and high-level social intercourse (although that may be a by-product), but instead to cater for a range of more run-of-the-mill activities, including economic exchange. In this respect, the case studies showed that, rather than being a dirty word, commercialisation is often the stuff of life.

The seriousness with which public realm is now being taken in places such as the City of London is in no small part due to the new development model introduced through developments such as Broadgate and Canary Wharf from the mid 1980s onwards. These developments established a competitive environment with public space at its heart, the benefits from which gradually came to be appreciated in the public sector as well, with some public authorities gaining the competitive bug. Today, with the exception of incidental spaces, new public spaces in London are most often extensions of wider developments that, in effect, give rise to them. They both support and are supported by those uses, whether commercial, cultural, community-oriented or residential, often with total management practices to match. In this, they provide important amenities in a modern city that greatly enrich the lives of their users.

As the case studies demonstrated, this is a model used in private, pseudo-private and public schemes alike, in part responding to changes in wider society. Thus London society has clearly evolved over the period covered by the research (from 1980), with London becoming more cosmopolitan, more white-collar, more international and, arguably, more divided (economically) than ever before. Along with these changes have come the spread of new technologies, new freedoms, some new social tensions, and, as the case studies showed, the spread of some types of 'third place' social locations (cafes, health clubs, restaurants) and the decline of others (notably traditional pubs and working men's clubs). In the public sphere, new forms of public gathering are apparent, for farmers' markets, big screens, new forms of public arts performance events, many more cultural and other festivals, alternative markets, and so forth.

All these trends were readily apparent in the design, development, use and management of London's contemporary public spaces, and all reinforced, rather than undermined, the position of traditional public space in London. Society is clearly changing, but adaptable public space and entrepreneurial public space managers have shown themselves adept at capturing and exploiting the new potentials unleashed, not least the demand for more leisure opportunities and the desire that more of these opportunities should take place out of doors.

Different groups seek different spaces with different purposes

Although many critiques of public space stem from the concern that the benefits of public space should be available to all, users are realistic about the nature and limitations of spaces. They accept that different spaces have different purposes and will attract different audiences. Indeed, there seems to be little desire that all spaces should be equally attractive to all and a general acceptance that users who do not fit in with societal norms and behaviours will not feel welcome.

All the evidence suggests that London remains an unequal city. As long Londoners live by the market, private space in the city will be differentiated by ability to pay. Inevitably, this will spill over from the private to the public realm, and so expecting a totally equal and non-exclusive environment is simply fanciful (the rich will go to Bond Street and the poor to Commercial Road), unless society changes the way wealth is distributed and reverses almost 2,000 years of how London has developed as a market-led entrepreneurial city. Yet, the research demonstrated that as the market is not the only provider of public space in London, because corporations and pseudo-private organisation have a social agenda and conscience (alongside their commercial one), and because, ultimately, the state has powers (in most cases) to shape even the products of the private sector, in general a clear set of wider 'public-interest' objectives are being met by contemporary public spaces in London.

Moreover, although different groups seek different spaces, all (without exception) seek spaces that are clean, well maintained, safe and secure. In general, these characteristics are being delivered across London's public spaces, with private and pseudo-private organisations particularly cognisant of these agendas. By contrast, the sort of edgy 'liminal' urban experience so lauded in some of the public space literature (see Chapter 10) does not seem to be an experience aspired to by many everyday space users.

Yet if there is a tendency for critics to laud a form of 'idealised' public space, then policy makers and regulators have also sometimes been guilty of attempting to fix a particular blueprint for public space. 'Urban renaissance' policies, for example, have perpetuated a vibrant, urban, continental ideal, despite the fact that continental European cities (even the densest of them) are typically surrounded by spaces of many different characters, from quiet and relaxing to animated and sensually energising. There is little reason to think that London's contemporary spaces could or should be any different, and this is a view strongly supported by public space users. London, for example, has long possessed spaces for public gathering, political expression and dissent, and these persist through to today. They are generally different, however, to those used for shopping, work, and living.

Needless to say, where a space starts out is not always where it ends, and it is difficult to predict how any space will fare over time. In this respect, it is important to allow room for the unknown and unexpected and respond appropriately, for example accommodating the skateboarders in Woolwich and in the process giving meaning to a space where none existed before (see Chapter 7). In this respect, some spaces need time to mature, to find their constituency, and some seem to perform better as time goes on. A key lesson may be to avoid thinking every public space intervention is permanent, and instead embracing temporary uses and spaces in order to gauge how they perform.

Things are on the up – only time will tell

Whether the sorts of contemporary spaces (new or regenerated) examined in this book will turn out to be superior or inferior to the types of spaces that London is rightfully famed for will only become apparent over time. In recent years, there has certainly been a flourishing of public space projects across London, both small and large. Yet comparing new with old is like comparing apples with oranges – or, more particularly, garden squares with what has become a new dominant model, the piazza, or urban square.

Such a task is made all the more difficult (and pointless) by the fact that many of the historic spaces that we experience today are quite different from how they were originally built, both in their design and ownership. Moreover, many less successful spaces (particularly in recent years) have been swept away altogether. What survives is the very best (or at least the most robust) of the past, setting a high standard against which to assess the combined output of the present, a proportion of which will invariably fail the test of time. In this regard, public space never reaches a finite end state but will continue to change. This may extend to entire redesigns where spaces obviously fail (e.g. Royal Arsenal Gardens), but may also imply updating as technologies, pressures on the city, and aspirations change, or simply as responsibilities are redefined. On this issue, history has shown

that, over time, public spaces in London have a tendency to move from private to public ownership and management, and this may eventually be the fate of many of the new private and pseudo-private spaces being created today.

In this regard, one method to measure success will be longevity, implying that those spaces that are most adaptable and amenable to change are the most successful. But whether, for example, we will still be using corporate headquarters and the spaces around them in 150 years is as yet unknown. Furthermore, spaces can be successful at points in their lifespan and not at others, or, like Gabriel's Wharf, may be designed to be temporary from day one. Therefore, all that can be concluded for now is that London has changed and that, in different ways, for different audiences, traditional public spaces are firmly back on the agenda. In this position, they are being associated with almost every form of development type in London.

TO CONCLUDE: IS IT REALLY THAT BAD?

Through in-depth empirical investigation, the research has suggested that many of the critiques are somewhat wide of the mark when it comes to London, and, on that basis, that the counter-arguments may offer a more accurate view of the city today. Thus the sorts of whole-sale homogenisation, privatisation, securitisation, commercialisation, sanitisation, exclusionary and formulae-driven approaches to public space that are so criticised in the literature have proven to be largely illusory in London, at least as regards the over-inflated claims made about their impact on the creation, recreation and experience of public spaces.

This, of course, does not by itself render the critiques meaningless, not least because they consistently raise issues about who the 'public' are in public space. In this regard, even surveying user opinion may not give a fully representative view of the merits, or otherwise, of public space if some potential user groups are routinely excluded from space. This did not seem to be the case in London's public spaces, although the scope of the work did not extend to seeking out such groups for interview. Based on the views that were obtained, however, a gap between public (user) opinion and theoretical discourse was clearly evident.

12.10 Mile End Park green bridge – multilayered public space

Returning to the question with which this book began – Public space, is it really that bad? – the simple but very clear answer is 'No'. Public space designers, developers and managers sometimes get it wrong, sometimes quite disastrously, and much public space in London remains neglected, invaded and scary, and, for these reasons, exclusionary and in desperate need of upgrading, but, in the main, the sorts of public spaces that are being created and recreated in

contemporary London are finding a ready constituency of users who, on the whole, greatly value these new spaces of the city. As such, there is no unwritten agenda to subvert the experience of public space in London, and stakeholders, whether public or private, typically have very clear and complementary aspirations to deliver long-term social, economic and environmental value through their projects (**12.10**).

12.11 St Paul's Churchyard (adjacent to Paternoster Square) – in 2011/2012 the space was occupied by anti-capitalist protesters, replacing the usual throng of tourists and City workers

The multiple complex spaces of a global city

From this positive affirmation about what is being achieved, and a recognition that much remains to be done, it is critical to recognise that what marks out a global city such as London is the sheer diversity of spaces on offer. Arguably, therefore, whilst smaller cities with a less diverse range of public spaces will need a higher proportion of spaces that offer something for everyone and where consequently the critiques may hold greater resonance, London and other large cities can afford spaces of difference and diversity that do not all attempt to cater for every member of society.

Thus, as the research has shown, the multiple complex spaces of a global city such as London each have different purposes, just as rooms in a house or buildings in a city have, and it would be foolish to try and design all according to some idealised blueprint for the perfect public space in order that each be equally appealing to all. Spaces take on different flavours as a result of the different groups of interests that create them or the particular range of uses they are intended to serve. What is more, these characters change over time, just as surrounding land uses and ownerships change, or as spaces are appropriated by new groups or abandoned by old (**12.11**). Occasionally, spaces take on a life of their own that may leave them as unrecognisable from what

was originally intended. This process may take many years or decades and may be cyclical. In London, the garden squares began as glorified parking courts, mutated into private gardens for the rich, and then (at least some) became public parks. Covent Garden Piazza began as an exclusive space for aristocracy, evolved into a market space for all and sundry, then into an avant-garde tourist experience, and today is mutating back to an exclusive space, this time for the retail needs of the rich (see Chapter 7).

For users in such a city, the choice is also diverse, with spaces of business, consumption, community, the domestic sphere, the civic city, and all manner of culture and entertainment to choose from, as well as every mix of these, and of course the option to shun public space altogether and retreat into the private sphere. This should be something to celebrate, and in London needs celebrating a little more.

The multiple complex spaces of an opportunity city

This positive picture sits within a political economy in which society has increasingly demanded more and better-quality public spaces, although has not always been willing to either deliver or manage those spaces itself. Instead, on the back of a successful business model in which public space is increasingly viewed as a critical value-adding asset to a range of economic, infrastructural, social and cultural concerns, the private sector and a range of pseudo-private organisations in London have risen to the challenge – latterly alongside a rejuvenated public sector – to usher in a new typology of public space. As these are often entirely new public spaces where none existed before, it seems churlish to complain when they do not match up to the impossible high standards of a largely mythical view of public space from the past, or to grumble when the public sector's own new, refurbished and reclaimed spaces evolve to meet the needs of an increasingly affluent, mobile and demanding populace.

On occasions, the critiques of public space are clearly motivated by an ideological position that crudely equates private development with profiteering and a disregard for socio-economic context, and public sector attempts to emulate such practices as cut from the same cloth. The research revealed that such perspectives fail to take account of both the crude economic incentives for private interests to deliver something better and more sustainable, but also the profound interest of professionals closely associated with projects (often for many years) to create something of lasting value – real places. Public spaces are anyway created through often complex partnerships between a wide range of players – public, pseudo-private and private – and sweeping generalisations about motives are likely to be misconceived.

The multiple complex spaces of future London

Fundamentally, there is nothing wrong with helping people feel safe and secure, or providing clean and commercially vibrant environments for people to enjoy. Nor is there anything inherently immoral about privately owned and managed public spaces. In essence, the private and pseudo-private processes of space creation are nothing more than the contemporary reincarnations of the opportunities that such interests have always found in London and that have become set in stone (quite literally) in the public spaces of the city. Unless the political economy of the city changes radically (which seems

unlikely in the near future), then the variety of processes unpacked in Chapter 11 show every prospect of continuing, as do some of the dangers of over-design and over-management that they periodically give rise to.

Particular problems may ensue, for example when owners and managers seek to use the privilege of ownership to exclude those who in the everyday spaces of the city would not be excluded, or to impose codes of behaviour that go beyond societal norms. Although the research found generally little explicit evidence of such behaviours, during the London-wide analysis the principal investigator and researchers were prevented from taking photographs on a number of occasions (once in entirely public space), a ready indicator that petty and seemingly unjustified management practices do exist. However, despite their somewhat bedraggled and unkempt appearance after days cycling around London analysing its spaces, no other restrictions were ever imposed on the research, and private and public interests alike were always very ready to be involved in the work.

On the basis of the research, calls in some quarters to ban all new private or pseudo-private public spaces in favour of an under-resourced public sector seem both unnecessary and undermining of the tradition of opportunity that has informed so much of London's public space. There does, however, seem to be a case to adopt a simple

12.12   Charter for Public Space Rights and Responsibilities

All public space users have the right to:
- **roam freely**
- **rest and relax unmolested**
- **associate with others**
- **use public space without the imposition of petty local controls on drinking, smoking, safe cycling, skating and dog-walking**
- **collect for registered charities**
- **take photographs**
- **trade (if granted a public licence)**
- **demonstrate peacefully and campaign politically**
- **busk or otherwise perform**

Public space users have a responsibility to:
- **respect the rights of others to conduct their business unhindered and unmolested**
- **respect public and private property**
- **act in a civil and safe manner at all times**
- **keep the peace**

Owners and managers of public space have a responsibility to:
- **respect and protect the rights of all users**
- **keep spaces safe within the context of the actions of any reasonable person**
- **keep spaces clean and well maintained**
- **keep spaces open and unrestricted at all times (or otherwise in line with regulatory stipulations)**

12.13   Incidental space outside the Zimbabwe Embassy on The Strand – a space used for many years by demonstrators against the regime of Robert Mugabe

12.14 Queen Elizabeth Olympic Park – London's future spaces

Charter for Public Space Rights and Responsibilities in London and elsewhere (**12.12**). Such a Charter would apply to all spaces, both existing and those still to come, that a reasonable person would regard as public, whether privately or publicly owned. This would cover all spaces that during daylight hours are (usually) open and free to enter.

Irrespective of such a Charter, if one looks at what sort of city London has become, and postulates about where it is going in the future, then London is first a city in which public space in all its forms has increasingly become the crucible in which the public life of the metropolis is played out (**12.13**). Second, it is a city in which these trends look likely to continue into the future with major additions to its network of public spaces at developments, including the Olympic Park (**12.14**) along the Lea Valley, King's Cross, Greenwich Peninsula, at Nine Elms, and along the new Crossrail system. Moreover, despite the austerity being felt across the public sector at the time of writing, a number of London's boroughs look set to continue investing in their own public realm networks, potentially leaving others, with no such a commitment, behind.

The multiple complex spaces of cities today

The empirical analysis presented in this book has focused on London, but the big themes it seeks to question are universal, as is the questioning approach it seeks to espouse about public space. To avoid falling into the same trap as others who have over-generalised on the basis of limited specific cases and/or contexts, extrapolating them as if they represent global and unstoppable trends, the detailed London-based findings should be treated with caution. It is possible to say, however, that the sorts of theory and assertions wrapped up in the critiques of public space should always be challenged and tested in the light of local circumstances, and, insofar as they have been found wanting in London, it is likely that they will be found wanting elsewhere also. No matter how eminent the original author, a theory based on theory alone is just that – theory. It can challenge us and make us question what we do, but should never be blindly accepted or applied to contexts far beyond the original discussion.

The same goes for empirically derived findings. Thus the findings and discussions in this and the previous chapter will clearly have resonance in other UK cities, also (although a little bit less so) in other European cities, and (although a little less again) in cities in the USA, Canada, Australia and other Western countries. Their application to developed Asian contexts will need careful interpretation, and they are likely to be less applicable in the non-developed world. Equally, however, they will be more relevant to large and global cities such as London, a little less to smaller cities, and perhaps not at all to towns and other settlements in which the variety and mix of public space is more limited.

There is, however, one key finding from the research that it can confidently be asserted will apply elsewhere: all cities (large and small) are made from multiple complex evolving spaces, most of which will present evidence of the sorts of issues encompassed in the critiques, as they always have. This is the nature of cities. Thus the endlessly stimulating diversity of public spaces across the world needs to be nurtured and protected against pressures (if and where they exist) to undermine the key qualities that give a sense of 'publicness' and that continue to make traditional public spaces so attractive to their users. At the same time, there will never be a one-size-fits-all utopian model of public space, and any critiques and aspirations – including those made in this book – need questioning and testing in the light of local circumstances. Long may that be so!

BIBLIOGRAPHY

A+UU (Architecture + Urbanism Unit) (2003) *Housing for a Compact City*, London, GLA.

A+UU (2005) *Commissioning a Sustainable Well-designed City*, London, GLA.

Akkar Ercan M (2010) 'Less Public Than Before? Public Space Improvement in Newcastle City Centre', in Madanipour A [Ed] *Whose Public Space? International Case Studies in Urban Design and Development*, London, Routledge.

Allmendinger P & Haughton G (2009) 'Commentary: Critical Reflections on Spatial Planning', *Environment & Planning* A, 41(11): 2544–9.

Association of London Government (2004) *Liveable London – A Cleaner and Greener Capital*, London, Association of London Government.

Atkinson R (2003) 'Domestication by Cappuccino or Revenge on Urban Space? Control and Empowerment in the Management of Public Spaces', *Urban Studies*, 40(9): 1829–1843.

Aurigi A (2005) *Making the Digital City: The Early Shaping of Urban Internet Space*, London, Ashgate.

Baeten G (2009) 'Regenerating the South Bank', in Imrie R, Lees L & Raco M [Eds] *Regenerating London: Governance, Sustainability and Community in a Global City*, London, Routledge.

Baird G (2008) 'The New Urbanism and Public Space', in Haas T [Ed] *New Urbanism and Beyond: Designing Cities for the Future*, New York, Rizzoli International: 120–3.

Ball T (2008) 'No Call for Change', *Building Design*, 12 August: 10.

Banerjee, T. (2001) 'The Future of Public Space: Beyond Invented Streets and Reinvented Places', *APA Journal*, 67(1): 9–24.

Barry J (2003a) 'Little Georgian Gems', *Evening Standard*, 18 June: 8.

Barry J (2003b) 'Circling the Square: Bloomsbury's Residents Can Now Use Their Gardens. About Time Too, Says Jane Barry', *Evening Standard*, 22 October: 9.

BBC News (2008a) 'Parliament Piazza Plan Scrapped', http://news.bbc.co.uk/1/hi/england/london/7547311.stm.

BBC News (2008b) 'CCTV Boom, Failing to Cut Crime', http://news.bbc.co.uk/1/hi/uk/7384843.stm.

BDP Planning (1996a) *London's Urban Environment: Planning for Quality*, London, HMSO.

BDP Planning (1996b) *Technical Working Report: London's Urban Environment, Planning for Quality*, London, Government Office for London.

Bentley I (1999) *Urban Transformations: Power, People and Urban Design*, Routledge, London.

Beunderman J, Hannon C & Bradwell P (2007) *Seen and Heard: Reclaiming the Public Realm with Children and Young People*, London, Demos.

Bindmans (2010) 'Press Release 8 June 2010: Parliament Square Peace Protesters Win Round One in Eviction Fight', London, Bindmans LLP.

Bingham J (2010) 'Parliament Square Peace Protesters Cling on as Bailiffs Move in', 20 July, http://www.telegraph.co.uk/news/newstopics/politics/7899657/Parliament-Square-peace-protesters-cling-on-as-bailiffs-move-in.html.

Binney M (2001) 'Square Route Solution to a Green Metropolis', *The Times*, 11 June : 3.

Birch A (2008) 'Hawkins Brown on the Parliament Square Debacle', *Building Design*, 5th December: 15.

Blakely EJ & Snyder MG (1997) *Fortress America: Gated Communities in the United States*, Washington DC, Brookings Institution Press/Cambridge MA, Lincoln Institute of Land Policy.

Bloomfield R (2010) 'Olympics Legacy Design is Radically Revised', *Building Design*, 8 October: 3.

Boddy T (1992), 'Underground and Overhead: Building the Analogous City', in Sorkin M [Ed] *Variations on a Theme Park*, New York, Noonday Press: 123–53.

Bowie D (2010) *Politics, Planning and Homes in a World City*, London, Routledge.

Boyer M (1994) *The City of Collective Memory: Its Historical Imagery and Architectural Entertainments*, Cambridge, MA, MIT Press.

Bremner C (2007) 'Top 150 City Destinations: London Leads the Way', Euromonitor Global Market Research Blog, 11 October, http://www.euromonitor.com/Top 150 City Destinations London Leads the Way.

Briffault A (1999) 'A Government for Our Time? Business Improvement Districts and Urban Governance', *Columbia Law Review*, 99(2): 365–477.

Buchanan P (1988) 'What City? A Plea for Place in the Public Realm', *Architectural Review*, 1101(November): 31–41.

Building Design (2008a) 'Lords Blast Boris on Parliament Square', *Building Design*, 3 October: 3.

Building Design (2008b) 'Parliament Square Paving Bugged Boris', *Building Design*, 18 July: 3.

Building Design (2008c) 'Mayor Axes Flagship Parliament Square Plan', *Building Design*, 11 July: 3.

Burton E & Mitchell L (2006) *Inclusive Urban Design: Streets for Life*, Oxford, Architectural Press.

Butler T (2003) *London Calling: The Middle Classes and the Re-making of Inner London*, Oxford, Berg.

Butler T (2004) 'The Middle Class and the Future of London', in Boddy M & Parkinson M [Eds] *City Matters: Competitiveness, Cohesion and Urban Governance*, Bristol, The Policy Press.

Butler T & Lees L (2006) 'Super-gentrification in Barnsbury, London: Globalization and Gentrifying Global Elites at the Neighbourhood Level' *Transactions of the Institute of British Geographers*, 31(4): 467–87.

CABE (Commission for Architecture and the Built Environment), Empire Square [n.d.] 'Case Studies: Empire Square, Borough, London', http://www.cabe.org.uk/case-studies/empire-square.

CABE, Kensington High Street [n.d.] 'Case Studies: Kensington High Street, London', http://www.cabe.org.uk/case-studies/kensington-high-street.

CABE, Somerset House [n.d.] 'Case Studies: Somerset House, London', http://www.cabe.org.uk/case-studies/somerset-house.

CABE, Trafalgar Square [n.d.] 'Case Studies: Trafalgar Square – Evaluation', http://www.cabe.org.uk/case-studies/trafalgar-square/evaluation.

Calabi D (2004) *The Market and the City: Square, Street and Architecture in Early Modern Europe*, London, Ashgate.

CAPCO (2010) *Capital & Counties Properties PLC Interim Management Statement for the Period 1 July to 9 November 2010*, London, CAPCO.

Carmona M (2001) *Housing Design Quality: Through Policy, Guidance and Review*, London, Spon Press.

Carmona M (2006) 'Coming Soon to a Public Space Near You ', *Town & Country Planning*, 75(3): 84–5.

Carmona M (2009a) 'The Isle of Dogs: Four Waves, Twelve Plans, 35 Years, and a Renaissance of Sorts', *Progress in Planning*, 71(3): 87–151.

Carmona M (2009b) 'Urban Design and the British Urban Renaissance, Part 4: King's Cross, Central London, Docklands and the Thames Gateway', *Urban Design Quarterly*, 109: 9–13.

Carmona M (2010a) 'Contemporary Public Space: Part One, Critique', *Journal of Urban Design*, 15(1): 123–48.

Carmona M (2010b) 'Contemporary Public Space: Part Two, Classification', *Journal of Urban Design*, 15(2): 157–73.

Carmona M (2011) 'Shaping Local London', *Urban Design*, 118(Spring): 32–5.

Carmona M & de Magalhaes C (2009) 'Local Environmental Quality: Establishing Acceptable Standards in England', *Town Planning Review*, 80(4–5): 517–48.

Carmona M & Freeman J (2005) 'The Groundscraper: Exploring the Contemporary Reinterpretation', *Journal of Urban Design*, 10(3): 309–30.

Carmona M, Heath T, Oc T & Tiesdell S (2003) *Public Places Urban Spaces: The Dimensions of Urban Design*, Oxford, Architectural Press.

Carmona M, de Magalhaes C & Hammond L (2008) *Public Space: The Management Dimension*, London, Routledge.

Carmona M, Davis M, Scott F, Gort J & Mellis H (2010a) *High Street London*, London, Design for London.

Carmona M, Tiesdell S, Heath T & Oc T (2010b) *Public Places Urban Spaces: The Dimensions of Urban Design*, 2nd Edition, Oxford, Architectural Press.

Carr S, Francis M, Rivlin LG & Stone AM (1992) *Public Space*, Cambridge, Cambridge University Press.

Cassidy M (2010) 'Seizing the Day', *New London Quarterly*, Autumn, 4: 71–3.

Castells M (1996) *The Rise of the Network Society*, Oxford, Blackwell.

Catt R (1995) 'Residential Squares', *Structural Survey*, 13(4): 16–20.

CBRE (2010) *UK Retail Outlook 2010*, London, CB Richard Ellis.

Chatterton P & Hollands R (2002) 'Theorising Urban Playscapes: Producing, Regulating and Consuming Youthful Nightlife City Spaces', *Urban Studies*, 39: 95–116.

Chelsea Society (2010) *Chelsea Society Newsletter*, May: 33.

City of London (2007) 'Street Scene Challenge: The Monument – City of London Revitalises Its Most Historic Landmark', City of London News Release, 15 January, http://www.cityoflondon.gov.uk/Corporation/media centre/files2007/Street+Scene+Challenge+-+The+Monument.htm.

City of London, History [n.d.] 'History of the Government of the City of London', http://www.cityoflondon.gov.uk/Corporation/LGNL Services/Leisure and culture/Local history and heritage/Buildings within the City/Mansion house/History+of+the+Government+of+the+City+of+London.htm.

Clark G (2002) 'London in the European Financial Services Industry: Locational Advantages and Product Complementarities' *Journal of Economic Geography*, 2(2): 1021.

Clout H [Ed] (1991) *The Times London History Atlas*, London, BCA.

Clout H & Wood P (1986) *London: Problems of Change*, London, Longman.

Cochrane A (2007) *Understanding Urban Policy: A Critical Approach*, London, Sage.

Coin Street Community Builders (2002) *There is Another Way*, London, Coin Street Community Builders.

Coin Street Community Builders (2008) *Coin Street Community Builders, A Very Social Enterprise*, London, Coin Street Community Builders.

Coleman A (1985) *Utopia on Trial: Vision and Reality in Planned Housing*, London, Shipman.

Collins M (1994) 'Land-use Planning Since 1947', in Simmie J [Ed] *Planning London*, London, Routledge.

Colson J (2009) 'Review of David Bowsher, Tony Dyson, Nick Holder & Isca Howell (2007) *The London Guildhall: An Archaeological History of a Neighbourhood from Early Medieval to Modern Times*', http://www.history.ac.uk/reviews/review/766.

Compton N (2002) 'Welcome to Fortress London', 22 March, http://www.thisislondon.co.uk/home/article-910182-welcome-to-fortress-london.do.

Corbett N (2004) *Transforming Cities: Revival in the Square*, London, RIBA.

Coupland A (1992) 'Every Job and Office Job', in Thornley A [Ed] *The Crisis of London*, London, Routledge.

Covent Garden Area Trust [n.d.] 'History', http://www.coventgardentrust.org.uk/aboutus/history/

Crang M (1998) *Cultural Geography*, London, Routledge.

Crawford M (1995) 'Contesting the Public Realm: Struggles Over Public Space in Los Angeles', *Journal of Architectural Education*, 49(1): 4–9.

Cunningham C & Jones M (1999) 'The Playground: A Confession of Failure?', *Built Environment*, 25(1): 11–17.

Daubney K (2008) 'Capital Design Body Absorbed in Agency', *Planning*, 1 August: 3.

Davenport J (2007) 'Tens of Thousands of CCTV Cameras, Yet 80% of Crime Unsolved', 19 September, http://www.thisislondon.co.uk/news/article-23412867-tens-of-thousands-of-cctv-cameras-yet-80-of-crime-unsolved.do.

Davies M (1992) *City of Quartz*, New York, Vantage.

DCLG (Department for Communities and Local Government) (2006) *Valuing Planning Obligations in England*, London, DCLG.

DCLG (2007) *The Contribution of Neighbourhood Management to Cleaner and Safer Neighbourhoods*, London, DCLG.

De Magalhaes C & Carmona M (2009) 'Dimensions and Models of Contemporary Public Space Management in England', *Journal of Environmental Planning and Management*, 52(20): 111–29.

Dean J (2007) 'Livingstone's 100 Public Spaces', http://www.ajspecification.com/Buildings/Section Page/?CI Building ID=633&CI Section ID=2490&CI Article ID=686.

Defra [n.d.] http://www.archive.defra.gov.uk/sustainable/government/progress/regional/summaries/39.htm.

Design for London (2010) *Royal Docks: A Vision for the Royal Docks Prepared by the Mayor of London and the Mayor of Newham*, London, London Development Agency.

DETR/CABE (Department of Environment, Transport & Regions and Commission for Architecture & the Built Environment) (2000) *By Design: Urban Design in the Planning System: Towards Better Practice*, London, DETR.

DfT (Department for Transport) (2007) *Manual for Streets*, London, Thomas Telford Publishing.

Dines N (2009) 'The Disputed Place of Ethnic Diversity', in Imrie R, Lees L & Raco M [Eds] *Regenerating London: Governance, Sustainability and Community in a Global City*, London, Routledge.

Dines N & Cattell V (2006) *Public Spaces, Social Relations and Well-being in East London*, Bristol, The Policy Press.

DTZ (2008) *Retail-led Regeneration: Why it Matters to Our Communities*, London, British Council of Shopping Centres.

Duany A & Plater–Zyberk, E with Speck, J (2000) *Suburban Nation: The Rise of Sprawl and the Decline of the American Dream*, New York, North Point Press.

eastlondonhistory (2010) 'Watney Market', eastlondonhistory.com, http://eastlondonhistory.com/watney-market/

ECOTEC (2009) *Urban Design London Skills and Training Evaluation Study, Final Report*, London, ECOTEC.

Edwards M (2010) 'King's Cross, Renaissance for Whom?', in Punter J [Ed] *Urban Design and the British Urban Renaissance*, London, Routledge

Ellickson (1996) 'Controlling Chronic Misconduct in City Spaces: Of Panhandlers, Skid Rows and Public-Space Zoning', *Yale Law Journal*, 105(March): 1172.

Ellin N (1996) *Postmodern Urbanism*, Oxford, Blackwells.

Ellin N (1999) *Postmodern Urbanism*, Revised edition, Oxford, Blackwells.

English Heritage (2000) *A Campaign For London Squares*, London, English Heritage.

Engwicht D (1999) *Street Reclaiming: Creating Liveable Streets and Vibrant Communities*, British Columbia, New Society Publishers.

Farrell T (2007) *Manifesto for London: 20 Propositions*, London, The Architectural Review.

Farrell T (2010) *Shaping London: The Patterns and Forms That Make the Metropolis*, Chichester, Wiley.

Flusty S (1997) 'Building Paranoia', in Ellin N [Ed] *Architecture of Fear*, New York, Princeton Architectural Press: 47–59.

Forster A (2010) 'Shared Surface Plan for Exhibition Road Axed in Favour of "Safe Space"', http://www.rudi.net/node/21479.

Frank A & Stevens Q (2007) *Loose Space: Possibility and Diversity in Urban Life*, London, Routledge.

Fulcher M (2010) 'London Projects Scrapped as LDA Funding Cuts Bite', http://www.architectsjournal.co.uk/news/daily-news/london-projects-scrapped-as-lda-funding-cuts-bite/8605447.article.

Fyfe N [Ed] (1998) *Images of the Street: Planning, Identity and Control in Public Space*, London, Routledge.

GC Partnership (2007) 'Euston Station Piazza Pavilions', http://www.gcpartnership.co.uk/kcc euston.html.

Gehl Architects (2004) *Towards a Fine City for People: Public Spaces and Public Life – London 2004*, Copenhagen, Gehl Architects.

Gehl J & Gemzoe L (2001) *New City Spaces*, Copenhagen, The Danish Architectural Press.

Giddens A (2000) *The Third Way and its Critics*, Cambridge, Polity Press.

GLA (Greater London Authority) (2007) *Housing Provision in London 2005/6: Annual Monitor*, London, GLA.

GLA (2010) 'Transforming London's Great Outdoors', 1 October, http://www.london.gov.uk/blog/transforming-londons-great-outdoors.

GLA, BIDs [n.d.] 'Business Improvement Districts', http://www.london.gov.uk/london-bids-links.

GLA, Parliament Square [n.d.] 'Improving the Square', http://www.london.gov.uk/parliamentsquare/improve.

GLA, Trafalgar Square [n.d.] 'Trafalgar Square – A Brief History', http://www.london.gov.uk/priorities/art-culture/trafalgar-square/history.

GLA Economics (2006) *Retail in London*, London, GLA.

Glancey J (2003) 'It's a Jumble Out There', 3 November, http://www.guardian.co.uk/artanddesign/2003/nov/03/architecture.regeneration.

Glass R (1964) *London: Aspects of Change*, London, MacGibbon & Kee.

Glyn S (2006) 'Streets Ahead in the City', *Planning in London*, 59(October–December): 39–31.

GMVSucks [n.d.] 'Greenwich Millennium Village Sucks!', http://www.gmvsucks.com/about-us/.

Goheen P (1998) 'Public Space and the Geography of the Modern City', *Progress in Human Geography*, 22(4): 479–96.

Goldsteen JB & Elliott CD (1994) *Designing America: Creating Urban Identity*, New York, Reinhold.

Goodman P (2003) *The Garden Squares of Boston*, Lebanon, NH, University Press of New England.

Gospodini A (2004) 'Urban Morphology and Place Identity in European Cities: Built Heritage and Innovative Design', *Journal of Urban Design*, 9(2): 225–48.

Government Office for London (1996) *Strategic Guidance for London Planning Authorities (RPG3)*, London, HMSO.

Graham S (2001) 'The Spectre of the Splintering Metropolis', *Cities*, 18(6): 365–8.

Graham S & Marvin S (1999) 'Planning Cybercities? Integrating Telecommunications into Urban Planning?', *Town Planning Review*, 70(1): 89–114.

Guide Dogs (2009) '£300k Sloane Square Shared Surface Street Slammed', Guide Dogs for the Blind Association 'Say No to Shared Streets' Campaign, 19 February 2009, http://gdbass.netefficiency.co.uk/index.php?id=247.

Gyford J (1994) 'Politics and Planning in London', in Simmie J [Ed] *Planning London*, London, Routledge.

Hajer M & Reijndorp A (2001) *In Search of New Public Domain*, Rotterdam, NAI Publishers.

Hall P (1994) 'London 1994: Retrospect and Prospect', in Simmie J [Ed] *Planning London*, London, Routledge.

Hall P (2007) *London Voices, London Lives: Tales from a Working Capital*, Bristol, Policy Press.

Hall P (2011) 'London Tops-up Northern Coffers', *Planning*, 1 July: 40.

Hall P & Imrie R (1999) 'Architectural Practices and Disabling Design in the Built Environment', *Environment & Planning B: Planning & Design*, 26: 409–25.

Hamilton F (2008) 'Boris Johnson to End London's Hobbit Habit with 50,000 New Homes', http://www.timesonline.co.uk/tol/news/politics/article5198945.ece.

Hamnett C (2003) *Unequal City, London in the Global Arena*, London, Routledge.

Hamnett C & Whitelegg A (2007) 'From Industrial to Post Industrial Uses: The Loft Conversion Market in London', *Environment and Planning A*, 39(1): 106–24.

Heath P (1998) 'Civilising Westminster's Streets and Squares', *Planning in London*, 24(January): 14–17.

Heathcote E (2007a) 'What's So Good About British Architecture?', *Financial Times*, 31 August, http://wiki.epfl.ch/lapa-studio/documents/0708 LON/ft_whats_so_good_about_uk.pdf.

Heathcote E (2007b) 'Modernism is Modernised', 9 June, http://www.ft.com/cms/s/0/9cf2c316-1625-11dc-a7ce-000b5df10621.html#axzz1Cnsy5gn6.

Hebbert M (1998) *London: More by Fortune than Design*, Chichester, Wiley.

Hempel L & Topfer E (2004) 'Working Paper 15: CCTV in Europe, Final Report', http://www.urbaneye.net.

Henley W (2008a) 'Ken Attacks Boris Over Design Policy', *Building Design*, 8 August: 7.

Henley W (2008b) '100 Public Spaces Axed in London Design Shake-up', *Building Design*, 1 August: 1.

Hillman J (1988) *A New Look for London*, London, HMSO.

Hoggart K & Green D [Eds] (1991) *London: A New Metropolitan Geography*, London, Edward Arnold.

Hopkirk E (2009) 'London's Journey into Space', *Building Design*, 27 November: 8–9.

Hurst W (2009) 'Boris Bashed over "Pocket Money" for Great Spaces', *Building Design*, 13 March: 1.

Hurst W & Barney K (2009) 'Revealed: Bust-Up with Boris Made Lord Rogers Quit', 20 November, http://www.thisislondon.co.uk/standard/article-23772331-revealed-bust-up-with-boris-made-lord-rogers-quit.do.

Imrie R & Hall P (2001) *Inclusive Design: Designing and Developing Accessible Environments*, London, Spon Press.

Imrie R & Sakai A (2007) 'Governance in Private-Spaces', *Town & Country Planning*, December: 448–50.

Imrie R, Lees L & Raco M (2009) 'London's Regeneration', in Imrie R, Lees L & Raco M [Eds] *Regenerating London: Governance, Sustainability and Community in a Global City*, London, Routledge.

Jackson N (2003) *The Story of Paternoster: A New Square for London*, London, Mitsubishi Estate.

Jacobs J (1961, 1984 edition) *The Death and Life of Great American Cities: The Failure of Modern Town Planning*, London, Peregrine Books.

Jenkins S (1975) *Landlords to London: The Story of a Capital and its Growth*, London, Constable.

Johns R (2001) 'Skateboard City', *Landscape Design*, 303: 42–4.

Johnson B (2008a) 'Building a Better London', http://www.backboris.com.

Johnson B (2008b) 'Protecting Our Local Environment: A Cleaner Greener London', http://www.backboris.com.

Johnson B (2008c) 'Making London's Mayor Accountable', http://www.backboris.com.

Jones Lang LaSalle (2008) *Prime High Streets Europe*, London, Jones Lang LaSalle.

Keller L (2007) *Triumph of Order: Democracy and Public Space in New York and London*, New York, Columbia University Press.

Kennedy R (1991) *London: World City*, London, HMSO.

Knox P (2005) 'Creating Ordinary Places: Slow Cities in a Fast World', *Journal of Urban Design*, 10(1): 1–11.

Kohn (2004) *Brave New Neighbourhoods: The Privatization of Public Space*, New York, Routledge.

Lang J (1994) *Urban Design: The American Experience*, New York, Van Nostrand Reinhold.

LAPHC (London Assembly Planning and Housing Committee) (2011) *Public Life in Private Hands: Managing London's Public Space*, London, GLA.

LAPSDC (London Assembly Planning and Spatial Development Committee) (2004) *Designs on London*, London, GLA.

Lawrence H (1993) 'The Greening of the Squares of London: Transformation of Urban Landscapes and Ideals', *Annals of the Association of American Geographers*, 83(1): 90–118.

Lazell M (2007) 'Sloane Square Revamp Dumped by the Public', *Building Design*, 27 April: 3.

LDA (London Development Agency) (2010) *London Statement of Skills Priority 2011/12*, http://lseo.org.uk.

Leendertz L (2006) 'The Urban Gardener', *The Guardian*, 10 June: 72.

Lees LH (1994) 'Urban Public Space and Imagined Communities in the 1980s and 90s', *Journal of Urban History*, 20(4): 443–65.

Lefebvre H (1991) *The Production of Space*, London, Basil Blackwell.

Lewis P (2009) 'Seeing the Facts Behind the Fiction', 4 March, http://www.guardian.co.uk/commentisfree/2009/mar/04/surveillance-civil-liberties.

Light A & Smith JM [Eds] (1998) *Philosophy and Geography II: The Production of Public Space*, Lanham, MD, Rowman & Littlefield.

Livingstone K (2010) 'How Londoners Lost the Space Race', *Building Design*, 9 April: 9.

Llewelyn Davies (2000) *Urban Design Compendium*, London, English Partnerships/Housing Corporation.

Lofland L (1998) *The Public Realm: Exploring the City's Quintessential Social Territory*, New York, De Gruyter.

London First Retail Commission (2009) *Reinvigorating the High Street: Encouraging Retail Diversity and Supporting Town Centres in London*, London, London First.

London Pride Partnership (1994) *London Pride Prospectus*, London, Corporation of London.

Loukaitou-Sideris A (1996) 'Cracks in the City: Addressing the Constraints and Potentials of Urban Design', *Journal of Urban Design*, 1(1): 91–103.

Loukaitou-Sideris A & Banerjee T (1998) *Urban Design Downtown: Poetics and Politics of Form*, Berkeley, CA, University of California Press.

Low S (2006) 'How Private Interests Take Over Public Space: Zoning, Taxes and Incorporation of Gated Communities', in Low S & Smith N [Eds] *The Politics of Public Space*, New York, Routledge.

Low S & Smith N [Eds] (2006) *The Politics of Public Space*, New York, Routledge.

LPAC (London Planning Advisory Committee) (1994) *Advice in Strategic Guidance for London*, London, LPAC.

LSE (2007) *The Impact of Recent Immigration on the London Economy*, London, City of London.

MacCormac R (1990) 'Designing Cities with Democracy', *Architects' Journal*, 14 March: 70–9.

Mace R (2005) *Trafalgar Square: Emblem of Empire*, Cambridge, UK, Cambridge University Press.

Madanipour A (2003) *Public and Private Spaces of the City*, London, Routledge.

Madanipour A (2004) 'Marginal Public Spaces in European Cities', *Journal of Urban Design* 9(3): 267–86.

Madanipour A (2010) 'Whose Public Space?', in Madanipour A [Ed] *Whose Public Space? International Case Studies in Urban Design and Development*, London, Routledge: 237–42.

Malone K (2002) 'Street Life: Youth, Culture and Competing Uses of Public Space', *Environment and Urbanization*, 14(2): 157–68.

Manifesto Club (2008) 'Against the Booze Bans and the Hyper Regulation of Public Space', http://www.manifestoclub.com.

Marshall S (2007) 'City Limits: Rolfe Judd in Southwark', *Architecture Today*, 177: 18–26.

Mattson K (1999) 'Reclaiming and Remaking Public Space: Towards an Architecture for American Democracy', *National Civic Renewal*, 88(2): 133–44.

Mayor of London (2002a) *Making Space for Londoners*, London, GLA.

Mayor of London (2002b) *Squares Annual Report 2002: Trafalgar Square and Parliament Square Garden*, London, GLA.

Mayor of London (2004a) *The London Plan*, London, GLA.

Mayor of London (2004b) *Making London a Walkable City, The Walking Plan for London*, London, TfL.

Mayor of London (2005) *Squares Annual Report 2005/06: Trafalgar Square and Parliament Square Garden*, London, GLA.

Mayor of London (2008) *Planning for a Better London*, London, GLA.

Mayor of London (2009a) *Streetscape Guidance 2009: A Guide to Better London Streets*, London, TfL.

Mayor of London (2009b) *The London Plan: Spatial Development Strategy for Greater London. Consultation Draft Replacement Plan*, London, GLA.

Mayor of London (2009c) *The Mayor's Great Spaces*, London, LDA.

Mayor of London (2009d) *London's Great Outdoors: A Manifesto for Public Space*, London, LDA.

Mayor of London (2009e) *Better Streets: Practical Steps*, London, LDA.

Mayor of London (2009f) *Better Green and Water Spaces: Practical Steps*, London, LDA.

Mayor of London (2010) *London Housing Design Guide, Interim Edition*, London, LDA.

Mayor of London [n.d.] 'The Mayor's London Plan: Population Growth', http://www.london.gov.uk/shaping-london/london-plan/facts/.

Mean M & Tims C (2005) *People Make Places: Growing the Public Life of Cities*, London, Demos.

Merrick J (2003) 'Not Hip to Be Square', *The Independent*, 11 November.

Merrifield A (1996) 'Public Space: Integration and Exclusion in Urban Life', *City*, 1(5): 57–72.

Metropolitan Police, Crime Figures [n.d.] 'Latest Crime Figures for London', http://www.met.police.uk/crimefigures/.

Middleton J (2009) 'London as a Walkable City', in Imrie R, Lees L & Raco M [Eds] *Regenerating London: Governance, Sustainability and Community in a Global City*, London, Routledge.

Miethe T (1995) 'Fear and Withdrawal from Urban Life', *Annals AAPSS*, 539(May): 14–27.

Minton A (2006) *What Kind of World are We Building? The Privatisation of Public Space*, London, RICS.

Minton A (2009) *Ground Control, Fear and Happiness in the Twenty-First Century City*, London, Penguin Books.

Mitchell D (1995) 'The End of Public Space? People's Park, Definitions of the Public Democracy', *Annals of the Association of American Geographers*, 85(1): 108–33.

Mitchell WJ (1996) *City of Bits: Space, Place and the Infobahn*, Cambridge, MA, MIT Press.

Morris H (2009) 'High Streets See Dramatic Increase in Pound Stores', http://www.planningresource.co.uk/news/935801/High-streets-dramatic-increase-pound-stores/.

Moylan D (2010) 'Sloane Arranger', *New London Quarterly*, 3: 66–7.

Murphy C (2001) 'Customised Quarantine', *Atlantic Monthly*, July–August: 22–4.

Nairn I (1988) *Nairn's London: The Classic Guidebook*, London, Penguin Books.

Naser JL & Evans–Cowley J [Eds] (2007) *Universal Design and Visitability: From Accessibility to Zoning*, Columbus, OH, The John Glenn School of Public Affairs/National Endowment for the Arts.

Neale J (2007) 'The Standards Bearer', *Regeneration and Renewal*, 14 December: 15.

Németh J (2008) 'Defining a Public: The Management of Privately Owned Public Space', *Urban Studies*, 46(1): 2463–90.

Németh J & Hollander J (2010) 'Security Zones and New York City's Shrinking Public Space', *International Journal of Urban and Regional Research*, 34(1): 20–34.

New Economics Foundation (2004) *Clone Town Britain: The Loss of Local Identity on the Nation's High Streets*, London, New Economics Foundation.

Newman P & Thornley A (1997) 'Fragmentation and Centralisation in the Governance of London: Influencing the Urban Policy and Planning Agenda', *Urban Studies*, 34(7): 967–88.

Nicolaou L & Chaplin S (2010) 'The Thames Gateway: Alive and Well?', in Punter J [Ed] *Urban Design and the British Urban Renaissance*, London, Routledge.

Norman W & Ali R (2010) *Stuck on London's Hard Shoulder: Social Needs in a Fast Moving City*, London, The Young Foundation.

Oc T & Tiesdell S (1997) *Safer City Centres: Reviving the Public Realm*, London, Paul Chapman Publishing.

ODPM (Office of the Deputy Prime Minister) (2002) *Living Places: Greener, Safer, Cleaner*, London, ODPM.

Office for National Statistics (2010) Local Area Labour Markets: Statistical Indicators August 2010, London, ONS.

Oldenburg R (1999) *The Great Good Place: Cafes, Coffee Shops, Bookstores, Bars, Hair Salons and the Other Hangouts at the Heart of a Community*, 2nd edition, New York, Marlowe.

Olsen D (1982) *Town Planning in London: The Eighteenth and Nineteenth Centuries*, New Haven, CT, Yale University Press.

Parkinson J (2006) 'Holistic Democracy and Physical Public Space', *British Journal of Political Science* Conference, London, British Academy.

Pauling K (2008) 'Gabriel's Wharf', *Thames Pathway: Journal of a Walk down the River Thames*, http://www.thamespathway.com/chapter12/gabriels-wharf.aspx.

Pimlott B & Rao N (2002) *Governing London*, Oxford, Oxford University Press.

Planning Inspectorate [n.d.] http://www.planning-inspectorate.gov.uk/pins/appeals/local dev/index.htm.

Postles D (2004) 'The Market Place as Space in Early Modern England', *Social History*, 29(1): 41–58.

Pratt A (1994) 'Industry and Employment in London', in Simmie J [Ed] *Planning London*, London, UCL Press.

PropertyWire (2010) 'Analysts Confident that London Office Market Will Lead Commercial Property Recovery', 21 January, http://www.propertywire.com/news/europe/london-market-outlook-positive-201001213831.html.

Punter J (1990) 'The Privatisation of the Public Realm', *Planning Practice and Research*, 5(3): 9–16.

Punter J (1992) 'Classic Carbuncles and Mean Streets', in Thornley A [Ed] *The Crisis of London*, London, Routledge.

Punter J (2010a) 'An Introduction to the British Urban Renaissance', in Punter J [Ed] *Urban Design and the British Urban Renaissance*, London, Routledge.

Punter J (2010b) 'Reflecting on Urban Design Achievements in a Decade of Urban Renaissance', in Punter J [Ed] *Urban Design and the British Urban Renaissance*, London, Routledge.

Punter J & Carmona M (1997) *The Design Dimension of Planning: Theory, Content and Best Practice for Design Policies*, London, E&FN Spon.

Raco M & Henderson S (2009) 'Local Government and the Politics of Flagship Regeneration', in Imrie R, Lees L & Raco M [Eds] *Regenerating London, Governance, Sustainability and Community in a Global City*, London, Routledge.

Ramesh R (2010) 'London's Richest People Worth 273 Times More than the Poorest', 21 April, http://www.guardian.co.uk/uk/2010/apr/21/wealth-social-divide-health-inequality.

Rasmussen S (1948) *London: The Unique City*, London, Jonathan Cape.

Regeneration and Renewal (2008) '100 Public Spaces Project Cut by Boris', *Regeneration and Renewal*, 8 August: 2.

RIBA (Royal Institute of British Architects)/English Heritage (2005) *Capital Spaces: Transforming London*, London, English Heritage/RIBA.

RIBA London Region (2001) *Design for a Greater London*, London, RIBA.

Rice A (2004) 'Gates and Ghettoes: A Tale of Two Britains', 18 March, http://news.bbc.co.uk/1/hi/programmes/if/3513980.stm.

Roberts M & Lloyd-Jones T (2010) 'Central London, Intensity, Excess and Success in the Context of a World City', in Punter J [Ed] *Urban Design and the British Urban Renaissance*, London, Routledge.

Roberts M & Turner C (2005) 'Conflicts of Liveability in the 24-hour City: Learning from 48 Hours in the Life of London's Soho', *Journal of Urban Design*, 10(2): 171–93.

Rogers P (2010) 'Youth Participation and Revanchist Regimes, Redeveloping Old Eldon Square, Newcastle upon Tyne', in Madanipour A [Ed] *Whose Public Space? International Case Studies in Urban Design and Development*, London, Routledge: 51–8.

Rogers R (1992) 'London: A Call to Action', in Rogers R & Fisher M, *A New London*, London, Penguin Books.

Rogers R (2005) 'London's Urban Renaissance', in Hunt J [Ed] *London's Environment*, London, Imperial College Press.

Rogers R (2011) 'Creating Places for People – Transforming London's Public Realm', *Urban Design*, 118: 16–18.

Rogers R & Fisher M (1992) *A New London*, London, Penguin Books.

Ross M (2007) 'Design Team to Guard Public Space', *Regeneration and Renewal*, 22 June: 12.

Royal Commission on London Squares (1928) *Report of the Royal Commission on London Squares*, London, HMSO.

Russell B (2002) 'Streets of New York Safer than London, Says Mayor', *The Independent*, 4 September.

Rydin Y, Thornley A, Scanlon K & West K (2004) 'The Greater London Authority – A Case of Conflict of Cultures? Evidence from the Planning and Environmental Policy Domains', *Environment and Planning C: Government and Policy*, 22: 55–76.

Sassen S (1994) *Cities in a World Economy*, Thousand Oaks, CA, Pine Forge Press.

Schwartz M (2009) 'Are the British Any Good at Designing Public Space?', *Building Design*, 13 February: 7.

Sennett R (1977) *The Fall of Public Man*, London, Faber & Faber.

Sennett R (1990) *The Conscience of the Eye: The Design and Social Life of Cities*, New York, Alfred Knopf.

Shields R (1991) *Places on the Margin*, London, Routledge.

Shonfield K (1998) *At Home With Strangers: Public Space and the New Community*, Working Paper 8, The Richness of Cities: Urban Policy in a New Landscape), London, Comedia & Demos.

Shoup D (2005) *The High Cost of Free Parking*, Chicago, American Planning Association.

Simmie J (1994) 'Planning Implications of London's World-City Characteristics', in Simmie J [Ed] *Planning London*, London, Routledge.

Simmie J [Ed] (1994) *Planning London*, London, Routledge.

Sircus J (2001) 'Invented Places', *Prospect*, 81 (September/October): 30–5.

Smith N (2000) 'Gentrification', in Johnston R, Gregory D, Pratt G & Watts M [Eds] *The Dictionary of Human Geography*, 4th edition, Oxford, Blackwell.

Sorkin M [Ed] (1992) *Variations on a Theme Park: The New American City and the End of Public Space*, New York, Hill & Wang.

Sorkin M (2004) 'Urban Warfare: A Tour of the Battlefield', in Graham S [Ed] *Cities, War and Terrorism*, Oxford, Blackwell.

Sudjic D (2000) 'A Love Skate Relationship in Somerset House's Liberated Courtyard', 10 December, http://www.guardian.co.uk/theobserver/2000/dec/10/2.

Swadkin C & Virdee D (2007) 'Regional Productivity', in Camus D [Ed] *The ONS Productivity Handbook: A Statistical Overview and Guide*, Basingstoke, Palgrave Macmillan: 147–56 (also available at http://www.ons.gov.uk/ons/guide-method/user-guidance/productivity-handbook/regional-productivity/index.html).

Tames R (2005) *The Westminster and Pimlico Book*, London, Historical Publications.

Taylor D (2011) 'Critical Eye – Design Review in London', *New London Quarterly* (7): 77–80.

TfL (Transport for London) (2006) *Central London Congestion Charging: Impacts Monitoring Fourth Annual Report*, London, TfL.

TfL [n.d.] 'Legible London', http://www.tfl.gov.uk/microsites/legible-london/.

Thornley A [Ed] (1992) *The Crisis of London*, London, Routledge.

Thornley A (1999) *Urban Planning and Competitive Advantage: London, Sydney and Singapore*, LSE London Discussion Paper No.2, London, LSE.

Thorold P (2001) *The London Rich: The Creation of a Great City from 1666 to the Present*, London, Penguin Books.

Tibbalds Colbourne Karski Williams Monro (1993) *London's Urban Environmental Quality*, London, LPAC.

Tibbalds F (2001) *Making People-Friendly Towns: Improving the Public Environment in Towns and Cities*, 2nd edition, London, Spon Press.

Tiesdell S & Adams D (2004) 'Design Matters: Major House Builders and the Design Challenge of Brownfield Development Contexts', *Journal of Urban Design*, 9(1): 23–45.

Trancik R (1986) *Finding Lost Space: Theories of Urban Design*, New York, Van Nostrand Reinhold.

Travis A (2008) 'Tough on the Causes of Crime', 15 February, http://www.guardian.co.uk/politics/2008/feb/15/crime.london.

Trent C (1965) *Greater London, Its Growth and Development Through Two Thousand Years*, London, Pheonix House.

UDL (Urban Design London) (2011) *Review of Design Review and Neighbourhood Planning Approaches in London*, London, UDL.

UDL [n.d.] 'About UDL', http://www.urbandesignlondon.com/?page id=15.

UK National Statistics, London [n.d.]. http://www.ons.gov.uk/ons/rel/regional-trends/regional-trends/no--43--2011-edition/regional-profiles---summary---london.html.

UKBIDs [n.d.] National BIDs Advisory Service, http://www.ukbids.org/BIDS/index.php.

Urban Task Force (1999) *Towards an Urban Renaissance*, London, Spon Press.

Van Melik R, Van Aalst I & Van Weesep J (2007) 'Fear and Fantasy in the Public Domain: The Development of Secured and Themed Urban Space', *Journal of Urban Design*, 12(1): 25–42.

Vaughan R (2007) 'Interview, Peter Bishop Reflects on his First Year',

20 December, http://www.architectsjournal.co.uk/news/interview-peter-bishop-reflects-on-his-first-year-at-design-for-london/394701.article.

Walker B (2007) 'Rows Likely When Public Space Meets Private', *Regeneration and Renewal*, 22 June: 21.

Webster C (2001) 'Gated Cities of Tomorrow', *Town Planning Review*, 72(2): 149–70.

Webster C (2007) 'Property Rights, Public Space and Urban Design', *Town Planning Review*, 78(1): 81–101.

Whyte W (1980) *The Social Life of Small Urban Spaces*, Washington DC, Conservation Foundation.

Wikipedia, Riots [n.d.] '2011 England Riots', http://en.wikipedia.org/wiki/2011 England riots

Wikipedia, Squares [n.d.] 'Squares in London', http://en.wikipedia.org/wiki/Squares in London.

Willis B (2008) 'Spaces in Boris's Policies', *Regeneration and Renewal*, 22 August: 21.

Wilson E (1995) 'The Rhetoric of Urban Space', *New Left Review*, A: 209.

Wilson J & Kelling G (1982) 'Broken Windows', *Atlantic Monthly*, March: 29–36.

Woodman E (2007) 'The New Face of Festival Hall', 24 February, http://www.telegraph.co.uk/culture/music/classicalmusic/3663365/New-face-of-the-Festival-Hall.html.

Woodman E (2010) 'The Man Who Built the City of London', *Building Design*, 27 August: 10–11.

Woolley H & Johns R (2001) 'Skateboarding: The City as a Playground', *Journal of Urban Design*, 6(2): 211–30.

Woolley H, Carmona M, Freeman J & Rose S (2004) *The Value of Public Space: How High Quality Parks and Public Spaces Create Economic, Social and Environmental Value*, London, CABE Space.

Worpole K (1999) 'Open All Hours, Like it or Not', *New Statesman*, 26 April: xxvi–xxvii.

Worpole K & Knox K (2007) *The Social Value of Public Spaces*, York, Joseph Rowntree Foundation.

Zukin S (1991) *Landscapes of Power: From Detroit to Disney World*, Berkeley, CA, University of California Press.

Zukin S (1995) *The Cultures of Cities*, Cambridge, MA, Blackwell.

Zukin S (1998) 'Urban Lifestyles: Diversity and Standardisation in Spaces of Consumption', *Urban Studies*, 56(5–6): 825–39.

INDEX